DISCIPLINE SURVIVAL KIT
for the
SECONDARY TEACHER

Julia G. Thompson

THE CENTER FOR APPLIED
RESEARCH IN EDUCATION
West Nyack, New York 10994

Library of Congress Cataloging-in-Publication Data

Thompson, Julia G.
    Discipline survival kit for the secondary teacher / Julia G.
Thompson
        p.   cm.
    ISBN 0–87628–434–9
    1. Classroom management.   2. Education, Secondary.   3. Teacher
effectiveness.   4. Teacher-student relationships.   I. Title.
LB3013.T56   1998
373.1102'4—dc21
                                            98–21381
                                               CIP

Acquisitions Editor: *Susan Kolwicz*
Production Editor: *Tom Curtin*
Interior Design/Formatting: *Dee Coroneos*

© 1998 *by* The Center for Applied Research in Education

Printed in the United States of America

10 9 8 7 6 5 4 3

ISBN 0-87628-434-9

ATTENTION: CORPORATIONS AND SCHOOLS

The Center for Applied Research in Education books are available at quantity discounts with bulk purchase for educational, business, or sales promotional use. For information, please write to: Prentice Hall Special Sales, 240 Frisch Court, Paramus, NJ 07652. Please supply: title of book, ISBN number, quantity, how the book will be used, date needed.

THE CENTER FOR APPLIED RESEARCH
IN EDUCATION
West Nyack, NY 10994

On the World Wide Web at http://www.phdirect.com

ACKNOWLEDGMENTS

I am grateful to my editor, Susan Kolwicz, for her hard work, insight, and patient guidance in the preparation of this book.

Thanks again to the faculty, staff, and students of Churchland High school for their support and encouragement—something all teachers everywhere need every day.

Special thanks are due to those family members and friends who generously shared their time and knowledge.

ABOUT THE AUTHOR

Julia Thompson received her B.A. in English from Virginia Polytechnic Institute and State University in Blacksburg. She has been a teacher in the public schools of Virginia, Arizona, and North Carolina for over twenty years. She has taught a wide variety of courses including freshman composition at Virginia Tech, all of the secondary English grades, mining, geography, reading, home economics, math, civics, Arizona history, physical education, special education, graduation equivalency preparation, and employment skills. Her students have been diverse in ethnic groups as well as in age, ranging from remedial seventh graders to adults. Ms. Thompson is currently teaching English at Churchland High School in Portsmouth, Virginia. She is a member of the Virginia Association of Teachers of English.

ABOUT THIS SURVIVAL KIT

As school boards across our country struggle to meet the escalating demands of a rapidly changing student population, increasingly difficult tasks are delegated to overburdened secondary classroom teachers. No longer do our students sit in neat rows while we deliver expert information. Often secondary teachers face unruly students who appear to be on the brink of violence. The dismaying prospect of trying to impose order on chaotic classrooms could rob even the most stalwart educators of satisfaction in their profession. The altruistic dreams that inspired us to choose education as a career vanish in the daily grind of the unpleasant realities created by out-of-control students.

However, many teachers across our country are coping beautifully with the recent, anxiety-provoking changes in education. These teachers manage their students' difficult behavior with skill and grace. Their students are successful and they, themselves, find a great deal of personal satisfaction in the positive learning environment that they have established in their classrooms. The dreams that they had when they chose education as a career are everyday realities. These secondary teachers have found successful ways to help their students become self-motivated and self-disciplined.

Discipline Survival Kit for the Secondary Teacher provides busy teachers of students in grades 6–12 with a useful desktop reference filled with essential techniques necessary to manage the wide range of problems and responsibilities related to discipline in the secondary classroom. It serves as a practical guide to solving many of the behavior management problems that secondary teachers in every school across our nation encounter each day. The timely, school-tested solutions in *Discipline Survival Kit for the Secondary Teacher* help you develop a classroom climate where cooperative students can focus on positive behaviors rather than negative ones. Experienced and novice teachers alike will find strategies, activities, tips, and tools that provide solutions to many of the frustrating problems involved in managing student behavior.

Specifically, the goals of this *Kit* are to:

- Put you back in control of your class,
- Help you create the kind of motivational environment where mannerly conduct and successful learning are the order of the day,
- Provide you with up-to-date solutions to some of the most common discipline problems that are unique to secondary classrooms,
- Save you time with an array of easy-to-use charts, forms, checklists, and reproducible materials,
- Help you guide students toward more successful collaborative relationships with you and with each other,
- Enable you to reduce disruptions and effectively manage student behavior,
- Show you how to use some of the sound discipline practices that other teachers have found successful,

- Help you motivate your students to take the initiative for their own learning, and
- Increase your confidence in your ability to find the satisfaction that a career in education can bring.

Within the *Kit* are a broad range of topics designed to help teachers move beyond controlling a crowd of unruly adolescents to teaching a group of self-disciplined students who love learning. The information in each section helps you meet the challenges that your students bring to school each day. For example,

Section One:	Your role as a classroom leader and how you can become a proactive teacher,
Section Two:	The organizational skills necessary to establish a positive learning environment from the first day forward,
Section Three:	How to maximize class time and to minimize disruptions,
Section Four:	Ways to promote positive discipline practices by teaching your students how to relate better to you, to other adults, and to each other,
Section Five:	Various methods that you can use to prevent discipline problems,
Section Six:	What to do once misbehavior has occurred in your classroom,
Section Seven:	Practical solutions to a broad range of specific problems that many secondary teachers encounter,
Section Eight:	How to begin the process of moving your students towards becoming self-disciplined learners, and
Section Nine:	More on the teacher's important role in the discipline process and how to reach your full potential as a classroom leader.

There are many ways that busy secondary teachers can use this resource. You can browse through it section by section, gathering ideas to fit your own classroom situation. You could use the table of contents to find advice quickly in a particular chapter that addresses a concern that you have at the moment. Or you can use it to analyze the discipline problems happening in your classroom. The most effective use of the information in these pages, however, would be to enable you to create the kind of positive classroom environment where the teacher is in control and where students are engaged in the enjoyable process of becoming lifelong learners!

Julia Thompson

CONTENTS

Section 3

DOOR TO DOOR: USING CLASS TIME WISELY / 71

Section 4

A PARTNERSHIP APPROACH TO DISCIPLINE / 99

Section 5

PREVENTING DISCIPLINE PROBLEMS / 145

Section 6

DEALING WITH PROBLEMS ONCE THEY OCCUR / 203

Section 7

STRATEGIES FOR SOLVING SPECIFIC PROBLEMS / 249

Section 8

MOVING BEYOND CROWD CONTROL TO PROMOTE
SELF-DISCIPLINE / 305

Section 9

THE MOST IMPORTANT FACTOR IN DISCIPLINE: THE TEACHER / 337

Section 1

THE DISCIPLINE DILEMMA: CROWD CONTROL OR SELF-DISCIPLINE?

In This Section . . .

Many capable teachers today find themselves facing increasingly difficult discipline problems. Even the most dedicated teachers are sometimes perplexed about what steps they should take when a problem arises. "The Discipline Dilemma" and "The Historical View (The Good Old Days)" explore some of the reasons for this problem that so many of us face.

In "Today's Schools: Problems We All Face," you'll see that you are not alone with the problems you may be experiencing in your class.

Explore the issue of punishment and the ways that you can move beyond its negative effects to a more productive way of handling classroom problems in "Why Punishment Alone Just Doesn't Work," "Harmful Punishment Practices," and "Moving Beyond Punishment to Better Discipline Practices."

Next, you'll learn about the most powerful tool that teachers have in creating a positive discipline climate in "What Every Teacher Should Know about Adolescents," "The Basics of a Good Teacher-Student Relationship," and "Teaching the Basics of a Good Teacher-Student Relationship."

If you are one of the thousands of secondary teachers who may feel confused about just what constitutes a well-disciplined class, then "The Characteristics of a Well-Disciplined Class" and the questionnaire that accompanies it will help you decide.

The next step in resolving the discipline dilemma is to take a close look at yourself and the way you perform in the classroom. "The Introspective Teacher" and the three self-assessments that follow it suggest ways that you can begin to redefine your role in the classroom.

"Attitudes for Success" can reveal some of the qualities you already possess that make you an effective classroom leader.

Finally, in "Becoming a Proactive Teacher," you will be able to define the personal qualities that will help you on your way to creating the most positive classroom environment possible.

"A load of books does not equal one good teacher."

—Chinese proverb

THE DISCIPLINE DILEMMA

This is a book about classroom discipline. This is not a book about lesson plans or grading papers or writing objectives on the chalkboard each day. It's not about taking attendance or delivering lectures or even about designing fair test questions.

Instead, it is about an issue far more puzzling and complex than any of these. It's about being sent to the principal and sassing the teacher and passing notes in class. It's also about teen substance abuse and bullies and students who bring weapons to school.

These problems have plagued teachers for as long as students have been coming to school. If you have discipline problems during the school year, take heart. Everyone who teaches does. *Everyone.*

We long for a positive discipline climate in our classes. Everything runs smoothly when that happens. We teach well. Our students learn what we want them to learn. The school day is a joyful, satisfying experience.

When the climate is a negative one, however, even our best lesson plans are useless. We can't teach because our students are too disruptive to pay attention. We do not enjoy these frustrating days. We endure them. Our students do, too.

With this in mind, it's understandable that the word "discipline" usually has a very unpleasant connotation for most of us. Our hearts sink at the thought of coping with discipline issues. We tend to think of "discipline" in the same way we think of the word "misbehavior": discipline referral, disciplinary detention, or being sent to the office for discipline action.

"Discipline" in this book is not a negative. Quite the opposite is true. In this book the word "discipline" means the systematic and positive training you provide for your students to help them develop self-control. It is the means by which we have orderly classrooms and successful students.

Fortunately, the discipline dilemma that all teachers face has solutions. We can take control of our classes. We can have a positive learning environment in our classrooms.

This book offers a wide variety of ways to create a peaceful and productive classroom. It's about how to manage the students in your class with sensitivity and dignity so that there is harmony in your classroom instead of strife.

This book is also about the most important factor in the discipline dilemma—the teacher. In many ways we are the most idealistic people in our community. When other adults see a group of teens loitering on the sidewalk just wasting time, we don't seem to notice the silly clothing and too-cool hairstyles. Instead, we see the future.

Somewhere in our teacher training, we acquire the unique gift of "potential sight." Instead of sullen juvenile delinquents, we see what others can't: potential doctors, teachers, accountants, lawyers, soldiers . . . our colleagues-in-waiting. Perhaps it is this gift that makes us struggle in the face of so many obstacles to help our students become the people we know they can be.

THE HISTORICAL VIEW (THE GOOD OLD DAYS)

It happens quite often. All it takes is a tough day and a few weary teachers. They huddle together around the snack machine or slump dejectedly on those lumpy second-hand couches that eventually find their way into every teachers' lounge in North America.

Sooner or later the topic of conversation will move from a rehashing of the day's problems to the perennial favorite: the "good old days" in education.

According to legend, life was much easier for teachers in years past. Well-dressed, hard-working children sat silently in neat rows. They either worked independently on their daily assignments or wrote down every word of the lecture delivered by the instructor. These legendary pupils always did their homework, never asked for a hall pass, and raised their hands before speaking in class discussions.

If an infraction of school rules occurred, punishment was swift. The worst thing that could happen to a student was a summons to the principal's office. Best of all, guilty children were sure to be punished again when school authorities notified their parents. Both parents and children valued the importance of an education in the good old days.

Those flawless students were never absent, wouldn't have dreamed of being tardy, and absolutely never talked back to an adult. They even brought their books to class every day.

These stories always end the same way. With a despairing sigh, the weary teachers sadly shake their heads and chant in unison, "These kids today . . . . What is the world coming to?"

While these teachers' lounge tales of the good old days are just a bit too unrealistic to be an accurate portrait of the classrooms of yesteryear, there is some truth to them. Schools today are very different places from the schools of earlier times. Our schools reflect the tremendous social changes that have altered the lives of many people in recent decades. They also reflect the intense efforts that educators have made in an attempt to solve the many problems that have kept schools from being as successful as they could have been in the past.

Contrary to the conventional wisdom expressed by weary teachers after a trying day, our schools are not getting worse. Instead, many positive changes in education in recent years have created schools that are a significant improvement over the educational institutions of the past. Here are just three of the recent improvements.

1. Across our nation educators reach out each school year to all students regardless of the factors that excluded many people from school success in the "good old days." Economic status, race, and gender—to name a few—are no longer the barriers to education that they once were. Separate, but unequal, is rapidly fading.

2. Teachers engage in the great effort to educate every child with great patience and belief in the future. We even offer the benefits of an education to those students who do not hesitate to let us know through a variety of disruptive behaviors that they are not at all interested in either an education or becoming productive citizens.

3. Today we know more than ever about which teaching strategies are effective in helping our students learn. One of the most obvious examples of how schools have changed for the better over time is in the discipline methods that many of us now use. The methods of the past, while admittedly effective in controlling the school population of the day, had some inherent faults.

In the past teachers controlled their classrooms with a variety of punitive methods that began with the "Teacher Look." This technique, familiar to us all, was an unwavering stare directed at a pupil who was perhaps only *contemplating* misbehavior. Other discipline strategies ranged from verbal reprimands to expulsion from school. In between these two extremes lay the old standbys: public humiliation, sarcasm, hundreds of sentences to copy, oceans of red ink on student work, threats, and corporal punishment. For many reasons these discipline strategies were not effective.

When teachers became aware that the traditional, punitive methods were no longer working, a variety of highly-touted strategies became the topics of faculty workshops in school district after school district. Many of these new methods were passing fads that quickly faded as teachers realized that the new strategies were not always as effective as the workshop leader had promised.

The outcome of these changes is that practical teachers, armed with discipline methods that were no longer working, did what capable educators have done throughout history. They blended what was working in the old methods with what was successful in the new. They realized that punishment was no longer the deterrent to bad behavior that it was once believed to be and that passing trends, while not always successful, could offer suggestions for a more humane approach to the problem of school discipline.

The result is that most effective teachers today take a balanced approach to discipline in their classrooms. They encourage productive student behavior through a wide assortment of strategies rather than focus on controlling a classroom of disruptive students through threats of punishment.

TODAY'S SCHOOLS: PROBLEMS WE ALL FACE

In spite of the encouraging changes that recent reforms have brought to education, one aspect of our jobs has not yet changed and probably never will—we still have discipline problems.

Problems with discipline are inevitable in our profession given the nature of the students we teach and the purpose of our work. In fact, according to national surveys, discipline problems are among the most frequent complaints that many teachers have about their jobs.

The comforting news is that you are not alone with your discipline problems. We *all* experience them—even those teachers who seem to have perfectly behaved students!

Many of our discipline problems, surprisingly enough, are not directly caused by our students. Many are caused by other educators, parents, the physical conditions in schools, and by our own inability to always cope adequately with the rigorous demands of our profession.

Here are just some of the discipline problems that many secondary teachers in today's schools have to handle in the course of their professional duties. The problems in this list are ones that are not always directly caused by students who misbehave, but are the result of other factors teachers have to manage in order to maintain a positive learning climate.

1. Ineffective local discipline policies

2. Overworked and unsympathetic administrators

3. Parents who do not support school personnel

4. Trendy but impractical solutions to discipline problems

5. Overcrowded classes

6. Buildings that need repairs and better maintenance

7. Too little productive time with students

8. Stacks of tedious paperwork

9. Lax teachers whose problems with classroom management spill over into our classes

10. A generation and culture gap between students and teachers

11. Students who are unsupervised by their parents

12. Uncertainty over the right action to take when problems occur

13. Textbooks and other materials that are not relevant

14. The loss of a feeling of safety at school

15. Students with overwhelming family problems

16. Not enough equipment that is not hopelessly outdated

17. Fatigue

18. Being unable to contact parents easily by phone

19. Exhausting class schedules

20. Frequent class interruptions

21. Teacher distress and burnout

Education today remains as it always has been—a mixture of good intentions and some pretty discouraging problems. Successful teachers, however, have developed ways to deal with their problems more efficiently than those teachers whose classes are chaotic. Successful teachers *do* have discipline problems just like the rest of us, but they have found ways to make the potentially negative impact of them as minimal as possible.

WHY PUNISHMENT ALONE JUST DOESN'T WORK

Teachers who want to create a well-disciplined class realize they cannot do this by using outdated practices. It is only natural that we tend to model our teaching styles on the experiences we had in school. We want to recreate for our students the positive experiences that we enjoyed. We want to inspire them as we were inspired. We want to shape their lives as school shaped ours.

But in our attempts to do this, we sometimes recreate the negative experiences that we had in school as well. Punishment is used often—far too often—in public schools today. It is, in fact, the most often used discipline practice in secondary schools across our nation.

Punishment is a historical tradition in childrearing. We have been taught that if we "spare the rod," we "will spoil the child" even though research has shown time and time again that spanking has an adverse effect on almost every child. Yet very few adults can say they were never spanked when they were children.

Another reason that punishment is used often in schools is that parents and children both expect it. Teachers who decide to never resort to punishment may seem to be too nice or too weak to be effective classroom leaders.

The problem is that punishment often does work—in the short run. If you want to establish brief control of a class, setting an example by severely punishing one pupil will quickly cause the others to sit up and take notice that you mean business.

Few graduates can recall school years that didn't include at least some hours wasted in tedious drudgery and meaningless work. Many can recall embarrassing moments at the hands of an insensitive teacher. Many graduates can also clearly remember an unfair incident in a class long after the weighty content of the course has been forgotten.

Many adults look back with nostalgic fondness on particular teachers who were very strict. These tough teachers held their students to very high standards of conduct and taught their subject matter thoroughly and well. Class reunions abound with fond stories about these respected teachers. More careful consideration, however, indicates that those tough teachers are revered only if they were caring, knowledgeable, and fair as well as strict.

If the modeling that we attempt for our students includes crowd control mainly through punishment and the fear of punishment, then it is not likely that we will be successful in creating the kind of positive classroom environment that we want. Rising dropout rates and the increase in the numbers of at-risk students are only two serious indications that we need to move away from discipline practices that are mainly punitive to take a more humane approach to our students.

Problems Facing Teens Today

Our troubled student population is a reflection of the sometimes chaotic social climate of our times. Problems in the home and community have profound effects on school life. Teachers have come to recognize that many of our students do not live simple lives. Many teens, even those who appear stable and carefree, grapple with problems at home and with their peers that would daunt even the most stalwart adult. Large numbers of our students are forced to assume responsibilities for which they are ill-prepared to cope.

Some of the problems facing teens today are ones that just a few years ago were not so widespread as they are now. Many teachers have struggled to help a pregnant teen, a child who has been thrown out of the home by frustrated parents, a student attending class while on house arrest, or one who works long hours after school not for luxuries, but to help support the family. Many of our students do not have basic social and academic skills, positive values, or even a realistic view of life. They do not live with caring families who can help them reach for a future.

In the face of these severe problems, attempting to scare a student into good behavior with punishment would be laughable if the situation were not tragic. With the failure of many of the social institutions that helped support education in the past, teachers everywhere have come to realize that we must find new ways to reach our students.

Punishment only hurts the teacher-student relationship. Pupils who are severely punished are not going to be humiliated into good behavior. Their self-esteem is so damaged that many will lose interest in school. Punishment, because of its negative energy, teaches students that they are not likely to succeed. It destroys trust. Punitive discipline is no longer a sign of strength, if, indeed, it ever was.

Positive Student–Teacher Relationships

The most powerful weapon available to secondary teachers who want to foster a favorable learning climate is a positive relationship with our students. When teachers interact in a collaborative and supportive way with students, pupils will respond in kind with fewer disruptions. Confrontational or punitive teachers are simply unable to be good role models for today's students.

A peaceful classroom where individuals have enough encouragement, praise, and attention for positive behaviors is a productive one. Disciplining students through punishment does not provide encouragement. It does not provide praise . . . and it certainly does not focus on positive behavior. Punishment does not create a productive class of happy students who work well with each other and with their teacher.

Even worse than this failure is the unexpected danger in discipline practices based solely on punishment. Misbehaving students can react violently when they lose face in front of their peers. Punishment almost guarantees embarrassment. What sensible teacher, when given other and more successful options, would rely on punishment?

If these practical reasons are not enough to make sensible teachers reconsider their discipline policies, then consider the larger philosophical issues of the art of education. Isn't it better to teach students how to control their own behavior rather than to be a teacher who assumes the role of controller for a classroom of active teens? If we don't provide our students with the skills, motivation, and practice to become responsible and productive citizens, then we have failed to fulfill the basic purpose of our profession.

Following in Figure 1-1 are examples of harmful punishment practices.

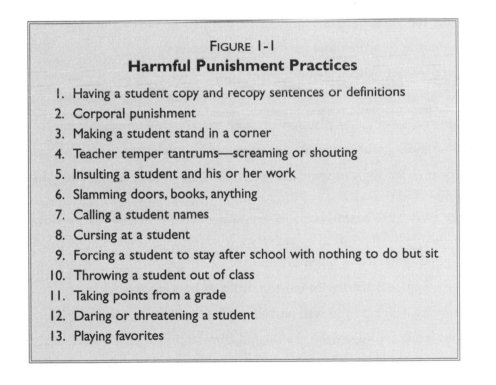

FIGURE 1-1
Harmful Punishment Practices

1. Having a student copy and recopy sentences or definitions
2. Corporal punishment
3. Making a student stand in a corner
4. Teacher temper tantrums—screaming or shouting
5. Insulting a student and his or her work
6. Slamming doors, books, anything
7. Calling a student names
8. Cursing at a student
9. Forcing a student to stay after school with nothing to do but sit
10. Throwing a student out of class
11. Taking points from a grade
12. Daring or threatening a student
13. Playing favorites

MOVING BEYOND PUNISHMENT TO BETTER DISCIPLINE PRACTICES

Teachers who want to have the rewarding experiences that teaching secondary students can provide have discovered that sound discipline practices are necessary for the attainment of that goal. Punishment is not an effective classroom control tool if it is used in place of the more beneficial and useful methods available to us.

Contrary to what many teachers have been taught to believe by their past school experiences, punishment is only effective when it is used in conjunction with a wide host of other methods. Since the incorrect application of punishment results in the creation of an adversarial relationship between teacher and student, it is much better to move beyond punishment as the main tool of our classroom control techniques.

One of the lessons teachers have learned from the reforms in education in recent years is that we will have much more success with our students if we focus on building positive relationships. The benefits of this are undeniable for teachers who are able to reach the kind of job satisfaction that they dreamed about when choosing a career and even more for the students who experience the thrill of an exciting school day where interesting discoveries are made and their opinions are valued.

The alternative actions in this list are not intended to be used in place of punishment when punishment is truly warranted, as in the case of violence or blatant disregard for safety. Instead, these alternatives are meant to serve as a springboard for your own ideas on better ways to handle discipline problems.

55 Ways to Handle Discipline Problems

1. Praise only the good behavior and ignore as much of the bad as you can.

2. Call a parent or guardian and get help for a problem.

3. Hold a conference with the child.

4. Listen to the student's version of the incident before taking any action.

5. Determine on a course of planned ignoring to extinguish misbehavior.

6. Ask the offending student what consequences he or she should have to pay.

7. Ask student to list for you some alternative actions that he or she could have taken to prevent misbehavior.

8. Move the student to a time-out area in another classroom in order to cool off and prevent further trouble.

9. Reward good behavior as often as you can.

10. Make a student feel worthy of trust in order to prevent misbehavior.

11. Post your class rules on the wall and then take the time to teach them.

12. Keep your students busy from the second they step into your room until they leave.

13. Discuss the class rules periodically—daily at first and then less frequently thereafter.

14. Move to stand near a child who is off task.

15. Smile at a student who is getting ready to misbehave.

16. Give a potentially troublesome child a position of leadership in the class.

17. If a perennially fidgety child is getting restless, send that student on an errand to channel the energy productively.

18. Put friends close together so that the more able ones can help the less able ones.

19. Change a lesson plan to something more exciting. Always have a backup plan handy.

20. If an exciting school event is causing your class to be out of control, go with the flow and plan assignments that will channel that high energy into productive outlets.

21. If the infraction is minor and a true slip in judgment on a student's part, offer reassurance that you know it won't happen again.

22. If students do not bring the necessary materials to class, arrange a system for lending the materials with collateral.

23. Make sure the lesson is exciting. Students who are interested in a lesson will usually not misbehave.

24. Create a reasonable policy about students who need to leave the room and enforce it.

25. Set behaviors for the entire group and reward them when the goals are met.

26. Offer tangible rewards for good behavior at unpredictable times.

27. If you see a student successfully struggling with temptation in class, be sure to say a quiet word of praise afterwards.

28. Be emotionally accessible for your students. Warm and friendly teachers have fewer misbehaviors than grouchy ones.

29. Give a child a second chance. Sometimes a warning can be very effective.

30. Remind students often of their future goals so that they have a good reason to stay on track.

31. Hold class award ceremonies at appropriate times to recognize the good deeds of your students.

32. Be gracious when accepting an apology.

33. Make your lessons as fascinating as possible. Even the dullest material can be interesting in the hands of a gifted teacher.

34. Use the "Revised Teacher Look." Glance in mild puzzlement at a potential problem student and shake your head slightly. The signal should be clear that you expect the student to focus on the lesson.

35. If a group is having trouble settling down, say, "I'll give you exactly two more minutes to finish getting to work." Then time them.

36. Laugh. You have a sense of humor, so use it.

37. Use inspiring mottoes and messages to remind your students to behave.

38. Be so soft-spoken, kind, and polite that your students would be ashamed to raise their voices at you.

39. Give students as many options about their work as you can without sacrificing your standards. Students who can choose wisely are learning to be self-disciplined.

40. Ask an offender to explain the class rule that was broken.

41. If a child has recurring problems or severe ones, involve other support personnel such as counselors or social workers.

42. After an incident has occurred, examine your own actions. Did you do something to cause the misbehavior?

43. Establish a clear procedure for class routines.

44. Teach your students how to work well in a group. Even very young pupils can be taught such good behavior as controlling noise level.

45. Control the pace of a lesson carefully. If it is too long or is too rushed, then problems are likely.

46. Post conspicuous notices to remind students to stay on task.

47. Reexamine your classroom rules. Are they working? What do you need to change?

48. Make sure the consequences for good and bad behaviors are clearly spelled out.

49. Stay on your feet and move around the room.

50. Move a student to another seat.

51. Reinforce the good behavior of as many students as you can.

52. Ask a troublesome pupil to help another student with an assignment. Both should benefit.

53. Make sure your students understand the criteria for success on an assignment so that they will work well.

54. Reinforce as many good behaviors as you can.

55. Discuss social issues with your pupils. They need to talk to caring adults about trust and responsibility.

FACTS EVERY TEACHER SHOULD KNOW ABOUT ADOLESCENTS

If outdated practices are no longer working and if we see the need for promoting self-directed behavior, then where do teachers begin the transformation of their classes?

Fortunately, the splashy headlines about youthful criminals aren't always a true picture of our students. Many of us were drawn to our profession for a variety of reasons that are not at all connected to the living, breathing, baffling adolescents we encounter daily.

We may have chosen education for those other reasons, but the chances are that we remain in its daily grind because of our students. Rare indeed would be the hard-hearted teacher who has not been touched by the simple decency of a child. If we want to create a sound, workable discipline policy for our classrooms, then we must begin with the pupils entrusted to our care.

Although making broad generalizations about any group is a risky business, there are some relevant character traits that many secondary students share. These traits can have a significant impact on the success or failure of a classroom discipline policy.

In the following list, you will find a few of the shared character traits of many adolescents, together with the chief challenge each one poses for the classroom teacher. This will be followed by three very brief suggestions for making sure that each character trait has a positive effect on your classroom.

Peer Pressure Is Intense for Teens

It is no surprise to teachers that teens are greatly influenced by their peers. Adolescents turn to their peers for support and guidance. Unfortunately, the guidance they receive is not always helpful.

THE CHALLENGE:

To give students the positive values that will enable them to resist negative peer pressure.

HOW TEACHERS CAN HELP:

1. Create positive identities for all of your students by including team-building exercises in collaborative work so that students can learn to work together in a positive way for a common goal.

2. Create positive peer pressure by allowing students to participate in the creation of class rules. Involving them in this process will encourage them to work together to enforce them.

3. Bring in current articles for class discussions about positive values that your students can develop for themselves. Use them to discuss the choices they make about almost every aspect of their lives and the positive and negative outcomes of those choices. You can extend the impact of these discussions by displaying these articles on a bulletin board. They will serve as visual reminders of the values you want your students to develop.

A Teenager's Emotional Energy Is High

The world of adolescence is a technicolored one. Emotions and experiences that are familiar to most adults are brand new for your students. This makes teens easily impressionable, sensitive, moody, and excitable.

THE CHALLENGE:

To channel this intensity into productive outlets.

HOW TEACHERS CAN HELP:

1. Build in class activities that allow students to be active and involved. Role-playing, panel discussions, and games are good ways to begin.

2. Use the time that might be wasted at the end of class for a forum to discuss teens' current concerns. Even a brief discussion can give your students some options to the unacceptable responses they might make to events in their lives.

3. Adjust your own attitude. Learn to view adolescents as joyful and vigorous rather than annoying. Laugh with them. Use that mixture of relief and nostalgia that you feel when you recall your own teen years to guide you now.

Having Fun Is Very Important to Secondary Students

The competition that many educators feel with the entertainment value of popular culture, the music industry, and television is real. Many students, used to attractive fast-paced entertainment, grow restless when they are expected to concentrate for a long time.

THE CHALLENGE:

To engage our students' attention fully for an entire class period.

HOW TEACHERS CAN HELP:

1. Divide lesson plans into 10-minute blocks of time and include several shorter activities in a lesson.

2. Use a variety of activities to make class interesting for yourself and for your students. Don't be afraid to be creative and a little off-the-wall.

3. Include music, art, and other bits of popular culture in your lessons. Have students fill out questionnaires to find out their interests.

Secondary Students Don't Always Use Time Wisely

Students in the secondary grades are very busy people. They have after-school jobs, active social lives, and a dizzying round of family, sports, and community activities. Even though they may fill their days with numerous activities, many teens tend to choose activities that offer short-term gains rather than long-lasting benefits.

THE CHALLENGE:

To guide students in making wise use of their time.

HOW TEACHERS CAN HELP:

1. Watch out for the signs of trouble—sleepiness, inattention, poor performance in class—and talk with the student. If the problem persists, contact the child's parents or guardians for help.

2. Work with your students to set long-range and short-term goals for themselves. Help them determine what activities need to take priority if they are to reach their goals.

3. Focus on time-management techniques in your class to help students stay on track. Show your students how to use a daily planner, a syllabus, and a personal calendar.

Adolescents Want Their Schooling to Have a Practical Purpose

Secondary students are intensely pragmatic about the work they are assigned in school. Vague assurances that "You will need this when you get to college" just do not provide the relevance that many students need to do their best work.

THE CHALLENGE:

To make students understand why they need to learn the material in a lesson.

HOW TEACHERS CAN HELP:

1. Follow sound educational theory and design lessons around a clearly stated objective and a strong anticipatory set. Use this to motivate your students to want to learn the material. (Make sure that you yourself know just how they will need this information. Just because "it is part of your district's curriculum" is not a convincing reason.)

2. Include as many real-world applications for the knowledge and skills that you teach as you can. Build in the connections to past learning and to what the students have learned in other classes.

3. At the end of class, ask students to brainstorm ways that they can use the material in the day's lesson before midnight.

Adolescents Do Not Want Absolute Freedom

Secondary students need and want guidance from caring adults. They need us to be positive role models who show them how to build constructive relationships with others and to manage the sometimes troubled course of their lives.

THE CHALLENGE:

To provide support and guidance for a large group of needy young people.

HOW TEACHERS CAN HELP:

1. Be a positive role model yourself. Studies have shown that positive and helpful teachers tend to create positive and helpful students. Modeling stable behavior is a good way to begin.

2. Set reasonable limits on the behaviors you will and will not tolerate. When your students test those limits, you have an opportunity to teach them—by your example—how to set limits for themselves.

3. Be accessible for your students. Have planned time after school when you can meet with them or sponsor a school organization. Above all, be a friendly adult who cares about their concerns.

Insecurity Is a Far-reaching Problem

Even the toughest adolescents are not always as sure of themselves as they would like us to think. Their confidence is a thin shell that is easily cracked by anxiety, failure, or the fear of failure.

THE CHALLENGE:

To make students feel more confident about their ability to succeed in school.

How Teachers Can Help:

1. Involve all of your students in your lessons. Many children have learned the fine art of being invisible in a classroom. Be sensitive to their fears and shyness, but get them engaged in positive activities where they can succeed.

2. Be positive with your students. Focus on their good points. Make sure you let them know about the good things they do. Students have no reason to try harder if a cranky teacher is going to criticize them anyway.

3. Begin a unit of study with activities that are easier to complete successfully than the ending ones. When students see they can do the work, they tend to try harder to complete assignments.

Mistakes Usually Arise from Inexperience

Contrary to what we may believe on a day when nothing is going right, our students do not get out of bed with the intention of failing our class and upsetting as many teachers as possible as soon as school begins. Students miscalculate the amount of time that it will take to complete a project or they say the wrong thing to the wrong person at the wrong time. These errors and countless others just like them are the ones made by young people who are trying to figure out the complicated business of living.

The Challenge:

To reduce the negative effects of the mistakes that your students make.

How Teachers Can Help:

1. Spend time each day showing students how to do their assignments. Many of them don't know how to break down a long-term project into manageable sections, for example, and need teacher guidance.

2. Teach your students that mistakes are part of living. We all make them. Be quick to apologize when you make yours. You'll set a good example if you do.

3. Be patient. Try not to overreact. Consider whether the error was intentional or accidental. There is a big difference, for example, between a swear word whispered to another student in the back of the room and one shouted at you.

Teens Need to Be Treated as Worthwhile People

Our students want the same things other humans want: to be taken seriously. Handling discipline problems in as dignified a manner as possible will show your students that you value and respect them.

The Challenge:

To foster mutual respect through courtesy.

How Teachers Can Help:

1. Refuse to fall into the trap of backing a misbehaving child into an emotional corner. Do not become confrontational if you want to treat your students with respect.

2. Never belittle a student's hairstyle, manner of dress, way of speaking, ideas, beliefs, aspirations, or any other personal quality. There is a big difference between correcting a student's error in a professional manner and making fun of that student, even if you were only joking.

3. Listen. Listen. Listen.

THE BASICS OF A GOOD TEACHER–STUDENT RELATIONSHIP

All of us have had the experience of having a teacher who seemed to have a magic way with students. Those classes were always the ones in which we did our best and the ones we enjoyed the most.

We can also recall those teachers we did not like and who made the class a trying experience. Many of us, even though we are reasonable adults, will admit that there were classes where we did not try very hard because we did not like our teachers. These strong memories should signal to all teachers that it is very important for us to establish a strong personal relationship with our students.

The first thing we must do is realize how powerful the desire to be treated with dignity is in our pupils. Adolescents who are searching for independence, in particular, need to have adults in their lives who take their fragile self-images seriously. This does not happen as often as it should in a culture that tends to exploit teens for their spending power or by adults who view them as overly-emotional creatures in comic-book clothes.

We also need to teach our students how to treat us with respect. Many students are just not accustomed to speaking to adults in a polite tone because they have not been taught at home the social skills they will need to succeed. Teachers should not condemn students for this failure of manners, but need to show them by example and gentle encouragement that respect must be mutual.

Effective teachers cultivate a positive view of life in general and about our students in particular. It is impossible to be a gloomy person and a good teacher at the same time. Your students need positive values to model. Those teachers who can't see that their students are worthwhile people lack an essential ingredient for successful human relations. Strong teachers are those compassionate and enthusiastic individuals who genuinely enjoy children and the art of teaching in spite of the frustrating daily grind we sometimes face.

We teachers also need to assume our roles as classroom leaders. It is teachers who set the tone for what happens in a class. Take charge! Students do not run your class—*you do*. You have the right to teach and your students have the right to learn. Take responsibility for this and you and your students will benefit.

TEACHING THE BASICS OF A GOOD TEACHER–STUDENT RELATIONSHIP

If you ever doubt that the effort and time you spend in teaching your students how to treat you with respect is a worthy use of class time, consider this: many employers state that the chief reason they fire employees is not job performance, but because the employees simply could not get along with co-workers or supervisors.

Someone neglected to teach those fired employees the importance of mutual respect and the basics of a positive relationship with other people on the job. This doesn't surprise many secondary teachers because this is the same problem we see causing disruptions in our classrooms. We can, however, prevent students from disrupting class and from losing jobs later on in their lives because they do not understand how to relate well to others.

Don't doubt that the effort we make in teaching our students how we want them to behave isn't vital to the success of the class. Many of them don't know how to relate well to adults and will engage in a long series of disruptions in order to test the limits of your rules and patience.

The process of teaching your students how to respond appropriately to you in class begins when you plan your rules and expectations before the first day of class, and it continues until the last day of the term.

You must also be very patient. Bad behavior is not learned in a day and it can't be unlearned as quickly either. One useful technique is to plan a small exercise every day that stresses the importance of a particular good behavior and how it can affect the students' relationship with you and with their classmates.

Here are five 10-minute activities for you and your students to try.

1. Hold a class discussion on why it is important for teachers and students to get along well with each other. You can begin by having students brainstorm some of the benefits of cooperation to each group.

2. Have students role-play correct and incorrect responses to such classroom situations as a boring guest speaker, an interesting guest speaker, or a disagreement with a teacher over a grade.

3. Put these questions on the board for your students to react to as an opening exercise for class: What are the three qualities teachers value most in their students? What are the three qualities students value most in their teachers?

4. Take photos of your students when they are being most helpful to each other and to you. Display them as a reminder of the importance of cooperation.

5. Stage frequent 1-minute extemporary speech opportunities for your students to present their views on topics related to mutual respect, positive relationships with bosses, honesty, the qualities of a good employee that they can learn in school, and how to disagree respectfully. Include other topics geared to allowing them to think about their relationships with teachers and peers.

There are countless other ways to build a good teacher-student relationship. Your students should be involved in classroom chores from the very first day onwards. They can help take care of shared materials and equipment, they can maintain the class in an orderly fashion so that it is tidy at the end of the day, and all students should have a hand in managing the smooth flow of the routines and procedures of the class.

Teaching students to respond to you respectfully even when you disagree on something is also a necessary part of the relationship between teacher and student. One way to do this effectively is to have your students elect a spokesperson or two to represent their interests in any disagreement they might have with you. These representatives can speak for the others to lobby for a change in a due date, for example, or a questionable test item.

You can have your students take their complaints to their spokesperson first. The spokesperson then states the students' case in a logical and calm manner. You will not only eliminate much whining and complaining, but also offer a sound model for conflict resolution if you incorporate this system into the culture of your classroom.

In addition to the classroom activities that you can use to teach good human relations, there are also other things you can do to foster positive relationships with your students. Here are twelve more brief techniques for you to consider.

1. Look at a problem from your students' view before acting.

2. Stress the values that you *share* with each other rather than your differences as often as you can.

3. Reward good behavior as often as you can. Make sure your students know what it is that they are doing right if you want them to continue.

4. Learn your students' names quickly. Teachers who don't know their students' names after a few days are rightly regarded with suspicion by the majority of their students.

5. Build your students' self-esteem by seeking their opinions.

6. Have high behavior and academic expectations for all of your students.

7. Encourage your students to reach their goals in life as well as in your class.

8. Make a point every day of making every child in your class feel important. Speak to each one every day. Call on all students. Praise their efforts. Celebrate success.

9. Display a sincere interest in their well-being both in and out of class. Ask about their successes in other classes. Help your students deal with peer pressure. Attend after-school functions when your students are involved.

10. Don't be overly familiar. Teachers who use excessive street slang or who attend their students' parties in an attempt to be friendly don't model the kind of mutual respect that students want their teachers to show.

11. Never argue with your students. Discuss problems in a calm manner away from the presence of other students whenever a difference threatens to turn into an argument.

12. Dress as professionally as the other teachers in your school district do. A professional and businesslike appearance will make it easier for your students to take you seriously.

THE CHARACTERISTICS OF TODAY'S WELL-DISCIPLINED CLASS

Should we worry about our students chewing gum? What should teachers do about those students who wear hats to school? How should we handle students who occasionally use mildly offensive language?

We wonder what to do about these and the countless other offenses that can occur during the school day. Are these the issues that should concern us or should we instead focus on the more serious problems confronting our students? After all, dealing with gum is rather silly when guns in the classroom are a real concern for many teachers.

Discipline issues today are neither simple nor self-evident. In the wake of the recent changes in education, many teachers have been left somewhat confused about how to define a class that is well-disciplined. Behaviors that used to be unacceptable no longer seem to be as serious as they once appeared.

Even though we may not always be certain about the definition of "well-disciplined," most educators are in agreement about what it is not. We certainly know when things are not going well in a classroom.

Misconduct referral notices from schools across the country are remarkably uniform in the types of behaviors that teachers and administrators do not find acceptable in schools. A quick survey of these reveals just a few of the serious misbehaviors that we do *not* want our students to engage in:

- violence
- disrespect for authority
- failure to complete work
- bullying
- dishonesty
- tardiness
- truancy

No sensible teacher wants to deal with these and their unpleasant aftermath. We know that these behaviors signal significant disruptions in the learning process and in the success of all of the students in our care.

Since we know what "well-disciplined" isn't, what then are the characteristics of a class where good discipline is the order of the day? Although there are as many hallmarks of a well-disciplined class as there are teachers and classes, a few of the most significant ones fall under the following five broad categories.

The Physical Environment Is Invitational

In a well-disciplined classroom, the room itself is appealing. Many of us teach in cramped and overcrowded rooms without even enough chalk, much less expensive equipment such as computers. Despite these restrictions, effective teachers can manage to create an environment where students focus on learning. Desks can be arranged to encourage collaboration as well as independent work. The walls showcase displays of student work. Traffic-flow problems are minimal and materials are readily available. The atmosphere in the well-disciplined room is as businesslike and comfortable as possible.

Students Understand the Rules and Procedures They Are Expected to Follow

The teacher has obviously given much thought to planning and establishing a well-organized learning climate. Class rules, procedures, and notices of upcoming activities are posted in convenient places to help students stay on track. Encouraging mottoes remind students of their goals and responsibilities. Students follow class routines for daily chores without nagging. In a well-disciplined class, students understand what they are expected to achieve each day and how they are to go about it.

Students Are Actively Engaged in the Pursuit of Knowledge

There is movement and laughter and noise. Active learning generates a much higher noise level than the silent classrooms of the past. Students are up and out of their seats while engaged in a variety of interesting activities that encourage thought and discovery. They certainly do more talking than the teacher does on most days. A well-disciplined class is a place where no child sleeps or sits idly waiting for dismissal.

There Is a Persistent Tone of Mutual Respect

Teachers and students treat each other with obvious mutual respect. This is evident in such nonverbal interactions as body language and tone of voice as well as in what students and teachers say to each other. Students speak with confidence because they feel their opinions are valued. Students in a well-disciplined class also respect their classmates. They have been taught ways to appreciate each other's unique contributions to the class as well as appropriate ways to resolve conflicts. There is a general sense of togetherness created by unflagging courtesy.

Students Take Responsibility for Their Learning

In a well-disciplined class, students are led by their teachers, but they are not coerced into good behavior through threats of dire punishment. Instead, they are encouraged to understand the importance of choosing good behavior and its lasting rewards over the short-term thrills of bad behavior.

Teachers employ a variety of collaborative strategies to promote responsible decision-making and create self-reliant students. In this class self-directed students not only encourage each other, but they also work with their teacher to achieve academic and behavioral goals that they themselves have helped to establish.

HOW WELL-DISCIPLINED IS YOUR CLASS?

The *reproducible* on page 20 will help you decide if your classroom is as well-disciplined as you think it could be. Be honest with yourself when filling in the sheet.

HOW WELL-DISCIPLINED IS YOUR CLASS?

If you are still not sure if your classroom is as well-disciplined as you think it could be, use this list to compare what happens in your class with just a few of the many things that happen in a well-disciplined class.

Put a "+" in the space beside the good behaviors that you can feel confident that your class already practices. If you need to work on a less-than-successful characteristic, put a "−" in the space. While no class is perfect, a well-disciplined class will earn far more positive marks than negative ones.

_____ When you're not there, students stick with class routines.

_____ Your students help each other. You can count on them to help you, too.

_____ Your students talk more than you do, but their conversation is mainly about the classwork they are doing. Their energy is focused on the assignment.

_____ No one shouts or nags. Everyone, including you, remembers to be polite.

_____ Students don't condone their classmates' bad behavior.

_____ Students take pride in their work. Work areas are left tidy at the end of class.

_____ The noise level is often high, but it's the noise of enthusiasm.

_____ There are practical problems to solve about real-world experiences. Community issues are part of the class.

_____ Everyone is involved. Everyone is valued. Diversity is not just tolerated, but celebrated.

_____ Students have long-term and short-term goals for their lives and you show them how to translate their goals into reality.

_____ The work is challenging, but students can be successful.

_____ You don't call students to order. They start to work as soon as they enter the room.

_____ Individual student needs are recognized in the mixture of activities designed to promote learning as well as in the variety of discipline strategies used in the class.

_____ Students perceive you as a warm and friendly person who treats them with firmness and fairness.

_____ You have a well-organized plan for preventing discipline problems and for dealing with them once they do occur.

THE INTROSPECTIVE TEACHER

In many ways education is a paradoxical profession. We are surrounded by lively and energetic people. We work five days a week and the majority of us have long summer vacations. Despite these perks, however, teaching is routinely ranked as one of the most stressful of all occupations, usually listed somewhere between air traffic controllers and cardiologists.

Another of the paradoxes of our profession is that while we work with other people for hours each day, teaching can be a very lonely job. We vanish into our classrooms early in the morning and do not emerge to even speak with another adult until much later in the day. Almost all of the decisions we have to make are choices that we have to decide upon without the benefit of consulting another adult.

Unlike many other occupations, we are almost never evaluated by our peers and not very often by administrators. Those of us who want to become more proficient at our jobs quickly learn that we must become skilled at self-assessment.

Much of our self-evaluation is done informally. We may just make mental notes along the lines of, "Tomorrow I have to separate Bobby and Kevin" or "Next year I should check the lunch menu to make sure I don't show that food parasite film on spaghetti day again!"

We keep file folders with little reminders clipped to the handouts that we have used for each unit of study. Almost all of us have notepads on our desks, write ideas all over the handouts that we pick up at workshops, and jot copious notes on our lesson plans about what worked and what didn't.

In order to be effective classroom leaders, however, these informal habits of self-evaluation may not be sufficient to enable us to create the kind of positive learning environment that we want. We need to use our tendencies toward introspection to first establish and then achieve our professional goals.

The *three reproducibles* included for you here (pages 22-27) are intended to do just that. The first two ("5-Day Self-Assessment for Negative Behaviors" *and* "Classroom Leadership Self-Assessment") are assessments designed to help you evaluate your current discipline practices and determine your strengths and weaknesses. The third assessment ("Setting Goals for Improving Your Classroom Leadership" *with* "Self-Assessment Sheets") is designed to help you get a start on setting goals for yourself so that you can create the kind of classroom that you want.

5-DAY SELF-ASSESSMENT FOR NEGATIVE BEHAVIORS

In this self-assessment you'll find 30 behaviors that do not signal a successful day at school for you or for your students. Since it is difficult to complete this form while you are teaching, take a few moments at the end of the day to rate yourself for negative behaviors. Put a check in the column under each day that you find yourself engaging in one of these negative behaviors.

	M	T	W	TH	F
1. Nag					
2. Threaten					
3. Raise your voice					
4. Allow your students "free time"					
5. Phone a parent or guardian while you were upset					
6. Fail to improve a lesson plan					
7. Fail to build relevance into a lesson					
8. Fail to greet students at the door					
9. Fail to hold a closing activity					
10. Lose your temper					
11. Point at a pupil or show other negative body language					
12. Single out a pupil for punishment					
13. Call students names, even in jest					
14. Talk over student noise					
15. Assign punishment work					
16. Allow students to sleep in class					
17. Fail to return graded work					
18. Allow a parade of students to leave the room					
19. Fail to contact a parent or guardian when you know you should have					
20. Allow a bad behavior from one pupil and not from another					
21. Talk negatively about a student in front of other students					
22. Neglect to change a plan that wasn't working					
23. Talk more than your students					
24. Fail to include higher-level thinking skills					
25. Allow some students to be uninvolved as long as they didn't cause trouble					
26. Fail to have an exciting lesson					
27. Fail to say something positive to each student					
28. Permit students to ignore you					
29. Have to deal with serious misbehavior					
30. Have a bad day					

CLASSROOM LEADERSHIP SELF-ASSESSMENT

Use these broad questions about your role as a classroom leader to evaluate your effectiveness in creating the positive learning climate that will lead to productive student behavior.

Read each question to analyze your effectiveness in that category. Use the space beside each to record your score.

Rate yourself on a scale of "1" to "5." A ranking of "1" is the lowest score that you can earn and a "5" is the highest.

1._____ Am I doing enough to prevent discipline problems from beginning?

2._____ Are the daily routines in my class easy to follow?

3._____ Are the class rules effective?

4._____ Do I enforce the class rules consistently?

5._____ Are my behavior and academic standards high enough?

6._____ Are the plans I have for dealing with discipline problems workable?

7._____ Have I helped my students set long- and short-term goals for themselves?

8._____ Do I work with my students to help them achieve their goals?

9._____ Do my students have enough relevant and challenging work to do?

10._____ Is the instruction designed to develop higher-level thinking skills?

11._____ Am I helping my students grow intellectually and socially?

12._____ Am I using all of the resources and support personnel available to me?

13._____ Do I include every student every day?

14._____ Do I treat my students with sensitivity and respect?

15._____ Do I present myself as a good teacher: concerned, committed, and professional?

SETTING GOALS FOR IMPROVING YOUR CLASSROOM LEADERSHIP

Use the information you have gained from your self-assessments to focus your efforts to improve your classroom leadership. After you have determined your strengths and weaknesses, you can begin setting goals for improving the areas that are not as strong as you would like for them to be.

By using the form that follows, you can begin your program of self-improvement in a systematic way. Here are the steps to take that will enable you to do this.

Step One: Use the self-assessments in this section to determine your discipline strengths and weaknesses.

Step Two: Write out your problem as you perceive it to be in response to the question on the sheet.

Step Three: List two strategies you think will help you solve this particular discipline problem.

Step Four: Begin to implement your strategies so that you and your students can benefit.

Since improving our teaching skills is a daily process for even the most experienced teachers, you should photocopy this form and refer to it throughout the school year. An area of concern that you might need to work on right now may not be of the same importance to you later on.

Here's a sample from the reproducible to help you get started in your quest for improving how you manage the discipline issues in your class.

SAMPLE SELF-ASSESSMENT

10. Is the instruction designed to develop higher-level thinking skills?

   I need to include more activities that are above the knowledge or comprehension levels.

Strategies

   a. **use the suggestions in the teacher's edition for including higher-level activities**

   b. **begin to think about how to include real-life and hands-on activities in every lesson so that students move at least to the application level**

Self-Assessment Sheet

1. Am I doing enough to prevent discipline problems?

   _____
   _____

   Strategies

   a. _____
      _____

   b. _____
      _____

2. Are the daily routines of my class easy to follow?

   _____
   _____

   Strategies

   a. _____
      _____

   b. _____
      _____

3. Are the class rules effective?

   _____
   _____

   Strategies

   a. _____
      _____

   b. _____
      _____

4. Do I enforce the class rules consistently?

   _____
   _____

   Strategies

   a. _____
      _____

   b. _____
      _____

5. Are my behavior and academic standards high enough?

   _____
   _____

   Strategies

   a. _____
      _____

   b. _____
      _____

6. Are the plans I have for dealing with discipline problems workable?

_____

_____

Strategies

a. _____

_____

b. _____

_____

7. Have I helped my students set long- and short-term goals for themselves?

_____

_____

Strategies

a. _____

_____

b. _____

_____

8. Do I work with my students to help them achieve their goals?

_____

_____

Strategies

a. _____

_____

b. _____

_____

9. Do my students have enough challenging and relevant work to do?

_____

_____

Strategies

a. _____

_____

b. _____

_____

10. Is the instruction designed to develop higher-level thinking skills?

_____

_____

Strategies

a. _____

_____

b. _____

_____

11. Am I helping my students grow intellectually and socially?

_____

_____

Strategies

   a. _____

_____

   b. _____

_____

12. Am I using all of the resources and support personnel available to me?

_____

_____

Strategies

   a. _____

_____

   b. _____

_____

13. Do I include every student every day?

_____

_____

Strategies

   a. _____

_____

   b. _____

_____

14. Do I treat my students with sensitivity and respect?

_____

_____

Strategies

   a. _____

_____

   b. _____

_____

15. Do I present myself as a good teacher: concerned, committed, and professional?

_____

_____

Strategies

   a. _____

_____

   b. _____

_____

POSITIVE TEACHER ATTITUDES THAT PROMOTE STUDENT SUCCESS

Education today remains as it always has been—a mixture of good intentions and some pretty discouraging problems. Successful teachers, however, have developed ways to cope with their problems more efficiently than those teachers whose classes are chaotic. Successful teachers do have discipline problems, but they have found successful ways to minimize their potentially negative impact.

Conventional wisdom tells us that it isn't the problems we face that determine our successes or failures. It is our attitude about our problems that ultimately determines whether our teaching is a success or a failure.

Here are some attitudes you can adopt today that will immediately make a difference in your classroom. The benefits of taking control of your attitudes are numerous and satisfying.

1. While goals keep your students focused on the big picture, you also need to develop professional goals for yourself. Having a few worthwhile goals will provide direction and focus to your school day.

2. Make it your goal that every one of your students will have a positive attitude about your class every day.

3. Make it your goal that you will begin each school day with a positive attitude about your career, your students, and your daily responsibilities.

4. Being an optimistic person doesn't mean that problems don't exist or aren't serious. A positive attitude just means you are working on a solution in a productive and efficient way.

5. Take responsibility for your attitude about your class and about your teaching duties. When you realize you are the most important factor in creating a solution to some of the discipline problems that you experience, then you are on the right path to that solution.

6. Problems move you forward when you choose to work to solve them. When you experience discipline problems, don't be discouraged; they stimulate you to use your creativity and talents to create a well-disciplined classroom.

7. Show your students that you believe learning is an enjoyable and worthwhile activity and that you expect them to share this attitude.

8. Spend your energy on the larger problems first and allot less of your energy for the small ones. Choose to deal with those problems that will give you the greatest benefit right away. Prioritize to save your energy.

9. Small attitude changes often create bigger patterns of success. For example, many teachers claim that one of their classes is a terrible class. When they stop to look at the situation clearly, they do not have a terrible class. What they have is a class with many well-behaved students in it and just a few who are not.

10. It is important that you earn the respect and affection of your students. Students who like their teachers will be much more willing to cooperate with them.

11. Since discipline problems are inevitable, you will do well to accept them as challenges and not as stumbling blocks to success.

12. Teachers must genuinely like their students and see them as worthwhile beings. You must not only appreciate their individual differences, but in order to be a successful teacher, you must communicate your appreciation, affection, and acceptance to your students.

BECOMING A PROACTIVE TEACHER

There's usually at least one in every school. Even in the most violent and out-of-control schools, there is usually at least one classroom that is a haven of peace and productive behavior. In this room, students engage in interesting learning activities that keep them coming back for more.

The key to these classes does not lie in their physical environment or in the time of day when they meet or even in the students who cross the threshold. The key to these classes can be found in the teachers who create them. These teachers don't just react to the school environment, they shape it. They take charge.

Keep in mind, as these successful teachers do, that sound class management and instructional practices can prevent many of our problems. If you doubt this, look at any two teachers who share the same students. One may experience significantly fewer discipline problems than the other. The difference is not in the pupils, but in the way those two teachers manage their students. One is a proactive teacher and the other is not.

Proactive teachers are the ones who accept responsibility for the success or failure of their classes. When we can accept that almost all of the discipline problems that can happen in a classroom can be prevented or at least made better by teacher action, then we are on the way to becoming proactive teachers.

On the other hand, those teachers who blame society, the media, parents, and other teachers for the problems they experience are only stalling. They are not making the necessary efforts to change the things that can be changed in their classes.

Teachers who decide to develop positive relationships with their students, who decide to seek out and use alternatives to punishments and threats, who decide to cope with the problems that we all share—these are proactive teachers. These teachers are free to make positive changes in their school days because they have accepted responsibility for their actions. These are the teachers who choose to make a difference in the life of a child.

There are five simple steps you can take to become a successful proactive teacher. They are neither complicated nor difficult, but they do require a mental commitment on your part.

Step One

Become thoroughly familiar with the course content. If you don't know the material you are supposed to teach, then your teaching will lack authority. Secondary students are quick to spot teachers who do not know the material and they are justified in having no patience with such teachers.

Step Two

Quickly get to know your students. If you know your students, you will be better able to establish the kind of rapport with them that you need in order to be a better teacher. Proactive teachers have a sound working knowledge of adolescent behavior in general and of their own students in particular.

Step Three

Don't rely on punishment for control of your classes. Instead, what you need to do is learn as much as you can about the various disciplinary practices that are available to you. You need to know what your options are and when you should choose each.

Step Four

Present yourself to your students and to your colleagues as a professional educator. That means doing all of the things good teachers do—maintain order, be very organized, teach innovative lessons, and provide your students with the kind of adult role model that they need.

Step Five

Take responsibility for your attitude about the discipline problems in your classroom. Let go of the negative thoughts you have about your students and about the past experiences you have had with them. Concentrate on the positive steps you can take to help your students become self-disciplined.

"Each goodly thing is hardest to begin."

—Edmund Spenser

Section 2

GETTING READY TO MAKE A GOOD IMPRESSION

In This Section . . .

The first few weeks of a school term are exhilarating and exhausting for most teachers. These crucial weeks are vital to the success of the rest of the time that we have with our students.

In "Getting Ready to Make a Good Impression," "What Your Students Really Want from a Teacher," and the student questionnaire, "Design Your Ideal Teacher," you will be able to gather information that will take the guesswork out of the image you want to present to your students.

The "Organizational Tasks Checklist" will help you keep up with the dozens of projects and chores you have to accomplish in order to get the school term off to a successful start.

Learn more about the important role that rules and procedures play in helping teachers create successful discipline climates in secondary classrooms. You'll learn how to create, teach, and enforce the rules and procedures that will be the backbone of your successful program all term.

The usefulness of a pleasant physical environment and the ways to achieve one are available to you in "More than Moving Furniture: Creating an Environment for Learning" and "The Hows and Whys of Seating Charts." You'll learn how to turn any classroom into a more productive work place.

The first-day-of-school jitters can often wreak havoc with our most carefully prepared lessons. Learn how to have a successful first day with your students in "The First Day of Class: Face to Face for the First Time," "25 Activities for the First Day of Class," "Student Information Form," and "Student Checklist for the First Day of Class."

Follow this first-day success with some of the tips you can learn from "The First Week of School: Five Successful Days" to make sure every student in your class gets off to a great start.

Since it's so important for teachers to be able to call students by name, you'll find some tips for this in "Quick Tips for Learning Your Students' Names."

You'll also make school success easier for your students to achieve in "Starting Off Right: Teaching the Text" and the survey that accompanies it.

In "Creating a Student-Centered Atmosphere in Any Room" you'll find ways to make your students comfortable and willing to achieve the success you have planned for them.

Finally, you'll learn how to take care of the most overworked person in a school at the start of a term—yourself—when you learn how to have a "Sound Mind in a Well-Rested Body" even during the hectic start of a new term.

"The beginning, as the saying goes, is half the work."

—Plato

GETTING READY TO MAKE A GOOD IMPRESSION

Most beginnings are a fine mixture of regret and anticipation. While we long for the safety of what we are leaving behind, we look forward to the promise of what lies ahead.

For teachers, the start of a new school term is an especially bittersweet mixture. We miss the comfortable routines of our long summer days while at the same time we begin to anticipate the promises that lie ahead of us in the new term. Few times of the year are as exciting or as stressful.

At the start of a new term, teachers are asked to do things that are almost impossible. We have to be extremely active at school—moving desks, fixing bulletin boards, putting up banners, and hauling hundreds of student textbooks from storage. Many of us learn how to do these demanding physical chores in our new school clothes because a parent might drop by before the term starts to discuss one of our students with us.

We also face an exhausting paperwork load. We not only have an entire course to plan, but we also have to find out as much as we can about our students and what they do and don't know about our subject. We know that the success of our school year lies in finding out as much as we can about them as quickly as we can in order to hold chaos at bay.

As if these two huge responsibilities weren't enough, we also have to spend the first few days of the new term impressing a room full of suspicious young strangers who are as nervous and excited as we are. Somehow we have to convince them that they will have an enjoyable term of meaningful learning experiences that will be of far more benefit to them than what they assure us they would rather be doing: hanging out with their friends at the mall or watching late-night cable television channels.

No wonder so many teachers report significant sleep disturbances at the start of a new term. Few teachers have not awakened in a panic from the teacher anxiety nightmare—the one where we are standing helpless in front of our class trying to get our students to pay attention to us while they riot happily around the room.

In spite of the seeming impossibility of our task at the start of a new term, somehow teachers throughout the years have managed with grace and dignity to create the kinds of classrooms and learning experiences for students that we all want. These organized, well-prepared, and dedicated teachers got their students off to a good start. You can, too.

WHAT YOUR STUDENTS REALLY WANT FROM A TEACHER

Many students have very clear ideas about what they expect their teachers to do and to look like. One of the best ways for you to find out what your students expect from you is to survey them. (See the *reproducible* "Design Your Ideal Teacher" on page 35.) You will probably find that the results of your survey will be similar to the following list of teacher traits that students value. If you know what it is that your students really want from you, then it will be easier for you to establish the kind of productive relationship with them that you want.

The start of the term is the best time to begin working on these traits if you want to be the kind of proactive and fair-minded teacher who has a minimum of behavior problems to deal with in the course of a school day. Use this list to begin to examine how you measure up against your students' vision of the ideal teacher.

The ideal teacher:

1. Enjoys students.
2. Doesn't just hand out assignments, but teaches the material.

3. Emphasizes the material and doesn't push, push, push grades.

4. Gives students a syllabus.

5. Uses lots of different techniques such as skits and films.

6. Has a great sense of humor.

7. Understands pupil problems and tries to help.

8. Acts like an adult and not a child.

9. Keeps promises.

10. Makes sure everyone understands the instructions for an assignment.

11. Is not too strict.

12. Makes everyone feel welcome in a class.

13. Is organized.

14. Spends time after school to help students who need it.

15. Returns papers promptly.

16. Offers extra credit to raise grades if necessary.

17. Is friendly and fair.

18. Uses a pleasant voice.

19. Knows the subject matter.

20. Admits when he or she is wrong.

21. Stays open-minded.

22. Is enthusiastic about the subject.

23. Is willing to listen to both sides of an issue.

24. Has a reputation for giving challenging work.

25. Isn't a pushover. Keeps misbehaving students in line.

26. Keeps everyone busy.

27. Learns everyone's name right away.

28. Does not have favorites.

29. Gives students a voice in class decisions.

30. Is polite to everyone all of the time.

DESIGN YOUR IDEAL TEACHER

If you were in charge of creating the perfect teacher, what qualities would you include? Here is your chance to express yourself!

Think for a few moments about the qualities you have appreciated in your teachers in the past and the qualities you would like to see in all of your future teachers.

Use the categories below to design your ideal teacher. Your answers should be thoughtful and serious because they will help me decide how I can be a good teacher for you this term.

Category	*Preferences*
Types of Assignments	
Preparation for the Future	
Class Rules and Procedures	
Homework Assignments	
Relationship with Students	
Attitudes that Inspire	
Organization of the Class	
Testing Techniques	
Problem-Solving Techniques	

Do you have any other advice for me? _____

_____

_____

ORGANIZATIONAL TASKS CHECKLIST

The *reproducible* on the following pages will help you keep up with the many projects and chores you have to accomplish in order to get the new school term off to a successful start.

ENFORCING SCHOOL RULES

There is a need for rules whenever people are expected to work in harmony. A school where all of the adults can agree on and abide by an established set of rules is a much more productive and pleasant place than a school where everyone does whatever might be workable at the moment. School rules are guidelines that can make life more agreeable for all of those people who are governed by them.

There is strength in unity. Teachers and students alike must abide by school rules. Although you may have important classroom rules, it is your responsibility to make sure your students know and understand the larger set of rules that governs their behavior. The suggestions here are designed to help you teach your students the importance of school rules and to guide you in enforcing them.

1. Make sure you know and understand the school rules. It doesn't do anyone any good to have rules written in a faculty handbook if you don't make yourself thoroughly familiar with them.

2. Follow the school rules yourself with cheerfulness and enthusiasm. Set a good example for your students and colleagues.

3. The time to begin to teach school rules is at the first class meeting. Waiting for a week or two sets a bad precedent that will make changing student attitudes more difficult. Don't just assume that your students know the rules; take the time to make sure everyone understands them. Your students should not break rules because no one cared enough to teach them.

4. After you have made sure your students know what the school rules are, go a step further and make sure your students understand the need for everyone to work together.

5. Don't tell your students the benefits of following rules. Instead, get them to work together to generate a list of the positive things that happen when all students cooperate in following the rules. Post this list as a reminder to everyone.

6. Another effective way to make students see the need for cooperative behavior is to have them survey adults in the community about the rules that govern their work places. This will help students see that rules are a part of everybody's work day and not just a set of arbitrary "tortures" for adolescents.

7. Follow the rules yourself. If your students can't chew gum or drink soda in class, then you shouldn't either. Model the behaviors you want your students to have.

8. Set a positive climate for enforcing school rules by praising your students when they follow them. When all students are on time for class or are particularly well-behaved at a pep rally, for instance, take time to thank them for their cooperation.

ORGANIZATIONAL TASKS CHECKLIST

There are many, many tasks that all teachers in almost any school have to accomplish before the term begins. Some of us are so overwhelmed by the seeming impossibility of completing all of them that we almost lose sight of what's really important at this time of year—getting our students off to a good start. Here's a quick checklist for teachers who want to stay organized during this hectic time.

1._____ Learn your schedule. Post a copy of bell schedules for your students.

2._____ Get a large calendar to keep track of student birthdays and school events.

3._____ Create a syllabus or planner for your students.

4._____ Make sure the clock is working. Better check your timer, too, so that games and short activities go well.

5._____ Learn about school activities such as contests, drives, assemblies, and other events planned for this term so that you can plan around them as well as encourage your students to participate.

6._____ Obtain or photocopy as many of the forms you will need for the term as you can. You will probably need some for attendance, health, collecting money, conduct, and parent conferences, among others.

7._____ Pick up the supplies that the district provides for you.

8._____ Purchase the supplies that your school district does not provide for you.

9._____ Get your school wardrobe in order. You should dress as professionally as the other teachers in your district.

10._____ Make a list of anticipated classroom-management problems so that you can create solutions for them.

11._____ Even if you are a seasoned veteran teacher, read the policies, rules, and expectations for teachers.

12._____ Read your faculty handbook and make notes on items that directly affect you.

13._____ Find out what is expected of you this year in the way of special duties such as hall duty or lunch duty.

14._____ If you are an experienced teacher, mentor a beginning teacher. If you are a beginning teacher and your school has no formal mentoring program, find a few respected teachers who will agree to help you throughout the year.

15._____ Join professional organizations.

16._____ Pay attention to fire drill and emergency information. Learn the procedures and be prepared to teach them to your students.

17._____ Although you should aim for perfect attendance, create a substitute folder just in case you might have to miss school.

ORGANIZATIONAL TASKS CHECKLIST *(cont'd)*

18._____ Taking attendance is a time-consuming procedure. Spend time figuring out how to streamline this daily chore so that you can be fast as well as accurate.

19._____ Plan the resources you will need and how you will go about arranging for guest speakers, media presentations, and other enriching experiences for your students.

20._____ Arrange the forms you will need for documenting parent or guardian contacts and other information.

21._____ Set up your plan book and your grade book. If you are using a computerized version of either, be sure to check out the format with a supervisor to make sure you are in compliance with district policy.

22._____ Outline the entire course content so that you know what you will teach.

23._____ Outline the course content for each grading period.

24._____ Plan your units of study.

25._____ Plan the first three weeks of lessons. Try to stay three weeks ahead.

26._____ Plan the procedure you should follow in order to issue textbooks.

27._____ Set up your classroom with good management strategies in mind.

28._____ Decorate your classroom so that students will be welcomed.

29._____ Decide on the way you will weigh and determine grades. Publish it on a poster or a handout for your students.

30._____ Make up a personal first-aid kit for yourself.

31._____ Study the class rolls as soon as you can to become familiar with names.

32._____ Make up your seating chart for the start of the term.

33._____ Set a professional goal for yourself. Write it down and plan how you are going to achieve it.

9. Be consistent in your enforcement of school rules. Playing favorites or making unfair exceptions sets a very poor example for everyone. You will have trouble enforcing rules when you need to if you are inconsistent in enforcement.

10. Many school rules today involve weapons and violent behavior. Be sure to teach your students how to handle confrontations that could escalate into something much more serious. For example, students need to know how to report a weapon at school.

11. There is no excuse for a teacher to break the school rules. Even if you disagree with a rule, continue to enforce it while you go about getting it changed to something better. If you see that a rule is no longer working at your school, offer to lead a committee to work with the administration to find a solution or an alternative.

CREATING CLASSROOM RULES

Ever since chalk was invented, teachers have used it to write sets of classroom rules. We know that we need classroom rules in order to maintain the kind of positive learning environment where our students can flourish. As necessary as they are, however, creating, teaching, and enforcing classroom rules is not always easy.

In order to be effective, classroom rules have to do several things all at once. They must:

1. cover the entire range of possible student misconduct,
2. appeal to students,
3. fit within a school district's policies for student behavior,
4. be stated simply enough for all students to understand them,
5. be enforceable,
6. satisfy parents,
7. create an orderly classroom,
8. be as fair to as many people as possible, and
9. be easy to remember.

You may be tempted not to take the time to create rules if you think students who are in secondary school should already know how to behave properly. You're right. They should. But they don't.

Unfortunately, even older students do not always know what you expect from them and they are not talented mind readers. To complicate matters further, other teachers have different behavior expectations for the students that you share.

Why should we go to the trouble of creating a set of rules for our students? The first issue you have to resolve for yourself when you begin to consider your rules is just why you need them. There are several sound reasons for establishing a set of rules that will guide your students.

■ *Reason One:* Rules show your students the importance of good behavior if they are to work productively. If you want to increase the number of positive behaviors in your class and decrease the number of negative ones, then you need to make students aware of the necessity of committing themselves to choosing to obey the standards you have for your class.

■ *Reason Two:* Rules give students and teachers a common language for the set of expectations that each has for the class. Even the most experienced educators can be surprised at the gap between the behaviors they believe that their students should exhibit and the behaviors those students engage in when left to just figure out things for themselves.

■ *Reason Three:* Students and teachers need rules spelled out clearly if they are to work together to generate a balance between permissiveness and punishment. Rules do this when they are *consistently* and *fairly* enforced.

■ *Reason Four:* Rules protect our right to teach and the right of all students in our classroom to have a positive environment for learning because rules set limits and give us all guidelines. Rules make us secure because—once established—they protect the safety of students, teachers, and property.

■ *Reason Five:* As a final argument for taking the time and going to the trouble to create a set of rules, consider your students. Even though they appear to be in a state of constant rebellion against all types of authority, students do not want—nor do they need—total freedom. The pupils in your class want guidance from caring adults who show them respect and consideration.

In addition to understanding why you need classroom rules, another factor you need to give some serious consideration to when you create rules is how involved you want your students to be in the process.

How to Involve Students in the Process of Creating Rules

Experienced teachers of all grade levels will agree that the best possible way to create class rules is with the wholehearted cooperation of all students.

The reasons for this are simple. When you let students have a say in deciding what the class rules should be, you set an example of trust and confidence in your students. Another reason to involve a class in this process is that students will be more likely to follow rules that they have created for themselves. There will be a group pressure in place that keeps many students from breaking the group's rules.

If you do decide to allow students to create rules for themselves, begin by asking a series of questions designed to get them thinking about what could benefit them all. Some questions to ask include:

1. What makes a student behave well in some classes?
2. What behaviors do you notice students with good grades exhibiting?
3. What are some behaviors you know will hurt a student's chances of doing well?
4. What limits should we set to make sure everyone can do well?
5. What rules do you think would work well for us here?

What to Do When You Don't Want to Involve Students

If you are not comfortable with allowing your students to create class rules, then don't involve them. Some classes start the term unable to successfully handle the mature responsibility of such a procedure. If this is the case for your class, you can still involve them in creating rules, but this can be done later in the term when they have settled into the routines of your class.

In this case, you should create a workable set of rules for them at the start of the term, teach these rules, and consistently enforce them. When you are ready for your students to participate in creating or refining rules for themselves, you can have students examine the current rules and modify them.

Stating Rules Positively

After you have begun the process of getting your students to think about the areas you would like to have the rules cover, you are then ready for the second step: how to state them.

State your class rules in a positive way. Instead of saying "Don't write on the desks," phrase the same thought as "Show respect for the property of others." With this slight change in wording, the emphasis is now on what your students *should* be doing, not on what they should *not* do.

Instead of stating "Don't play around before class starts," try "Be in your seat and working when the bell rings," whereby the tone is pleasant and broad enough to cover a wide range of activities. The positive message conveys a tone of mutual respect that is lacking in the "do not" statements.

Determining if Your Rules Will Be Successful

If you are still not sure if your rules are appropriate for secondary students, here are a few examples that might help you determine if your classroom rules will lead to self-directed learning.

1. Bring your materials to class every day.
2. Be working on your opening assignment when the bell rings.
3. Be prepared to do your best in class each day.
4. Help your classmates and yourself by respecting the rights of all students to learn.

It is also important that you select just a few rules so that your students will have no trouble in remembering and honoring them. You will find that it is easier for you and your students to follow five or six well-expressed broad rules rather than a larger number of detailed ones. If your rules are reasonable, few in number, broad in scope, and stated positively, then you are well on your way to creating a positive classroom atmosphere.

Determining Appropriate Consequences

After you have created the rules and stated them in the very best way possible, you now have to consider the consequences your students will face if they break them. Begin this by discussing with your students the intangible rewards everyone will enjoy when everyone follows the rules. Next, ask your students to help you determine what should happen if the rules are broken.

Ask your students for their advice on assessing how the rules should be enforced. Be careful to state that you intend to take their comments under advisement so that you are not forced to agree to anything on the spot with which you are uncomfortable. Don't give in to student pressure that compromises the strength of your carefully thought-out rules.

When you discuss consequences with your students, whether or not they are involved in determining these, make sure the consequences are ones you can enforce comfortably. They should fit the crime in a natural way. Consequences should also follow a simple pattern of escalating punishments for escalating offenses.

For example, writing 1,000 sentences for the first tardy to class is not appropriate because it is excessive, does not fit the crime, and will make students dislike writing. A more appropriate consequence would be a warning for the first tardy to class, a 10-minute detention for the second time, and a 20-minute detention for the third time. The punishment is not only appropriate, but it also grows more severe with each infraction of the rule.

If you are still not sure about the effectiveness of the classroom rules you have established, use the questions in the following list to guide you as you examine each one.

1. Is each rule necessary to the smooth management of your class?
2. Is each rule reasonable and age-appropriate?
3. Are you willing to consistently enforce each one?
4. Is each one stated as positively as possible?
5. Are your class rules consistent with school policies?
6. Can your students recite the rules from memory or do you have too many?
7. Are students committed to honoring the rules?
8. Do your students understand the consequences and rewards associated with each one?
9. Are the consequences appropriate?
10. Can your students cite examples that define each broad rule?

TEACHING CLASSROOM RULES

A perfect list of rules is useless if your students don't know them or don't understand them. You'll find that most broken rules are momentary lapses on the part of students. You can help them with this by raising their awareness of the rules and of the importance of following them. The way to do this is to *teach the rules*. You'll also find that one of the three important areas concerning classroom rules—teaching them—is the most important step if you want an orderly classroom. It's also the easiest one to overlook as you focus your energy on teaching the material in your curriculum.

Use the following techniques to establish the balance between firmness and respect for your students. This is not a one- or two-day event, but rather a process that continues until the end of the term. Use these to get started in the right direction and let your creativity and teaching skills take over as you make sure your students understand what they are supposed to do to honor the rules of your classroom.

1. Design a plan for teaching the rules to your students as you would design a lesson plan to teach any other information. Explain the behavior, model it, have students practice it, and then reinforce it.

2. Be friendly, serious, and firm when you introduce the topic of classroom rules to your students. Now is not the time to confuse your students by joking or treating the subject lightly.

3. Send a letter with a copy of the rules home so that parents or guardians can understand what the classroom rules are, what consequences are involved, and how they can support you and your students. It will pay to have parents and guardians informed and working with you from the first day forward.

4. Enlarge a copy of your rules and display it. There should also be a copy in each student's notebook. In order to get your students to pay attention to the rules, leave blanks for them to fill in as you discuss the rules.

5. Compare the classroom rules that govern your students with the rules that face all of us as employees. Relate classroom rules to the world of work as often as you can so that your students understand that the rules they have in your class are similar to the ones they will live by when they are adults.

6. Focus on the rules and on teaching and reinforcing them during the first three weeks of the term to ensure that your students take them *and you* seriously. Don't neglect to return to the rules as needed throughout the term.

7. Enhance your presentation of classroom rules by involving your students in active roles. Rather than sit through a droning lecture from you, they can role-play situations where rules are broken, list positive and negative consequences of rules, hold a debate about the need for various rules—any activities that engage your students in active learning.

8. Check for student understanding of the rules by having your students explain the rules to you. This would be a good time to have them think of new examples or benefits of each one.

9. Hold sessions periodically where you and your students review the rules that they have listed in their notebooks. Checking for understanding every now and then will make students aware of the rules of the class and thus better able to abide by them.

10. Offer alternatives to students who break class rules. Teach them not just to stop a negative action, but to replace it with a positive one. You encourage self-discipline and redirect student energy when you do this.

ENFORCING CLASSROOM RULES

Enforcing your classroom rules is as important a step in creating the kind of classroom environment you would like to have as are creating and teaching them. Effective enforcement of the rules will make the difference in your classroom between order and disorder or between a positive or a negative atmosphere.

Much of what we already know about enforcing classroom rules is simply common sense—you have to be consistent in enforcement from the first day of the term until the very last day. If you are not consistent, you will confuse students. They will not be able to see the connection between the rule and their behavior unless you bring it to their attention through consistent enforcement.

Here are some strategies designed to help you be more effective at enforcement. Use them to encourage your students to follow the rules that govern your class.

1. Deal with a broken rule immediately. Waiting will confuse students who are expecting to see you take action.

2. Don't threaten students who break a rule. Calmly enforce the rule.

3. Don't lecture, argue, fuss, or give undue attention to rule-breakers. Enforce the rule.

4. Be clear with your students. When you have a rule, mean it. Show this by making sure you enforce all rules.

5. Call parents or guardians if you see that a student is having problems with a particular rule. They can be very helpful when asked to intervene early.

6. When a student breaks a rule, follow a quick 5-step procedure:
   Step 1: Have the student state the rule. Ask, "What rule have you broken?"
   Step 2: Clarify the rule so the student can see that it applies to this situation.
   Step 3: Have the student tell you the reason for the rule.
   Step 4: Have the student tell you the consequence.
   Step 5: Put the consequence into action.

7. Establish a routine for the ordinary procedure of business in your classroom so that it is easy for your students to work within the rules. You can find some suggestions for these routines in Section Three.

8. When a student has broken a rule for the first time, question the student privately to make sure he or she understands what rule was broken.

9. Be aware of the trouble spots in your class day. Before class, transition times, and when some students finish an assignment before others are some of the better-known trouble times. Work out solutions to these so that the rules can stay unbroken.

10. Students often misbehave for valid reasons. Check to see why your students are breaking a rule. Students may misbehave because they need attention from you or their peers. Students also misbehave because they need more clearly defined limits or because they are lacking sufficient motivation to improve their behavior. If you know these, then you can provide these basic needs for all of your students.

11. Sometimes students don't observe rules because doing so is not a priority for them. You must make it a priority for your students to be governed by class rules. Doing so will help your students be self-governed.

12. Be patient. Your students are going to backslide as well as perform better than you expect. Enforcing rules is a long-term commitment.

13. One way to make enforcing the rules easier for everyone is to keep the infractions small. Try to keep situations from escalating into major disasters whenever you can.

14. When you are enforcing rules, don't tell the offending student the rule he or she has just broken. Instead, ask the student to recall the rule for you. This is more effective in creating a permanent change in students.

15. Don't hesitate to put the rewards and consequences for your class rules into place. Having a class reward early in the term will show your students that you are serious about the rules that govern your class.

16. Call attention to good behavior as often as you possibly can. Rewards can be an effective way to encourage students to follow rules.

17. It is tempting to make exceptions to your rules. Before you make exceptions, think carefully. You have to balance the needs of the group with the needs of the individual student who broke the rule.

18. Be friendly but firm when you set limits for your students. Sometimes we err by being too permissive. Here is a quick checklist for you to use to see if you are too permissive with your students. This is a common pattern of permissiveness. Is it yours?

    Step 1: You ask students to cooperate with you.

    Step 2: You wait while they disregard your request.

    Step 3: You repeat your request in a louder voice.

    Step 4: You wait while they disregard your request again.

    Step 5: The cycle repeats itself until you lose your cool.

19. One effective technique to enforce rules consistently is very easy: Chart the rules that are frequently broken. Simply make a checklist with a grid to record each infraction as it happens. You can do this by writing the rule on the board and putting a checkmark next to it whenever it's broken. Often the act of recording the infractions will serve to make students aware of the rules they often break.

20. If you find you are having trouble enforcing a particular rule, you may want to ask yourself these questions to see how to get back on track.

    Question 1: Do all students understand this rule?

    Question 2: Is the rule too vague or too broad?

    Question 3: Do students understand and accept the need for this rule? Can they see how it is necessary for the smooth running of the class?

    Question 4: Has your enforcement of this rule been consistent or have you sent a confusing message by allowing too many exceptions?

CHECKLIST FOR RULES, PROCEDURES, AND EXPECTATIONS

One of the best ways to insure that your students are attending to the rules and other important information that you give them at the start of the term is to have them fill in a worksheet as you go over the rules and information. (See next page.) This practice has several advantages over just talking to your students.

One advantage is that it forces students to become active learners while you are teaching them the rules, procedures, and expectations you have for them. Instead of passively listening to yet another teacher drone on and on about how they are supposed to act, your students will be forced to attend to what you are saying.

Another advantage is that your students will have a written record of just what they are supposed to do. When a student breaks a rule, you can ask that pupil to check the rule on the handout. Because they have written the answers themselves, students are far more likely to recall them.

A final advantage of such a worksheet is that you communicate to your students early in the term that you are a serious teacher who has given lots of thought to the way you want your students to act in class. When you are able to effectively communicate this to your students, you are then on your way to helping them become self-disciplined.

MORE THAN MOVING FURNITURE: CREATING AN ENVIRONMENT FOR LEARNING

During those tight budget times in education, it's not easy to arrange our rooms in the ways that we would like. Drastic spending cuts have all but eliminated the art supplies we had grown accustomed to in more affluent times. Other problems also affect how we set up our rooms. Because we have students with diverse needs, we need to be responsive to a wide variety of physical needs and learning styles.

We struggle to make a workable physical environment in spite of overcrowded classes and having to share classroom space with other teachers and their pupils. As difficult as it is to arrange the classroom, however, creating an environment for learning has a significant impact on the discipline climate in your room.

However, even with these serious problems, there are many things you can do to create an environment that encourages positive discipline in your classroom. Your room should reflect your pleasant, professional attitude and encourage your students' efforts to be successful. Careful planning and organization will insure that your students are comfortable and ready to work while they are in your room.

When you are deciding how you want your room arranged, consider three important elements: the traffic flow, the space you need for yourself, and the physical arrangement of the desks.

STUDENT CHECKLIST FOR RULES, PROCEDURES, AND EXPECTATIONS

Name _____ **Class** _____

Teacher _____ **Period** _____

1. When does class begin? _____ end? _____

2. Is seating by chart assignment or by student choice? _____
   _____

3. Behavior upon entering classroom:
   _____ visiting with friends allowed
   _____ board work to do
   _____ other:

4. Time to clean room: _____ pack up: _____

5. Behavior upon leaving classroom:
   _____ leave at bell
   _____ leave when this signal is given: _____

6. What to do when tardy: _____

7. How to request permission to leave the room: _____
   _____

8. Procedure for turning in assignments: _____
   _____

9. Policy for making up missed work: _____
   _____

10. What to do if you don't have your homework: _____
    _____

11. Testing schedule: _____
    _____

12. Cheating policy: _____
    _____
    _____

13. What you should bring to class each day: _____
    _____

STUDENT CHECKLIST FOR RULES, PROCEDURES, AND EXPECTATIONS *(cont'd)*

14. What to do if you don't have materials: _____

_____

15. Procedure for trash disposal: _____

_____

16. What to do if you need a tissue: _____

_____

17. Policy about gum and food: _____

_____

18. Where to find homework assignments: _____

_____

19. Location(s) of clock(s): _____

_____

20. Area(s) of room off-limits to students: _____

_____

21. Where to find shared materials: _____

_____

22. When it is *not* okay to talk: _____

_____

23. Additional information: _____

_____

_____

_____

_____

_____

Traffic Flow

The first of these elements, traffic flow, has a serious impact on classroom management. Concerns that appear minor when you first begin thinking about them soon escalate into major distractions. If the trash can is in the back of the room near your desk, for instance, instead of near the door, students will not be able to dispose of trash on the way out at the end of class. Instead they will make trips to the back to dispose of trash causing a distraction for other students.

Five strategies are listed here to help you consider the problems of traffic flow in your class and how you want to begin to solve them.

STRATEGY ONE. The best way to begin dealing with the problems of traffic flow is to identify the routine events that are predictable in your class. Some of these will probably be:

1. entering and leaving class
2. passing papers
3. using the stapler or hole puncher
4. sharpening pencils
5. disposing of trash
6. getting materials
7. speaking with you privately
8. picking up a hall pass
9. getting papers back from you
10. checking information on the bulletin board

You should plan the most efficient ways for your students to do each of these routines. If you put a stapler and hole puncher near the trash can, for example, students will mill around less than if these three were in three different areas of the room. You can increase the efficiency of your design by putting these near the door and adding a tray for students to put their completed work in on the way out of or into the room. Adding a bookcase or table for shared supplies and an information bulletin board will create an efficient student area and reduce the unproductive traffic in your class.

STRATEGY TWO. Another routine event you can predict and you need to consider in setting up your room is a relatively private place for students to visit with you and to pick up hall passes or other paperwork. If you place your desk at the back and add an extra chair beside it facing you and turned away from the class, then you have created the space that you need.

STRATEGY THREE. Instead of having students pass papers to the front of the room and then you collect them, it is much more efficient to direct the flow of papers to the student nearest your desk. Have that student neatly stack them on your desk. You'll not only be more efficient, but you will also reduce the confusion in the class because you will still be able to monitor and move around the room instead of waiting for papers to come to you.

STRATEGY FOUR. If passing out texts or work folders is a routine event in your class, place them near the door for students to pick up as soon as they enter. The area near the door is often an area that is overlooked when teachers set up their rooms, but it is an area that can be extremely useful if you plan carefully. Use this area to post your syllabus or the nightly homework reminders that you want students to notice on their way out.

STRATEGY FIVE. In addition to the disruptions that come from within our class-rooms, you can reduce the interruption from without by placing an envelope or fold-er on the outside of your door. Many people can leave papers and notes for you rather than knocking, entering, interrupting, and disrupting.

The Space You Need for Yourself

The space you need for yourself is another important element to consider when you are setting up your classroom. You need a place in which it is convenient for you to work and to store the materials you will not need to share with your students. Your desk is an impor-tant part of your work day. Set it up as efficiently as possible to meet your needs. Teach your students not to take anything from it without asking your permission first. This will be easier if you provide a stapler or other materials and supplies for them in another part of the room.

The most obvious mistake that many teachers make when setting up a room is to place the teacher's desk at the front of the room in front of the chalkboard. This is an easy mistake to make because it has been a tradition in secondary schools for years. It has out-lived its usefulness. When you place your desk at the front, you invite the invasion of your private space by students who enter or leave the classroom and you block the board at the same time. If you place your desk at the back of the room or in one of the back corners, you will be able to monitor students from your seat during quiet times. Students won't know when you are watching them. You will also discourage students who might be tempt-ed to pick up a teacher's edition from your desk as they crowd past at dismissal.

The Physical Arrangement of the Desks

The third element to consider when creating your desired physical environment is the arrangement of student desks. The configuration of student desks will play a large part in the success or failure of the discipline climate that you establish in your classroom.

Some arrangements, such as small groups or circles, encourage students to talk with each other. Others, such as the traditional arrangement of rows facing the front, encourage students to focus on the teacher. Throughout the term you and your students will use dif-ferent arrangements for different purposes, but there are a few principles that should guide you in deciding which arrangement will work best for you at any given time.

1. First of all, you must be able to see every pupil's face. A well-organized grouping where half of the class sits with their backs to you is not a functional one if you want to catch and hold their attention.

2. Your students must also be able to see you. If you have to speak from the back of the room or from a point where a shorter student's view of you is blocked, then you should reconsider the desk arrangement.

3. Another important consideration when setting up desks involves the distractions in your classroom. If your students use pencils, don't block the sharpener. Glare from a window will also distract many students. Other distractions to work around can include the door, the trash can, blasts of hot or cold air from vents, areas where materials are stored and shared, noise from the hall, and your desk.

4. Another point to consider when you're deciding how to arrange desks is movement. Will you be able to move around the room easily? Will your students?

5. Pay attention to where you spend most of your time in a class period. If you are like most secondary teachers, you probably spend most of your time at the front of the room. This will affect your desk arrangement because you will need to be able to arrange desks in such a way as to encourage your less able students to stay on task and to be successful.

6. Be careful not to put student desks too near a wall or a chalkboard. These areas are often targets for vandalism.

7. Even if your room is overcrowded, you should plan to have at least one extra desk if at all possible. You'll find that it will come in handy if your students need it for a prop, if you need to isolate a student, or if you have a classroom visitor.

8. Many teachers have found that starting the term with seats in the traditional rows is a good idea. Such an arrangement is orderly and businesslike. It sends the message that you want students to focus on you and not on each other; it thus promotes an orderly climate from the beginning. If you number the desks, you'll find it easier to arrange a seating chart and to put the room back in order after students are finished working in groups.

9. As the term progresses, you'll need to move students into various activities. You'll need different patterns for small group work, class discussions, debates, guest speakers, and for video viewing.

10. It is important to make a final test of your seating chart and of your room arrangements. Sit in the desks in your room. Can you see the board? Can you tolerate the glare? What about the other distractions? Will your students be comfortable and productive in the environment that you have created for them?

THE HOWS AND WHYS OF SEATING CHARTS

Arranging the furniture in your classroom into functional and attractive patterns is an exercise in futility if you don't use a seating chart. No matter how skillfully you set up the physical environment, no matter how well-planned your lessons, no matter how dynamic your delivery—if your students don't focus on learning, then they are wasting their time and yours.

Many experienced teachers who went through teacher training in not-so-recent years were taught that seating charts would discourage students' creativity and impair their ability to function well in the classroom. With utmost sincerity, we left our universities determined not to hinder our students' search for knowledge. With naive dismay, we watched as our idealistic intentions created havoc.

Anyone who has ever stood in front of a class with no seating chart has watched what can go wrong when students choose to sit wherever they please. Students from the same neighborhood choose to sit with each other—resulting in painfully obvious ethnic divisions. Students fight over seats. Talkative students sit together so that they can chat with greater ease. Less able and unmotivated students sit in the back in an often successful quest for anonymity. Easily distracted students invariably choose seats near the door, pencil sharpener, or window. Students with special needs who should sit near you wind up somewhere in the middle where they are quickly lost. The noise level reaches new highs.

As you can see, there are many convincing reasons to use a seating chart. Putting your students in assigned seats right away shows them that you are organized and well-prepared from the first day forward. You can begin with an alphabetical arrangement since you may not know your students. This seating arrangement will enable you to learn names very quickly.

Seating charts also allow you to mix your students into a team instead of allowing them to sit in cliques. Assigned seats can mix low-ability students with high-ability ones, distraction-prone students with peers who stay on task, boys with girls, talkers with quieter students, and members of different ethnic groups in your class.

You can use seating charts to handle medical problems smoothly. Students with poor vision or who need extra help can get it if you arrange the room to accommodate their needs. You can also cope with the difference in the sizes of your pupils if you assign seats to make sure that tall students are not blocking the view of shorter ones. You can also deal with the physical size of your pupils with greater sensitivity. If a student is extremely large, that student will be uncomfortable in a small desk.

With a seating chart, you can move the pupils who need help staying on task near where you spend most of your time—probably near the front of the room if you are like most secondary teachers. Placing these pupils near you and away from attractive distractions will help them stay on task and allow you to pay attention to all members of the class instead of just to the needy ones.

Assigning seats also provides security for those timid students who don't want to argue with more aggressive classmates over seats. This is especially important with those less-capable students who may want to sit near you to concentrate, but who aren't comfortable with speaking up about it. Assigning seats removes another barrier between your students and their chances for a successful day in your class.

THE FIRST DAY OF CLASS: FACE TO FACE FOR THE FIRST TIME

For secondary students getting ready for the first day of a class is an involved process. They spend hours planning their wardrobes, getting new school supplies, and worrying about us.

Before the start of a new term, secondary students spend hours working the teen grapevine to find out as much information as they can about their new teachers. Fortunately for us, much of this teacher folklore has little basis in reality. Most of us don't give *tons* of homework *every* night or an *impossible* test that counts *one hundred percent* of the grade every *Monday*.

Because it is crucial that this first day go well so that you and your students can get off to a good start, you must present yourself to your new students in as positive a manner as possible. Fortunately, this is not difficult to do if you focus your plans and activities around a few important priorities.

Here is a list of a few of the most important priorities that should guide you when you plan the first day of class with your students. With each priority you'll find three quick pointers to help you achieve it.

Priority One: Take Charge of the Class

1. Have a seating chart already made up so that after you greet students at the door, you can then direct them to their seats.

2. Settle down your students right away. The best way to do this is to have them immediately begin work on an assignment that is posted on the board or is on a handout that you provide as they enter the room. This lets students know you are prepared and businesslike.

3. Quietly but firmly stop any misbehavior as soon as it begins. Most students will not misbehave on the first day of class because they are not sure of you or of their classmates. Use this to your advantage by being alert to the first sign of misbehavior and acting quickly.

Priority Two: Alleviate Your Students' Fears

1. Make sure the room number and your name are posted for all students to see as they walk along the hall. As you stand at the door, greet each student pleasantly. Check schedules if you have to in order to make sure they have found the right room.

2. Be a pleasant and smiling teacher who obviously likes teaching and students. Make eye contact. Be upbeat. The old advice about not letting your students see you smile until Thanksgiving is no longer useful.

3. The lesson you teach on the first day should be an interesting one that students can complete successfully. Encourage your students to think they will be able to do the work you have planned for them.

Priority Three: Engage Their Minds

1. Have plenty of work for your students to do. Even veteran teachers have been caught short at one time or another by underplanning. Plan to use every minute of the class. Make sure you include a short and reasonable homework assignment that will continue the day's learning and get them back into the homework habit.

2. Make sure you use various modalities in your first lesson to stimulate your students' thinking. Encourage them to work with others as well as work alone and to answer orally as well as in writing. Involve their five senses if you want a successful learning experience.

3. Make sure at least one part of your day's activities includes a written assignment. This will promote an orderly working environment and provide information for you.

Priority Four: Complete Your Paperwork

1. Use your seating chart to check attendance. Calling roll orally when you are not sure of pronunciation can cause disruptions as well as waste time.

2. If you have students complete the "Student Information Form" (given later in this section), you will find it easier to recall their names and to plan the next set of lessons. You will also have all of the personal information you need in order to speak to a guidance counselor, an administrator, or a parent or guardian.

3. Use the time when your students are doing a written assignment to complete any paperwork you have to turn in before the end of the period.

Priority Five: Begin to Teach the Class Routines

1. When it is time for your students to turn in their first assignment, show them the procedure you want them to follow not only then, but from now on.

2. Show your students how you want them to do their homework. Spend time going over the directions so that everyone knows what to do. If you want homework to be a successful experience for your students and less of a headache for you, spend time on the first day to make doing homework well important to your students.

3. At the end of the class period, remind your students of how you want them to enter the room from now on. Show them again where they can expect to find their opening exercises. Spend this time to also show them how you will dismiss them at the end of class. Run through the signal that you will use to dismiss them.

25 ACTIVITIES FOR THE FIRST DAY OF CLASS

1. Have students fill out an information form. One is included in this section for your use.

2. Make it easy to learn names by having every student sit in an assigned seat and wear a name tag.

3. Photograph students in their new school clothes for a class scrapbook.

4. Hand out the checklist entitled "Student Checklist for the First Day of Class" on page 59. Go over it together.

5. Show examples of the supplies students need for class. Keep your requests simple so that everyone can afford school supplies for your class.

6. Pass out a scrap of paper and get students thinking about the class rules by asking every student to write out one rule they would like to suggest for the class to follow.

7. Explain how you want class to begin every day. Model it with an assignment on the board for students to do right now.

8. Give them one minute to think about this question before responding: "What can you contribute to our class to make it a better one for everyone?"

9. Issue textbooks and have students complete the "Textbook Survey" included at the end of this section.

10. Put students in pairs and ask them to tell the other student one thing they like to do and can do well. Have students then introduce each other to the class and tell what their talents are.

11. Ask students to write a letter to you describing three things you really need to know about each of them in order to teach them well.

12. Make old magazines and newspapers available so students can create a class mural of things they have in common. If you already have the construction paper on the wall, students just have to cut out photos and words that describe their strengths and talents, and glue them for instant room decoration and student motivation.

13. Ask students to tell you what they already know about your subject or your class.

14. Choose one of the student inventories from Section Four and start getting to know your students.

15. Ask students to describe what they want to learn from your class this year.

16. Assign homework that is reasonable in length and not dependent on the school supplies that you want them to purchase other than pen or paper. Make sure students know why they are doing homework and exactly how to do it well. Tell them how you intend to grade it.

17. Go over some of the basic procedures you expect students to follow in your class from now on. You can use the "Checklist for Rules, Procedures, and Expectations" from this section (see page 47) to keep all students on task.

18. Your students could interview each other following some of the suggestions from "Breaking Barriers by Breaking the Ice" from Section Four. See page 123.

19. Send students around the room to find out what they have in common. Some areas to explore could be: past school experiences, neighborhoods, likes and dislikes, foods, goals in life, study methods, pet peeves, pets, fashion styles, or favorite subjects.

20. Put students in triads to work together to determine what ten values or beliefs they have in common. Share some of these with the rest of the class.

21. Get started on a class motto. Students can work in pairs to come up with suggestions that everyone can vote on.

22. A very quick activity is to have your students create bookmarks for younger students with good advice about how to succeed in school. At the end of the day you can take these bookmarks to an elementary school for distribution.

23. Pass around a 12-month calendar for students to use to record their birthdays.

24. Distribute a copy of the syllabus to each student. Show students how to use it to plan their work and to anticipate upcoming lessons.

25. Teach an action-packed, fascinating lesson about your subject. It should last 8–10 minutes and completely engage their interest. Your students should leave your room on the first day with new knowledge and with a desire to know more about your subject.

Student Information Form

Having students complete this information form on page 58 or one that you create to meet your own particular needs is a useful activity for several reasons. When you need to contact a parent or guardian, the information will be right in your files—not just in the office at the other end of the building. You'll save time and trouble if you have this information handy. You will also benefit from having a record of your students' schedules so that you can find them quickly during the day. For example, you may need to return lost textbooks or other materials they may have left behind in your class, but know they will need for homework.

You can use this form as an opportunity to include a real-life experience in your classroom even as early as the first day of class. Don't just hand out this form and tell your students to fill it out. Instead, talk with them about how many employers are concerned about job applicants who are not able to correctly fill out forms. If your students see this form as an application for your class, then you can turn even this simple activity into a learning experience for them.

The first day of class is also an opportune time to give students the checklist. By filling this out, they will know what supplies they need for the class, what they need to do that night, what to bring the next day, and more.

THE FIRST WEEK OF SCHOOL: FIVE SUCCESSFUL DAYS

The first week of school is a lot of fun for students and teachers. Often students are still unsure of us and are still on their very best behavior. They still remember to bring all notebooks and supplies to class. No one has lost the textbook yet.

We are still trying to win over our students with careful preparation and lessons designed to please even the most discriminating adolescent. Since we don't know them very well, we tend to treat our students with more than our usual kindness and courtesy during the first few days.

The first week of school is also difficult for both students and teachers. Everything we teach is new to our students and everything they do is new to us. Often we're shocked at how much they don't know, haven't been taught, or don't understand. We have endless clerical tasks to perform, lessons to revise, and more work to do than at almost any other point in the school year. Our school responsibilities are overwhelming and exhausting.

Here is a list of the basic responsibilities secondary teachers face during the first week of school. Whenever you feel overwhelmed at the tasks facing you, just take a look at the list and use it to stay organized. The better organized you are and the more efficiently you run your classroom, the easier you will find it to create a classroom climate that will promote good discipline and successful achievement.

25 Basic Teacher Responsibilities

1. Learn your students' names. Try to do this by day three—at the latest!

2. Teach five successful lessons.

3. Establish, teach, and begin enforcing classroom rules.

4. Make sure everyone knows the school rules.

5. Make sure all students have the necessary supplies.

6. Issue textbooks or other school-provided materials.

7. Present yourself as a caring teacher five times.

8. Teach pupils the procedures and routines for your class.

9. Take action to stop small behavior problems from becoming large ones.

10. Send a letter home to parents or guardians. A sample is given for you to adapt for your own students in Section Four on page 106.

11. Check permanent records and make note of anything that will help you be a better teacher.

12. Give and grade *meaningful* homework.

13. Pay attention to information that the guidance counselors and school nurse send about your students.

14. Set up a folder for each student so that you can keep all information, notes, or documentation handy and organized.

15. Set up your grade book or grade program.

16. Start right away to make sure every student in your class feels important and part of the classroom community.

17. Help every student feel that he or she can be successful in your class.

18. Teach your students how to organize their notes and notebooks.

19. Make sure everyone knows where to go and how to act during a fire drill. You might have one this first week.

20. Arouse curiosity at the end of class as well as at the beginning so that students will want to return to your room.

21. Help your students set long-term and short-term goals for themselves.

22. Make every new student who is added to your class feel welcome.

23. Make sure students new to the building know how to find their classes.

24. Be accurate with attendance and other records. Paperwork is as important now as it will ever be.

25. Plan how to make the second week of school even more successful than this one!

STUDENT INFORMATION FORM

Your full name: _____

What you want me to call you: _____

Your home phone number: _____

Your birthday: _____ _____ _____
              month   day   year

Your age: _____ Your student number: _____

Your brothers and sisters: _____

_____

Your hobbies: _____

_____

Your goals after high school: _____

_____

What clubs or sports you participate in _____

_____

Name of your parent(s) or guardian(s): _____

_____

What is their relationship to you? _____

Which parent or guardian would you like me to contact if I need to call home?

_____ _____ _____
        title   first name   last name

Please tell me the occupation and business phone of each of your parents or guardians.

Mother _____ _____
            occupation   business phone

Father _____ _____
            occupation   business phone

Guardian _____ _____
            occupation   business phone

What is your address?

_____ _____ _____ _____
        street address   city   state   ZIP Code

What were your grades last year?

    Subject _____ Grade _____

    Subject _____ Grade _____

    Subject _____ Grade _____

    Subject _____ Grade _____

    Subject _____ Grade _____

    Subject _____ Grade _____

What is your schedule this term?

    Subject _____ Teacher _____

    Subject _____ Teacher _____

    Subject _____ Teacher _____

    Subject _____ Teacher _____

    Subject _____ Teacher _____

    Subject _____ Teacher _____

STUDENT CHECKLIST FOR THE FIRST DAY OF CLASS

Teacher's Name _____

Subject _____

1. My assigned seat is: _____

2. The supplies I need to purchase for this class are: _____
   _____
   _____

3. Tonight I need to do these things for this class: _____
   _____
   _____

4. One important thing I learned today is: _____
   _____
   _____

5. I need to bring these things to class tomorrow: _____
   _____
   _____

6. Other notes: _____
   _____
   _____
   _____
   _____
   _____
   _____
   _____
   _____
   _____
   _____
   _____
   _____
   _____

QUICK TIPS FOR LEARNING YOUR STUDENTS' NAMES

Want to appear foolish in front of a group of students? Stand in front of the class on the first day of the term and say, "Hey, you—the boy in the blue shirt. . . . No, the other boy, the one near the window. . . . No, the one with the blond hair. . . . Yes, you—please turn around." Teachers of every teenager in the nation shudder at the potential for disaster that lurks just beneath the surface of a calm class during those first few days of class when we aren't quite sure of our students' names.

Any experienced teacher knows one hard and fast rule about the first few days of school: learn names as quickly as you can! The reasoning behind this advice is that you want to be able to get the year off to a good start by stopping misbehavior as soon as it begins. You will do this more easily if you know students' names.

There are even better reasons for learning names as quickly as you possibly can. Knowing your students' names on the first or second day of class is a signal to your students that you take them seriously enough to value them as individuals. Taking the time and making the effort to learn everyone's name is also a very friendly thing for a teacher to do. It impresses students and their parents. Finally, when you show that you care enough to learn everyone's name right away, you reassure those students who are anxiously trying to figure out what kind of teacher you will be.

Don't underestimate the importance of names. Students resent teachers who repeatedly call them by the incorrect name. Doing so makes pupils feel worthless at a time when they are struggling to find their identities and when they are most uncertain of you and what your class will be like.

Take care to spell a child's name correctly, to pronounce it correctly, and to use a friendly voice when you say it. Be very careful if you have taught several members of the same family not to call a pupil by the name of a brother or sister. No doubt about it, learning names is one of the most important tasks that secondary teachers have to do well at the start of a term.

Learning all of those names is not so very hard if you use some of the strategies listed here. These quick tips will make it possible for you to go home on the first day of the term confident that you know the students in your class well enough to create a positive classroom atmosphere that will get the term off to a good start for both you and your students.

13 Quick Tips on Learning Students' Names

1. Put some mental energy into this activity. Even though you will have many, many other responsibilities taking up your class time at the start of the term, putting forth the effort to learn names is important.

2. Get yourself organized. Get name tag materials and seating charts ready. Study class rolls carefully as soon as you receive them so that you can at least be familiar with the names before the first day of the term begins.

3. Have students sit in assigned seats for the first few days. If they change their hair styles or other noticeable physical characteristics, you will still be able to call your students by name if they are in their assigned seats.

4. Have them wear name tags for the first few days or until you are sure of everyone's name. You can purchase those self-stick ones or you can use neatly cut scrap paper to either tape or pin the tag to a shoulder. Provide markers and ask students to write their first and last names on the tags in big, bold letters. Of course you should be sure to return the courtesy by wearing a name tag yourself. If your students seem reluctant to take wearing a name tag seriously, ask them to name local businesses where employees are expected to wear identification badges. Once you stress how helpful the name tags will be in helping you learn names and the importance of identification badges in the workplace, their hesitation should vanish.

5. One of your opening exercises should be to have students fill out an information form such as the one provided for you in this section. Use this form to help you learn names by reviewing it as soon after class as you can. Reading about your students while their images are still clear in your mind will help you connect the name on the form to the face in your room.

6. Take the information form and actually rewrite their names in a list that follows the seating chart. If you are overwhelmed, try learning only the first names for the first few days of class.

7. Focus on features that *don't* change when you are trying to learn names. Learning that the girl in the red shirt is named Xiang is a great idea until the next day when Xiang wears her new purple shirt to class.

8. On your roll write a note beside some names during times when your students are working independently of you. Writing "tall" beside Pietro's name or "big smile" beside Eugene's name will help you recall them quickly.

9. Ask your students to say their names for you. Look them in the face and concentrate as you say their names back. Don't do this in front of the class, but do it when they are working together or on independent assignments. Go around the room student by student and then try to go over them one more time before class is over.

10. Use icebreakers and opening-day exercises to help you focus on learning names. If students interview each other and then introduce their partners to the class, pay attention to the names and any information that will help you recall them later.

11. After school on the first day of class, reread your roll and the notes you have made about their names during class. Visualize each student to the best of your ability, trying to create a strong association between the face and the name in your mind.

12. If you can't remember a student's name, admit it and ask for help. When the student says the name, recite it and then repeat to make sure you can recall it.

13. Make a game out of remembering names. Involve your students in the game to make sure they also know each other's name. If you want to create a community of scholars, it's important to make sure they know each other by name.

STARTING OFF RIGHT: TEACHING THE TEXT

Helping students learn about the resources locked away in their textbooks is an activity often overlooked by many teachers. We seem to assume that our students go home on the first day of class with their new books and spend hours looking through them, trying to figure out what the course will be like.

While many students do take the time to look over their books, most do not. These are the same students who ask us seven times in a class period to tell them on what page a certain chapter begins rather than look in the table of contents. They don't understand the big picture of what it is they are supposed to learn. This failure on our part creates discipline problems rising from student failure and frustration.

We can help our students get acclimated to our class and to the information that we want them to have at the end of the term if we show them how to use their textbooks. The *reproducible* "Textbook Survey" included here begins with general questions that could fit almost any text. These are questions 1-12. The remaining questions are suitable for a literature book, but are included here to give you some ideas about how to adapt this form to your own teaching situation.

CREATING A STUDENT-CENTERED
CLASS ATMOSPHERE IN ANY ROOM

There are many names for this teaching phenomenon. *Student-centered learning*, the *user-friendly class*, and *invitational teaching* are just three of them. Whatever the name, the result is the same: a place where students and teachers can work in a safe and pleasant environment as partners in the exciting process of learning and preparing for the future. The important word here is "partners."

These havens exist everywhere and anywhere. You don't need a huge operating budget, gifted and willing students, or cooperative colleagues to make your classroom a friendly place. What you do need is the right attitude, a clear vision of what you want to happen, and the willpower to put your plans into effect.

In a student-centered class, your pupils are not just passive receptors of your expert knowledge. Instead, you and your students work together to discover and learn. Although a student-centered class is often noisy and full of activity, much more learning is going on than in the more traditional classrooms.

Make no mistake. The teacher still needs to be a strong and powerful force in the classroom—probably more so than in a traditional class. However, your role now is that of facilitator, collaborator, and coach working with students, rather than being the expert who holds and withholds the information that students need.

It's easier to switch from a traditional class format to a successful student-centered one than you might think. The discipline problems that face teachers who insist on the old ways of nonproductive teaching just don't happen when you begin to involve your students in a positive way in the class activities.

TEXTBOOK SURVEY

Name _____ Class _____

1. What is the complete title of your text?

   _____

   _____

2. What is the complete name of each author?

   _____

   _____

3. Into how many sections is your book divided?

   _____

4. Who is the publisher of your book?

   _____

5. What is the latest copyright date of your book?

   _____

6. What is the first word on page one?

   _____

7. What are the titles of two of the most interesting sections or chapters listed in the table of contents?

   _____

   _____

8. How many items are there in the index under these letters:
   K_____,   M_____,   S_____,   P_____,   and   Q_____?

9. What seems at first glance to be the most interesting chapter? Why?

   _____

   _____

   _____

10. List three things you already know about the subjects covered in your text.

    _____

    _____

    _____

11. List two of the books that the authors used to write this one. You'll find them in the bibliography section.

    _____

    _____

TEXTBOOK SURVEY *(cont'd)*

12. How are the big sections of this book broken down into smaller sections of information?

_____

_____

_____

13. What are the three most interesting illustrations? Why do you find them interesting?

_____

_____

_____

_____

_____

14. What insights, knowledge, or skills do you think the authors want you to gain from their work?

_____

_____

_____

15. What parts of the book will be most helpful to you? Why?

_____

_____

_____

_____

_____

_____

_____

27 Techniques to Create a Student-Centered Class Atmosphere

Here are some techniques you can use to develop your own version of the kind of class where you and your students are partners in learning.

1. A student-centered class can begin on the very first day of class before your students have time to settle into their passive routines. Plan ahead so that your students don't have a chance to fall into bad habits.

2. Focus on meeting the immediate and future needs of your students when you plan your lessons. Students are intensely pragmatic about their studies and want to know how they will use the information you want them to know. Provide good answers for them when they ask, "Why do we have to know this?"

3. Students should do more talking than the teacher. You should listen to your students more than you ever have before.

4. Be courteous. Greet your students at the door and welcome them into the room. Tell them good-bye when they leave.

5. Value and foster student creativity whenever you can.

6. Plan to lead students to discover the information that you want them to have rather than just telling them dry facts in a lecture format. Focus on the higher-level thinking skills for successful learning.

7. A student-centered class is one in which there is a great deal of mutual sharing of ideas and opinions.

8. Plan events together—free time as well as assignments. Seek students' advice as often as you can in deciding how you would like the classroom to be run.

9. When you deal with students who have special needs, focus on what these students are able to do, not on what they can't do. Anytime you deal with a child's strengths, you are helping that child grow.

10. Search quotation anthologies in the library for inspiring messages for your students. Prepare a few banners or signs for your class with these messages. Put one on the board every day for you and your students to enjoy. An even better idea is to ask your students to bring in an inspirational saying about life and then give them the materials to create a poster to display.

11. In a student-centered classroom where there is a persistent tone of mutual respect, everyone knows—and follows—the school rules as well as the classroom rules.

12. Decorate your room with student work. Students enjoy seeing their work on the wall far more than they enjoy an expensive poster that you might purchase. Students feel a sense of pride and ownership when theirs is displayed. When you display student work, display everyone's. If you hang only the best examples, you could be accused of favoritism, which will do more harm than good.

13. Keep recycled paper, construction paper, crayons, markers, and other simple art supplies on hand to help you display student work. Some types of work that make good displays are projects, group-generated lists, cartoons, "sponge" activities that have

developed far beyond the original assignment (see Section Three), posters that your students create, inspirational sayings, thank-you notes, and anything else your students could be proud to display.

14. Have a sense of humor. Some teachers never laugh with their students. Don't be one of them.

15. Involve your students in the routines of the classroom. They need to assume some of the responsibilities for running things if they are to feel a part of the whole process of the class.

16. Make your lessons interesting. Be unpredictable. Break up the pace. It's hard to make your students feel welcome while you are boring them at the same time. Many small and large discipline problems disappear in a classroom when the lessons are engaging.

17. Teach your students how to work well together to provide each other with help and encouragement.

18. Work to create the atmosphere where your pupils are comfortable enough to ask you questions or to take risks that might lead to mistakes.

19. Call parents or guardians to say nice things about their children.

20. Design lessons so that your students' craving for success is satisfied.

21. Take a positive approach. Show your approval in both large and small ways. Even older students like stickers and other little rewards.

22. Use standard English when you talk with your students. It shows your respect for them.

23. Admit it when you make a mistake.

24. Play favorites—only make sure that *all* of your students know they are each your favorite.

25. Watch the words you use around your students. A word such as "ignorant," even when used in jest, is not a word that will enhance your reputation as a friendly teacher.

26. Create an information board where you display relevant information from the faculty handbook: bell schedules, menus, dress code information, the honor code, fire drill procedures, sports schedules, and other information your students want to know about.

27. Survey your students periodically so that you can determine that the image you believe you have is the one you *really do* project. You may be shocked to discover that your students don't think of you as a friendly teacher at all. Surveying your students is a terrific way to help you improve your teaching and to create the kind of positive student-centered class you want. You can use the "Teacher Effectiveness Report Card" in Section Four for this purpose.

A SOUND MIND IN A WELL-RESTED BODY

University scholars have spent a great deal of time researching teachers and the seriousness of our responsibilities at the start of the school term. Their research shows that it is necessary for teachers to create as many positive experiences as possible from the first meeting with their students.

Especially at the beginning of the term, teachers have to be multi-talented: flexible, organized, efficient, quick-witted, energetic, creative, intuitive, and resourceful. We are expected to tackle problems that would scare a Hollywood daredevil, perplex an Army general, and depress Mary Poppins.

Of course, many of us handle the start of the term with ease. The teachers who do well at the start of the year have learned how to successfully cope with one of the most important paradoxes in education—in order to take care of the needs of so many others, we need to think about ourselves.

At the start of the school year a teacher's energies are directed outward towards the needs of students as we strive to make them comfortable, welcome, secure, and motivated to try their best. But what about us? Who is looking after the teachers who are so busy looking after their students? In trying to meet the needs of others, our own are often lost in the shuffle.

If you would like to have a more productive and enjoyable beginning to your school year, you need to pay attention to your most valuable asset—yourself. You need to use this stressful time to strengthen your coping skills and make sure that taking care of your own well-being is an integral part of your daily routine. If you want to get the new school term off to a good start, you need to spend some time taking care of yourself.

30 Tips for Good Mental Health

Here are a few mental health tips designed to help all teachers soar through the trials of those first exhausting weeks of school with ease. Use them to help you as you cope with the unique pressures of the teaching profession.

1. Hit the "Back to School" sales. Even if you teach in a school that uses a form of year-round scheduling or block scheduling, you should use this time to stock up on the supplies your school district doesn't provide for you.

2. Check your alarm clock to make sure it's still working. One of the hardest adjustments we have to make this time of year is getting up much earlier than usual.

3. Wear comfortable shoes to teach. You'll be on your feet all day.

4. Spruce up your professional wardrobe. You will want to make a good impression on your students.

5. Take care of as many of your regular household projects in advance of the start of school as you can. You will find life more pleasant if you don't have a jillion small house projects to do on top of trying to get used to a new term.

6. Now is not a good time to plan an important social event—such as a major household move, a wedding, or a family reunion. Try to take it easy until you are used to the demands of school.

7. Get enough sleep. Many of us suffer from disturbed sleep at the start of school because we are still on a summer timetable or because our minds are still racing with the demands of the day even while we sleep. You need rest if you are going to do your job well.

8. Eat well. Don't skip lunch in order to get work done. Take a break and relax a little. If you are planning to take vitamins, you might want to start now.

9. During the school day, get some fresh air and take a brief "sanity" break. It's tempting to work until we are exhausted in the mistaken hope that we will get it over with more quickly. If you take a break, you will work more productively.

10. Expect to be very tired. Even veteran teachers are shocked at just how exhausted they feel at the end of the day during the first few weeks of the term. If you know that you will be tired, you can plan around your slump times and figure out a better work schedule for yourself.

11. All work and no play makes. . . . Be sure to keep your day in balance. Even though you have lots and lots of work to do now, you still have time for some fun. Go to the gym and work out. Take a walk. Go swimming. Play with your child or pet. Enjoy the day.

12. Keep a running "To Do" list of all the chores you need to do. Remember to record all paperwork chores that need to be handled efficiently on your list.

13. Get a calendar/planner like the ones you encourage your students to use so that you can keep track of all your meetings, conferences, and appointments.

14. Make it a point that you will leave your desk clean at the end of the day. You won't dread morning chores if you can discipline yourself to do this.

15. Grade papers promptly. Letting papers that need to be graded pile up will just make you frustrated. Do a few each day and keep ahead. You will feel much lighter in spirit.

16. Get to work a few minutes early and stay a few minutes late each day until you are comfortable with the press of your workload.

17. Set priorities for the work that needs to be done. Planning a wonderful lesson for each day of the week is a priority item; cleaning out the supply closet is not.

18. Figure out your personal needs at school. You need to have a safe place to store your belongings. You need to decide on a place where you will always place your keys so that you don't have to go through a stressful search. Paying attention to these small matters will help make your days run more smoothly.

19. If you are one of the many, many teachers who suffers from stage fright before the first day of class, take heart. Many of us worry about the impression we will make on our students and about how the first day will go. If you act confident, things will be easier for you.

20. Talk over your school concerns with colleagues. You don't have to haunt the teachers' lounge in order to find supportive people at work.

21. Learn your students' names. It's anxiety-provoking not to be able to call out to a student who is misbehaving.

22. Don't be one of those unprofessional people who chat or do busywork during meetings. Pay attention even if you have heard it all before.

23. Set professional goals for yourself and write out a plan for achieving each one. Let this year be the one where you write a grant proposal, solve a funding problem, or finally decide on the best way to handle all of the paperwork.

24. Make sure all of your students have the materials they need to get their work done well.

25. Prepare a syllabus for your students. This will make your life easier in many ways.

26. Overplan! You can't have too much for your students to do during the first weeks of class. You still are not adjusted to their pace. It is far, far better to have extra work than to have extra time at the end of class.

27. Make a folder of emergency plans just in case you have to be absent. Store these in a safe place so that all you have to do in an emergency is tell your substitute where to find them.

28. Nip trouble in the bud. It's far easier to deal with *one* student who is misbehaving than with several.

29. Plan what you want your students to know at the end of the term and begin designing interesting lessons to accomplish this.

30. Try to get at least two weeks ahead in your plans and in photocopying or arranging for guest speakers, films, or other resources. If you can stay ahead, you will avoid the misery of last-minute rushing.

"Without a shepherd sheep are not a flock."

—Russian proverb

Section 3

DOOR TO DOOR:
USING CLASS TIME WISELY

In This Section . . .

While you don't have to be so time-conscious that you distress yourself and your students, there are many ways that secondary teachers can use this most valuable resource more efficiently. In "From Door to Door: Why Every Minute Counts" you'll learn why it's important to use class time fully. You'll go even further with this exploration when you read "Taking a Minute-by-Minute Approach to Class Time" and use the reproducible that goes along with it. Learn even more techniques for better time use in "20 Ways to Make Every Minute Count."

The importance of class routines is a topic that many secondary teachers already understand. Refine your own use of routines with "Establishing Control through Class Routines," the reproducible "Student Sign-Out Sheet" and "How Classroom Routines Promote Self-Discipline."

Next, you can improve the way you begin class with the tips in "The First Ten Minutes of Class" and by using the form "Self-Check for Improving Class Time Management" to see how you are already doing and where you can improve.

If transitions are times in your class—as in so many others—when students tend to be disruptive, then the suggestions in "Reducing Disruptions through Effective Time Management" and "50 Sponge Activities to Keep Students Engaged in Learning All Period Long" will help with suggestions for you to use.

Just as important as the start of class is the ending—the last ten minutes in particular. Use the "Improved Class Time Management" to see how you are doing already in the way you use this block of class. You'll find suggestions for making the ending a productive time for your students in "The Last Ten Minutes of Class" and in the more general "What to Do When Waste Time Causes Problems."

Finally, teach your students to manage their time more wisely on your journey to help them become self-directed learners. For this you'll find "Power-Packed Time-Management Tips for Students," "Student Calendars," "Student Time Schedule/Planner," and "You Are in Control!" to help them gain control of the time they have in class and at home for studying.

> *"I recommend you to take care of the minutes,*
> *for the hours will take care of themselves."*
>
> —Lord Chesterfield

FROM DOOR TO DOOR: WHY EVERY MINUTE COUNTS

According to the headlines in newspapers across our nation, educators are being held accountable for a wide range of social problems by citizens who are increasingly concerned about the fate of our children. Low test scores, high dropout rates, rising adolescent drug use, teen pregnancy, illiterate graduates with no work ethic, violent classrooms—we are not expected just to cope with these, but to remedy them. More than ever, teacher performance is under scrutiny by a society that wants a quick fix for the huge problems facing our youngsters.

Although being held accountable for such a seemingly impossible task is daunting, dedicated teachers rise to the occasion every day. We work hard to establish order in the chaotic world of teenagers. Too few adolescents are guided by caring adults who show them the rudiments of a fulfilling life, much less how to reach their fullest potential. We teachers need to do our share and then some. There is much to do and much that we can offer.

We can't control many of the negative aspects of our profession—inadequate facilities, students without basic skills, those who live with daily violence at home, overcrowded classrooms, endless paperwork—but there is one very important factor over which we do have control: time. Teachers have door-to-door control over the ways our students use the all-too-few hours they spend with us in our classrooms. Teachers control whether class time is wasted or used wisely. Teachers can either engage students in relevant and successful learning activities or condemn them to sit and stare helplessly at the clock. While some time is unavoidably wasted in unproductive or disruptive classroom activity, we can and should work to minimize this loss.

We can arrange to have students engaged in a variety of learning tasks, developing and refining a positive attitude about their academic responsibilities, or we can allow disruptive behavior to occur because our students have nothing productive to do for significant amounts of time each class period. We do our students a serious disservice when we neglect to engage them in meaningful learning activities for the entire class period. Classroom misbehavior is only one of the unavoidable results of this disservice.

TAKING A MINUTE-BY-MINUTE APPROACH
TO CLASS TIME

Many teachers, experienced as well as novice, encounter significant and disturbing discipline problems each day in their classes in spite of long hours spent in planning and preparation. They have done everything their teacher training and experience tells them to do to reduce behavior problems, but they still have to confront difficult or disruptive students daily.

One step you should take to gain control of your class is to examine how your students actually use the time they have while they are in your classroom. In many ways this is the opposite of planning a lesson. When you plan a lesson, you are likely to think more about the subject matter than about your students and what they will choose to do. You are also dealing with what you would like to see happen in your class rather than what actually will happen in spite of your careful planning and preparation.

When you keep a chart for several days of the student activity in your class, you will be gathering data to support the vague suspicions you might have about the times when productive and nonproductive behavior happens in your class.

STUDENT TIME-USE SELF-CHECK FORM

Name _____   Class _____

Beginning and Ending Times _____

Time in Minutes	On-Task Behaviors	Off-Task Behaviors
1–10		
11–20		
21–30		
31–40		
41–50		
51–60		
61–70		
71–80		
81–90		

What can I do to increase the on-task behavior?

_____

_____

_____

_____

What can I do to decrease the off-task behavior?

_____

_____

_____

_____

Use the "Student Time-Use Self-Check Form" on the previous page to record the behaviors you can observe during a class period. Try to do this for several days to determine what patterns exist in the connection between time use and behavior in your class. Once you become aware of the time periods when students seem to be most likely to engage in negative behaviors, you can then begin the process of reducing or eliminating these unproductive behaviors by substituting productive ones.

20 WAYS TO MAKE EVERY MINUTE COUNT

1. Plan and teach lessons that are focused around a clearly-stated objective that is published for your students.

2. Teach your students that you are the person who decides when class will begin and end—not a bell. This will reduce disruptions and wasted time near the end of the class period.

3. Don't call roll out loud. Check attendance by scanning the room while your students are working independently.

4. Assign an appropriate amount of work. Fifty math problems may not be as effective as 15 done correctly. Finding the appropriate pace of a lesson is not an easy thing to do, but careful pacing will prevent frustration and wasted time.

5. Have alternative assignments for those students who finish an assignment ahead of the others. Many students waste precious time waiting for others to finish.

6. Make sure the topics you assign are relevant and necessary for your students' immediate and future needs. Your students should understand their importance.

7. Plan your classes so that students are engaged from the minute they enter the room until you dismiss them. Giving "free time" at the end of class is a practice with enormous potential for trouble.

8. Resist the temptation to be distracted during a lesson by students who want to chat or otherwise stray from the topic.

9. Establish and follow a routine set of procedures for daily classroom chores. When students know how to manage classroom routines, they will be more likely to stay on task.

10. Be careful not to interrogate students who are tardy or who are otherwise misbehaving in front of the class. Work to minimize disruptions, not call them to the attention of everyone else.

11. Be flexible. Many teachers who are very well-organized like to stick with a lesson plan even if it isn't working. This is evident in those classrooms where students are sleeping, tuned out, or disruptive. Don't be afraid to change a lesson plan in the middle of class if you see that your carefully made plans are not working. Always have a backup plan.

12. Plan lessons that are exciting and have real-world applications so that students will stay focused.

13. Give immediate feedback so that students know how they're doing and can proceed with confidence. Research shows that the sooner students know how they did on an assignment, the better.

14. Become the most organized and well-prepared teacher that you know. Don't waste your students' time because you are not ready for class.

15. Arrange your activities so that your students can work together as often as possible. Students who are taught to work well together are much more likely to be productive than those students who never have a chance to collaborate successfully with others.

16. Strive to interact positively with every student every day. Show your students that their welfare is important to you if you want to encourage on-task behavior.

17. Recognize that not all of your students will have the same abilities and background knowledge. Many teachers waste precious time because they assume students have common background knowledge and can learn at the same rate. If you spend time assessing your students' previous knowledge before beginning a unit of study, you will be much better at designing lessons that will fulfill the needs of each student. Build in lesson components that will address the varying learning rates of your students.

18. Don't allow small misbehaviors to continue or to escalate.

19. Raise your students' awareness about the importance of using time wisely.

20. Teach your students the skills they need to become self-disciplined. If your ultimate goal is that your students will govern their own behavior, then you need to spend time teaching the social skills that will lead to this. Students who are not self-disciplined waste everybody's time with misbehavior and unproductive activity.

ESTABLISHING CONTROL THROUGH CLASS ROUTINES

One of the easiest ways to decrease the amount of negative behavior and increase the amount of positive behavior in your class is to provide a comfortable set of class routines for your students. Being consistent in the way you manage routine tasks will save you and your students valuable hours of wasted time and eliminate many of the discipline headaches that a less-organized class experiences.

At the beginning of the term, establish a few simple procedures for routine classroom activities and then spend a sufficient amount of time teaching these procedures to your students. The extra time you spend teaching your students how you want them to perform these routines will reward you with saved class time, less confusion, comfortable students, and more efficient learning. All of these, of course, result in a marked decrease in discipline problems and an increase in productive activity.

Make sure, also, that your students understand *why* it is necessary to follow these routines so that their cooperation can be whole-hearted.

Passing Out Papers

At the start of class, have all of the materials that you and your students will need for class ready so that no one will have to wait while you shuffle papers. Either give your students the handouts for the day as you greet them at the door or place all of your students' work in folders that they can pick up at the start of class.

Shared Supplies

1. Provide your students with a stapler, scratch paper, a hole puncher, and a supply of tissues located in a convenient place so that they won't have to waste time trying to find these.

2. Establish a shared bank of materials and supplies such as pens, pencils, paper, and extra textbooks so that those students who find themselves unexpectedly caught short will be able to settle down to work quickly. While there are many ways to set up such a bank, one of the easiest is to have students who want to participate bring in materials that can be shared. Put a student or two in charge of collecting and maintaining the collection. Before class starts, students who need to borrow items will check with those classmates who are in charge. At the end of class, the students who are in charge assume responsibility for seeing that the borrowed materials are returned. This system allows students to work together to solve a problem that has immediate consequences for them. It also promotes self-discipline rather than involving you.

Giving Written Directions

1. At the start of class, have written directions on the board in the same place each day so that your students know what is expected of them.

2. Use numbered step-by-step directions to keep students on task. Word the information as simply as possible.

3. Develop a few key words in your directions that will serve as signals for your students.

4. Check for understanding when you go over directions with your students. Often, in spite of our best efforts, what we think we are saying isn't what our students understand at all.

5. Provide your students with a checklist if the directions are lengthy or complicated so that they can cross off each task as they complete it.

Students Leaving the Room

1. Allow only a very few students to leave class. Be reasonable, but be clear in your expectations that leaving the room is not to be a daily occurrence without just cause.

2. Establish and follow a fair policy for students who need to sign out of your room.

3. Set a limit on the amount of time that students may spend when they have checked out of your room for any purpose.

4. If you are fortunate enough to work in a small or peaceful school where generic hall passes work well enough to be approved by your supervisors, then use one. If not, be sure to complete an official hall pass with the student's name, destination, and the time he or she left the room. An official pass will make students more aware of the necessity to hurry back and not stray from the intended destination. In either case, students should not leave the room without a pass from you.

5. Make sure students who are leaving know when they are expected to return.

6. Collect the hall passes when students return and note the time of return. File these passes just in case you need them later for documentation purposes.

7. Sometimes students who see their sign-out times noted on a chart will be more careful not to abuse the privilege because a chart increases their awareness of the amount of time they actually lose from class when they need to leave the room. A "Student Sign-Out Sheet" that you can use for this purpose is included. (See next page.)

Collecting Papers

1. Create a pattern for paper collection. Students should either pass their papers to someone sitting near your desk or to the same collection point every day so that no one will have to get up and walk around. Passing papers to the front of each row is not as efficient as having all papers passed to a central collection point.

2. If you choose to collect papers when you stand at the door at the end of the class to dismiss your students, ask them to tell you one relevant fact from the day's lesson as a final review as each one hands you a paper.

3. Encourage the student who dawdles over a test to finish by setting a reasonable time limit for completing it.

4. Encourage your students to produce accurate, neatly done work. It saves time when they do a job right the first time rather than having to do it over.

Checking Attendance

Never waste your students' time by calling the roll out loud. While taking attendance is very important, it should be done in the most efficient manner possible. Calling the roll every day is not efficient because it provides students with limitless opportunities to misbehave as they sit with nothing to do but watch you and the rest of the class interact one person at a time. You should check attendance by referring to your seating chart while either your students complete their start-of-class assignments or later in the class period.

HOW CLASSROOM ROUTINES PROMOTE SELF-DISCIPLINE

Anyone who has ever substituted for a colleague who was absent knows how important classroom routines are. Those classes where students know what to do and how to go about it are pleasant and productive places. By the time students are in secondary-level classes, they are more than ready to assume responsibility for many routine tasks.

In a well-managed secondary class the wise teacher will use the abilities of all students to the best advantage in creating a self-disciplined classroom environment. Below are seven reasons that should convince you that taking the time to establish and teach your students to follow routine procedures is a sound way to get students to govern their own actions.

1. Students begin on-task behavior as soon as they enter the room and continue to be focused throughout the period.

STUDENT SIGN-OUT SHEET

Class _____

Beginning Date _____   Ending Date _____

Student Names	Time in Minutes That Students Were Out of the Room											
	1	2	3	4	5	6	7	8	9	10	11	12
1.												
2.												
3.												
4.												
5.												
6.												
7.												
8.												
9.												
10.												
11.												
12.												
13.												
14.												
15.												
16.												
17.												
18.												
19.												
20.												
21.												
22.												
23.												
24.												
25.												

2. Students understand exactly what you expect of them every day and what they have to do to meet those expectations.

3. Students can focus on relevant learning activities rather than on how they are supposed to complete daily chores.

4. Students learn how to be better organized themselves by watching an adult model efficient behavior in the workplace.

5. Students assume responsibility for their own work without being nagged by yet another impatient adult authority figure.

6. Students are comfortable and happier when they work within the framework of classroom routines. Comfortable and happy students are less likely to be disruptive.

7. Students interact with each other and with you in positive ways because you have established an atmosphere of mutual cooperation in your classroom that makes this possible.

THE FIRST TEN MINUTES OF CLASS

The first ten minutes of every class are crucial in getting your students off to a constructive start. During these first minutes you establish the tone of the class for your students whether you realize it or not. If you have done the careful preparation that is required for a successful class, then this brief time can be used to get your students focused on learning.

Students who are focused on learning and achieving instead of trying to figure out what to do will be less likely to engage in disruptive misbehavior. During the first ten minutes of class you can avoid many discipline problems by providing your students with a comfortable and predictable routine that varies in content but gives them the necessary stability to perform well academically and behaviorally.

Help your students focus their attention on the activities in your class by giving an anticipatory set that will pique their interest. There are many small assignments that you can have your students complete in the first ten minutes that will prevent behavior problems when they focus on the day's lesson or will review the previous day's work.

Use your creativity to design small assignments that serve as anticipatory sets; it's not hard to find ones that would be suitable for your class. The following 25 suggestions can be adopted to fit the needs of your students and of the day's lesson. You can ask your students to:

1. Make a quick outline of their notes.
2. List important facts.
3. Quiz each other.
4. Write a paragraph.
5. Predict the day's learning.
6. Draw a diagram, flow chart, or bar graph.
7. Make a set of flash cards.
8. Write a fact on the board.

9. Combine information with another student.

10. Draw a cartoon.

11. Summarize the reasons why something happened.

12. Judge the suitability of something.

13. Illustrate important information.

14. Create a test question.

15. Write marginal notes for an essay.

16. Take a mini-quiz.

17. Use a highlighter on their notes.

18. Create a mnemonic device.

19. Read a newspaper or magazine article.

20. Label a map.

21. Brainstorm.

22. Scan the day's reading assignment.

23. Make a list of reasons to study the day's topic.

24. Solve a puzzle.

25. Explain an illustration.

Use the "Self-Check for Improving Class Time Management" *reproducible* to see how you are presently doing and where you can improve in managing those first ten minutes of class. (See next page.)

REDUCING DISRUPTIONS THROUGH EFFECTIVE TRANSITIONS

Because students have grown accustomed to the fast pace of modern life with its intense barrage of mini-messages, they can grow bored very quickly with a lesson that seems to last too long. Wise teachers have learned to create a positive learning environment by designing daily lessons around several brief activities. While this decision is a very sensible reaction to the discipline problems caused by student disinterest, it can create problems of its own: transition periods where students with nothing to do waste valuable learning time by entertaining themselves and each other with inappropriate behavior.

Transitions are difficult because they require that students mentally close out one task, prepare for the next one, and then refocus their mental energies on the new topic. Some students find it difficult to do this several times during one class period.

One useful technique for increasing the level of student concern about wasted time during transitions is to set a time limit for the transition and to actually time your students. Students who are told by a teacher who is watching the clock that they have only one minute to switch from one activity to another are more likely to move more quickly than those students in a less-structured situation.

SELF-CHECK FOR IMPROVING CLASS TIME MANAGEMENT

Class _____

Date _____

FIRST TEN MINUTES OF CLASS

Activities Planned	*Estimated Time to Complete Each*	*Actual Time Each Required*
1.		
2.		
3.		
4.		
5.		

Off-Task Behaviors Observed

_____

_____

_____

_____

_____

Positive Behaviors Observed

_____

_____

_____

_____

_____

Proposed Solutions for Improving Time Management

_____

_____

_____

_____

_____

You can also reduce the number of discipline problems in your classroom if you design activities that flow naturally from one to the next with a minimum of interference from you. Your students become self-disciplined when they assume the responsibility for following the directions and making the transition an integral part of the lesson.

Another way to encourage self-discipline during transition times is to provide your students with a checklist of the things they need to accomplish during the class period. Early in the term you should teach your students how to use a checklist to keep track of their daily tasks. Figure 3-1 is a sample for an American history class to give you an idea of how to set up a useful checklist.

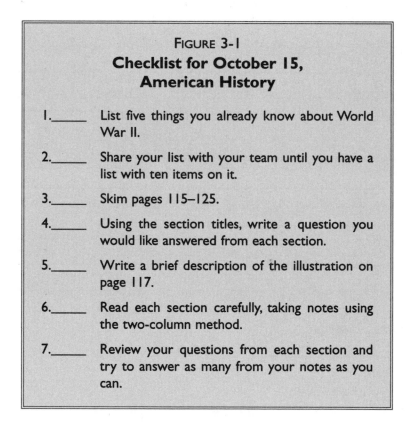

FIGURE 3-1

Checklist for October 15, American History

1._____ List five things you already know about World War II.

2._____ Share your list with your team until you have a list with ten items on it.

3._____ Skim pages 115–125.

4._____ Using the section titles, write a question you would like answered from each section.

5._____ Write a brief description of the illustration on page 117.

6._____ Read each section carefully, taking notes using the two-column method.

7._____ Review your questions from each section and try to answer as many from your notes as you can.

A final solution to the problem of wasted class time is to give students productive activities to convert their useless waiting time into learning opportunities. Even these small blocks of time can be productive and enjoyable for you and your students if you use brief learning activities to keep students involved in actively thinking and learning. These activities, called "sponge" activities, can add interest and motivation to a lesson as well as add new information. Read on to find out more about these "sponges."

50 "SPONGE" ACTIVITIES TO KEEP STUDENTS ENGAGED IN LEARNING ALL PERIOD LONG

"Sponges" are useful ways to "soak up" time that would otherwise be wasted in your classroom when students are forced to wait for others to begin class, to settle down to work, or to finish an assignment. You can use sponges to keep your students engaged in independent learning activities while significantly decreasing the amount of time they could otherwise spend engaged in disruptive behavior. Even though these activities are designed to be brief, their impact on the productivity in your classroom can be significant.

Students will often find these activities exciting enough that they will do them without protest and look forward to the break in routine. The sponges here are written in the form of directions for students to follow. Adapt, adjust, or add information to use these to create other activities that will keep your students involved in productive learning all period long.

1. Look over your notes from yesterday's lesson. Circle the key words.

2. List five things that you can recall we did in class yesterday.

3. Pick a partner and play a quick game of "hangman" with your vocabulary words from this unit of study.

4. Make quick flash cards to review the vocabulary words we have studied this week.

5. Pretend that the essay question on the board is a real test question. Write out your answer just as if you were taking a test.

6. Open your book and read the first three paragraphs from yesterday's lesson. What is something new that you learned today that you hadn't realized yesterday?

7. List ten words associated with the lesson we are currently studying.

8. What is your objective for this class today?

9. Write out a study skill that you have recently mastered.

10. Time a classmate while that person intently reviews yesterday's lesson. Switch roles and repeat.

11. Scan your text and find . . . (Provide your students with specific facts or information to seek. This is an excellent review technique.)

12. Here's your word of the day: _____. Copy and define it and then use it correctly in a sentence.

13. What is the most important quality for a good student to have?

14. Supply the missing words in this cloze exercise. (Find a reading assignment that is appropriate for your group and then cloze it.)

15. Unscramble these vocabulary words.

16. What do you need to accomplish this week? Make a "To Do" list for this week's activities.

17. Looking back over this week, what did you really learn?

18. List ten things you learned in class today.

19. Read this short newspaper article and respond to it in your journal.

20. Practice the process of elimination on these multiple-choice questions.

21. Complete these analogies that relate to the lesson we are going to study today.

22. Look over the first three paragraphs of your homework reading last night. Write a brief paraphrase of them.

23. What are the underlying principles of the lesson we are studying?

24. What is the correct procedure for . . . ?

25. Justify the rule about . . . .

26. Defend your position on . . . .

27. Defend your teacher's position on the topic of . . . .

28. How can you modify _____ so that it is more efficient?

29. Proofread this paragraph and make as many corrections as you can.

30. What solutions do you have for the problem of _____?

31. Demonstrate the proper way to _____.

32. How does what you learned in this lesson really apply to your life?

33. Why is it necessary for successful people to use time wisely?

34. Pick a partner and show that person how to use one fact from the lesson that you learned in this class yesterday.

35. There are seven errors in the reading passage you were given as you came into the classroom. Can you find them all?

36. Take two of the vocabulary words you have been studying this week and use them both in the same sentence.

37. Write one of the key words from this lesson on a scrap of paper. Pass it to a classmate. Time that person as he/she has only one minute to tell you five important things about it.

38. Why is it useful to learn the information in the unit we are now studying?

39. Pick a partner and brainstorm a list of all the ways you can use the information that you have learned in this class in the last three days.

40. What did you learn in another class this week that you can use in this class today?

41. What have you learned in this class lately that you can apply to another class?

42. Take the items on the board and group them according to a criteria that you devise based on the information in yesterday's lesson.

43. What are some of the assumptions you had about today's class?

44. Using what we learned in class today as proof, justify the reason for . . . .

45. Create a wordsearch puzzle that you will share with a friend tomorrow. Use the key words from today's lesson.

46. Use all of your vocabulary words to create a quick short story.

47. Create a fair test question about the information you have learned today.

48. Take this list of words and create relationships among them.

49. Ask a classmate a question about the current lesson that will absolutely stump that person.

50. List as many ways as you can that you are like the people we have studied in today's lesson.

Use the "Improving Time Management" *reproducible* to help you plan for these "sponges" and transitions. (See next page.)

THE LAST TEN MINUTES OF CLASS

The last ten minutes of every class period can be ones where your students are either engaged in misbehaviors of varying degrees of seriousness or engaged in positive and productive behaviors that indicate self-discipline. You can take several steps to insure that your class provides your students with a sense of satisfaction.

First of all, establish a routine for the end of class so that students know:

■ you won't detain them,
■ they will have to clean up after themselves,
■ they are expected to continue their good behavior,
■ they will have a very limited amount of time to pack up their things,
■ there will be a closing exercise for them to complete every day, and
■ they will be dismissed at a signal from *you*, and not by the bell.

There are many benefits from having a well-structured closing to your class. The biggest benefit, of course, is the marked reduction in misbehavior. Here is a simple two-step plan for ending class that you can follow if you want those last minutes to be as productive as the earlier ones.

IMPROVING TIME MANAGEMENT WITH TRANSITIONS

Class _____

Date _____

Activity One

Objective:

Description:

Estimated Duration:

Actual Duration:

Transition Used:

How successful was the transition in increasing learning and reducing misbehavior?

Activity Two

Objective:

Description:

Estimated Duration:

Actual Duration:

Transition Used:

How successful was the transition in increasing learning and reducing misbehavior?

IMPROVING TIME MANAGEMENT
WITH TRANSITIONS *(cont'd)*

Class _____

Date _____

Activity Three

Objective:

Description:

Estimated Duration:

Actual Duration:

Transition Used:

How successful was the transition in increasing learning and reducing misbehavior:

Activity Four

Objective:

Description:

Estimated Duration:

Actual Duration:

Transition Used:

How successful was the transition in increasing learning and reducing misbehavior?

IMPROVING TIME MANAGEMENT
WITH TRANSITIONS *(cont'd)*

Class _____

Date _____

Activity Five

Objective:

Description:

Estimated Duration:

Actual Duration:

Transition Used:

How successful was the transition in increasing learning and reducing misbehavior?

Activity Six

Objective:

Description:

Estimated Duration:

Actual Duration:

Transition Used:

How successful was the transition in increasing learning and reducing misbehavior?

Step One: Closing Exercise (8 Minutes)

There are many last-minute exercises you can have your students do in the brief time that you allot for this. Here are 15 suggestions to help you design closing exercises that will work with your students.

1. Ask your students to chain together five facts that they learned in class today.

2. Review a list of key words for the next day's assignment.

3. Have your students write a quick explanation to you of the most interesting aspect of the day's lesson.

4. Teach your students a new word related to the day's assignment.

5. Hold a rapid-fire drill on the relevant facts from the lesson.

6. Hold a quick vocabulary, review, or spelling bee.

7. Play a game for bonus test points.

8. Ask a student to explain the directions for the homework assignment one more time.

9. Unveil a final thought for the day that you have hidden on the board under a sheet of paper all period long.

10. Challenge your students to do some independent research about the topic under study.

11. Have your students read and comment on a brief passage related to the day's topic.

12. Show an upbeat cartoon on the overhead projector.

13. Ask students to thank someone in their group for a specific action.

14. Ask for a prediction of what they will learn at the next class meeting.

15. Have students write out five things they learned in class and share their list with a classmate.

Step Two: Dismissal (2 Minutes)

After the closing exercise is completed, you should have two minutes for your students to get ready to be dismissed at your signal. During this time they should have a daily routine to follow. The routine you establish for them should include:

1. disposing of the trash that has accumulated during the class period.

2. stowing away books and materials, and

3. checking under desks to see that nothing is left behind.

It is perfectly okay to allow talking at this time if students stay in their seats and keep their voices down. You can teach this part of the closing routine to your students by timing them often at first and rewarding the class for successfully completing it.

One mistake that many teachers make is to allow students to just jump up and bolt for the door when the bell rings. You need to teach your students that *you* will dismiss them and that they should wait for your signal. You do not need to detain them after the bell has rung in an obvious power display in order to make the ending of your class productive.

At the very end of class, you should move to the door and speak to every student as the class leaves. By doing this you will prevent any last-minute flareups of misbehavior. You will also show your students that they have a teacher who models the concern and courtesy that they need to leave the class with a feeling of well-being.

Use the "Self-Check for Improving Class Time Management" *reproducible* on the following page to see how you are presently doing and where you can improve in managing those last ten minutes of class.

WHAT TO DO WHEN WASTED TIME CAUSES PROBLEMS

PROBLEM:

The lesson is not appropriate for the ability of every pupil.

POSSIBLE SOLUTIONS:

1. Assess students to make sure that lack of ability or basic skills is the problem and not just a lack of motivation.

2. Check the reading levels of the students and provide extra help with reading assignments if students are poor readers.

3. Allow flexible deadlines so that students who need longer to complete the assignment can take more time.

4. Provide interesting enrichment assignments to those students who have mastered the material quickly.

5. Provide a variety of assignments to appeal to everyone's strengths. Pay attention to the importance of learning styles in reaching as many of your students as possible.

6. Encourage students to work together in groups so that they can help each other.

7. Provide as many hands-on and real-life experiences for your students as your subject matter allows.

8. Offer study sessions after school and encourage other teachers in your building to join you in after-school tutoring.

9. Don't lower your expectations for students who are struggling. Encourage and support their efforts, but don't give up or allow them to.

PROBLEM:

Students are distracted by an upcoming event such as a holiday, the prom, or a pep rally.

POSSIBLE SOLUTIONS:

1. Prepare yourself mentally for the change in your students so that you can remain in control of the situation.

2. Channel that energy into productive activity. If students have engaging lessons, then they will be more likely to stay focused. Design your most productive lessons for the times of the school term when you anticipate distractions.

SELF-CHECK FOR IMPROVING CLASS TIME MANAGEMENT

Class _____

Date _____

LAST TEN MINUTES OF CLASS

Activities Planned	Estimated Time to Complete Each	Actual Time Each Required
1. _____		
2. _____		
3. _____		
4. _____		
5. _____		

Off-Task Behaviors Observed

_____

_____

_____

_____

_____

Positive Behaviors Observed

_____

_____

_____

_____

_____

Proposed Solutions for Improving Time Management

_____

_____

_____

_____

_____

3. Now would be a good time to pull out those puzzles that students enjoy solving if you want them to work quietly.

4. If you don't mind noise, engage your students in some of the low-tech games described in Section Five.

5. Try to design a lesson around the theme of the upcoming event so that your students can be excited and productive at the same time.

6. If students are normally well-behaved, tell them they can have a set amount of time to chat and be excited. Set a time limit with them and tell them that when the limit is up, you expect them to settle down to work without fail. Often just a small amount of time—three to five minutes—is all that they need to clear their minds to settle to work. Students will also appreciate your understanding.

PROBLEM:

Students lose interest in a lesson because it seems to take too long to do.

POSSIBLE SOLUTIONS:

1. Break long-term assignments into manageable blocks of work so that students can see that each small step leads to a finished product.

2. Try to divide your class time into 15-minute blocks so that students can have a change of pace.

3. Use graphic organizers to help students see where an assignment is leading. Some students just need to see a visual representation of what you expect them to do before it makes sense to them.

4. Use the checklist suggested earlier (see Figure 3-1) so that students can feel they are accomplishing something and moving ahead with purpose.

5. If students are working in teams, have one student in charge of keeping everyone working productively.

6. When possible, allow students a choice of activities. You don't have to change or eliminate activities, but if you allow students to choose which of three activities that they want to do first, for example, then they are likely to stay on task.

7. Set time limits for completing tasks within a class period. This encourages students to work towards a goal.

8. Sometimes a tangible, extrinsic reward will motivate students who might stray from an assignment to stay busy to complete it.

PROBLEM:

Students are disruptive while they are waiting for further instructions or for a classmate to finish an assignment.

POSSIBLE SOLUTIONS:

1. Design your instruction so that students have a series of tasks rather than just one thing at a time.

2. Designate a spot on the board or some other place in the room where students are to check for further instructions.

3. Give students a long-term project, such as reading a library book or completing a series of puzzles, if they have finished their work.

4. Make it a part of the culture of your classroom that students work from beginning until the end instead of just until they have done the assignment for the day.

5. Put students in study teams to work together; they tend to work more efficiently.

6. Always provide an enrichment assignment for those students who complete work early. Make this a habit when you are writing lesson plans.

7. Encourage those students who find an assignment easy to help those who don't.

8. Be careful to place the homework assignment on the board before class starts so that students who want to get started on it early may do so. Be clear with them that it is okay to start homework in class only if they have finished their other work.

9. Give your students a checklist of assignments so that they can work on a series of assignments rather than having to consult you after each step.

PROMOTING SELF-DISCIPLINE THROUGH TEACHING TIME-MANAGEMENT SKILLS

It is not enough for teachers to become efficiency experts who don't waste a second of their students' time if those same students don't understand how to be efficient themselves. Good discipline practices involve more than crowd control. We need to give our students the time-management tools that will lead them to assume the responsibility for their own behavior and progress.

There are many ways to accomplish this. One of the most popular is to teach a generic unit on study skills with a strong component of time management built in. The problem with this method is that often it is taught in isolation from practical applications for students and is abandoned once the unit of study is complete.

A more effective method is to engage students daily in discussions about how they can use their class time and study time more efficiently. Begin the process of moving your students towards self-discipline with the four time-management tools included here.

Tool One: Time-Management Strategies for Students

The first tool is a list of 27 time-management strategies for secondary students. The reproducible is written in the form of quick tips for students to follow. Adapt it for use in frequent, brief discussions in which you and your students share insights on the best ways for them to accomplish their academic tasks. Although it is by no means a complete list, it will get you off to a good start. (See *reproducible* on the following page.)

Tool Two: Calendar for Student Planning

The second item, "A Monthly Planner," (page 95) will help your students learn to control how they use time. Reproduce copies of this form for your students to keep in their note-

27 POWER-PACKED TIME-MANAGEMENT TIPS
FOR STUDENTS

- Prioritize your time. You'll have to make choices about your activities if you want to do well in school.

- Avoid stress, burnout, and failure by planning your work.

- Pack your school materials the night before so that you won't have to scramble early in the morning.

- Use a planning calendar to keep track of all the tasks you have to accomplish each day.

- If you don't have a syllabus or a planning calendar, be sure to write down your homework instead of just trying to remember it.

- Learn the material the first time you see it. Don't delay your learning until the night before a test.

- Use your class time fully. If you have a few minutes to spare in class, use that time to review your notes or to start your homework rather than to just stare at the clock.

- Study your most difficult or boring subject first while you are most alert.

- Think of the little blocks of time that most of us waste as potential work time. When you have an extra 15 minutes, plan to use it for a quick review of your notes.

- Work steadily. Cramming all night is not productive.

- Learn to use a computer. You'll get the job done much faster than if you try to do everything by hand.

- When you have a big project to do, set deadlines for accomplishing parts of it well in advance of the final deadline.

- Pace yourself by watching the clock during a timed assignment.

- Set aside a 2-hour block of time each night for studying. Even on the nights when you don't have assignments, you should spend this block of time reviewing and studying.

- Avoid study sessions that last for hours. After a while your concentration begins to lag. Instead, take a 3- to 5-minute break every 30 minutes or so.

- Become aware of the time of day when you are most alert and use it to study efficiently.

- Complete your homework the night before it is due. Don't count on stealing time from other classes to finish what you should have done at home.

- Schedule several small bits of time to finish a long-term project. Try to turn in your projects early.

- Don't spend too much time on a particular subject if this causes you to neglect other topics.

- Do all tasks well the first time so that you won't have to repeat them.

- Become aware of just how and when you procrastinate. Take the steps necessary to get this bad habit under control.

- Use your daylight hours to study as often as you can. Most people are more alert then.

- Allow enough time to study. Five minutes before a big test just isn't enough.

- Looking over your notes is a huge waste of time. Study actively with a pen in hand. Write down the information!

- Learn to concentrate. In class and when you are studying at home, make sure you focus your energy into learning.

- Attend class. Those students who attend class do better than those who don't. Be one of them.

- Make "doing your best" a priority. *You* are the person who determines your present and your future.

A MONTHLY PLANNER

Month: _____   Year: _____

Sunday	Monday	Tuesday	Wednesday	Thursday	Friday	Saturday

Notes

books. It can be a valuable part of your efforts to help your students if you and they begin to use it together to plan, to raise awareness about time use, to focus attention on upcoming events, to use time wisely, and to stay on task.

Tool Three: Time Schedule

The third time-management tool is a schedule for your students to complete with information about how they actually use their time. Once students have charted their activities after school for a week, you and they can begin to see where problems with time management occur. At that point you can reissue the schedule to your students and ask them to use it not as a diary of their time, but as a planner. You can work together to improve the ways your students spend their after-school hours when you show them how to plan their days. (See *reproducible* on following page.)

Tool Four: The "You Are in Control" Questionnaire

The final time-management tool is a *reproducible* questionnaire that you can give to your students periodically at the end of class. This questionnaire is designed to help students realize that they make choices constantly about how they use time. It will guide them into thinking about ways that they can make more intelligent choices for themselves. (See page 98.)

When your students begin to realize that they have choices and begin to make wiser ones about how they use time, then you know you have successfully incorporated time-management concerns into the culture of your classroom and that your students are becoming self-disciplined.

"Time enough always proves little enough."

—Benjamin Franklin

STUDENT TIME SCHEDULE/PLANNER

Date _____

Time	*Activity*
4:00 P.M.	
4:30	
5:00	
5:30	
6:00	
6:30	
7:00	
7:30	
8:00	
8:30	
9:00	
9:30	
10:00	
10:30	
11:00	

YOU ARE IN CONTROL!

Date _____   Class _____

APPROPRIATE BEHAVIOR DURING CLASS

1. What happened in class today that was a good use of your time?

   _____

2. What was your attitude during class?

   _____

3. How did your actions and attitude affect your grade?

   _____

   _____

INAPPROPRIATE BEHAVIOR DURING CLASS

1. What did you do that wasted your time?

   _____

2. Complete this statement: I estimate that I wasted _____ minutes in class today.

3. How did your attitude and actions affect your grade?

   _____

   _____

SOLUTIONS

1. What attitude changes can you make?

   _____

   _____

2. Which time-management skill should you improve?

   _____

3. What are three alternative actions you can do to improve your behavior and grade in this class?

   a. _____

   b. _____

   c. _____

Section 4

A PARTNERSHIP APPROACH
TO DISCIPLINE

In This Section . . .

One of the most important skills we can have at school—as well as in other areas of life—is relating well to other people. Section Four offers suggestions for improving our relationships with our colleagues, with the parents or guardians of students, and with our students.

"Why Cooperation with Other Professionals Is Important for Effective Discipline," "Why We Can't Do It Alone," "Working Well with Your Supervisors," and "Joining Forces with Colleagues" all explain various ways that we can establish our discipline climate through strengthening the professional relationships we have with others at school.

Another important area of human relations that is very important for teachers is building a strong partnership with parents. Read "Building a Strong Relationship with Parents," "A Sample Letter to Parents," "How to Have a Beneficial Parent Conference," "Documenting Parent Conferences," and the reproducibles "Parent–Teacher–Student Progress Checkup" and "Parent Contact Documentation Form" to find out how.

By far, however, the most important relationship we need to establish is with our students. The first steps you can take to do this can be found in "20 Actions that Let Your Students Know You Care" and "The Importance of Modeling Good Behavior."

Learn practical suggestions for handling confidential information and for soliciting helpful feedback from students in "What to Do When a Student Confides in You" and "Getting Feedback from Students." The "Teacher-Effectiveness Report Card" is a reproducible designed to help your students let you know how well you're doing in a productive manner.

"Conducting Useful Student Conferences" explains all of the details that need to be worked out when you hold a conference with a student and you want it to be absolutely successful.

If knowledge is indeed power, then the student inventories included in this section will grant you both. All four inventories will help promote a successful relationship with students because they allow you to find out about them in a friendly and nonintrusive way.

Building a strong working relationship with students who may want to engage in a power struggle is the topic of "Class Leaders and the Power Struggle."

"The Importance of Teaching Courtesy" and "Arming Our Students: Teaching the Art of the Alternative Response to Rude Classmates" focus on the ways you can help students develop more courteous and positive relationships with each other and with you.

Finally, in "The Interactive Class," you'll explore games to increase the pleasant ways that you and your students interact with each other.

"No man is wise enough by himself."

—Plautus

WHY COOPERATION WITH OTHER PROFESSIONALS IS IMPORTANT FOR EFFECTIVE DISCIPLINE

Contrary to what many other professionals believe, we teachers do not pick up our book-bags and head out to ivory towers every morning. While it is true many of us have the entire summer off, many of us spend our unpaid vacation days taking classes to meet recertification requirements. While it may be true that our work days are over in mid-afternoon (at least on the days when there is no faculty meeting), we stagger to the parking lot at the end of the day with our bookbags filled with hundreds of ungraded papers.

We work in an environment that is unique, true. But schools share an important challenge with all other professions where people work closely together. We deal with many, many people during the work week and we must cooperate successfully with each one.

To complicate matters, schools are not just job sites, but complex communities composed of students and the adults who care for them. Each school is a mixture of old and young, cheerful and cranky, competent and struggling. School communities also extend far beyond the walls of the building into the homes of staff members and students.

The stakes are also higher in a school than in most businesses. If there is a mistake on an assembly line, quality control personnel can simply toss the product aside. For us, the product of our labors is infinitely more precious. Cooperation with others is one of the most important factors in our success.

The need to cooperate well with others seems to grow greater every year as school districts struggle to help an increasing number of students in more and more ways. Just a few years ago a school nurse was still a novelty in many schools. Now we have a growing array of clerks, technical assistance staff, remediation specialists, social workers, vocational counselors, psychologists, media specialists, environmental control personnel, paraprofessionals, attendants, police liaison staff, security guards, drug rehabilitation counselors, and computer wizards.

Secondary teachers know that each of these people plays an important role in the school community. Cooperating well with our colleagues, with parents and guardians, and with our students is not only crucial to the success of the entire school, it also has a direct and very significant impact on the success of the discipline program within the four walls of our classrooms.

WHY WE CAN'T DO IT ALONE

1. Schools are communities—not just of children, but of many different types of people.

2. The job of coping with class responsibilities is just too complicated to do it without help. We can't be experts in every area.

3. We need to build positive relationships with others if we want them to be able to offer us help when we need it.

4. We need the insights that others can offer us.

5. Every person in the building can offer a unique and valuable contribution to solving student behavior problems.

6. Strong adult influences can help students fight peer pressure. The more positive adults that we can enlist, the better.

7. Our students learn polite behavior and positive interactions by watching how we relate to each other.

8. When the adults in a school get along well with each other, the trickle-down effect has a positive influence on students.

9. Behavior—both good and bad—does not occur in a vacuum. A pupil's behavior is often influenced by what has happened earlier in the day, the week, the year.

10. We will all have at least one impossibly difficult student over the course of our professional careers. When you're not being successful with a student, it is important to know who you can turn to for help. The mark of a professional is to know when to seek assistance.

WORKING WELL WITH YOUR SUPERVISORS

If you want to be the best teacher to your students that you possibly can, then you will have to work well with your supervisors. The administrators who make up the supervisory staff for your school district and for your school building depend on faculty members to make things run smoothly.

Sometimes this happens and sometimes it doesn't. In either case, it is up to you to do all you can to work well with your supervisors. You will depend on them not only for leadership and guidance, but for practical help in dealing with discipline dilemmas as they arise.

If you want to establish a partnership that will be effective in creating the kind of positive learning climate you want for your class, then you will need to take action to foster a positive working relationship with your supervisors. Fortunately, this is not very difficult. You can use many of the following suggestions to establish a working partnership with not just your supervisors, but with all of the people you meet in the course of your school day.

1. Remember to be professional if you are angry and speaking with an administrator. You should appear competent and concerned, not out of control.

2. Once you have referred a child to an administrator, your part is over. Don't criticize the actions taken or not taken by an administrator once you have turned a child over to the office staff for disciplining.

3. Conduct yourself in a professional manner each day. Not only will this make an administrator's daily job easier, but, when your professional reputation is solid, that administrator will find it easier to help and support you if you make mistakes.

4. Model the respect you expect your students to show towards an administrator no matter what your feelings about that person might be.

5. Don't threaten your students with "the office." Doing this will only weaken your own efforts to maintain control of your classroom.

6. When an administrator asks you to take on extra duties or responsibilities, do so if you possibly can.

7. Administrators are responsible for the entire school, while you are responsible for only a small part of it. Try to see yourself as part of a larger process and you'll find it easier to understand some of the policies or decisions that you might otherwise find confusing or troubling.

8. Familiarize yourself with the procedures and policies outlined in your faculty handbook. This simple action will prevent you from making avoidable mistakes and having to deal with administrators in a negative way.

9. Make an appointment when you need to speak with administrators. Just dropping by the office may catch them at inconvenient moments and your problem won't receive the attention that it deserves.

10. Never lie to an administrator. When you've made a mistake, admit it.

11. If you work in a large school, you will deal with a number of administrators. Get to know each one so that your working relationship will be productive. Find out their discipline philosophy or methods so that you can work well together.

12. Accept the fact that the administrators you work with are not always going to act in ways with which you agree. Public criticism of their actions will not change the situation and can seriously damage your professional reputation. Think before you criticize.

13. If you need help with a problem, don't wait until it's too late to involve an administrator. Don't let a small problem become a large one before seeking assistance. Find out early in your relationship the point at which your administrators want you to involve them in discipline problems.

14. Share your successes with administrators. Creating good public relations is a large part of their job. You can make this job easier by letting them know about successful and innovative events in your classroom.

JOINING FORCES WITH COLLEAGUES

What the Cooperative Teacher Does

1. Arrives early and leaves late
2. Keeps sensitive material confidential
3. Strives for personal perfect attendance
4. Joins committees and works hard
5. Works well with supervisors and support staff
6. Does paperwork neatly, accurately, and promptly
7. Is a good hall buddy
8. Does favors whenever possible
9. Has good manners even on bad days
10. Shows respect for other teachers
11. Assumes responsibility

12. Generously shares materials and equipment
13. Has school spirit
14. Joins the parent–teacher and other professional organizations
15. Tackles school improvement projects
16. Is a staff cheerleader
17. Enjoys friendly socializing with colleagues
18. Asks
19. Knows what to do

And Doesn't Do

1. Arrives late and leaves early
2. Is always first with gossip
3. Often misses school for flimsy reasons
4. Forgets that there's a scheduled faculty meeting
5. Believes that school policies apply to others
6. Takes three weeks to grade and return papers
7. Causes other teachers to bang on the wall to get things to quiet down
8. Asks for favors whenever possible
9. Has bad manners even on good days
10. Undermines other colleagues in creative ways
11. Blames everything on the school board, parents, and television
12. Constantly runs out of necessary materials and supplies
13. Leads the rush to the parking lot at the end of the day
14. Thinks that the only people who know anything about education are teachers
15. Is the reason so many school-improvement projects are necessary
16. Can complain more loudly and more often than any other staff member
17. Still isn't sure of everyone's names
18. Demands
19. Is still trying to figure out the photocopier

BUILDING A STRONG RELATIONSHIP WITH PARENTS

Never underestimate the importance of dealing well with the parents or guardians of your students. All parents have the right to be informed about their child's academic and behavioral progress. Parents can also be enormously helpful to you. After all, these are the people who know more about your students than anyone else. Many secondary teachers think that because their students tend to act very independently that they are, in fact, independent creatures. Most are not.

While secondary school parent-teacher groups may not be so large as primary ones, don't be misled into thinking that it isn't important to reach out to parents. Secondary students have parents who are as concerned about the welfare and educational status of their children at this point in their lives as they were when they were younger. These are the people who want the best for their children and who look to teachers for help in navigating the turbulent waters of adolescence.

Without doubt, parental support has a major impact on students' attitudes about school. Many secondary teachers realize early in their careers that those students whose parents are involved in their education consistently perform better academically than those students whose parents are not as involved as they should be. It is the responsibility of teachers to be the first to reach out to involve parents or guardians in school life.

Establishing a good working relationship with parents also makes classroom discipline much easier to achieve. When students know that the important adults in their lives are united in their attempts to help them achieve their potential, students are less likely to misbehave and more likely to achieve success.

Working well with parents is just good sense if you want to create a positive learning environment in your classroom. Always remember to treat all parents with respect even though not all of them are alike in how they express concern about their children. If you make a point of helping parents feel successful about their children, you will find them more willing to work successfully with you.

23 Strategies for Working with Parents

Use the following strategies to improve how you present yourself to parents or guardians so that you can establish the kind of working relationship with them that you want.

1. On the first day of school send home a letter that explains your policies on various classroom issues. The first parent contact should be a positive one. Be very careful to explain your homework policy if you want parents or guardians to help you with this area. A sample letter is included in Figure 4-1 on page 106.

2. Write neatly or type it when you send any letter to a parent. Have someone proofread for you so that you appear as professional as possible.

3. Call parents or guardians when their children are successful as well as when you need their help in solving a problem. Send home positive notes. When parents hear good news from school, they realize you are trying to help their children achieve. Parents who only hear from teachers when there's trouble quickly learn to dread conversations with us.

4. Be a good listener when you talk with parents. Often parents are just as confused and worried about a child's behavior as you are. Listen carefully; together you can be a strong team.

5. When you talk with many parents, you must realize that their own unpleasant experience with school and with their child's previous teachers may color their view of you. Be as positive and professional as possible to help these parents overcome their negative feelings.

FIGURE 4-1
Sample Letter to Parents

Dear Parents,

With this letter I would like to introduce myself as your child's English 9 teacher this year. I have been a teacher at CHS for the last fifteen years. I am originally from Southwest Virginia and I graduated from Virginia Tech.

On September 23, I would like to welcome you to the PTSA Back-to-School night. I am looking forward to meeting you and showing you our texts and the classroom. Please attend if you have an opportunity to do so.

This year will be an exciting one for my students and me. We'll study literature, usage, grammar, study skills, vocabulary, and writing. I have planned many activities that I hope will encourage my students to succeed.

Many parents ask about homework assignments for their teenagers. While there may be other times when assignments and long-term projects will take lots of time, there is a routine that I try to follow as closely as possible to insure that students benefit from their homework. Every Monday, Tuesday, Wednesday, and Thursday night you can expect to see your child doing homework for this class. The assignments are listed on the syllabus that students are required to keep in their notebooks.

If you have any questions or if any problems arise, please contact me at school: 686-2500. I will be glad to speak with you if you just give me a call or send in a note.

I look forward to working with your child this year. I also look forward to meeting you and learning how I might be of help to you and your child.

Sincerely,

Mrs. Thompson

6. Be quick to involve parents when there is a problem with a student. Many parents complain that teachers let problems get out of hand before calling home. This is understandably easy to do if you and the student are trying to work out the problem, but it is not a good practice. If you notice a drastic drop in a grade, for example, notify the parent or guardian as soon as possible.

7. If a student's problem is a serious one, set up a conference so that you and the parents can discuss the situation face to face. Be as flexible as you can in arranging time for this conference with parents. Make sure parents have plenty of advance notice about meeting times.

8. When you have to contact a parent about a problem, be as specific as possible. Don't tell a parent that the child is "acting funny," for example. Instead, give examples of what the child has done that causes you concern.

9. If a parent calls you, return the phone call as soon as possible. Do not let even 24 hours go by without talking to the parent. To do otherwise is rude and harmful to your relationship with the child and the parent.

10. Call parents at work if necessary. When you get them on the line, have the courtesy to ask if they have the time to talk to you at that moment.

11. When you call a parent at work, be very careful about the message that you leave. Do not involve a person's co-workers in personal business about one of your students. This violates the child's privacy and is unprofessional on your part.

12. It's not a good idea to give out your home number to all parents. You should protect your privacy and personal life. Keep relationships with parents on a professional level.

13. Have a specific goal in mind when you speak with a parent. Don't ramble in your conversation. Try to keep the parent focused on solving the problem also.

14. Make sure you have followed school rules and have the proper documentation in place when a parent calls to question you about something in your class.

15. If there is a death in the family or another kind of emergency, call parents to offer assistance in helping your student through the crisis. This small gesture will let them know you care about the welfare of their child.

16. Work with several other teachers to create a schoolwide "Parents' Board" in the lobby of your school for displaying information and articles of interest to parents.

17. Never become confrontational with parents, even when they are confrontational with you first. Instead, show your concern and caring.

18. Never talk about another person's child when you talk with a parent. This is not only unproductive and unprofessional, but it will also get back to the child or the other parents quickly.

19. Immediately document any contact that you have had with a parent or guardian whether it's a phone call, conference, or letter. You might need this information later.

20. Write a thank-you note after a conference or after a phone call to thank the parents for their concern and time.

21. Encourage parents or guardians to visit your class as volunteers or as guest speakers.

22. Send out a monthly newsletter to parents that describes class activities. You could invite parents to share ideas and comments.

23. If a parent or guardian requests weekly or even daily progress reports, comply with this request willingly. Set up a system with the child where the student is responsible for bringing you a paper to sign at the end of class each day or week with the information on it that the parent requested. You can make this even easier for yourself if you use the "Parent–Teacher–Student Progress Checkup" reproducible on the next page.

PARENT–TEACHER–STUDENT PROGRESS CHECKUP

Student Name _____ Class _____

Date	Teacher Comments	Parent Comments

HOW TO HAVE BENEFICIAL PARENT CONFERENCES

Parent conferences can produce high-level anxiety for all of the parties involved: parents, teachers, and the students who are the cause of the occasion. Parents who are summoned to school may feel that their years of child-rearing decisions are under attack. Teachers dread that parents will question every decision that they've made since student teaching and then call in auditors to check over their grade books. The students who misbehaved to the point that the important adults in their lives are meeting—usually behind closed doors—relive every mistake that they've ever made since kindergarten while they wait to see just how long they'll be grounded. At least that's what happens on television sitcoms.

Of course the reality of parent conferences is quite different. There are many different ways for parents and teachers to meet to work together for the well-being of a child. The most informal way is a chance meeting, perhaps in the mall or at a social gathering. Parents and teachers can also get together at parent-teacher functions and back-to-school nights. A more structured conference happens when a parent and a teacher speak with each other on the phone to solve a problem that has arisen. The most formal and structured type of conference is also usually the most effective: a face-to-face meeting.

Teachers who want to communicate well with parents or guardians realize that parents want to be reassured that their child is doing well and can succeed in school. Even though this may not be the current state of affairs with their child, parents want teachers to work with them and with their children to make this happen. We need to connect solidly with the parents or guardians of our students if we intend to create a positive learning climate in our classrooms.

One way to have a beneficial conference is to make sure our goals for the conference are clear. There are five important goals for every successful parent conference:

1. You should present yourself to parents or guardians as a friendly teacher who has their child's best interests at heart.

2. You should strive to create a "we" atmosphere of cooperation and friendliness.

3. Parents should leave with a sense of satisfaction—that all of their questions have been answered and that all of the points they wanted to cover were covered.

4. Both parties should have a sense of mutual respect and an understanding of each other's problems.

5. A workable solution to the problem has been agreed upon and everyone involved intends to work together to help the student.

In addition to these five goals, there are many other things you can do before and during a conference to make sure that the result is what you want it to be. By working together with parents and students, you can have the peaceful and productive classroom climate that you want. The very best public-relations instrument that any teacher can have is a room full of well-behaved and satisfied students busily engaged in the task of learning.

Before the Conference

1. Make sure you have a clear purpose for the conference.

2. Plan the points you want to cover.

3. Get together samples of the student's work.

4. Go over the student's cumulative record and report card to familiarize yourself with information that the parents already have.

5. Establish a rough estimate of the student's strengths and weaknesses as well as any special aptitudes.

6. Find out about the student's performance in other classes.

7. Try to anticipate the parents' questions and concerns.

8. Create a seating arrangement that will be comfortable for parents. Sitting together around a table is much more comfortable and friendly than expecting parents to sit in student desks while you sit at yours.

9. Make sure you have pen and paper for notetaking. Have some handy for parents, too.

10. Mentally rough out a plan of action that you would like to discuss.

11. Make sure you remain calm before and during the conference. Becoming agitated will not only upset you, but it will also interfere with the rapport you want to establish in order to create a solution to the problem.

12. Make a neat "Do Not Disturb" sign and post it on your door so that you can meet with parents without distractions.

During the Conference

1. Be considerate. Meet the parents in the school office and escort them to your room unless you are sure they know the way.

2. Be prompt.

3. Greet the parents cordially and express your appreciation for the fact that they came to the conference. This will create a tone of goodwill that you should strive to maintain throughout the conference.

4. Do not try to impress parents with your knowledge of educational terms and jargon. Use language that will make parents comfortable.

5. Begin the conference with positive remarks about their child. Talk about the student's potential, aptitude, special talents. Focus on strengths even if the reason for the conference is a serious breach of conduct. Do not lose sight of the fact that this child is very important to the parents.

6. Convey the attitude that the child's welfare is your primary concern.

7. State the problem in simple, factual terms and express your desire to work together on a solution for the good of the child.

8. Allow upset or angry parents to speak first. After parents have had the opportunity to say all of the things that they have probably been mentally rehearsing on the way to school, then and only then, can they listen to you or begin to work on a solution to the problem.

9. Show examples of the student's work that illustrate the problem. If the problem is not directly work-related, be prepared to discuss specific examples of misbehavior.

10. If this is a problem that you have talked about before, perhaps informally or over the phone, share any improvement.

11. Tell the parents what you have done to help correct the situation.

12. Listen to the parents. If you want a solution to the problem, give them your full attention throughout the conference. Your nonverbal language is crucial to the success of a parent conference. Be attentive, friendly, and positive.

13. Encourage parents to express their ideas. You need their insight and help.

14. Ask parents questions that will direct their thinking. These questions can also keep everyone focused on the problem at hand and on solutions to it.

15. Summarize the points of the conference at the end. Be sure to outline what you will do and what they will do to help their child be more successful in school.

16. Determine how you will follow up on the conference and keep them up to date.

17. Express appreciation again for their concern and the time they have spent with you in the conference.

After the Conference

1. Immediately document the conference either with your notes or by filling out the parent contact form included in this section. Don't wait to do this because your memory may play tricks on you later.

2. Write out the steps that you, the student, and the parents will take now that the conference is over.

Mistakes to Avoid

1. Don't make parents defensive and don't become defensive yourself.

2. Don't talk about other students or compare their child with others.

3. Don't talk about other teachers, the principal, or the school district unless you are complimentary.

4. Don't become angry. It won't accomplish anything.

5. Don't try to outtalk parents. They need to feel comfortable expressing themselves around you. Don't interrupt, either. Both trying to outtalk and interrupting are just plain bad manners.

6. Don't make parents uncomfortable by asking questions that are too personal.

7. Do not allow parents to become abusive. Sometimes angry parents lose control. As soon as you see this happening, end the conference as gracefully as you can and involve your supervisor. Do not remain alone with parents who are angry to the point of abusing you.

8. Don't neglect to document the conference and file your notes.

9. Don't neglect to follow through on the promises that you have made to the parents during the conference.

10. If you have learned confidential information during the conference, keep it confidential.

DOCUMENTING PARENT CONTACTS

Sometimes it appears as if the stacks of paperwork that teachers are expected to do reach the ceiling. There are countless forms for just about every interaction we have with our students.

It is an unfortunate part of the discipline process that we have to protect ourselves in this way, but we do. It's just good sense to keep accurate records of when you have communicated with parents. Especially at the end of a school term, you might be expected to provide proof that you have enlisted the aid of parents or guardians as well as others in your efforts to help a particular student.

In June you may not remember that you contacted a parent in September. It is horrifying to think you could be accused unjustly of not doing all that you could to help a student, but it can happen. It does happen every year in countless cases where frustrated parents and children look for a simple cause to a complex problem.

Just a few minutes of planning and paperwork will save you time, enhance your professional credibility, and prevent problems when an administrator or parent wants proof that you have fulfilled one of your most important professional duties.

More important than these, however, is the chief reason for you to keep accurate records of all of your parent contacts. You will be better able to help all of your students if you contact parents when you need to and work out plans for preventing and dealing with discipline problems.

Since so much of the paperwork we have to do is time-consuming and tedious, it pays to make it easy whenever we can. Keeping a record of the times you communicate with parents does not need to be time consuming. One way to do this is to document parent contacts in a standard format.

Photocopy the "Parent Contact Documentation Form" so that you have one for each student. Whenever you communicate with a parent, simply pull out a copy of the form, fill it out, and file it in a folder with the other paperwork you have for that particular student.

THE TEACHER–STUDENT LINK

Many teachers who have traveled abroad to third-world countries have had the opportunity to observe the schools in those countries. Often these teachers return home appalled at the unendurably primitive conditions in which teachers are expected to teach and students are expected to learn.

They describe classrooms with no chalkboards, supplies, texts, electricity, or even enough potable water for comfort. Students study at benches or sit on the ground for many hours after walking long distances to school. Teachers and students suffer together from the extremes of weather in schools without any sort of efficient climate control.

Even though they may be appalled at the conditions they observe, teachers also are awed by the superior learning they witness taking place. They recount stories of dedicated students who turn in work that is not only insightful, but beautifully written in a perfect script.

Students and teachers with no books somehow find a way to read the world's greatest literature. Students and teachers with no calculators solve incredibly difficult mathematical problems. Students and teachers with no current periodicals manage an astounding grasp of the world's political events.

PARENT CONTACT DOCUMENTATION FORM

Student _____

Parent _____

Date and time of contact _____

Type of contact:

_____ phone call

_____ letter

_____ detention notice

_____ home visit

_____ informal meeting

_____ meeting with administrator

_____ meeting with counselor

_____ other: _____

Person initiating the contact: _____

Topics discussed:

_____

_____

_____

Steps parent will take:

_____

_____

_____

Steps teacher will take:

_____

_____

_____

Additional notes:

_____

_____

_____

Somehow those resourceful teachers and their students have achieved what seems impossible to us. They have achieved the truest aim of education—learning that will lift us far above our sometimes uneasy daily lives. The question that faces us is an important one. How can we attempt to duplicate the learning success created by those inspiring teachers in our own state-of-the-art classrooms?

Successful learning is not dependent on such modern essentials as computer networks, interactive texts, competitive sports, or even photocopiers. Students everywhere need to enter into an important partnership with their teachers. The personal link between teacher and student is essential for successful learning and for a class climate geared to self-discipline.

The following strategies are designed to foster this necessary link. Many of them seem to be almost instinctive acts by excellent teachers who are mindful of the fact that one of the biggest complaints unsuccessful students have about school is that no one seems to care about them. These teachers reach out to students because they know the secret to a successful class is their personal relationship with each child.

33 Ways to Develop the Teacher–Student Link

1. Take the time to get to know your students as people.

2. Use a kind voice when speaking with them.

3. Set up your classroom where you can walk around to every desk and stay away from the front of the room.

4. When a student speaks to you, stop what you are doing and listen.

5. Be clear about your role as a teacher who will enable students to achieve their dreams.

6. Use humor. Laugh when funny things happen in your class.

7. Show your appreciation for the good things your students do.

8. Stress that you won't give up on your students.

9. Allow your students to get to know you. Often our students are convinced that we sleep in the teachers' lounge all night and eat only lunchroom food. They need to see your human side.

10. Agree with them as often as you can.

11. When there is a problem, don't automatically assume a student is at fault. Listen to your students as they tell their version of events before passing judgment.

12. Move your desk to the back of the classroom. This small action signals a user-friendly attitude to many students.

13. Call home to parents or guardians when good things happen.

14. Share your feelings with your students and allow them to share theirs.

15. Use positive language with them. Be careful not to appear negative or critical.

16. Take notice of the special things that make each student unique.

17. Stop and chat with pupils anytime: when you are monitoring their progress, in the hall or cafeteria, or even when you are away from school.

18. Create opportunities for success every day.

19. Speak to every student each day. Include every one in class discussions.

20. Make pens, paper, and extra books available when students need a loan.

21. Set aside an afternoon or morning for "office hours" when you can provide extra help for those students who need it.

22. Offer small perks whenever you can.

23. Be sincere, generous, and tactful in your praise.

24. Keep students busily involved in interesting work.

25. Be a well-prepared and well-organized teacher who takes the time to present interesting lessons.

26. Call home when your students are absent more than one day to see what's wrong.

27. Set limits for your students. They need a comfortable framework in which to operate.

28. Talk with students when you notice a change in their behavior or attitude. If a normally cheerful student, for example, seems distracted or upset, there's a good reason for the change.

29. When students confide in you, follow up on it. Ask about how they did on the history test that was troubling them or check to see if their grades have improved in math class.

30. Be concerned enough for their futures to help them set long-term goals.

31. Involve pupils in projects that will improve the school or community.

32. Focus on students' strong points, not on their weaknesses.

33. Stress that you and they have much in common: goals, dreams, and beliefs.

20 ACTIONS THAT LET YOUR STUDENTS KNOW YOU CARE

1. Find a large 12-month calendar and have your students put their birthdays on it. Those students who have birthdays during holidays can mark a day they would like to use to celebrate the event. On the day, put a "Happy Birthday!" message on the board. At the beginning of the term you should spend some time at the computer to design a card for your students. Photocopy these and have them ready for your students.

2. Praise and reward your students often as individuals and as a class.

3. Use your very best manners in dealing with your students. Insist that they do likewise.

4. Pay attention to your students' health. When a child seems ill, send that student to the nurse. If a child has to miss several days of school, call home to see how he or she is doing. When homebound work is requested, be prompt in sending it out and include a get-well card.

5. Speak to your students when you see them in the hall or in the neighborhood. Often their social skills won't be up to yours, so take the initiative to be friendly.

6. Ask after their family members. If you have taught brothers or sisters (or even a parent) of one of your students, ask about them. If you know that a family member is ill, show your concern.

7. Use a simple sentence—such as "What can I do to help you?"—that projects a caring attitude.

8. Send home a note when good things happen to a student in school. Share your pride with the family.

9. Write notes to your students. Write on their papers and use plenty of stickers.

10. Take photographs of your students and put them on the wall for all to see.

11. Be accessible to help your students before or after school. Offer student help sessions on a specific day each week. You don't have to stay for a long time, but you can help those students who may be struggling.

12. Tell your students that you like them. Take a few moments after a long week to recount all the good things they have done. This simple action will increase the likelihood of having another good week.

13. Seek their opinions. Give your students lots of opportunities to share their ideas with you.

14. Attend school events. If your students are playing in a football game or performing in a band concert, go to show your approval and appreciation for their hard work.

15. If a student is featured in the newspaper for something good, clip out the article and post it for everyone to see.

16. Lend materials for those students who have accidentally forgotten theirs.

17. Ask your students to tell you about their weekends or holidays. This is easier if you ask them to write about it.

18. Allow your students to have a voice in the classroom. Listen to them. It's easy to provide opportunities for this. For example, you could give them a choice of due dates or a choice in types of test questions.

19. Notice and compliment changes in personal appearance. Be sincere even if the change is not to your personal taste: "That third nose ring really adds something to your face" or "Green hair doesn't work for everybody, but it is becoming on you."

20. Set responsible behavior limits for everyone and be fair in expecting everyone to abide by them. This "tough love" approach to classroom control will set a positive tone that underlies all other discipline actions that you take.

THE IMPORTANCE OF MODELING GOOD BEHAVIOR

"What we *do* is much more important than what we say." If you doubt this saying, just look at some everyday teacher actions from the viewpoint of students. We should all be alert to the message that our actions send to our impressionable students.

- ■ "My teachers tell me not to eat in class, but they drink coffee."
- ■ "My teachers tell me to pay attention in assembly programs, but they grade papers."
- ■ "My teachers tell me not to interrupt, but they interrupt if it's just students talking."
- ■ "My teachers tell me not to raise my voice, but they shout at my classmates and me."
- ■ "My teachers tell me to listen respectfully, but they keep on writing when I'm trying to talk to them."

Model the behaviors you want to see in your students!

WHAT TO DO WHEN A STUDENT CONFIDES IN YOU

When a child turns to us for help, solace, or advice, we are being trusted with a part of that child's heart. It's one of the reasons we go into education.

Although the situation varies from child to child, the educator's responsibility is the same. We have to find out the best way to help the child while remaining emotionally uninvolved enough to be part of the solution—and not part of the problem. This is not an easy task for anyone, but it is a necessary one.

When a student confides in you, you will have to handle the situation in one of two ways. What the student tells you will determine what actions you will need to take. You will either need to involve other professionals or you will be able to provide counsel yourself.

When You Need to Involve Others

1. As a teacher you are legally obligated to protect the safety and well-being of all your students. When a child confides that he or she is in a situation that threatens either safety or well-being, you must involve other professionals. Begin by taking what the child says seriously. Inform a guidance counselor of what the child has told you. If your school does not have a guidance counselor, then contact an administrator. These fellow professionals should then contact the appropriate social agency to help your student.

2. What type of confidences warrant the involvement of others? Contact a counselor if the information involves: sexual abuse; physical abuse; neglect; pregnancy; threats and intimidation by family member, neighbor, or peer; substance abuse; illegal activity; depression; and anything else that seems serious enough to indicate that outside support is necessary.

3. If a child confides to you that he or she is considering suicide, it is critical that you react to this emergency without delay. Even if the child's remarks don't seem particularly sincere to you, react as if they are a shout for help. This is certainly a situation where the saying "Better safe than sorry" should apply.

4. If a student begins a confidence by trying to make you promise not to tell anyone else, do not agree. Be clear with the child that you can't promise this, but that you can and will accompany him or her—if necessary—to talk with counselors, parents, or administrators and that you will remain accessible and involved.

When You Can Provide Counsel

1. If the information the student confides in you is something that is troubling, but does not require outside assistance, still remain cautious in your approach. Keep in mind that you are a professional educator and an adult. Do not let your emotions at the moment influence you to act in any other way. Your student may see you as a friend, but you must remain a professional educator in the way you handle the situation.

2. Protect yourself with common sense. Talk to the student in a place that can't be misconstrued. Keep the door to your classroom open, for example, if you are meeting there. Also be careful at this emotionally charged time about how you touch a student. Many students just need an opportunity to talk with a sympathetic listener.

3. Another common-sense strategy is to imagine that your words of advice could be printed in the daily newspaper. Would you sound like a wise counselor in public? Don't open yourself to public humiliation by acting in less than a professional way.

4. Many of the problems faced by your students will be caused by troubled peer relationships. Listen to these problems and do your best to give sensible as well as sensitive advice. Encourage your students to be self-confident and tolerant whenever you can.

5. Make sure you don't make a situation worse by agreeing with a student's poor assessment of another student. You do not need to engage in gossip with the student. Instead, provide advice that is based on common sense. Encourage your students to take responsibility for themselves and for their emotions.

6. Listen sympathetically to your students and to their parents or guardians whenever you can. Make the advice that you give an extension of the principles you promote in your classroom.

7. Resist the temptation to reveal details about yourself and your private life to a student who confides in you. Focus on the child's problem, not on your personal situation.

8. Remember that the one expression that will turn your students off quickly is, "Well, when I was your age . . . ."

9. After a child has confided in you, don't mention the secret in the faculty lounge. A student's trust is a precious thing. Don't violate it.

10. Be sympathetic, but do not criticize the student's parents or other teachers. This is unprofessional as well as counter-productive.

11. Many student problems can be dealt with by helping students put the troubling events into perspective. Encourage your students to see beyond the problems and emotions they are experiencing at the moment. Help them see that their problems will fade in time. This is good advice for all of us to follow.

GETTING FEEDBACK FROM STUDENTS

Have you ever looked at old photos of times when you thought you looked great—only to be horrified at your appearance? It's funny how stylish we thought we looked with our long sideburns, bell-bottomed jeans, miles of love beads, green and purple streaks in our hair, or even go-go boots, but the old photos show us a very different reality. Usually our reaction is an agonized cry to family members, "Why didn't somebody *tell* me?!"

The truth is that we often think we present one image to the world but, in reality, the image is not at all what we expect it to be. When we're teaching, it's especially important that we present an image that will help our students succeed—and we often think we do. When we are trying to work as a team with our students, however, we need feedback from them about just how well we're doing.

Often our students are reluctant to speak up in class for a variety of good reasons. Fear of ridicule by peers, shyness, fear of rejection, unwillingness to hurt our feelings, or the inability to think quickly are just a few of the insecurities that plague students. We can certainly benefit from hearing what our students have to say if we allow them a safe outlet for expressing themselves. You should not end a lesson by asking a classroom of students, "Well, how did I do?" if you want a helpful answer.

There are several effective ways you can get useful feedback about your teaching from your students.

1. The most commonly used one is also the least formal: pay attention to their reactions. If a class acts bored, the chances are good that they are. If they seem interested and involved, the chances are also good that they are both of those.

2. Another way to find out how you're doing is to ask your students to write out a reaction to the class. You could do this on a test as one of the essay questions or as a closing exercise to class. Try asking one of these questions:

   ■ What advice do you have for me when I teach this unit again?

   ■ If you were the teacher, what would you do differently about teaching this lesson? Explain your reasons.

   ■ What did you find most interesting and helpful about this lesson?

3. A third way to build a team atmosphere in your class and get feedback from your students at the same time is one that many teachers find helpful. Try using a suggestion box. You can benefit from the advantages of having one in your classroom if you use common sense in establishing it for your students. Try the following techniques for setting one up in your room:

   ■ Decorate a box neatly so that your students will take it seriously. Shoe boxes are the ideal size.

- Place the box and a stack of small slips of paper near the door so that students who want to respond to you through the suggestion box can do so in relative privacy.

- Empty the box yourself at least once a day. Don't allow students to do this because the writing inside is directed to you and is not meant to be read by others.

- A good place to begin with teaching your students to use a suggestion box is to get them to write slips at the end of class where they comment on the activities of the day or ask questions. This will begin to get them in the habit of communicating with you directly.

- Be sure to tell your students when you want them to sign their names to their suggestion box writing. Start with having them sign their writing if you are not comfortable with the maturity of your class and their ability to treat the privilege of a suggestion box responsibly.

- Teach your students to be careful of the content of their suggestions. Stress that there is to be no foul language or other unpleasant writing for you to deal with.

- Suggest some things they might want to write about: the activity in class, the homework assignment, the topic being studied in class, test questions or format, or necessary personal information.

- The suggestion box should be an open issue for discussion in your classroom. Thank those students who make sensible suggestions for you and for the class, but be sensitive enough that you don't mention names.

4. A fourth way to reach out to your students and to show that you value their opinions enough to ask for feedback is to issue a "Teacher-Effectiveness Report Card" for them to complete about you. If you think back to your college days, you probably had to complete lots of these for your professors. The principle is the same for your class. Use the sample report card either as is or adapt it for your situation. Use it as often as you need to in order to listen to what your students have to say about your performance in the classroom. (See next page.)

CONDUCTING USEFUL STUDENT CONFERENCES

Ours is a society that values its mentors. Even very young children are familiar with many images of wise elders counseling young people. Literature, art, and the media provide us with traditional portraits—grandfathers teaching youngsters to fish, grandmothers passing along family recipes, and parents teaching their children to ride a bike or drive a car. Along with these traditional, family-oriented images are the less traditional ones where someone who is not a family member is the trusted counselor—police officer, minister, doctor, and teacher.

Our students need us to provide them with mentorship. They need us to work with them on a one-to-one basis even though most of the work we do with our students is done with groups of various sizes. One of the best ways to do this kind of mentoring in a school setting is by holding a conference with a student.

There are many times in the course of the term when you will need to confer with a student or with groups of students. Some of these times may be when you are helping them plan long-term projects or improve their performance by completing other academic assignments.

TEACHER-EFFECTIVENESS REPORT CARD

Please take a few minutes to think about this class and your teacher's performance as an instructor. Give your reaction to the following items by placing the number from this scale in the appropriate blank.

4 = excellent
3 = above average
2 = average
1 = below average

_____ 1. There is a reasonable amount of homework that consists of assignments designed to increase or reinforce knowledge.

_____ 2. There is a variety of evaluations—tests, quizzes, papers, and other assignments.

_____ 3. My teacher is a good listener who tries to be fair to all students.

_____ 4. My teacher is available to provide extra help either before or after school on designated days.

_____ 5. The class presentations are interesting and helpful.

_____ 6. Explanations are thorough; my teacher is patient.

_____ 7. There is a variety of activities during the course of a week.

_____ 8. My teacher helps me set and achieve goals for myself.

_____ 9. The class behavior is geared to cooperation and not misbehavior.

_____ 10. I am busy all of the time in this class.

_____ 11. My teacher communicates subject knowledge well.

_____ 12. There are class rules and policies for us all to follow.

_____ 13. My teacher models courteous behavior.

_____ 14. My teacher inspires me to do my best.

Additional comments:

_____

_____

_____

_____

_____

_____

Conferences can also be very useful in establishing a positive working relationship with a student who has misbehaved. When the two of you can sit down together without the rest of the class as a distraction and can work out a solution to the problems that the student has been experiencing, then conferences are powerful tools for positive discipline. You can begin to provide the mentorship that your students need.

17 Strategies for a Successful Student Conference

Holding a conference with a student is not difficult, but it can be more successful if you plan ahead to take some positive actions to guarantee success. The following strategies will be most effective if you are working with a student who has already misbehaved and who you think is mature enough to respond well to a conference.

1. Arrange a time for the conference that is agreeable for you both. Be sure to show respect for your student's schedule by being as cooperative as possible about the time. It is also a good policy to set in advance an ending time for the conference. Fifteen minutes should be a reasonable amount of time for most conferences.

2. When you arrange a place for meeting, remove as many distractions as possible. Other students should not be in the room waiting and listening; however, it is not a good idea to meet one-on-one with a student behind closed doors.

3. Make the meeting place comfortable for you both. Offer pen and paper for taking notes. Sit side-by-side in student desks or at a table. Avoid unpleasant situations where the student sits slumped while you are free to pace.

4. When the student arrives for the conference, be courteous in your greeting. If you are relaxed and calm, then it is likely the student will also be relaxed and calm.

5. Begin your meeting by stating that the purpose of the conference is to decide upon a solution to the problem. Avoid blaming and rehashing your disapproval if you want to solve the problem.

6. Take the initiative by stating the problem as you see it. Take time to not only discuss the negative aspects of your student's behavior, but to stress the positive attributes that you see in your student as well.

7. Focus on the behavior itself, not on the personality traits of the student. Avoid name calling or labeling.

8. Let the student then state his or her side of the story. Listen attentively. Take notes.

9. Restate the problem in your own words to make sure you understand the problem and to show your sincere interest in solving it.

10. Be positive but firm in conveying that the responsibility for change is the student's. Offer help and support to encourage a resolution.

11. Together with your student work out a plan that will help solve the problem. Brainstorm together if needed. Ask questions that lead to a solution: What could you do instead? How could you handle the situation better?

12. Agree on a plan that satisfies both of you. Restate it so that you both have a clear understanding. Make sure the plan is simple to carry out.

13. Once again affirm that you are willing to offer help in solving the problem.

14. In calm, matter-of-fact terms, explain the negative consequences that the student will have to deal with if he or she does not carry out the plan.

15. Be very clear that you have put past misbehavior behind you and that you do not hold a grudge.

16. At the end of the conference, ask the student if there is anything else that needs to be said. Offer a chance to listen once again.

17. Be courteous in thanking the student for deciding to work with you. Express your optimism that better days lie ahead for you both.

BREAKING BARRIERS BY BREAKING THE ICE

It goes without saying that getting to know your students is important for positive classroom discipline. There are many ways to find out what you need to know about them as quickly as you can. Some of the more traditional ways are by going through student permanent records, contacting parents, and talking with other teachers who have already taught your new students. You could also hold private conferences with as many of your students as possible, but it is not easy given the time constraints that bind us so at the start of the school term.

Other time-tested ways to try to learn as much as you can about the people with whom you will be expected to work well with for an entire term are student inventories and surveys. Four of these are included on pages 127–135 for you to use or to adapt for your classes.

One of the best ways to get to know your students, however, is by observing them as they get to know each other. A classroom where students know each other well and value the contributions that each one can make is a classroom where many obstacles to success just don't exist.

Don't assume that your students know each other, even though they may tell you that they've grown up together or are even best friends. To create a positive learning climate, instill in your students the sense that they are all members of the same team. At the same time, your teacher's "radar" can be actively trying to find out as much as you can about your new students.

To do this, you will need to design activities that get your students to share information and collaborate in a positive way while you learn as much about them as you can. If you want to break some of the barriers to a successful discipline environment in your class, try some of these activities.

22 Icebreakers

1. Begin to get to know your students by having them fill out an information form on which you ask for the basic information you should have on file for each child: phone numbers, the names of parents or guardians, addresses, class schedule, and other necessary data. Instead of having each child fill out a personal one, put your students in pairs and have them complete a form for each other. Include questions designed to get them talking with each other about topics that you choose. For example, you might ask them to relate a story about academic success or to list three important study habits. A "Student Information Form" is included in Section Two.

2. You'll be surprised at how many of your students don't know their classmates' names, especially their last names. If you spend some time playing a chaining game where students try to recite each other's names in an unbroken chain, you'll eliminate this problem. You can have a silly reward (a funny sticker?) for the student who can successfully name all of the students in the class. You can even use this technique later to show your students effective ways to memorize facts.

3. After you have met with your students for a few days, assign each one to a permanent study team. This group will watch out for each other all year. When you review, this is the group that will work together. They should exchange phone numbers so that absent students know who to call to get missing notes and assignments. The possible tasks that study teams can perform in your class are limited only by what you choose for them to do based on their maturity and ability. This technique is a positive way for students to support each other while focusing on the study skills needed for success in school. **Note:** If you notice the chemistry in a group is not working, don't hesitate to switch students to a more cooperative grouping.

4. Have your students create personal ads for the type of study mates they seek before you create the study team. Older students, in particular, enjoy this activity. After your students have been introduced to each other, give a quiz to the entire class where you ask them to match people with their hobbies, past histories, or any other information that comes to light.

5. During the first week of class, you can get your class rolling by creating a class newsletter. In this activity, your students can share a variety of ideas with each other depending on the discipline you teach and the ability of your students. Use some of the information your students uncovered in their interviews, facts they discover about the school, interviews with other students about various topics, interviews with other teachers, cartoons, predictions, and anything else you and they decide would be worthwhile to include. Keep the tone upbeat and stress the value of working together as your students complete their newsletter.

6. Be sure to spend time at the start of the term assigning the classroom duties and responsibilities that your students can take care of for the good of all.

7. Take photographs of your students and post them.

8. Ask those students who claim they already know each other well to write out 20 facts about each other for you to read.

9. Put your students into groups of three and give each group a bag with several common objects in it. Each group could combine the objects in some new way. Your students can name the invention as well as make up a marketing plan for it that they present to the class. The point of this exercise is not just to help your students develop their creative-thinking skills, but to help them see the value of working together.

10. Make it a point to focus on your students' strengths by asking them to reveal what they do well. (Too often we focus on what they lack.) You'll be pleasantly surprised at the skills your students already possess.

11. Place a large map on the board and mark each child's birthplace on it. Give small rewards for the silly topics in this exercise: who was born closest to the school, who was born farthest away, or who was born in the most unusual place.

12. Send your students in teams to interview other people about the school. They can find out its history, information about new teachers, unusual facts about its architecture, or other information designed to have them working together while finding out about the overall organization of which they are now a part. You might want to publish this information in writing, in a simple class presentation, or in a video.

13. Spend some time having your classes create a class motto.

14. Have your students bring in magazine pictures and words that indicate things that are of value to them. Combine these into a giant collage that shows how your students can be different yet still part of the whole.

15. Put your students into pairs to determine ten things they all have in common. You can make many activities from this simple activity depending on the ability level of your students. Go beyond the obvious to deal with the mental traits they share, past experiences, future goals, problems, successful attitudes, or whatever traits you want to focus on at the moment.

16. Have your students create some wise advice that they display on mini posters to inspire them all year. You can also take this same wise advice and publish it in a booklet to be shared with younger students if it's appropriate for them.

17. Get your students working together to benefit someone less fortunate or to participate in a cause that's bigger than the classroom.

18. Post a large calendar and have students record their birthdays on it. Establish a simple ritual that you and your students follow to celebrate each one.

19. During the first week of the new term, your students could create a time capsule to be opened in the future on a date that you can all agree. In the time capsule, include photographs of your students, videotapes, letters, and other objects that will reveal what your class is like as they begin the term.

20. Have your students bring in their baby photos to display. This is not only an excellent icebreaker, but it is also an attractive way to decorate your room.

21. Put your students into small teams and have them illustrate a school-success topic in a cartoon panel that you provide for them. They should generate the story line using the actual members of their team as the characters. Stick figures are acceptable for those teams who are not gifted in drawing. The point of this assignment is to have them focus on school success while working together. Display these for the enjoyment of all.

22. Don't forget that as your students are learning about each other, they also need to learn a little about you. While you should not reveal overly personal information, let your students see that you have a human side to your personality also.

Interview Projects

A popular icebreaker is to have students interview each other at the start of class. While this technique usually ends in students introducing each other to the class, it is such a widespread activity that much of its appeal is fading. Revive this excellent idea with some ingenious twists of your own or you can try some of the following suggestions.

1. Instead of just having students mumble a series of facts about each other to the class, have your students write descriptive paragraphs about each other that you then photocopy into a booklet for all of your students to read. This is the most intently read document that you will present all year. Make sure it's successful by giving specific guidelines about the types of material you want emphasized in each paragraph. You'll also need to be very specific about the appearance of the work so that it can be photocopied easily.

2. Another twist on this topic is to have each student interviewed by two others who then write paragraphs, which you publish. The differences in the interview questions asked by each should give your students plenty of discussion topics.

3. A successful way to get students chatting together productively in the interview is to give each one a common object and ask that student to interview the other one in order to determine what the second team member and the object have in common. When your students present their findings to the class, be prepared for the fun that you'll have as you watch your students compare each other to egg beaters, tissues, or whatever silly objects you can find.

4. Yet another spin on the interview project is to videotape your students making their presentations about each other. Plan this assignment carefully; you should be able to have your students working together productively in no time.

Use the following *reproducibles* to assist your students with their interview projects.

STUDENT INVENTORY: IMPRESSIONS

Name _____ Date _____

1. My greatest asset is _____
   _____

2. The nicest thing I ever did for anyone was _____
   _____

3. The nicest thing anyone ever did for me was _____
   _____

4. One question I have about life is _____
   _____

5. One thing I've always wondered about is _____
   _____

6. My teachers last year will tell you that I am _____
   _____

7. My friends will tell you that I am _____
   _____

8. People like me because _____
   _____

9. One thing most people don't know about me is _____
   _____

10. I am an expert on _____
    _____

11. I want to know more about _____
    _____

12. When I am 25, I will _____
    _____

13. Five years from now I will _____
    _____

14. When I want to, I have the ability to _____
    _____

15. A famous person I admire is _____ because _____
    _____

16. The bravest thing I ever did was _____
    _____

STUDENT INVENTORY: IMPRESSIONS *(cont'd)*

17. I have trouble dealing with _____

_____

18. I appreciate it when teachers _____

_____

19. I am proud of my _____

_____

20. I like _____ because _____

_____

21. I really need to _____

_____

22. My favorite class is _____ because _____

_____

23. My friends make me laugh when they _____

_____

24. My pet peeve is _____

_____

25. When I am sad I _____

_____

26. The most stressful thing in my life is _____

27. The most influential person in my life is _____ because _____

_____

28. If I had one hundred dollars I would _____

_____

29. I am named for _____

_____

30. It was easy to learn _____

_____

STUDENT INVENTORY: IMPRESSIONS *(cont'd)*

31. It was difficult to learn _____
_____

32. I have no regrets about _____
_____

33. I want to know more about _____
_____

34. A friend once showed me how to _____
_____

35. I like _____ music because _____
_____

36. My favorite color is _____ because _____
_____

37. One dish I can cook well is _____
_____

38. I show self-respect when I _____
_____

39. What is a mistake that taught you a lesson? What lesson did you learn?
_____
_____
_____
_____
_____

40. What is an obstacle that you face? How do you plan to get around it?
_____
_____
_____
_____
_____

STUDENT INVENTORY: ATTITUDES

The right attitudes are crucial for success in school and in life. This inventory will help you make a check of which ones you already have underway and which ones could use a bit of work. Get your pencils ready!

Study the list below and decide how you stand in relation to each of the positive attitudes that create successful students.

1. Color the space under "1" if the attitude does *not* apply to your school life at all.
2. Color the space under "2" if the attitude applies to your school life *some* of the time.
3. Color the space under "3" if the attitude applies to your school life *most* of the time.

1	2	3	
			Kind
			Patient
			Curious
			Strong-willed
			Able to concentrate
			Flexible
			Respectful of evidence
			Skeptical
			Ambitious
			Open-minded
			Ready for change
			Tolerant of ambiguity
			Confident
			Sincere
			Honest
			Understanding
			Compassionate
			Persistent
			Inventive
			Hardworking
			Thorough
			Willing to be a pioneer

STUDENT INVENTORY: ATTITUDES *(cont'd)*

1	2	3	
			Brave
			Self-disciplined
			Able to laugh easily
			Able to laugh at self
			Sensitive
			Generous
			Fair-minded
			Respectful of others
			Respectful of self
			Respectful of authority
			Neat
			Able to maintain self-control
			Loyal
			Creative
			Articulate
			Values the importance of an education
			Able to follow through on an idea
			Energetic
			Able to work on a team
			Willing to help others
			Alert
			Able to achieve long-term goals
			Optimistic
			Punctual
			Respectful of social values
			Independent
			Able to request help
			Able to admit mistakes
			Cooperative
			Easy-going

1	2	3

A deep thinker

Friendly

Healthy

Able to act with common sense

Hungry for knowledge

Cheerful

Trustworthy

Willing to try

Imaginative

Empathetic

Willing to take a risk

Appreciative

Practical

Given to detail

Forgiving

STUDENT INVENTORY: REACTIONS OF OTHERS

What others would tell you about me . . .

1. My favorite teacher last year would say _____
    _____
    _____

2. My parents would say _____
    _____
    _____

3. My grandparents would say _____
    _____
    _____

4. My neighbors would say _____
    _____
    _____

5. The security guard at the mall would say _____
    _____

6. My future children would say _____
    _____
    _____

7. My youngest relative would say _____
    _____
    _____

8. My oldest relative would say _____
    _____
    _____

9. My pet would say _____
    _____
    _____

10. My girlfriend/boyfriend would say _____
    _____
    _____

11. My best friend would say _____
    _____
    _____

STUDENT INVENTORY:
REACTIONS OF OTHERS *(cont'd)*

12. The lunchroom staff would say _____

_____

_____

13. The teacher who taught my hardest class last year would say _____

_____

_____

14. My future mate would say _____

_____

_____

15. My coach would say _____

_____

_____

16. The custodians would say _____

_____

_____

17. My remote control would say _____

_____

_____

18. The clerks at the store I go to often would say _____

_____

_____

19. My parents' neighbors would say _____

_____

_____

20. My future employer would say _____

_____

_____

STUDENT INVENTORY: STUDY SKILLS

Rank each statement as it applies to you by putting the appropriate number in the blank.

4 = Always   3 = Some of the time   2 = Seldom   1 = Never

I use these study strategies:

_____	Tape recorder
_____	Flash cards
_____	Study with a group
_____	Study with one other person
_____	Study best alone
_____	Have a family member quiz me
_____	List what I need to study
_____	Plan long-term projects in steps
_____	Can take good notes from textbooks
_____	Study in quiet area
_____	Rewrite notes into my own words
_____	Recopy notes
_____	Have a plan for successfully taking tests
_____	Review within 24 hours of original learning
_____	Use colored pens to mark notes
_____	Will ask for help when I don't understand the work
_____	Make up missing work on time
_____	Turn in homework assignments on time
_____	Write neatly
_____	Take time to proofread
_____	Use a weekly study schedule
_____	Use a planner to organize study time
_____	Have a study buddy to consult about class events
_____	Make use of my biological clock to study efficiently
_____	Create my own study guides
_____	Aim for a specific grade in each class
_____	Work towards a future goal
_____	Predict accurately what will be on tests
_____	Spend enough time to learn the material well
_____	Have enough supplies at school
_____	Have enough supplies at home
_____	Have a well-organized study area at home
_____	Keep all old papers on file for tests and exams
_____	Write down my assignments
_____	Skim material before reading
_____	Focus well in class
_____	Come to class prepared to work
_____	Pass tests
_____	Take planned study breaks

CLASS LEADERS AND THE POWER STRUGGLE

While thoughtful teachers can appreciate and value the individual differences in their students' personalities, some personality traits can be harder to cope with than others. Class leaders are often individuals with such personality traits. Defiance, a strong need for power or attention, impulsivity, anger, and negativity are just a few.

Class leaders come in many shapes and sizes. The helpful student who offers to run errands or clean the board and the students who proudly announce that they just earned a perfect score on a test are the kind of leaders that all teachers welcome. We have no trouble smiling fondly at their charming little quirks.

On the other hand, negative class leaders are certainly not as enjoyable. The class clown who seems amusing at first, but then doesn't know how to quit; the hateful child who lashes out in anger at anyone at anytime; the openly defiant students . . . the list of less-than-ideal qualities can seem endless after a trying day spent battling for control of the class. There are several things you can do to help your class leaders be positive influences instead of negative ones.

The most obvious decision you need to make is whether you intend to engage the class leaders in a virtual hand-to-hand combat for control of the class or whether you want to win them over to your side. Trying to fight student leaders can have many more negative effects than positive ones. In the end it is likely that any victory you have will be short-lived.

If, however, you can forego the temptation to become another adult adversary for your students, you have a much greater chance of creating an orderly and productive classroom. Keep the following five techniques in mind when you are dealing with the power struggle that class leaders can generate.

1. The first step you should take is to identify your positive and negative leaders. Do this by examining their actions and the reaction of the rest of the class to them.

2. Turn negative leaders into positive ones with a delicate touch. What they want to do and are probably already pretty good at doing is simple: leaders want to lead. A wise teacher will give them plenty of constructive opportunities to do this—and there are plenty of opportunities to do this in every class period. Here are just some of the small actions you can take that will allow leaders to be productive instead of destructive influences in your classroom. Class leaders can:

   ■ monitor groups working on class assignments;

   ■ serve as a liaison for you and the class;

   ■ speak for the class at assemblies;

   ■ take class votes, collect monies, assume responsibility for issuing texts;

   ■ consult with other students about choices in due dates, projects, materials, and report these to you;

   ■ run errands, pick up supplies;

   ■ manage debates or panel discussions;

   ■ be the reporter from a small group to the class;

   ■ lead a class discussion;

   ■ serve as moderator in role-play situations;

- represent the class at schoolwide functions;
- be the person who makes sure everyone knows what the homework assignment is; and
- greet guests and be the helper when you must have a substitute.

3. Be as overwhelmingly positive with your class leaders as you can. Never belittle them. You'll only appear foolish as the rest of the class immediately takes sides sympathetically with their classmates. Praise them often when they are doing well or when they are making serious efforts to do the right things.

4. Reinforcing their positive behaviors is the best strategy you can take with class leaders. Gain their cooperation as well as the approval of the entire class when leaders accept that you want everyone in the class to succeed.

5. As a final suggestion for handling class leaders, it's important to maintain a level-headed approach to the problem. You won't be able to win over every student in spite of your obvious sincerity and very best efforts. It is unrealistic to expect otherwise of yourself and of your students.

THE IMPORTANCE OF TEACHING COURTESY

Transforming a classroom full of awkward adolescents into a community of learners is the dream of secondary teachers. We want our students to be pleasantly cheerful and polite to each other and to us.

In order to have our dream come true, we must teach our students the importance of courtesy and then we must insist that they treat others with exquisite politeness. Courteous behavior oils the machinery of the classroom: preventing discipline problems, building teams, and making everyone's day easier.

Successful teachers realize that classes are social groups. We often use this to our advantage when we are in the process of creating positive peer pressure. We teach our students that when we expect and encourage them to be courteous at all times, the payoff for everyone is in enhanced learning opportunities. We know that pupils who interact in a positive way take a vital step in creating a more successful classroom environment.

Savvy teachers use all of the tricks of the trade to create polite students. We can reward individuals and classes with little treats and effusive words of praise—especially at the start of the term—when we are trying to instill the importance of polite behavior in our students.

We can shamelessly use the power of peer pressure to steer students in the right direction as we try to be as supportive as possible of our students' needs to express themselves and to just be teenagers. We can allow them plenty of chances to express themselves without fear of sarcasm or ridicule from us and from their classmates. We can help our students clarify their goals and values and we can give our students lots of responsibility so that they can learn to be polite.

All of the tricks of our profession are useless, however, if we ourselves are rude. The most important technique for the secondary teacher who wants to encourage courtesy is to be a model of courtesy. In a hundred small acts every day we can model the kind of courteous behavior that we want from our students.

When a child slams a book, we can say, "Do I slam a book while you are talking?" "No." "Then please don't slam a book while I am talking." Being able to ask, "Do I treat you with disrespect?" and have the child answer "No" can be a powerful tool for the teacher who wants to foster courtesy in a student who is sometimes disrespectful of authority. It is with small exchanges and actions such as these that we show our students the kinds of behavior that will make their lives more successful.

Our students are far more observant of us and what we do than we can ever imagine. Use this awareness to your advantage to teach one of life's most important lessons—the absolute need for courtesy in a sometimes rude and unfeeling world.

ARMING OUR STUDENTS: TEACHING THE ART OF THE ALTERNATIVE RESPONSE TO RUDE CLASSMATES

"Did not!" "Did too!" "Did not!" "Did too!" "You wish!" "Don't hold your breath!" "Hey! I'm talking to you!" "Get out of my face!" "I'm gonna get you!" "He makes me *sooo* mad!"

By the end of the first day of school almost every secondary teacher, even those who teach seniors, has heard some form of these childish exchanges all too often. In many classes this type of interaction is a daily problem. A few students who have not been taught to be polite or respectful of others can create havoc when they react in an aggressive and angry way in response to what they perceive as slights from other classmates.

This tension at school has serious implications for all of us. News stories regularly report the devastating effects of our violent social climate on our younger citizens. Stories about teens having been murdered for such offenses as stepping on someone's shoe by mistake, or looking at a stranger "funny," no longer have the power to shock us that they once held.

We follow legislative debates about the increasingly prevalent practice of trying youthful offenders as adults. Many of us have trouble accepting that the children we see accused of robbery or cold-blooded murder don't appear to be very different from those mischievous youngsters in our class.

Far too few of our students enter secondary school with more than basic social skills. Many students do not understand how to be tolerant, how to get along well with the majority of their classmates, or even how to cope when people are rude to them. Most of our students are just beginning to learn the business of creating positive relationships with other people.

One of the ways we can help them acquire these social skills and create a pleasant classroom environment at the same time is to give our students some alternative ways to cope with bad-mannered classmates who are insulting, tactless, inconsiderate . . . in short: rude.

The list of responses here is not meant for those situations where a student's safety is in jeopardy or when a more serious response is required to stop potential violence. Instead, these alternatives are designed to help students deal with the smaller irritations caused by daily interactions with others. Some of these are simple. Some are simplistic. All are effective in teaching students that they do not have to answer rude behavior with rude behavior.

What to Do When Someone Is Rude to You

1. Smile mysteriously and say nothing.

2. Treat the remark with good humor and chuckle softly as if you found it amusing.

3. Ignore the person by walking away.

4. Tell a friend, a parent, a teacher, or a counselor.

5. Count from 1 to 10 five times.

6. Take six deep breaths. Exhale slowly.

7. Silently ask yourself what caused the rude person to be cranky today.

8. Chew a piece of sugarless gum. When your anger is under control, consider offering a piece to your offensive classmate.

9. Return rudeness with kindness! Pay the offender a compliment.

10. Plan how you can use this unpleasant situation in your next creative writing assignment.

11. Look at your watch and make a mental note of the time. Let five minutes pass before you allow yourself to speak back.

12. Go to the water fountain for a drink. Splash a few drops of cool water on your face while you are there. This will help you cool off.

13. Quickly write out all of the mean and hurtful things that you would like to say to the person who has hurt your feelings. Tear it into a zillion tiny pieces when you are finished and carefully throw them into the trash can.

14. Make yourself forgive and then make yourself forget.

15. Pretend you didn't hear an unkind remark.

16. Promise yourself a reward if you can resist the urge to retaliate.

17. Make a conscious decision to not let it bother you.

18. Mentally picture the rude person as a small fluffy mouse wearing a large silly hat.

19. Go for a jog around the block.

20. Place yourself in the shoes of the person who was unkind. Try to understand what caused it

21. Pat yourself on the back for staying calm.

22. Think of the last nice thing that someone said to you.

23. Turn to a classmate and pay that person a compliment.

24. Get out your calendar and find a time when you can fit rude people into your life.

25. Mentally make a list of four things you would like to say but are too mature to waste yourself on.

26. Repeat "I am in control of my attitude" 50 times.

27. List your ten best personality traits.

28. Think of a famous hero and ask yourself what that person would do in your situation.

29. Open a book and read a page before allowing yourself to respond. Read two pages if you're very upset.

30. Picture yourself walking across a beautiful field of freshly-fallen snow.

31. Ask yourself if this incident is really worth stressing yourself over.

32. Remind yourself of another time when you acted in a mature and responsible manner.

33. Picture yourself standing ankle deep in the surf, letting all of your troubles drift away on the tide.

34. Go to the gym and exercise for 30 minutes.

35. Imagine how wonderful it will be when you are attending your own graduation.

36. Say to yourself, "I can't let this bother me because my goal in life is to _____."

37. Mildly say, "I'm sorry. I didn't hear what you said."

38. Clench your left hand tightly and then relax it. Do this five times and let your troubles be relaxed, too.

39. Close your eyes and imagine that you are eating your favorite meal.

40. List ten things for which you are thankful.

THE INTERACTIVE CLASS

One of the easiest and best ways to foster cooperation among your students is very simple: give them plenty of carefully planned opportunities to interact well with each other. Classrooms where students engage in activities that require they work well together are classrooms where discipline problems are minimal.

Students who are engaged in working well together foster a sense of cooperation and self-discipline that is the result of their need to be active and not passive receptors in this type of activity.

Use the following strategies and activities to create a classroom where students are engaged in cooperating well with each other.

1. Create a collage in which your students have to bring in words and pictures on a topic. It can be a topic that you are studying or it can be about their interests. A wall mural is a great way to display these.

2. Have students create another group wall display. This time have them bring in a written statement of the contributions they can make to the class. Hand each student a bright sheet of paper and trace their handprints. After they cut out the handprint, ask students to write their names along the thumbs and then to write their contributions to the welfare of the class on the palms. When these are displayed, they serve as a bright visual reminder of the importance of cooperation.

3. Have student helpers as often as you can. These students need to be carefully coached for each assignment so that they are prepared to offer the best possible help to their classmates.

4. When you are seeking solutions to problems, involve the class in the act of brainstorming as many solutions as you can. Students who brainstorm in groups and then combine their brainstorms with other groups benefit from the interaction and mental stimulation that occurs.

5. Have cooperative groups role-play various scenarios when they are appropriate to the lesson at hand.

6. Have students check each other's work when it's appropriate and nonthreatening for them to do so.

7. Play chaining games to aid in memorizing as often as you can.

8. Have students work together to finish a story, an assignment, or a quiz when appropriate. One fun way to do this is to have students who are struggling with an assignment get help from classmates during a 15- or 30-second interval timed by you.

9. Create study buddies for each test or major review session.

10. Play team games with your students so that they can compete successfully in a controlled environment. Some of the more popular old-fashioned team games are described below.

RACES. Arrange all sorts of events around the concept of racing. In any case, you are encouraging your students to be the first to solve problems, look up words, learn information, or any other competition you devise.

BALL TOSS. Line up your students in two teams facing each other. As soon as a student correctly answers a question, that student tosses a soft foam ball to a student on the opposite team. Now that student must answer the next question.

GAME SHOWS. Popular trivia game-show formats can usually be adapted to your classroom with a minimum of modification. If you're stumped about how to go about doing this, just ask your students! Game-show formats can be used to review or introduce new material.

SPORTING EVENTS. Divide your students into teams and use the board to wage fierce games of football, baseball, soccer, or whatever sport is the current favorite in your classroom. Students advance play in the game not by actually moving, but by answering questions correctly or by completing assigned tasks.

CHAIN MAKING. To help students improve their memorization skills or to use some free time productively, play a chaining game. This is simply a sophisticated version of the old alphabet game where one player thinks of an object beginning with the letter "a" and the next player recalls that object and another beginning with the letter "b." Your students don't need to be restricted to letters of the alphabet, but can recall as many facts or dates as your lesson involves.

HANGMAN. This perennial favorite can be played in any classroom with a chalkboard and by students of almost any age. If you're not sure that you recall how to play this game, ask your students! Students will often entertain themselves in free-time situations in a classroom by playing a version of this childhood amusement.

SPELLING BEE. This game can be used for almost any lesson; it's certainly not restricted to just spelling. Place your students in two rows facing each other. Ask questions in sequence along the rows. Students who answer correctly stay in the game; those who answer incorrectly just sit down. This is a good way to review quick facts or to reinforce recall of vocabulary terms.

20 QUESTIONS. To play this game in your classroom, write the correct answer on a slip of paper and have students guess it with a series of questions. Keep count of the number of questions that they have to ask in order to figure out the answer. In this game, the lowest score wins.

NAME THAT TIME, BATTLE, ETC. This game is similar to "20 Questions" in that students try to guess answers with as few clues as possible. You should make up the clues in advance. On game day, you'll call them out one at a time. Be sure to mix up the difficulty level of the clues in order to keep your students engaged as long as possible.

FLASH CARDS. One of the most useful study techniques to teach your students is to use flash cards to learn new information and to review previously learned material. Either make flash cards large enough for the entire class to use all at once or have your students make up their own and use them in groups. Be sure to award points for the individuals or teams who guess accurately.

BOARD GAMES. Design your own board game to fit your topic. You can either make smaller boards and photocopy them for several students to play in a group or you can make a giant one for your entire class to play. Keep the rules simple, but have lots of color and excitement built into the game and the questions that you ask. The tasks you assign your students in a board game range from simply answering questions correctly to solving just about any sort of problem. You can also ask students to create their own board games.

SIMULATIONS. Although most simulation games are often sophisticated computer ones, you and your students can enjoy low-tech ones; which are simple to construct. Plan the scenario you want your students to enact, then involve them in it with a written description or by role-playing. A very popular version of this game is to have your students imagine that they are shipwrecked on a deserted island and have to plan ways to survive. Simulation games can be used to help your students think creatively, learn to work cooperatively, examine their values, or satisfy just about any purpose you have in mind when you create the game for them.

TIC TAC TOE. In this game, your students earn the right to play by answering questions or by solving problems.

UNSCRAMBLERS. This is a fun way to improve retention of facts, improve your students' vocabularies, or to teach correct spelling. When your students play this game, they fill in missing letters and unscramble mixed-up words in messages that you send them. This is a creative way to improve all sorts of skills and have fun at the same time. An alternative would be to have your students create their own messages to unscramble.

CHARADES. This age-old acting game is probably already one of your students' favorites. Use it to teach information about people, events, discoveries, literature, and any other topic that seems to lend itself to this format. Don't worry about brushing up on the rules. There's a very good chance that at least some of your students are already very good players. Their classmates will soon follow.

QUIZ BOWL. Set up a tournament of quick questions and answers involving as many of your students as possible. Make the Bowl as elaborate as you can with various levels of difficulty, several different rounds, varying scores, and other incentives designed to keep student interest piqued.

SHOPPING. Here is a useful way to use some of the junk mail that most of us receive. Plan a shopping trip for your students. Give each one a certain amount of "money" and a group of people to shop for. Hand them the junk mail catalogs and stand back. Your students will surprise you with the choices they make for their fictional recipients and probably with their own shopping skills. The benefits of this lesson include improved mathematical skills, clarification of values, and even increased vocabulary. Most of all, however, your students will be fully engaged in a meaningful learning experience.

OLYMPICS. Periodically you may want to review various concepts or material by holding an Olympics. You can let your imagination roam while creating the events or you can put some of your students in charge of creating and staging the learning events. In either case, your goal is to review information while having fun. Divide your students into various teams and keep a total team score. Recall as much as you can about the actual Olympics when creating your own events.

TRASHKETBALL. In almost any novelty store or catalog geared for games, you should be able to find and purchase a basketball hoop designed for a trash can. You can use this to keep your classroom clean or you can use it as part of the games you use for learning. Be sure to explain the rules for throwing paper into the hoop carefully and to communicate those rules clearly to your students to make sure that play is both safe and fun.

TREASURE HUNT. Stage a treasure hunt to have students figure out new information and get moving in a productive way at the same time. You can involve areas outside of your classroom for extra interest and to get your students really up and moving. There are endless variations of this game that you can play with your students to get them interested and engaged in a topic. If you are not clever at creating clues, assign a team of students who would do a good job to this task and to direct the hunt. The real treasure is the enjoyment and learning that your students will experience with this activity.

TELEPHONE. This child's game can be played to teach facts or introduce new information. Even older students will enjoy playing this game if it is played at top speed with emphasis on accuracy. To play telephone, have a student read a fact or series of facts from a paper that you have created. That student has to repeat the information to another and that student, in turn, tells another one. In the old version, the fun comes from the scrambling of the message. In the version you want to use, keep the information short and the number of repetitions limited to no more than five before checking to see that it is still accurate. You could have rows or small groups compete against each other.

STORYTELLERS. Even sophisticated older students can excel at this game if it is geared to their level. To play, one student begins a story, stops after a few sentences, and points to another student to continue the plot. You can use this activity to teach vocabulary, facts, the order of events, or other material.

PICNIC. One of the best ways to pull a class together is to have them plan and go on a picnic. Gear the activities in this game so that students learn about other cultures, food preparation, fractions and measurements, and each other. With careful planning on your part, a class picnic can be an engaging and meaningful lesson for everyone involved.

TALK SHOW. Have your students stage a talk show to interview characters in literature or history or in any other discipline. Choose your most outgoing and trustworthy student to be the host and let that student interview the guests about their problems or contributions. The audience of interested students will get as involved as if they were at an actual television talk show. Plan ahead to make sure that all of the participants have the information they need to succeed at this activity.

Classroom-Management Advice for Game Days

■ Make sure each activity has a sound educational purpose and isn't only to kill time in a pleasant way.

■ Modulate the intensity of the competition in your classroom by having teams play against teams. You should determine the team members so that no one gets picked last.

■ Try to structure your activities so that as many students as possible are involved at one time. Students sitting around watching other students play a game is not what you should aim for when creating a situation for maximum learning for everyone.

■ Teach good sportsmanship in advance of the game day. Be very explicit about how you expect your students to play.

■ Be concerned about safety. Stop any game as soon as it starts to become unsafe. Teach your students why safety is important and consistently enforce your safety rules.

■ Accept the fact that some games are much noisier than others.

■ Keep a running total of the various teams or individuals if you wish to keep scoring even.

■ You can be free for monitoring if you allow students to be scorekeepers and timers.

■ Make your games as realistic as possible with music and other props where necessary. Your students will find it easier to get into the spirit of the game if you take this little bit of extra effort.

■ Consider making ribbons that your students can use for bookmarks, stickers, and other inexpensive trinkets for prizes.

■ To determine who goes first—and other vital decisions—have your students draw numbers from a container that you keep on hand for this purpose.

■ Have your students work together to set rules and to plan scoring procedures. The more decisions they make and the more involved they become, the better the activity will be.

"'And how did Little Tim behave?' asked Mrs. Cratchit.
'As good as gold,' said Bob."

—Charles Dickens

Section 5

PREVENTING
DISCIPLINE PROBLEMS

In This Section . . .

Since most of the discipline problems that we face each day can be successfully prevented, this section is designed to provide you with as much information on the various prevention methods as possible.

The importance of skillful teaching and of taking necessary steps to prevent misbehavior are described in "Why Prevention Is Better than the Aftermath of Trouble," "Skillful Teaching Prevents Misbehavior," "Evaluating Your Lesson Plans for Successful Teaching," "Building Critical Thinking Skills," "Questions that Spark Critical Thinking," and "Perfecting the Art of Questioning."

Learn the practical uses of behavior contracts from the three reproducible samples that accompany "Successful Contracts" and "Behaviors that May Be Improved with Behavior Contracts."

Learn more about school safety in "Creating a Safe Environment for Your Students and Yourself."

Find out how to prevent problems through effective monitoring techniques in "The 'Up and at Em' Approach: Monitoring Students' Behavior" and "Monitoring on the Run: 20 Quick Techniques."

Since many discipline problems can result from group work that goes wrong, there are some useful suggestions included to help you in "Teaching Students to Work Well Together" and "Keeping It to a Dull Roar: Helping Students Learn to Control the Noise Level."

"How to Make Your Students Pay Attention to You" and "50 Actions that Will Grab Your Students' Attention" will both help you figure out ways to support on-task behavior.

Since misunderstandings about grades can often be a focus point for misbehavior, refer to "Averting Disaster: Helping Students 'Make the Grade'" and "Teaching Your Students How to Track Their Grades" as well as the reproducible form that helps students do this.

Some other problems that are often the cause of misbehaviors in secondary classes are addressed in the remainder of this section. Look to this information for help with evaluation, using a syllabus, homework, projects, and organizing notebooks.

Section Five ends with material to help you inspire your students: "Teaching Students to Make Good Decisions," "Getting Students Involved: Some Innovative Activities," and "How to Avoid an Awful Day at School."

> *"The object of punishment is prevention from evil;*
> *it can never be made impulsive to good."*
>
> —Horace Mann

WHY PREVENTION IS BETTER THAN THE AFTERMATH OF TROUBLE

Have you ever spent an afternoon watching an old cowboy movie on television? The kind with sweaty horses, a train robbery, gamblin' and whiskey drinkin', chuckwagons, gunfights, saloon girls in itchy satin dresses, and a stampede or two?

Without fail, at some point in the movie the good guys (white hats) will mill around on their horses and make plans to ambush the bad guys (black hats). The leader of the good guys always turns to his men and says, "Let's head 'em off at the pass, boys. They can't get past us there."

The same principle applies to preventing discipline problems in the secondary classroom. It's much better to keep the bad guys from getting past you by using strategies that head 'em off at the pass.

Preventing problems from getting started is only common sense. Discipline problems rarely happen in isolation. Once students start disruptive behaviors, their classmates may be tempted to join in. Crowd control is more difficult and less likely to succeed than planning ways to keep students engaged and interested.

Even small disruptions such as having to nag students to stop talking can snowball into hours and hours of lost instruction time for the other students in the class as well as for the misbehaving ones. These disruptions can be stopped early and with not much effort.

It is also much easier to plan ways to prevent, or at least to minimize, discipline problems than it is to have to deal with their aftermath. Serious discipline problems are dangerous. No teacher wants to deal with the terrifying consequences of violent students who may or may not be armed.

The toll that constant disruptions can take on even the most dedicated teachers is heavy. Many teachers leave our profession to look for other careers every year rather than have to continue to face an unruly mob. It is hard to find satisfaction in a workplace where rude and uncontrollable adolescents make a mockery of our ideals for a peaceful classroom.

We can—with some planning, organization, practice, and skillful teaching—prevent almost all of the discipline problems that could plague us. In this section you will find a variety of techniques and ideas that will help you be the "good guy in the white hat."

SKILLFUL TEACHING PREVENTS MISBEHAVIOR

In addition to creating a positive relationship with our students, the most powerful discipline tool for any secondary teacher is effective instruction. Teachers who plan exciting lessons and who have the love and respect of their classes are failures if they can't transfer knowledge to their students.

This problem has been around for as long as teachers have been. Remember the first time you ever heard the teacher axiom, "What you teach is not always what your students learn"? If you were an undergraduate, you probably didn't understand it. But any teacher who has taught for more than five minutes can verify the truth of this saying with rueful stories of carefully prepared lessons that completely confused entire classrooms of adolescents. Teachers will also be quick to tell you that a room full of confused students is neither a quiet nor a happy place, especially for the poor teacher whose lesson plans have suddenly gone awry.

On the other hand, good instruction will prevent many discipline problems. Appealing, well-structured lessons delivered with attention to what your pupils already know and what they need to learn are fundamental. Simply put, good teaching will prevent and poor teaching will cause behavior problems.

What should you do, then, to become better at delivering the knowledge and skills you want your students to have at the end of the term? The answer to this is easy. Begin with what you know already about your own successes and failures as a student. What can you recall from your student days about specific teachers and classes that were successful for you? Reminisce with a purpose.

After you have done this, make a list of the things you did as a student that made learning easy for you. What did those good teachers from your past do that made it work? What can you do when you are standing alone in front of your students that will help them learn the information you plan to teach?

The factors that make the delivery of instruction effective begin with planning and end with the final assessment. In between these two events are hundreds of opportunities for skillful teaching.

Use the following suggestions to make sure your instruction is as effective as you would like it to be. Most of these are just common-sense refinements of what good teachers already know and put into practice.

1. Talk less at your class and listen more to your students. Your lessons should be fun and interesting as often as you can make them so. Droning on and on will only interest you. Research has proved this many times, but teachers persist in their determination to talk to a large group of restless teens. Use your imagination and creativity to get your students talking while you listen and help them learn.

2. A good way to begin to make an effective delivery of instruction is to think of a new slant on old material. If you want to engage their attention, bend a viewpoint or two. Shake up your students!

3. Even though it should be automatic, many teachers just don't spend enough time in determining what their students already know about a subject. You need to do this so that you can help them link the new material to previously learned information.

4. Ask your students to explain to you the purpose of learning the material you want them to learn. You'll be surprised at the insights this technique will give you about their attitudes towards their work and their future. If you do this early enough in the unit of study, you can use their insights to build in relevance.

5. Very few secondary pupils are interested in arcane theories. They are, however, interested in themselves. Use this knowledge to your advantage by helping students relate new knowledge to their personal experience. Real-world experiences also help prevent discipline problems because students can see a reason for learning the lesson.

6. Students need to be taught to examine their beliefs. You certainly don't need to antagonize the community where you work by defying its cherished traditions and customs, but you do need to encourage your students to think about their lives and what they believe about their world. Teens are besieged by popular culture advertisements and music that challenge their thinking and beliefs. Shouldn't teachers have a voice also?

7. When you give instructions to your students, give them one at a time. Intelligent students, even those in advanced classes, have problems processing a flurry of directions. Take your time to make sure everyone understands what to do.

8. Include at least two instructional modalities, such as visual and tactile, in each lesson. If you can include more than two, then do so. Not all of the students in your class will learn at the same rate or in the same way. Help them learn by building in a variety of activities.

9. Use open-ended questions every day in your classroom if you want your students to be thinkers. You'll find a list of some open-ended critical-thinking questions later on in this section to get you started.

10. Don't just tell your students information. Keep asking questions until they discover information for themselves. It will take longer, but the results are worth it.

11. It's better for your students to learn a few things well than for you to rush them through an entire textbook in an attempt to cover every page. If you really want to improve the delivery of instruction in your classroom, remember that you are teaching *people*, not a subject.

12. Teach your students how to learn the information you are presenting right now. Delayed learning is a habit that students get into early. Teach them how to break the habit and how to be active learners right now. Make teaching study skills a part of the daily routine. A little work every day will teach your students to focus on learning the material now—not the night before a test.

13. Monitor! Don't wait until a lesson is over to see if everyone learned it. Check their progress. A quick and easy way to do this is to ask pupils to read their notes aloud so that others can fill in any missing gaps. Be sure to never, ever ask an entire class, "Does everybody understand?" Many teachers seem to do this reflexively, but it only wastes time.

14. Plan times where your students can work independently. Too often we are so concerned with making group work successful that we overlook the importance of independent study. Solitude and deep thought go together.

15. Keep everyone on the right track. There are lots of ways to do this. Provide students with a list of key words or main ideas to watch for. Use daily objectives and help your pupils set short-term goals for each lesson. Give them a syllabus or an outline of your lecture.

16. Practice is what students do. Input is what teachers do. Be sure to keep that distinction clear when you are trying to make the instruction effective. Keep your lessons structured so that you allow plenty of both.

17. Students have a keen eye for any assignment that they suspect might be classified as busy work. They can spot it as soon as you begin to write the instructions on the board. Gear all practice work to the successful completion of your objectives for the lesson if you want to reduce the possibility of mutiny.

18. Guided practice is a time in your classroom when teamwork is appropriate. Independent practice is the time for students to work by themselves. One is just as important as the other.

19. Don't grade independent practice work. Students should use practice time to perfect the skill they are working on. Do check it, however, to see who needs help in understanding the material.

20. Allow for the short attention spans of your students. You can complain all you want, but complaining has not yet caused students to focus for longer periods. Break your instruction into small chunks of manageable and useful information.

21. As soon as your students have mastered a skill, ask them to apply it to a new situation. This will be even more effective if the new situation is as close to real life as possible.

EVALUATING YOUR LESSON PLANS FOR SUCCESSFUL TEACHING

One of the first things undergraduate education students learn is that lessons in a well-planned sequence will lead students into a progressive acquisition of knowledge and skills. Lessons that are not well-structured, even though they may be original and interesting, just will not be effective in creating the positive learning climate that we want to establish in our classrooms. Careful lesson planning is the first step in our efforts to teach successfully and to head off any discipline problems before they can begin.

Before you ever begin to plan a unit of study, you must take time to consider what it is you really want your students to learn and just how you want them to achieve the goals you set for them.

Our discipline successes and failures also are closely tied to the lesson planning that we do. Students who are uninvolved in a lesson or who are confused about what to do will be more likely to be disruptive than those whose teachers plan lessons that meet their needs.

Here are some of the questions experienced teachers ask about the lessons they teach as they plan. Finding answers to these questions should lead you to a logical and well-planned sequence of daily lessons that will help you prevent discipline problems.

1. How does this material fit into the district curriculum for my discipline?

2. What do my students need to know about this subject?

3. Is this material appropriate for the needs of my students?

4. What do my students already know about this material?

5. What can I do to make this material interesting for my students?

6. What does the teacher's manual or any other resources suggest about the material and how to present it effectively?

7. How will this material help my students immediately? How will I lead them to decide this for themselves?

8. How will this material help my students become successful adults? How can I lead them to decide this for themselves?

9. What are the essential points of this material?

10. What is the purpose or objective for each section of the material?

11. What are the areas most likely to prove confusing?

12. What activities can I devise to engage my students in higher-level thinking skills?

13. Which parts of the material lend themselves to group work?

14. What homework assignments would be appropriate?

15. What sort of progress checks should I make to monitor how well students are learning the material?

16. What are some effective strategies to use to make sure my students retain this information?

17. How can I help my students see the real-life importance of this lesson?

18. How many class periods will this material take?

19. What's the fairest and most accurate way to evaluate student achievement?

20. What are some alternative assignments to consider if I've misjudged the time needed or if some of the activities that I've planned just don't work?

21. What preliminary work do I have to do—photocopying, reading, researching, etc.—before I can teach this material?

22. When the unit of study is completed, what should I do to change how I present this information next year?

BUILDING CRITICAL-THINKING SKILLS

One of the strongest movements in education in recent years is the new emphasis on critical-thinking skills. Unlike some recent educational fads that have had a deservedly short shelf-life because they can only be used for a few students, the new emphasis on critical-thinking skills applies to all students. Older teens as well as younger ones can benefit from activities that are designed to help them develop their thinking skills.

Critical-thinking and creative-thinking activities can enhance the learning in any classroom because, while they are enjoyable, they are also effective skills for increasing retention and successful performance. Those students whose teachers help them develop their critical-thinking skills are much more likely to be productive and on-task than those students who slog through rote memorization exercises. They are also far less likely to dream up ways to disrupt class than those frustrated students who liven up the lesson by acting out.

In order to expand their thinking skills, pupils need to have a knowledge of the subject matter, a knowledge of the various types of thinking skills you expect them to use, and plenty of opportunities for practice.

Be careful to avoid a common mistake made by many well-intended but misguided teachers. Don't teach critical-thinking skills in isolation from the other work your students do. Setting aside a day every month to focus on critical-thinking skills, for example, is not a good idea. Your students simply won't benefit from this. They need to practice critical thinking often in order to develop the skills. It is better to make critical thinking part of the everyday work in your class.

One of the easiest ways to begin to include critical-thinking activities in your classroom is to start slowly and then raise the awareness level of your students so that they begin to recognize the various levels of thinking they are expected to do in school and in life.

Here are some strategies for incorporating critical thinking into your class. Many of these ideas should help you prevent discipline problems from beginning because students are engaged in their work.

How to Raise Awareness

1. Your students need a copy of Bloom's Taxonomy to keep in their notebooks. You should also enlarge a copy and post it in your classroom. You will need the common vocabulary if you are to teach your students to think.

2. Have students get into the habit of labeling the question types in assignments to raise their awareness of the types of thinking they could be doing.

3. Another way to have students increase their levels of awareness about critical thinking is to have them make posters illustrating each type.

Some Pointers for Success

1. Encourage your students to be open-minded and tolerant when they listen to each other's ideas. Strive to build a community of trust in your classroom so that hesitant students will not be afraid to take risks.

2. In addition to being open-minded about each other's responses, your students should also work to be open-minded about ideas of their own that seem odd or far-fetched. All great inventions and discoveries begin with a fresh idea.

3. Put students in groups to brainstorm, to solve problems, to form a consensus, or any of the countless other activities that a group situation inspires in students who are working on their thinking skills.

4. Use critical thinking to help students unlock what they already know about a subject and then help them discover more on their own. Ask them to make connections between new material and previously learned information. It's especially effective if students can make these connections between subjects that do not seem to be related at all.

5. Teach your students to look beyond the surface. Have them study an object, such as a small piece of gravel, and collect ideas about it until they have exhausted every possibility. Students will be surprised at what their classmates noticed when they share ideas.

6. Give your students enough time to think when you ask them a question that is not just a recalling of facts. Allowing students to jot down possible responses will insure this.

7. Small details are important when students are practicing their critical-thinking skills. Teach your students to key in on these as well as on the "big picture."

8. Homework will be more effective if it involves critical thinking rather than rote exercises. Give meaningful homework assignments to spare you and your students from discipline problems.

9. Games, puzzles, riddles, time-management sponges, logic quizzes, and other lively exercises are perfect ways to stimulate your students' thinking skills.

10. Use time that might be wasted. Opening and closing exercises are good times to practice these skills with your students. Since this time is often wasted, you have nothing to lose in trying a brief critical-thinking exercise with your class.

11. Be sure to model the skill you are trying to teach so that your students understand the criteria for success. Lots of examples will reassure your students that they are on the right track.

12. Have your students deal with real-world issues as often as you can so that they can connect their textbook learning to their futures. Use advertisements and clippings from magazines and newspapers as well as audio-visual support whenever you can to stimulate your students' thinking.

13. Teach your students the research techniques that are appropriate for your subject matter and for the age level of your students. Students need to be able to retrieve and manipulate information quickly. Technology can also speed up this process if your students are computer literate.

QUESTIONS THAT SPARK CRITICAL THINKING

One of the easiest ways to involve your students in higher-level thinking skills is by asking open-ended questions designed to stimulate and direct thought. Open-ended questions provide a nonthreatening opportunity for your students to shine. Questions that require students to think, but at the same time have no real incorrect answers, will give your students confidence as well as practice in decision making.

In the list below you will find some general questions grouped according to Bloom's Taxonomy. These can be adapted to almost any classroom or to almost any group of students. Of course there are thousands more that you can use, but these should help you focus on the vital critical-thinking skills necessary for student success.

Comprehension

- What advice does your group have for my future students about this project?
- Write a summary of today's class notes in fewer than one hundred words.
- What are some things we can learn from this experience?
- What have your previous teachers done to help you review for an important test that we could try here?

Application

- What steps did your group take to arrive at that answer?

- What did you learn in another class today that you can use in this class right now?
- What did you learn in this class today that you can apply to another class?
- How can you apply what you have learned today in class to your own life right away?
- How will you use what you learned today in the future?
- How could you modify today's lesson to make it easier to remember all of the key issues in it?
- What organizational skills do you have that you can teach to the class?
- What are some logical ways to set up your notebooks for maximum efficiency?

Analysis

- What is the quickest way to learn the facts in today's lesson?
- What are the underlying principles that govern the lives of most of your classmates?
- What are the reasons for the behavior we studied today?
- Why should all students be treated fairly regardless of previous behavior?
- What are some of the things you could say to someone else who wants to cheat by copying your homework that won't make you feel awkward?
- Since I really wasn't clear in the way that I phrased that test question, what suggestions do you have for me?
- If I change the date of the test, we will be off schedule. What do you suggest we do about that?
- How do you think I should signal you to be quiet when you are working in your groups?

Synthesis

- Choose ten facts from today's lesson to create a puzzle to help a classmate review.
- Demonstrate the main point of today's lesson to a classmate.
- List the events that you just read about in the order that they happened. Now change the order of just one event and tell what the new outcome would be.
- Group the items on the board according to a criteria that you devise.
- If you were a newspaper reporter writing about the events in this class this week, what would the headline of your article be?
- Create relationships among these items.
- List as many ways as you can that you are like your classmates.

Evaluation

- Rate this class against the other classes that you have attended this week.
- What qualities caused the people in today's lesson to succeed?
- How do you know when you have done a job to the best of your ability?
- What are the errors in logic in the passage that you just read?
- Defend a classroom rule to a classmate whose opinion is very different from yours.

PERFECTING THE ART OF QUESTIONING

The art of asking questions well is one that takes time to develop. The right questions asked at just the right time can turn an ordinary class discussion into a memorable experience for students and teachers alike. This skill is one that all teachers can develop no matter what the age or ability level of their students. While it is a skill that takes planning and practice, it pays off in increased student enthusiasm and success.

Enthusiastic and successful students will create a positive learning climate with few disruptions. When you capture and hold the attention of all your students, a questioning session turns into a learning session for the entire class.

Happily, learning the art of asking questions well is not difficult. First, you must plan questions that are going to generate good answers. Develop ones that build on each other logically.

There are two types of questions that you will want to ask your students. *Recall questions* require a factual response based on previous learning. *Thought questions* require a more in-depth answer and can also be open-ended. Both kinds of questions, when handled with delicacy, help establish an atmosphere of trust in your classroom.

After you have decided on the questions you want to ask your students, teach your students the routine you want followed for questioning sessions before you ever hold the first one. When your students know what you expect from them, you will all benefit.

With practice you can set the stage for academic and social success in your classroom. Use as many of the following strategies as you can in each questioning session when you want to involve every student in your class in productive learning.

1. When you ask a question, it is crucial that you wait for a response. You must allow everyone enough time to think of a answer. After you have waited, call on a student to respond. This technique not only takes practice on your part, but you'll also need to train your students to wait for you to call on them and not to blurt out answers.

2. After you have asked a question and waited, call on a student by name. Remember that if you call a student's name before you ask the question, the rest of the class is automatically uninvolved in the questioning.

3. If you are in a questioning situation where all of your students are expected to give a response and one student refuses, still hold that student accountable by saying, "I'll come back to you." Be pleasant but firm if you want a response from every student.

4. Avoid responses from an entire group. You can't hear from everyone when your students shout out answers at once. Too many students successfully tune out when the group is expected to answer and individuals are not held accountable.

5. Don't follow a pattern when you call on students. A good way around this bad habit is to photocopy your roll book at the start of the term and use it to mark off your students' names as you call on them at random. You'll find this much more effective than just following alphabetical order or calling on students in rows.

6. You and your students should devise simple signals to yes-or-no questions. You could use thumbs up or thumbs down; one finger held up or two fingers held up; or any other signal that will help you engage each student's full attention.

7. When answer choices are limited to several categories, such as in a classification, make up response cards in advance.

8. Another excellent way to get all of your students fully involved is to ask them to write their answers before you call on anyone. You could have them put their pencils down as a signal that they are through writing. This technique also forces your students to think for themselves.

9. Never be sarcastic about a wrong response. Your students must be allowed to make mistakes.

10. Encourage your students to be responsive and to answer without fear of ridicule from you or from their classmates. Don't allow students to laugh at a classmate's incorrect answer. Instead, direct them to be helpful. Say, "How can you help _____ with this answer?"

11. Try to not repeat a question. Your students need to listen and stay focused. If your students don't seem to understand one of your questions, ask a student to rephrase it for you.

12. Teach your students to speak loudly enough for all to hear. Avoid repeating their answers for them. Instead, ask them to repeat.

13. Respond to every answer. If it's correct, say so. When it's an incorrect response, react calmly. If part of an answer is correct, then you must respond to that part. Continue until you have an answer that is entirely correct.

14. In order to keep your students engaged, it is necessary for you to move around the room as you question them. Standing near daydreamers often forces them to pay attention to you.

15. Practice drills can be lots of fun. Finding the correct pace is a challenge for most teachers. If your pace is too quick, you'll lose most of your slower students. If it is too slow, you'll lose some students to boredom.

16. An effective way to end class is with a 3-minute drill session. End the drill session by asking for a recap of the information covered in the drill.

17. Make sure you ask one question at a time. A shower of questions will only confuse your students.

18. An effective questioning technique is to poll your students on the issues you have just taught them. Forcing everyone to take a stand or to express an opinion will engage them more readily than if they are allowed to sit passively.

19. Design questions that will allow students to go beyond simple yes-or-no answers if you want to promote thinking and student involvement.

20. Consciously promote student interaction by asking some students to comment on the answers given by others. Setting up a crossfire situation will force them to think. It keeps everyone interested and the class lively.

SUCCESSFUL CONTRACTS

The idea of written contracts between students and teachers has been a proven success in classrooms for many years. Whether it's the promotion of positive behaviors or the elimination of negative ones, contracts are one of the most effective tools a creative teacher has.

Contracts between teachers and students can be as varied as student interests and your own creativity allow. You can easily add your own unique touches to the standard formats suggested in this section to help your students find success.

Although there are as many different types of contracts as there are teachers who use them, several basic types are determined by their function. You'll now find out about contracts in general, assignment contracts, group contracts, and behavior contracts.

By using these techniques, you should be able to experiment successfully to create a variety of contracts to meet a wide range of student needs.

In General

Although contracts differ from teacher to teacher and from situation to situation, they generally have common characteristics. Basically each contract should include:

- name of the student
- name of the teacher
- beginning and ending dates
- specific tasks to be performed
- degree of success expected
- immediate rewards
- future rewards
- consequences
- witness signatures
- student and teacher signatures
- any extra notes pertaining to a specific contract

Don't be afraid to have fun with a contract if the situation warrants. Use legal language and an elaborate typeface. Illustrations and places for students to make addendums also create interest. Do whatever you can to catch your students' attention and motivate them to improve the behavior in the contract or perform whatever task is required by it.

Assignment Contracts

Assignment contracts are special types of behavior contracts that can be especially effective for reviews, drills, work that is easily self-checked, when you sense that a class would like more choice in making decisions about their work, when you have a mature class, or when you want to help students reinforce their skills. There are many ways to design these depending on what you want each one to accomplish. In particular, these are excellent for students who like to work independently within a comfortable framework of your expectations.

Assignment contracts allow student choices about what they want to work on each day. In this type of contract, you decide what type of work needs to be done, but the students are allowed some freedom in deciding the order in which it is completed. In general, this contract should not last longer than a week before you bring everyone together for a common pooling of knowledge and review before assessing progress. A sample of this type of contract can be found on pages 227-228.

SAMPLE BEHAVIOR CONTRACT #1

I, _____, hereby declare on this date,

_____, that I agree to do the following:

_____

_____

_____

_____   _____

Student Signature   Teacher Signature

My efforts at meeting this goal will be considered acceptable and complete when:

_____

_____

_____

By successfully completing the terms of this contract, I will be rewarded by:

_____

_____

_____

_____   _____

Ending Date of Terms   Student Signature

                                                      _____

                                                      Teacher Signature

SAMPLE BEHAVIOR CONTRACT #2

Contract between _____ and _____
                                    Student   Teacher

agrees to _____

_____

_____

_____

Rewards: _____

_____

_____

_____

Consequences: _____

_____

_____

_____

Dates for Checking Progress: _____

The terms of this contract will end on this date:

_____

_____   _____

Student Signature   Teacher Signature

Behavior Contracts

Behavior contracts are designed to help solve discipline problems that are usually the result of a student's bad habits. Talking back, not doing homework, and other habitual misbehaviors respond well to this type of contract.

Begin with steps that are easily and quickly met. It is better to create a series of short contracts rather than one long contract since the object here is to help the student improve behavior; this is accomplished more easily in small, easily achieved steps. It is also effective to begin with tangible rewards rather than intrinsic ones in order to get the child used to the new behavior.

Make sure the student understands the problem that has resulted in the need for a contract and the alternative solutions to which you can both agree. The agreement between you must be explicitly stated in the written contract.

Another effective technique to use in the conference with the student in which you discuss this type of contract is to ask the student to restate the terms in his or her own words.

You can also enter into a contract with a parent and a child when the need arises. If a parent is actively involved in the solution to a problem, having that parent sign the contract is a good idea. The student will also take it more seriously.

Group Contracts

Using behavior contracts to motivate groups to perform better is an efficient way to create a positive classroom climate. Having an entire group sign a contract creates a sense of comradarie that makes students work together for the good of all.

Some teachers use group contracts after the set of classroom rules has been determined. (See the sample.) You might have your students sign individual copies to keep in their notebooks, while you have the class sign one large copy that is posted.

Use a contract to have students set successful goals for themselves at the beginning of each grading period. In addition to the grade they want to earn, have your students list the steps they need to take in order to meet their goals.

When your students are in groups, they will enjoy contracting out who is responsible for which tasks. When each member of the group sees the jobs to be done written out, the chances for the successful completion of those tasks become greater as students begin to see their part in the whole of a project. Signing a contract with group members creates a sense of responsibility in each member.

A good way to create a team spirit is to set up a contract in which all of the members work towards a common goal. For example, you might want to promote certain behaviors and eliminate others. If your incentive is appropriate, your students will help each other reach that goal.

SAMPLE GROUP CONTRACT

CLASS RULES CONTRACT FOR THE ENTIRE CLASS

We, the undersigned, understand the behavior expectations for this class and intend to faithfully abide by and be guided by them for the betterment of all concerned.

We hereby sign in good faith:

Witnessed this day, _____

_____
Signature of Teacher

BEHAVIORS THAT MAY BE IMPROVED WITH BEHAVIOR CONTRACTS

In addition to using behavior contracts as tools in solving major behavior problems, you can also use them to help eliminate minor disturbances.

The reason that behavior contracts work well on these smaller problems is simple: They force a student to attend to the problem. Once a student sees the problem behavior written out and agrees to take steps to solve it, that student is then aware of not just what's wrong, but how to fix it. Behavior contracts work because they give students alternatives to misbehaving.

The following list of annoying disruptions are examples of the kinds of misbehaviors that can be improved with contracts.

1. Tardiness to class
2. Forgetting to do homework
3. Putting head down during class
4. Speaking without raising hand
5. Mild and habitual backtalk to teacher
6. Not following procedure for beginning or ending class
7. Writing on desk top
8. Excessive restroom requests
9. Work not done neatly
10. Not having books and materials in class
11. Habitual inattention
12. Unorganized notebooks and materials
13. Chewing gum
14. Mild rudeness to other students
15. Balling-up paper when the teacher is talking

CREATING A SAFE ENVIRONMENT FOR YOUR STUDENTS AND YOURSELF

Even though it takes four years of hard work and many long hours to become a teacher, we all know that not all of the skills teachers need to know are learned in college courses. Much of what we need to do we learn by experience, through making mistakes, and by observing other educators in the daily routines of our profession.

Common-sense behavior is called for in our classrooms when we want to keep our students safe. The wise teacher will be guided by the sensible practices used by other teachers as well as by the formal education learned in those college courses. There are, however, a few common-sense safety practices that can almost be written in stone and that don't have to be learned the hard way.

Examine the following list of common-sense safety practices in order to determine which ones you can use to create a safe environment for your students and yourself.

1. Don't give your class or car keys to a student. Open the car door and the classroom door yourself and walk with the students whom you ask to help you carry things from your car.

2. It's wise not to give out your home phone number to your students even though it is a friendly thing to do. The problems that need to be solved after hours can probably be solved with *you* making the calls, rather than your students phoning you.

3. Stay at school with your students until their rides arrive if you are holding a group after school. They still need supervision. *Don't give your students rides home from school.*

4. Don't keep matches or other fire starters where your students can take them.

5. Lock out of sight all of your personal belongings as well as any money that you collect during the day.

6. If your classroom is not in use, keep it locked. No room should be left unattended with students unsupervised.

7. Openly take a stand against drugs, alcohol, and tobacco. Your students need to hear adults speak out against these.

8. If you suspect that a child has been abused, act at once. Send the child to a counselor.

9. Take seriously students who say they are suicidal.

10. Pay attention to which students have left your room with a hall pass. You are responsible for the students assigned to your care.

11. Keep your hall passes and other school passes in a safe place.

12. Discourage your students from taking such items as staplers from your desk. Instead, provide materials just for their use in another part of the room and teach students to respect your property.

13. Teach and enforce your rules and procedures on a daily basis until everyone understands your expectations.

14. Don't allow your students to have cards or other toys in class. They cause disruptions when your students should be focusing on productive work.

15. Report suspected guns or other weapons immediately.

16. Organize your room so that your students can find what they need quickly and with a minimum of confusion.

17. Listen to students who say they feel unwell. Send ill students to the school nurse or office as quickly as you can.

18. Keep adhesive bandages, tissues, and extra pens and paper on hand for your students to use.

19. Don't give students—of any age—hard candy. It's too easy for someone to choke on it.

20. Don't allow your students to have food or drinks in your classroom if this is against school policy.

21. If possible, teach with your door closed. You will minimize disruptions from outside of your classroom.

22. Deal with the bullies in your classroom. Never overlook one child tormenting another one.

23. Pay attention to notes from a doctor or from a parent about a potentially dangerous physical condition.

24. Constantly monitor the stress levels of your students.

25. Have zero tolerance for racial or other prejudices.

26. Keep scissors out of sight until you know your students very well. Even then be careful about potential weapons.

27. Return parent phone calls on the same day you receive them. It is not only courteous and professional, but the parent may have an important concern that needs to be addressed at once.

28. Keep teachers' textbook editions secure. If you should lose something of value, don't threaten your students. Instead, offer a reward for the first person to return it.

29. Realize that there is a reason why students misbehave. Do your best to discover and deal with the reason.

30. Don't use too much cologne or after-shave. Some students may experience allergic reactions if you do.

31. Never accuse a student of serious misconduct or cheating without absolute proof.

32. Treat your supervisors with professional courtesy. Keep them informed about things they should know.

33. Come to work on time. Don't miss school unless you have to.

34. Plan, plan, plan, and then plan for the unexpected.

35. Address other adults respectfully in front of students.

THE "UP AND AT 'EM" APPROACH: MONITORING STUDENTS' BEHAVIOR

Monitoring students is the reason teachers resign themselves to purchasing sensible shoes. Monitoring means getting up from behind your desk and staying on your feet all day to oversee your students. It means you are acutely aware of what each student is doing every minute of the class. It requires the hyper-alertness of a combat veteran, the patience of Job, and the stamina of an Olympic athlete.

Monitoring students is one of the most important skills successful teachers can master. At its worst, monitoring happens when a lecturing teacher pauses for breath and says, "Does everybody understand?"—obviously hoping that everybody does. It is not just an opportunity to reprimand students.

At its best, monitoring is giving door-to-door attention to your students. It is the famous "eyes in the back of the head" that is the hallmark of excellent teachers who can write on the chalkboard and tell a student in the back of the room to stop passing notes at the same time. It is one of the most important ways we can connect with our students. Monitoring enables us to reach each student because it helps every one of them feel important.

There are several good reasons for mastering the techniques involved in successful monitoring. Here's a quick baker's dozen of the advantages to being a good classroom monitor.

1. Problems can't get out of control.
2. You build rapport and a positive climate.
3. Students assume responsibility for behavior.
4. Everyone stays on task.
5. It reinforces good behavior.
6. You appear to be a good classroom leader.
7. Students take you seriously.
8. Your personal stress levels decrease.
9. It can eliminate cheating.
10. Learning moves forward.
11. You can show you care.
12. You deal with difficulties in a positive way.
13. It works.

If you are not sure you are monitoring as effectively as you can be, it's not hard to get started right away. Here are some strategies for you to use.

1. Unless you and your students are working together in a circle, stand up. *Move around.* This body language will make you seem accessible and relaxed.

2. Make sure you arrange the furniture so that you can monitor everyone. Students in the back of the room count on the fact that you will not notice what they are up to. Try to avoid long rows of neatly placed desks or groups of desks crammed so closely together that you have trouble getting to them.

3. The simplest request that teachers who are monitoring overlook is to ask their students to put their bookbags and other materials underneath their desks. If you remember this, you can move around without having to worry about tripping.

4. Pay attention to the *eye contact* you have with your students. Eye contact keeps them alert as well as involved in the classroom activity. You also send the nonverbal message that you find your students important when you look at them as individuals.

5. Stay relaxed and positive. A good monitor enables, facilitates, and helps—not prowls around irritably trying to catch a naughty child in the act.

6. Spread out your attention. Do you tend to focus on only a few students? Most teachers tend to do this. A good way to determine if you are guilty of this is to carry a photocopy of your class roll. When you speak with a student, place a check next to the

name. After doing this for a couple of classes, you should be more aware of the unconscious patterns in the way you attend to your class.

7. Be alert, also, to how much time you spend with each student. A student who spends 15 minutes in a conference with you has received considerably more attention and support than the students who only have your attention for less than a minute.

8. Be very careful that you don't ignore students who need help. It's easy to get bogged down in a crowd of students who need attention and overlook a student. If there are several who are waiting to speak with you, reassure them that you will get to them.

9. Don't allow long lines of students waiting to see you. A better solution is for students to put their names on the board so that you can then see them in order. You could also take a deli-counter approach and have students take a number. See them in the order of the numbers. You could also have those students who know how to help with a particular problem assist the others.

10. If you use monitoring to keep students on task, be sure to stand near them. A quick nod of the head, a light touch, a glance, or even a few quiet cautionary words are all it takes most of the time.

MONITORING ON THE RUN: 20 QUICK TECHNIQUES

1. Encourage students to work together to monitor their own group for noise, on-task behavior, and progress.

2. When students work in groups, assign the role of monitor to one student in the group.

3. Give students silly stickers, tags, or badges to wear when they have reached a certain point in the assignment.

4. When you are walking around the room, ask students to tell you five things they have just learned from the assignment.

5. If the work for the day involves several smaller assignments, create a "To-Do Checklist" of work for students to use and to show you their progress when you come by.

6. Project friendliness. Sometimes just a smile will get a daydreamer back on the job.

7. Offer a small reward to the students who reach a certain point in the assignment.

8. When conducting rapid-fire drills, don't be predictable. Ask a student a question, go to another student for the next question, and then return to the first one for the third question. This way no one is let off the hook just because of a correct answer.

9. Divide an assignment into small steps. Monitor by asking students to show you each step.

10. Put students' names on the board and have them check off their names as they prove to you they have met the assignment requirements.

11. Have students who are successful at an assignment put their names on the board as potential helpers.

12. Write a fact from the lesson on the board and have students add a different fact to it as they finish working. This is also a great way to review.

13. Say, "When I come by your desk, please show me the correct answer to _____."

14. Set a time limit for an assignment and walk around the room with the timer ticking or a stopwatch running. This usually helps students stay on task.

15. Ask, "At this moment, what are you doing that's right?"

16. Tell students that you intend to record the name of every student you see off-task when you make a check at random times. You can also record the names of all students who are on-task at the same time.

17. Ask, "How may I help you?"

18. Tell students that if they have a question about the work that other students might have also, they should write it on the board. You can address it when you get a chance.

19. If students tend to sit and play while waiting for you to check their work or answer a question, teach them that they are wasting time. They need to understand the difference between a delay and an abrupt halt.

20. Arrange signals for your students. If they have asked three other people for the answer to a question and still need help, then they can signal you by holding up a sign with a giant "?" on it. You could ask them to let you know their progress by thumbs up or thumbs down when you make a check.

Group Monitoring Form

Use this form when you need to monitor group work systematically and to focus on specific areas of concern. Although you can use this form to monitor any behavior that you want, some of the areas you might want to monitor are: on- or off-task behavior, noise level, progress, and specific assignment completion.

The sample form on the following page will help you get started.

TEACHING STUDENTS TO WORK WELL TOGETHER

One of the most successful techniques to gain popularity in classrooms across the nation in recent years is group work. Those teachers who have spent long hours perfecting this teaching strategy claim that it has revolutionized the learning process in their classrooms. On the other hand, those teachers who have not mastered this technique shudder at the thought of noisy, out-of-control students busily engaged in learning nothing. Group work can be an effective technique for preventing many discipline problems if students are taught how to work well together.

Using group work well in your classroom requires a great deal of planning, patience, and persistence on your part, but the rewards are worth the struggle. Students who work well together enjoy the experience and benefit from it. The following suggestions will help you master this teaching technique.

GROUP MONITORING FORM

GROUP	BEHAVIORS MONITORED	COMMENTS
1		
2		
3		
4		
5		
6		

General Strategies for Group-Work Success

1. Start small. A single, brief successful activity once or twice a week is better than several days of chaos.

2. Start with pairs or triads. Putting too many students in a group is a common mistake.

3. Have a very clear objective for the activity and make sure every student in the group understands this objective. A good way to guarantee this understanding is to have one person in the group take the responsibility of explaining it to the rest of the group.

4. Not every assignment will be successful when it's done by a group. Be careful to design activities that require that students work together.

5. Design activities that force your students to work together successfully. You could try these:

    ■ only give the necessary materials to one student so that all of them have to work together to get the job done

    ■ divide the task into various parts to complete a larger whole

    ■ give a reward for group success

    ■ give different members parts of the information that they must share in order to grasp the big picture

6. If the project is one that is fairly lengthy or involves several different parts, provide your students with checklists and deadlines so that they can stay organized.

7. Figure out your personal areas of concern about group work and begin to deal with them. Some areas that have caused other teachers problems are excessive noise, time off-task, group evaluation, and the lack of student responsibility.

8. Make sure every group member has a specific task and understands how to do it well.

9. Your students need to be taught the interpersonal skills necessary to work together well. For each activity you have students do, teach them a specific skill to practice. Some of these skills are listening well, developing an open mind about the opinions of others, asking questions, staying on-task, and taking responsibility for the work. An opening icebreaker is a good idea for each new group configuration even in a classroom where students know and like each other, but have not worked together as a team before.

10. Closely monitor your students while they are in groups. You might even have a checklist so that you can work to promote desirable behaviors or eliminate unproductive ones. Observe how students work together and make sure your students are doing so as productively as possible by offering assistance and suggestions when needed.

11. Teach students how to deal with their concerns, questions, or side issues that might be off-task behaviors by taking these to a designated area of the room. In this area, you should provide paper and markers or pens so that students can list them as topics with which they need help. This will allow group members to temporarily put these on hold to come back to later.

12. Have students begin their working together by developing a few ground rules for their own group. Give one or two as models and then ask students to create others.

13. Avoid the trap of having most of the work done outside of class. You can actively intervene and direct the process if students work in class. You will also find it easier to assign grades if you observe your students working together.

14. In a long or complex project, it's best to begin with brief activities that encourage group members to work together successfully.

15. Build in check points for lengthy projects. Make sure all students have met these mini-deadlines before going further. Students will be responsible at these points for keeping the teacher up-to-date about their progress.

16. It's obvious, but needs to be mentioned: Students must sit together and look at each other in order to work well together.

17. Make sure you create a classroom that is conducive to group work. Have chairs arranged in groups and materials handy to avoid traffic-flow problems.

18. After a group has worked together on an assignment, have the members discuss how well they worked together as a group. What were their strengths and weaknesses? What would they do differently the next time they worked together?

19. With the increased popularity of group work, some students can be confused about when it's okay to work together on an assignment and when it's not. Make sure you continue to be very clear about this with your students.

Group Selection

1. The least effective way to put students into groups to work together is to have them choose their teammates. Avoid this if you want to have your students fully engaged.

2. Although you can do brief teamwork sessions with random grouping or by having students "count off" for larger or more complicated projects, spend planning time creating group configurations that will be successful for your students.

3. A mixed group based on low-, medium-, and high-ability levels and interpersonal skills is often the most productive especially if you work with your students on the ways that you want them to interact with each other.

4. Stress that students are to work together, not be playmates. Tell them you have created teams based on this idea.

5. The size of the group will be dependent on several factors: the maturity of your students, the length of time they will be working together, the resources they will need, the type of task they will have to do, and the interpersonal skills your students already have.

6. With less able groups, use smaller groups where everyone can have an important part.

7. Try not to put friends together. Often students are comfortable working with their friends, but are not as productive as they would be if they worked with others.

8. Teach your students that working together is a big part of the real world of work and community that lies ahead of them. They are gaining the skills they need now to be successful later.

The Teacher's Role in Group Work

1. Set clear, measurable objectives for each activity.

2. Keep students on the right track by giving immediate feedback through constant monitoring. You will be most effective if you stay on your feet while your students are working in teams.

3. You should spend more time coaching and monitoring than delivering a lecture.

4. Solve problems or help your students figure out ways to solve problems.

5. Make sure resources are available to students.

6. Teach the skills students need to work together.

7. Organize students' work for maximum efficiency.

8. Provide deadlines and data so that you can fairly evaluate your students.

9. Deal with students who are reluctant to participate fully in the team. Some ways to do this are:
   ■ remove the offending students and have them complete the work by themselves
   ■ encourage them and offer a needed jolt of self-confidence
   ■ be very specific about the tasks they need to do
   ■ break the tasks into more manageable bits for students who may be overwhelmed
   ■ get to the root of the matter and help students resolve their differences if this is the problem
   ■ contact parents
   ■ be very fair when grading others in the group when one student has problems and the others don't

10. Give your students lots of examples to use as models.

11. Be a sounding board for ideas and problems.

12. Provide resources and materials as well as guidance.

13. Remember that group work doesn't become successful just on the days that students are working together. Its success begins on the first day of the term with the atmosphere that you establish for your classroom.

Evaluation Strategies

1. Be aware that this is probably the area of biggest concern for parents and students.

2. Don't just give a group grade. Be sure to give individual grades as well.

3. You will find it easier to evaluate your students fairly if the objective for the activity is measurable.

4. Keep a log of your students' progress as they work on each day's activity during the course of a long project. This way you won't have to try to recall the various contributions that each student made to the group's progress.

5. Make sure you divide the workload evenly among your students in a group and grade them evenly, also.

6. Give generous feedback as the group works on its project. Students need to be clear about their progress if they are to achieve success.

7. Give individual grades on tests on material that the group was supposed to master during the project. This will encourage individual accountability.

8. Encourage accountability and success by having the entire group work on a project. Then call on a student from each group to turn in a paper or to make a report to represent the entire group.

9. Avoid trouble by making the group grade only a portion of the entire grade.

10. Be careful that you do not reward students who do not put forth an appropriate amount of effort.

11. If a project is going to take several days to complete, give daily grades for working together. Base this on objective and measurable criteria that your students are made aware of in advance of beginning so that they understand what they need to do to achieve success.

Some Quick Group-Work Activities

1. Ask the entire class a question. Allow them to think about their responses. Have your students discuss their responses in a group and reach a consensus to share with the larger class.

2. Have a group list as many items as it can in a category that is under discussion. The group can do this easily if there is one only pen and one piece of paper that needs to be passed from student to student in the group.

3. Have students fill out each other's information sheets that you need for their records. This is a twist on the interview project that so many teachers like to use to open the term.

4. Have students work to answer questions and then explain their teammates' answers to the rest of the class.

5. Students can work together to complete a worksheet or drill exercise. Be sure to provide structure for this by assigning questions to the team members.

6. Have groups create master lists of information that they know about a topic either before you begin studying the material or as a review after your class has covered it.

7. Have students review for a test by drilling each other, comparing notes, or writing study guides together.

8. Have students outline the main points of a lesson and share their outlines with the group to check for accuracy.

9. Editing papers and checking for proofreading errors is a group task that makes a teacher's job of evaluating papers easier.

10. Assign a large topic to a group and have the members report on it through various methods. Make sure each member understands the part he or she is to play in presenting the final report.

KEEPING IT TO A DULL ROAR: HELPING STUDENTS LEARN TO CONTROL THE NOISE LEVEL

Maintaining an acceptable noise level in a classroom is not always an easy task. Our students seem to thrive in a noisy world of blaring radios, televisions, and music . . . often all playing at the same time. Their lives are full of ringing phones, conversations, and noise, noise, noise—and the louder the better. Just ask the parents of any teenager.

Unfortunately, this noise tolerance on the part of our pupils can have an adverse effect on the orderly, productive classrooms we want to have. More than one veteran teacher has had the unpleasant experience of having to shout to be heard above pandemonium.

You *can* have a classroom where the noise level is under control by teaching your students how to achieve the acceptable noise levels you want in your classroom. The following strategies can help you and your students as you learn to work together to create a classroom where the only noise is the sound of great minds at work.

1. Begin to teach the various types of noise levels to your students by dealing with distance. Teach them to pay attention to the one-foot voice, the two-foot voice, and a whisper. Model these acceptable levels and monitor until your students have internalized them.

2. Tell your students which noise levels are acceptable for each assignment you give them. Be specific and clear.

3. Play soft instrumental background music at a volume that can be heard all over the room. This will tend to quiet most students if you tell them that you need to always be able to hear the music over their voices.

4. Plan ways to signal your students when the noise level reaches an unacceptable level. Some arranged signals could be a gesture, a warning word from you, a warning mark on the chalkboard, or a quick flick of the light switch.

5. Learning to control the noise takes practice. Be consistent about practicing and enforcing the noise level you prefer. Monitor noise levels by moving around the room frequently to help students stay focused and working quietly.

6. When pupils are working in groups, teach them to talk only to the other people in their group so that they won't have to raise their voices to be heard. You can also put a student in charge of the noise level for that group.

7. Make controlling noise a team undertaking. You should not be the only person in the room concerned about the noise.

8. Take noise level into account when you plan. If a lesson is going to be a very loud one, you might consider moving to a location where you won't disturb the other people or classes around you.

9. Make sure your students understand when noise is unacceptable. Many of your students will think nothing of talking when you are giving oral directions or during a movie or even during a test unless you teach them not to do this.

10. Teach your students to be attentive listeners. If you teach your students how to listen well, then you will be closer to reducing side talking and background noise when these are inappropriate.

11. When your students are working together, keep the noise level down by putting them physically close to one another. Sounds simple? Many teachers overlook this easy way to control the volume.

12. Adjust your attitude about noise if you need to. Many students are comfortable working in noisier environments than adults tolerate easily. If you find yourself fretting about noise, examine your attitude before you make any sweeping changes.

13. Arrange your room into loud and quiet areas on days when there will be a variety of student activities in progress at the same time. Students who need to talk can feel more comfortable doing so if they move to an area of the room where they won't disturb a student who needs more peace and quiet to concentrate.

14. Lower your own voice. If you speak quietly and command attention at the same time, then your students will quiet down in order to hear what you have to say. Students tend to tune out their loud teachers whenever they can.

15. Learn to distinguish between good noise and bad noise. A noisy class may either be one where there's lots of productive talking and on-task behavior or it may be one where students are rudely ignoring the instructional directives for the day.

HOW TO MAKE YOUR STUDENTS PAY ATTENTION TO YOU

It happens to every teacher at some time or another. We lose our students. Not physically, of course; it's pretty difficult to misplace 30 or so rambunctious individuals. But while their bodies are still in the room with us, their minds have taken a little vacation from the lesson we have so carefully prepared. If we're lucky, all that goes wrong is that eyes glaze over and expressions of polite disinterest replace the focused attention that we strive to instill in our students.

If we're not lucky, pandemonium erupts and less enthusiastic teachers consider other career opportunities. The skillful teacher, however, will take pains to develop a full repertoire of strategies to cut the vacations short and put the class firmly back on track before too much vital learning time is lost.

Here are four mistakes many teachers make when trying to catch their students' attention. They are easy to avoid once you have made yourself aware of them.

Don't Talk Unless You Have Everyone's Attention

Many teachers talk *over* their students' activity. While students are getting materials ready, sharpening pencils, finding the page, or finishing a conversation, the teacher is in the front of the room giving directions or other information about the lesson for the day.

This is not a practice that encourages students to be self-disciplined or even polite. The message that it sends is that what the instructor is saying is not really important. It also usually results in either a student asking you to repeat the information or in students asking each other to explain what you have just said.

A BETTER CHOICE: Wait until you have everyone's attention before you address the class. Establish a signal with your students so that they know they are to stop what they are doing and listen to you. This can be an expression such as "May I have your attention, please" or another signal such as a place in the room where you go when you need to speak to the entire group. It's not enough to just establish this procedure; you have to teach it to your class and then consistently reinforce it.

Don't Repeat Yourself

It's one thing to clarify information or explain directions; it's another to have to repeat yourself for students who are not in the habit of listening attentively. Don't assume that your students are good listeners. Many have never been taught how to listen attentively.

A BETTER CHOICE: Say something once and teach your students to listen to you the *first* time. Take the time and teach listening skills throughout the term so that your students can develop them. Make this a part of the culture of your classroom and you will find yourself not having to repeat.

Don't Forget Your Audience

If you never vary the tone of your voice, if you mumble, if you talk with your back to the class, or if you talk to only one or two faces in the crowd, then you are more interested in what you are saying than in whether your students are learning the material. The best planned lessons in the world are useless if you forget that you are talking to an audience of living, breathing adolescents who are quick to disengage from a speaker they don't find interesting!

A BETTER CHOICE: Recall those public-speaking tips from your undergraduate Speech 101 class and apply them. Videotape yourself or simply record your voice. Study your presentation to make sure you are reaching your audience.

If you give your students work to do while you are speaking that will force them to interact with you, then you can be sure of engaging their attention. A handout with key words missing or with outlined notes to complete will encourage students to stay on track while you are speaking.

Don't Assume That Your Students Are Ready to Listen Just Because You Are Ready to Speak

Many teachers tell their students to turn to a certain page in the book and then immediately begin talking about the material on that page while students scramble to find paper and pens to take notes. Your students need time to prepare themselves and to settle down before they can listen well.

A BETTER CHOICE: Wait. Allow your students to get their notebook pages dated and other materials ready before you begin talking to them. If you just want them to listen and not write, ask them to clear their desks of all writing materials and books. Set the stage if you want to capture their attention.

50 ACTIONS THAT WILL GRAB YOUR STUDENTS' ATTENTION

There are countless ways to wake up and shake up your students. Prepared teachers take the time in advance of the lesson to prevent their students from being bored in class. They combine various techniques and try all sorts of bold new approaches to get their students engaged in a lesson. Don't be afraid to try as many as it takes to get your students in the fast lane to success when their attention begins to lag.

Although there are dozens of approaches to take, the following list includes some that are designed to meet the needs of just about every teacher. Mix and match and use these to experiment with the best ways to keep your students on task.

1. Put a humorous drawing on the board or on the overhead or give your students chalk and have them draw a sketch on the board of some of the facts of the lesson. You could also ask the right-handers to use their left hands and vice versa. Asking blindfolded students to draw some of the facts from the lesson also helps focus their attention.

2. Stage a confrontation. Have another adult come in and fake a high-stress situation that relates to the material the class is preparing to study.

3. Use Christmas tree lights or other colored bulbs to spotlight a part of the lesson.

4. Hold up a box and ask students to guess what's in it. Items can relate to the unit being studied.

5. Do you speak French? Pig Latin? Try speaking in another language for a sentence or two.

6. Write on the board three quotations that don't seem to be related to one another and ask not just how they are related to each other, but to the day's lesson as well.

7. Use music. Play raucous music or ask your students to identify sounds from a tape. Play bits and pieces of songs for students to put together to make sense of the lesson for the day. You can even sing to your students or have them sing to you.

8. Show a film montage.

9. Move the desks around or ask students to trade places with each other.

10. Hand out blindfolds and have your students put them on. Give them objects from the lesson for them to identify without peeking.

11. Hold a visualization session where your students imagine themselves as successful people, or on a deserted island.

12. Wear a costume to class or have your students wear costumes. Even simple accessories such as ties or hats can spice up a lesson.

13. Hand pupils a notice as they come in that says, "Today will be a silent communication day. No pupil is allowed to speak. All communication must be done through writing."

14. Create a giant puzzle from posterboard and magazine pictures you've collected and glued to the board. Assign each student a piece of the puzzle and then have them work together as a group to solve it.

15. Whisper or pantomine the directions you want your students to follow.

16. Pretend to be a talk-show host. Have props and procedures as close to the real thing as you can.

17. Ask students to identify the pieces of a word or sentence relevant to the lesson. Write the letters or words on construction paper. Then hand out these so that students can unscramble them to recreate the relevant word or sentence.

18. Promise a treat when the day's work is done correctly.

19. Time as many activities as you can. Students work efficiently when they work to the clock. You can also put a student in charge of timing an activity or ring a bell or buzzer when the activity is over. Another way to keep students focused through timing is to announce that a change of pace is about to happen and then begin a countdown. Timing pupils almost always causes them to focus on the activity at hand and mentally prepare for the upcoming change.

20. Videotape your students in action. Even a mundane activity is more interesting when your students are given the opportunity to "mug" for the camera.

21. Give pupils a checklist of the highpoints of the material they will be studying and ask them to tick off the points that are covered in your presentation.

22. When you ask students to take notes on the day's lesson, focus their attention with a list of the key words and phrases you want them to learn.

23. Announce that you intend to make deliberate errors on the board, on a handout, or in your speech and ask your students to catch you if they can.

24. Offer extra points for the first person to answer a question or for the person who can give the best answer.

25. Play a tape recording of yourself giving information or, even better, of your students giving information.

26. Show a videotape of other pupils modeling the same work you expect yours to do.

27. Get out the colors! Even older students enjoy using paints, crayons, and colored chalk to brighten a lesson.

28. Give your students soft play clay or other gooey stuff with a specific task to accomplish with it. It's hard to be bored and to play with something gooey at the same time.

29. Plan an imaginary field trip to the place under discussion. Your students can brainstorm all sorts of information with this activity.

30. Hand out lengths of ribbon or string and have your pupils tie them together, make shapes with the various pieces, or invent other activities that apply to the lesson.

31. Make name tags for your students. There are many different ways you can use this strategy in your classroom. Your students could role-play the names they have been given. You could place the tags on your students' backs so that they would have to work with other students to try to figure out the roles they have been given. You can also use name tags in group activities to assign various tasks.

32. Hand out pictures of people and have your students make guesses about the people in the photographs, match them up, notice specific details, or use them in other activities.

33. Revive that old game of telephone to get your students paying attention to the facts and figures in a lesson.

34. Have your students vote to respond to questions by signals, standing, holding up signs, or other ways that appeal to their sense of fun.

35. Counting down from 10 to 1 will alert even the most mature students that they need to focus on *you*, and not on their classmates or daydreams.

36. Ask someone to stand to answer a question. Be sensitive when doing this, however. Ask several students to stand—not just one child you want to single out.

37. Count off your students into teams.

38. Ask everyone to stand and do a series of silly movements such as touching their left elbows with their right hands or putting both hands on their heads. This will generally shake out the cobwebs.

39. Hand your students a newspaper or magazine with words missing and ask them to supply the missing information.

40. Show a cartoon that pertains to the lesson and ask students to create a caption for it.

41. Present a slide show. Even better, ask your students to prepare a slide show about a school event, a lesson in class, their interests, etc.

42. Present prizes for the best presentation, performance, answers, etc.

43. Hold a drawing for prizes.

44. Have your students make up signs or posters about the lesson.

45. Turn the lights low to signal a change of pace.

46. Ask riddles to stimulate interest.

47. Use computers in your classroom. Even the most routine tasks are more fun and are easier when students get to use computers to do them.

48. Give your students food to sample.

49. Put a list of words on the board and ask your students to determine what they have in common. Use this to change the pace of a lesson. Adding unlikely names or words to the list will force your students to stretch their minds.

50. Take photographs of your students in action during a lesson.

AVERTING DISASTER: HELPING STUDENTS "MAKE THE GRADE"

Although no student should be surprised at his or her final average in any class, many of them are. Some of their misunderstandings arise from wishful thinking, while others are created by teachers who don't sufficiently explain the criteria for success to their students. Many secondary teachers are puzzled when they realize their students seem to believe teachers pluck grades out of thin air to appear on their report cards.

This misunderstanding can be heartbreaking for everyone. There are few experiences as demoralizing for teachers, parents, and students as when a student fails a class. Even the students who seem to be the least concerned are miserable when they fail. When a child fails, many teachers assume responsibility and experience a sense of loss that few other professions can equal.

While academic failure is often the result of behavior problems, it also causes them. Students who know they are about to fail a class often lose heart and quit trying. This can have a devastating impact on class morale if the failing student realizes this early in the term and repeatedly lashes out at you or at the other students in the class. Parents, too, can be galvanized to anger or unreasonable action if they think *you* are the cause of the problem. The most significant impact, however, comes in the amount of time off-task that all students experience when you are trying to cope with a failing student.

The following strategies present ways for you to prevent discipline problems by helping your students pay attention to their grades and their impact on final averages. You should be able to use some of them in your efforts to not only keep your students from failing, but to also help them once failure is inevitable.

1. Provide a wide variety of assessments in order to satisfy as many learning styles as you can. Make it your goal to offer as many chances for success as possible. A list of alternative assessments is included later in this section to make this easy for you.

2. Make sure your students have many assessments in order to be as fair as possible. At a minimum, you should provide three or four grades per week.

3. Decide at the start of each grading period how you will weigh each type of assessment: homework, collaborative work, notebooks, quizzes, tests, individual projects, classwork, extra credit, and any other assessment you use. Post this information in a conspicuous position, discuss it often to remind your students, and then stick to it.

4. Your students need to know the criteria for success on individual assignments as well as for the entire grading period. Make sure you are careful to let all of your students know just what they need to do in order to succeed in your class.

5. Prompt feedback is an invaluable tool in helping students succeed. Return graded assignments as quickly as you can. Tests, quizzes, and other short assessments should be returned the next day. Aim for a 3-day maximum whenever you possibly can. Parents frequently complain (and with good reason) about teachers who are slow to return graded work.

6. Don't lower grades because a student has misbehaved. Be sure to grade what you have taught and not whether a student has annoyed you.

7. Make sure your grading policy is objective. For example, don't have a class participation grade that you determine at the end of each week. If you decide to have a class participation grade, be very specific about the criteria for success. You can count the number of times that a student changes into exercise clothes for a physical education class, for example. You'll have trouble justifying a grade based on how many times you think a student has answered questions correctly in class discussions.

8. Don't be petty when you compute a final average. Quibbling over a fraction of a point is beneath you and will not do anything to promote a positive attitude in your stu-

dents. Many, many students find it hard to forgive a teacher who is mean-spirited about point fractions.

9. If you find that a grade is a borderline, don't give into the temptation to "take" or "give" points. Whether you like a student or not should have nothing to do with the final average.

10. Never threaten a class with a difficulty of your course or with a particular assignment. Keep in mind at all times that you need to be positive and supportive in what you say to your students.

11. Never reveal a student's grade to an entire class, and discourage your students from sharing their grades with each other. Encourage them to respect each other's privacy in this way.

12. If you post grades at the end of a grading period, reconsider your policy. Students quickly figure out the averages of their classmates and so privacy is lost. You are also posting your entire grading scale for the world to interpret favorably or unfavorably, fairly or not. You probably don't want to have this discussed publicly. A more humane way to inform students of their grades is to have them drop by to discuss their final averages with you.

13. Make time throughout the grading period to discuss grades with your students. No one should be surprised when you compute final averages. You could even protect yourself by having students sign conference sheets indicating their awareness of their average on various dates.

14. Be accurate in your averaging. If you make a mistake, admit it, and correct the error immediately.

15. A simple way to compute final averages and to keep a running total of grades is to use raw scores on assignments to determine the final average. If you do this, you will create a large percentage and you won't have to recall how many times a test should count or other needlessly difficult procedures. Record the number of points earned and the number of points possible on each assignment as fractions, add them, and divide the denominator into the numerator to obtain the percentage. Here's a sample. The numerator is the points that the student earned and the denominator is the points that were possible for each assignment. This procedure makes it possible for you to compute a student's grade at any point in the grading period easily. You determine the weight of your assignments in advance and make sure that your students are aware of the importance of each assignment.

$$\underset{\text{test}}{\frac{95}{100}} + \underset{\text{quiz}}{\frac{40}{50}} + \underset{\text{project}}{\frac{60}{75}} + \underset{\text{homework}}{\frac{20}{20}} + \underset{\text{test}}{\frac{118}{125}} = \underset{\text{raw score}}{\frac{333}{370}} = \underset{\text{final percentage}}{90\%}$$

16. When you grade each assignment, make sure you tell your students both their raw scores and their percentages so that they have a clear idea of their success on each assignment.

17. Make sure you have followed your policy on making up missed work whenever a student is absent so that you not only encourage your students to succeed, but also insure that you are as fair as you can be.

18. If parents ask for weekly or even daily progress reports, then provide them. The few minutes this takes will more than reward you with greater student success.

19. Make sure parents and students understand that the responsibility for earning grades rests with the student, not with you. As an educator, your responsibility is to compute the average, not to give grades.

TEACHING YOUR STUDENTS HOW TO TRACK THEIR GRADES

The Grade Tracking Form (next page) is an easy way for you and your students to work together to keep a running progress check on their grades. Photocopy plenty of these for your students at the start of the term and have your students clip them into their notebooks.

Whenever you hand back a paper, ask your students to circle the grade. This forces them to pay attention to it. Then have them record the grade on the grade tracking form, being careful to fill in all of the spaces.

You will raise awareness of each grade's effect on the final average if you have students judge the impact in the last column. A "+" means the grade is now higher. A "–" means it is lower. A "0" means there is no significant improvement or loss because of the grade.

Once you help your students get in the habit of tracking their own grades, you help them see the connection between each assignment and their report cards.

AN ASSORTMENT OF EVALUATION TECHNIQUES

Good teachers have always been aware of the importance of evaluating their students' progress frequently and fairly. Long gone are the days when a few quizzes and a big test or two were considered effective evaluation tools.

Today we know there exists a wide variety of evaluation methods for us to use in determining how well our students are learning the material that we so painstakingly present to them. We are also aware that we need to use as many as we possibly can—as often as we can—in order to be as fair as possible to our students.

What may not be obvious is that by using a wide variety of evaluation techniques, you can prevent discipline problems. Many students who do not perform well on traditional assessments, such as exams or quizzes, do not react well to their poor performance. Many experienced teachers have had to cope with frustrated students who may have put in lots of effort, but who still failed. Often these problems can escalate as the poor frustrated student keeps trying and failing.

GRADE TRACKING FORM FOR STUDENT SUCCESS

Name _____

Class _____

My grade goal for this class is _____.

Two study strategies I am using are:

_____

_____

Date	Assignment	Grade	Weight	Impact

Even if we can't always avoid this unpleasantness, at least we can lessen its negative impact by offering many different types of assessments during a grading period. If what we really want for our classes is a positive learning experience, we need to offer an assortment of assessments to meet the needs and abilities of the diverse student populations in our classrooms.

While traditional assessments still have a valid place in any school, there is a wide variety of techniques that you can use along with them. Many of these techniques will meet the needs of your students. Start with just one or two that you think might be successful and then experiment.

- labeling maps
- labeling diagrams
- oral questions
- questions to be answered in complete sentences
- essay questions
- multiple-choice questions
- true-or-false questions
- matching questions
- putting items in order of importance
- putting items in chronological order
- research projects
- research papers
- self-evaluation
- students evaluating each other's work
- completion of checklists
- analogies
- teaching material to someone else
- posters
- booklets
- portfolios
- book reports
- questions designed to facilitate comprehension
- the number of correct responses in a class discussion
- completion of a project based on previous knowledge
- recognition of names in the news
- class newsletter
- organized notebooks
- restatement of material in students' own words
- reading more on their own about a particular topic
- worksheets
- contracts for work to be completed

- oral reports
- formal speeches
- problem solving
- models
- project progress reports
- letters to the media
- restating definitions
- creating definitions
- word games
- puzzles
- sentence completions
- questions generated independently
- identification of main points
- original writings
- classification of material into categories
- evaluating material for themselves
- combining various elements in a lesson
- recognizing characteristics
- recalling facts
- using context clues
- applying knowledge from one unit of study to another
- completing an experiment
- summarizing
- expressing opinions
- making comparisons
- drawing contrasts
- analyzing information
- debating issues
- constructing models
- paraphrasing
- illustrating ideas with words
- writing samples
- drawing maps
- drawing diagrams
- applying book knowledge to real-life situations

USING A SYLLABUS TO PREVENT PROBLEMS

Most of us can recall from our own college days the advantages of using a syllabus. We used a syllabus to plan projects and papers, keep track of daily assignments, anticipate the more interesting lecture topics, check due dates, schedule extra study time for tests, and just stay organized in general. Too few of us, however, pass these advantages on to our students for a variety of reasons, most of which deal with a lack of confidence in our ability to plan in such a structured fashion.

A syllabus not only helps students stay organized, but it also promotes self-discipline. Students who know what to do and when they are supposed to do it are much more likely to be better behaved than those who are confused or who don't know what they are supposed to do in order to succeed in your class. A syllabus allows students to take responsibility for their learning by letting them see the big picture of what they are supposed to learn. The benefits of a syllabus to you and your students far outweigh any reluctance you might feel for not giving it a try.

Use the sample syllabus form on the following page to get started or design one that better serves the needs of your students. When designing your own syllabus, don't just list study topics and dates. There are many things you can add to a syllabus to help your students become more organized and self-disciplined. Try adding some or all of these items to yours:

- simple drawings or cartoons
- a space for students to record their grades
- a space for classroom activities
- a space for homework assignments
- a space for class objectives
- inspirational messages

In addition to these items, you also need to teach your students how to use a syllabus. You'll have to work hard at first to get them in the habit of checking it instead of just asking you what's for homework, but the effort will soon be rewarded when you see your students begin to take responsibility for their work.

A syllabus can serve as a planner/organizer for your students if you show them how to use it for a personal planner, too. They can circle the dates on which they are absent from class, underline any make-up work that's due, and keep track of their goals in the class.

If you are not confident about using a syllabus, start small. Put a week's worth of work on your first syllabus and then expand it when you and your students are comfortably using it regularly.

One way to handle the problem of schedule changes is to build in flexible time. Allow an unscheduled day every two weeks or so to compensate for the time that is often lost to the numerous interruptions that seem to plague our school days. Be sure to use that day in productive activity, however, not just as free time simply because it was initially unscheduled.

Don't be afraid to change your syllabus, either. It's tempting sometimes to schedule more work than can be realistically accomplished in the allotted time. Don't hesitate to work with your students to drop, add, or shift items to the syllabus. In fact, your students will appreciate it if you check with them about their other class schedules and try to arrange user-friendly deadlines whenever possible.

Keep in mind that a syllabus can be much more than a listing of topics. It can be an effective tool for teaching your students time management, developing organization skills, and preventing discipline problems.

Syllabus

Date	Objective	Classroom Activity	Homework	Grade

HANDLING HOMEWORK HASSLES

One of the most troublesome parts of any teacher's day begins just as soon as the school day itself ends. Students who do not do their homework create huge frustrations for themselves, their parents, and their teachers. The bad news about homework is that it can be a giant headache for all parties involved. The good news is that homework does not have to be a problem. Through very careful planning on your part, by creating an awareness of the importance of the assignment, and by instilling a sense of confidence in your students, you can eliminate most of the problems associated with homework.

Work to find ways to make homework successful for students, their parents, and yourself as often as possible. Think of homework assignments in three steps: what you do before you make the assignment, what you do while making the assignment, and what you should do when the assignment is due.

Prior to the Assignment

1. Never make homework a punishment. To do this is not only unfair to your students, but they will not take the assignment seriously.

2. Make sure the homework you assign is relevant to the needs of your students and will further mastery of the objectives for the material under study.

3. Homework should be independent practice of a skill covered in class, a review of old material, or an in-depth enrichment. It should not be the introduction of new material.

4. Follow your district's policy on the amount and types of recommended homework assignments. If your district does not have a formal policy, then check with the other members of your department to find out the informal policy.

5. Spend some time thinking back to your own school days. What made homework enjoyable or miserable for you? How can you incorporate your own experience into your assignments?

6. Aim for assignments that students can do independently, can accomplish in a reasonable length of time, are interesting enough to engage their attention, are relevant, are useful, are based on an objective, and that provide practice or a deepening of understanding.

7. Expect that your students will help each other on homework assignments, even the ones you would prefer they do individually. Either allow them to consult with each other or create assignments that can only be completed by individual students working independently.

8. Have a very structured homework pattern for less organized students. Students should have a clear idea of which nights they need to schedule time for homework.

9. At the start of the term write a letter to the parents of your students explaining your homework policy so that they can work with you to benefit their child. A sample letter is included for you in Section 4.

10. Parents and guardians can be very powerful allies in avoiding homework hassles. Make sure you are all on the same side by: keeping parents informed, providing them with copies of your syllabus, alerting them quickly if a problem arises, and being very structured and organized about homework.

11. Be willing to change due dates if your students seem genuinely distressed or overwhelmed by the workload.

12. Don't allow students to do homework for other classes in your class. But don't snatch the papers and books from students who are caught doing this, either. Simply make sure they are put away and the student is back on task.

13. Take other teachers' assignments into account and be reasonable with the length of time your assignments will take.

14. Include your students in planning when particular assignments will be due, what material they need to practice, when major tests are given, and which types of review work they need whenever you can. While you do this you still remain the master planner, but your students have a much-appreciated voice in their homework decisions.

15. Create an informal and brief questionnaire at the start of the term to get your students thinking about homework: its importance and their attitudes about it. See the sample homework questionnaire that follows.

16. Give your students the tools they need to get their work done easily. Stress the importance of a quiet place to study at home, a storage place for papers and materials, setting aside time, getting organized, and planning how to accomplish the work. It's also important to discuss with your students how to handle study breaks and the phone calls that interrupt their study schedule. Students need help in handling their responsibilities.

Making the Assignment

1. The three or so minutes that you spend each day on making students aware of their homework responsibilities will be more than paid off in increased student success.

2. Make sure students know why they have to do each assignment so that they won't feel martyred to busy work. Before they begin it, your students should have a clear idea of what they should learn from each assignment.

3. Avoid confusion by making sure the directions are clear and your students know exactly what they have to do in order to succeed on each assignment. Take time to go over each set of directions so that your students know exactly what to do.

4. One of the most effective ways to get students to pay attention to their homework responsibilities is to include it on their syllabus. Each student should have a copy to keep in their notebooks. Arrange a checklist space for homework assignments so that your students can keep track of what they have accomplished. Write the homework objective on the board and have students copy it onto the syllabus.

5. Enlarge a copy of the syllabus and post it beside the door so that students can see it on the way out of your room. Highlight the homework assignment for the day to catch their attention.

6. Write the assignment for that particular night in the same place on the board each day. Near the end of class make a quick check to see if all students know what the night's work will be.

HOMEWORK QUESTIONNAIRE FOR STUDENTS

1. Why is homework an important component for classes at the secondary level?

   _____

   _____

2. Why is homework important for this class?

   _____

   _____

3. What types of homework assignments have you been given in the past few years? Please list as many as you can recall. Use the back of this sheet if you need more space.

   _____

   _____

4. What kinds of homework assignments helped you learn the material better than the others?

   _____

   _____

5. What kinds of assignments do you prefer?

   _____

   _____

6. Which nights of the week do you find it difficult to do your homework?

   _____

   _____

7. What kinds of assignments do you find difficult to do?

   _____

   _____

8. What do you think is a fair policy about late assignments?

   _____

   _____

9. On average, about how long do you spend on your homework each night?

   _____

   _____

10. What advice do you have for other students to help them complete homework assignments well and on time?

    _____

    _____

7. Ask students to explain to you what the homework assignment is, how to do it, and what they can gain from doing it.

8. You can end class by asking students to plan how much time the homework will take and what hours they intend to set aside to accomplish it. They should share this with each other. Ask a different student each day to explain the assignment to the class.

When the Assignment Is Due

1. Engage your students in discussions throughout the year in which you ask them to evaluate various assignments as to relevance, information learned, skills sharpened, or difficulty.

2. Have your students jot down how they studied: the time they began and ended, when breaks happened, in what order they did their homework, which assignments they found more successful than others, and other topics that will shed insight on the homework situation in your classroom.

3. Check homework at the start of class on the day that it is due. Most students are upset when they do homework that is never graded. Grading the assignments will help your students take their homework responsibilities seriously.

4. If you do not want to give a grade on the actual assignment, then you can give a quick quiz after you and your students have discussed the homework.

5. One way to avoid homework hassles while involving parents is to allow any student who does not have the homework completed to bring in the assignment without penalty if the child has a note from home stating that the parent is aware that the assignment is not yet complete. This note should be brought in on the day the assignment is *due*—not the next day or later. This act of understanding on your part will put the responsibility for the homework on the child while treating the parent and the child with respect.

6. A note or phone call home after the second missed or late assignment will often correct the problem. If it doesn't, at least you've contacted the parents and alerted students to the seriousness of their actions. A "Parent-Teacher-Student Homework Notification Form" is provided on the next page for your use.

7. Be reasonable when the unforeseen happens. A power outage that lasts for hours is good reason for not completing an assignment; a regularly scheduled soccer game is not.

8. Be aware that many students justifiably resent teachers who allow students to turn in late homework assignments without penalty. Determine a fair policy for late work in your classroom and make parents and students aware of your policy.

9. Hold students accountable for their work in a variety of ways. The loss of a grade is not enough to deter the determined student from not doing the assignment. Contact parents, create a fair late policy, and find other ways to make your students see the importance of completing their homework promptly.

PARENT–TEACHER–STUDENT HOMEWORK
NOTIFICATION FORM

Date	Homework	Teacher	Parent

TEACHING THE PROCESS OF LONG-TERM PROJECTS

In recent years even very young children in many schools have been assigned a wide variety of long-term projects to complete outside of class. These projects in the early school years can take a wide range of forms such as history booklets, science experiments, or even more creative topics such as dramatic presentations and poetry collections.

As students grow older their assignments become more complex and time-consuming, but the frustration involved in long-term projects for students, parents, and teachers does not diminish. Often these projects involve a bewildering amount of research, extracurricular resources, organizational skills, creativity, and controversial parental involvement—all of which can overwhelm even the best students.

Few experienced teachers have been spared the misery of seeing an innovative project that seemed promising on the day that it was assigned degenerate into a muddle of poor work turned in by discouraged students who are obviously relieved to get the assignment over with at last.

Long-term projects can be successful for everyone concerned when you teach your students how to achieve each step involved in completing these projects. With careful planning and by teaching the skills necessary for success, these assignments can fulfill their promise and become the enjoyable learning experiences they were designed to be.

1. Choose a topic and a format that are intrinsically interesting and appropriate for your students.

2. If you select topics and formats that are as close to real-life situations as possible, you'll motivate your students to succeed more easily than if you assign work that has little relevance to their present or future lives.

3. Allow as many choices as you can for your students when you design the project. If students choose their own topics, they are more likely to enjoy the project and be more successful.

4. Skills as well as knowledge are necessary to complete out-of-class projects. Give your students both of these vital components.

5. It is important to teach the process of working on a long-term project if you want students to do well on it. Recall the techniques *you* used when you did well on projects and use these to assist your students.

6. Be sure to allow enough time for your students to do a good job on their projects. In the daily press of work, it's tempting to hurry students so that we can move on to the next item on the curriculum that we are supposed to cover. Be careful that your students take the time they need to do excellent work on their projects.

7. Make certain all students have equal access to the resources necessary to complete the work. Transportation to a public library or finding money to buy art supplies may be problems for some. Be sensitive to the needs of your students, and offer assistance and intervention at the onset of the assignment.

8. When you make the assignment, be sure to include flow charts, checklists, and other visual aids to make the interim steps of the assignment clear to your students. Your students not only need to see the big picture of what it is you are asking them to accomplish, but they also need to see the smaller steps they need to take in order to achieve the final result.

9. Be sure to include a final criteria list for evaluating the final project. Students should have a clear idea of exactly what they need to do in order to succeed before they begin the assignment.

10. Between the time you make the assignment and your students begin working on it, encourage them to plan what they need to do to achieve success. Have students write out a project proposal for you to read in which they describe what they want to do, what materials and outside resources they need, how they are going to accomplish each step, and any other information you think is necessary to demonstrate that they have thought through each step of the work they are about to begin. Hold conferences with your students to discuss each proposal and resolve any potential problems before they can become serious.

11. Teach your students about plagiarism each time you assign a long-term project. Even very young students should be taught the importance of crediting the source for any work that is not their own.

12. Break a large project into smaller parts with separate deadlines and grades for each part.

13. Teach your students the skills necessary to successfully complete each smaller part of the whole assignment.

14. Time-management skills are vital to the success of any project. Work with your students to show them the error of procrastination and any other bad habits they need to eliminate in order to use their time efficiently.

15. Don't hesitate to show your students the shortcuts that will make the project easier. Work done quickly and easily is much more fun than work that is a struggle to slog through. Be careful to spell out what parts of the project are okay to complete with the help of others and what parts you expect your students to complete by themselves.

16. Take your students' artistic talents into account when you assign a creative project. Many students are intimidated by projects that demand lots of drawing or other artwork. While you certainly should discourage students from cutting pictures from books or magazines, there is nothing wrong with photocopying work or generating computer graphics for most projects if credit is given for the source.

17. Computer skills are wonderful timesavers for those students who can use computers to research or finish a project. Encourage your students to use the technology that is available to them in your school or community by allowing time for this and arranging for someone to teach them the specific computer skills needed for your project if you are not able to do so yourself.

18. Include as many models of each step in the project as you can so that your students know exactly what they should do. Don't just show them the final project; show them models of the steps in the process.

19. Be very specific when you explain what your students need to do at each point of the project process. Don't assume they know what to do to achieve the results you want from them.

20. Arrange time for frequent peer reviews of the steps in the assignment. Students benefit when they share ideas with each other. Also arrange your schedule so that you are available to students who need to consult with you.

21. Have your students explain the process and comment on their progress at each step in the project. They need to assess their own progress and plan what they need to do next in order to achieve the quality of work you expect.

22. Stress the importance of 100% accuracy and excellent work in the final product. Have high standards for the assignment and help your students achieve them throughout the project process.

23. Avoid an unpleasant experience for all parties concerned in the project by grading each part of the project as the steps are completed. One final grade is not as effective or as fair as several grades for the various skills and knowledge that students learn along the way to the final product. This will also alert students and their parents to the problems that arise early in the process so that these problems can be solved before they snowball into failure.

24. Design a long-term project so that your students must complete all of the steps. Students can become so bogged down that they fall behind and never get caught up. Avoid the inevitable result of this by helping your students accomplish each part of the assignment to the best of their ability before moving on to the next part.

25. Have students assess themselves at the end of a project. Ask them to reflect on the project and the parts of the process that they did well or which were troublesome for them. This will provide meaningful closure to the entire project process.

STUDENT NOTEBOOKS: ORGANIZING FOR SUCCESS

Teaching students how to organize their paperwork is an important responsibility for all teachers. Don't assume your students know how to keep their notebooks and other papers in order. Many of them have never been taught the skills necessary to keep themselves organized.

Make teaching organizational skills and notebook-keeping part of your plan to prevent discipline problems. Not only will you teach your students important organizational skills, but you will also create competent learners. Students with good notetaking and organizational skills are much more likely to do well than those whose idea of keeping up with papers is to stuff them into their backpacks or gym bags. Another benefit of teaching notebook-keeping is that it is a constructive activity that will keep your students engaged and on-task in class.

Spend a few minutes on this topic each week and you will be more than rewarded in the improved performance of your students. The following strategies are designed to help your students become more organized.

1. Keep your requirements for a notebook logical, sensible, and simple if you want your students to remain consistently well-organized.

2. Teach your students why they need to keep their papers in order. They need to see that this is an important lifetime skill, not just another hoop they need to jump through in order to pass your class.

3. Spend time each day at the beginning of the term to make sure students are getting off to a good start with organization. Make frequent periodic checks of their notebooks to make sure your students understand that keeping them organized should be a priority.

4. Encourage your students to purchase 3-ring binders. These are durable and can be used for years, while paper binders or folders often self-destruct in a matter of weeks.

5. After your students have purchased their binders, focus on the ways you want them to keep their papers and notes orderly. The easiest way to do this is to have students file each paper they have by its date. If you do this, your students will find it easy to review for tests by checking their work against the course syllabus.

6. Your students should color-code their notebooks for quick identification. Assign each subject its own color.

7. Taping the edges of binders will often extend the life of each notebook. So will encouraging your students to value their investment in their notebooks.

8. Teach your students to be businesslike in labeling the covers of their notebooks. They should neatly label their notebooks with their names, the subjects in their notebooks, and any other appropriate information that would enable anyone who finds a lost notebook to return it promptly to its owner.

9. Discourage student doodling, stickers, or other marks on the covers of notebooks only if you feel that they seriously distract your students from the task of keeping work in an orderly fashion.

10. Your students will also benefit from a recloseable pouch in their notebooks. In this pouch they can keep pens, pencils, and flash cards. You can show them how to make these pouches for themselves from small food storage bags if they are unable to purchase them.

11. Encourage your students to use pens. It's much easier to read than pencil after a few weeks of being filed in a notebook.

12. Have your students label every page in their notebooks so that they can immediately tell what it is. This labeling should include the date, since papers should be filed by date.

13. You might want to have your students separate papers into various categories such as test papers, homework assignments, or class notes. While this is one way to keep a notebook, students who file papers by date will find it easier not only to keep up with their papers, but they are more likely to see a logical progression in the development of what they have studied.

14. Encourage your students to use different colored inks or highlighters when they study their notes. "Looking over" their notes is not an efficient method of learning the material they have so neatly organized. Taking time to mark up or even rewrite material into their own words ensures greater retention.

15. Purchase a 3-hole puncher for the papers you return to your students. Students can't file them in order unless you have provided this service for them.

16. At the end of each grading period, have your students clear out their notebooks and transfer their papers to a set of files they have set up for this at home. This will keep their notebooks in better order, while the material they will need for big tests and exams is still safely well-organized.

TEACHING STUDENTS TO MAKE GOOD DECISIONS

It's ironic. One of the most frequently voiced complaints by adolescents in their endless struggle for independence is that too often they face unnecessary restrictions imposed by the powerful adults in their world. The irony of this situation lies in the misconception that many teens have about their lack of power.

Teenagers today have to make choices that were unthinkable in earlier times. We routinely expect even the most vulnerable and ill-prepared adolescents in our society to deal with issues and problems that have a serious impact on their lives and on our own.

We don't find it unusual that students have part-time jobs, plan their own school schedules, select and purchase their own clothing, drive their own cars, fix meals for themselves and other family members, care for siblings, or get themselves up and off to school each morning. For many teens, these choices are tough, but routine. Many handle them with surprising ease. Others do not.

The gamut of decisions that today's students have to make is not only tough, but sometimes unforgiving. Adults are no longer shocked at finding exhausted students working long hours in after-school jobs, involved in violent crimes, experimenting with illegal drugs, or being sexually active.

Unfortunately for the secondary teacher, too often these choices overwhelm students who are not prepared to handle the responsibilities that go along with so many options. The impact of students who make poor decisions for themselves can be devastating on a classroom.

One of the most joyful tasks teachers can undertake, however, is to guide students as they learn to make sound decisions in our classrooms and, ultimately, in their lives. Luckily for us there are many nonthreatening opportunities for teachers to help students make good decisions in the course of a school day.

There are many advantages to giving students safe options as often as possible. Here are just four of them:

1. When we allow them opportunities to make choices and then discuss the consequences of those choices with our students, we teach them to think about the actions they take.

2. Options increase students' problem-solving abilities while reducing the need for time-consuming and unpleasant power struggles.

3. Giving students choices can allow them to share ideas while working towards a common goal—a skill they will need as good employees when they are adults.

4. Another advantage to allowing students frequent options is that it shows you value their opinions, respect their uniqueness, and have faith in their ability to succeed. All three of these will increase your chances of having a peaceful and productive classroom.

If we want our students to become more self-disciplined, then the first thing we want is for them to make an intelligent choice about their attitude. Students need to realize they have tremendous power and control over almost every respect of school life. This power and control lies in their attitude. They can choose how they do their work, regard their classmates, treat their teachers . . . in fact, they have choices over all of their school day through their attitudes. Students with a positive attitude about their school day are pleasures to teach. Students with a negative attitude create our discipline problems.

We can help students in our classes make good choices about the attitude they want to have about something if we see this action on our part in terms of small steps. Many small good choices can add up to a positive pattern. We can and should offer all of our students plenty of opportunities to make wise decisions for themselves.

You do not have to lose control of your class while you help students make good decisions. It would be unwise to abandon your classroom to the whims of your students. The best way to promote sound decision making is to give students a limited range of choices. For example, instead of saying, "Do you want homework tonight?" say, "Do you need to do exercise three or exercise four or both of them for extra practice at home tonight?"

Here are some other safe ways to begin thinking about how you can give your students options. Making choices such as these will lead students to make good decisions for themselves as they struggle towards an independent adulthood.

1. "Which of these two assignments do you need to do first?"

2. "How should the teams for this task be set up?"

3. "Which day would be better for the test on this unit?"

4. "You may be excused from the room three times this month. How can you use those passes wisely?"

5. "Do you need to do this now or can it wait a few minutes?"

6. "Do you need more practice on this or should we count the next activity for a grade?"

7. "What could be a more efficient way to arrange our supplies?"

8. "What would be a better way to express that?"

9. "We have these things to accomplish next week. Would you like to help me plan which days we will do them?"

10. "What should we do about students who choose to break this rule?"

11. "You can have either the essay format or the objective format for your test. Which one would you prefer?"

12. "In what order do you want to answer questions?"

13. "Which nights next week will be better for you to do this homework assignment?"

14. "When someone is rude, what can you choose to do instead of responding with rudeness yourself?"

15. "You have ten minutes left. Please do either Exercise A or Exercise B."

16. "There are five essay questions for you. Answer any three of them."

17. "Would you like to do your review drill orally or in writing?"

18. "If you continue to do that, what will the result be?"

19. "Since you didn't do well on that quiz, what could you do now to make sure you do better on the test?"

20. "What is one choice you can make right now that will improve your future?"

GETTING STUDENTS INVOLVED: SOME INNOVATIVE ACTIVITIES

Although we may want to teach so skillfully that we rivet our students' attention from the first day of class until the last, sometimes teachers fall back on the same old handouts and activities that have been at least moderately successful in the past. Sometimes these less-than-fresh activities result in less-than-interested students with all of their attendant discipline problems.

Skillful teaching means lessons that promote interest, discovery, creativity, involvement, and—ultimately—success. If we want to promote self-discipline through skillful teaching practices, then we need to provide our students with activities that are innovative and challenging.

Fortunately, the possibilities are endless. Here is a list of activities that should help you get unglued from those activities you may have become accustomed to using. While these get your students busy discovering information for themselves, you will be able to enjoy the benefits of the positive learning climate created by pupils who are fully engaged in their work.

- Create an advertisement for a magazine or newspaper.
- Make up test questions.
- Rename an object.
- Create a puzzle.
- Solve a puzzle.
- Create a classified advertisement.
- Rewrite a story.
- Analyze a television show.
- Create a time capsule.
- Write an autobiographical sketch.
- Translate something into English or into another language.
- Create and wear a badge or button.
- Create a scrapbook.
- Hold a banquet.
- Make a timeline.
- Write a biography.
- Create a treasure chest.
- Invent a board game.
- Make a chart.
- Make a sculpture.
- Create an anthology.
- Design a bumper sticker.
- Write a caption.
- Make a mosaic.

- Hold a treasure hunt.
- Make a collage.
- Host a talk show.
- Create a wall of fame.
- Draw a comic strip.
- Stage a mock trial.
- Write a commercial for radio or television.
- Write a memo.
- Design a computer program.
- Have a panel discussion.
- Enter a contest.
- Hold a contest.
- Publish a cookbook.
- Make a video.
- Cook foods from another culture.
- Make a brochure.
- Design costumes.
- Debate an issue.
- Produce a children's book.
- Volunteer your services.
- Be a critic.
- Teach the class for the day.
- Invent a dialogue.
- Demonstrate how to do anything.
- Draw a diagram.
- Write an exposé.
- Hold a fair.
- Invent a new school cheer.
- Entertain invited guests.
- Take a field trip.
- Write a first-hand report.
- Put on a talent show.
- Make flash cards.
- Make a flip book.
- Write a parody.
- Make a tabloid newspaper.
- Create a flow chart.
- Create a class yearbook.
- Set up your own art gallery.

- Conduct a survey.
- Create a graffiti wall.
- Create a greeting card.
- Make a flag.
- Design a postage stamp.
- Write a letter to a well-known person.
- Illustrate a book.
- Interview someone.
- Invent a better way.
- Write a letter to the editor.
- Sing a song.
- Send a message in a bottle.
- Create a class newsletter.
- Make a map.
- Stage a play or class skit.
- Write the first installment of a novel.
- Observe an unusual holiday.
- Paint a picture.
- Stage an Academic Olympics.
- Write to a pen pal.
- Make a sketch book.
- Take photographs.
- Design a postcard and send it.
- Plan a journey.
- Hold a press conference.
- Hold a recognition ceremony.
- Create a shadowbox.
- Make up a questionnaire.
- Produce a puppet show.
- Create a television show.
- Invent a game.
- Make a flip chart.
- Decorate a bulletin board.
- Create a radio show.
- Read a book aloud.
- Design a T-shirt.
- Design a banner.
- Reenact an event.
- Pass a note.

- Make a tape recording.
- Role-play a situation.
- Open an information booth.
- Make a public service announcement.
- Hold an auction.
- Teach someone a new skill.

HOW TO AVOID AN AWFUL DAY AT SCHOOL

Step One: Be a Good Leader

1. Establish a warm and supportive class identity where students can work together as a team.

2. Provide an organizational framework to help students stay focused. Help them set goals. Use a syllabus or daily planner. Show them how to make and use "To Do" lists. Plan lessons around learning objectives.

3. Keep your students active! Use every minute of the class.

4. Do the unexpected. Include a variety of activities that will intrigue your students.

5. Don't make success an impossible dream. Start out with familiar material, then move on to more challenging assignments. Build their confidence.

6. Mix up the type of activities you include. Individual, cooperative, and competitive work during the same class period can be effective.

7. Let students have a voice in some of the decisions in the class.

8. Reward and praise as many students as you can when things go well.

Step Two: Get Help

1. Call on the support personnel at your school: guidance counselors, social workers, administrators. Turn to other teachers and coaches for advice.

2. Call a parent while the problem is still small.

3. Arrange a time-out situation with a nearby teacher. If you see that misbehavior is beginning, send the offending student to the other class to get back on track.

4. Be a good role model. Arrange guest speakers who are also good role models for your students. A little inspiration always helps.

5. Have students help each other learn something new.

6. Arrange for older students to visit your class and give advice, counseling, and support.

Step Three: Make an Attitude Check

1. Keep in mind that in spite of your very best efforts, not every student is going to like you or enjoy your class. Do the best you can and then go on.

2. Laugh at your problems. Even the most annoying problems at school have possibilities for humor. Look for the lighter side of a problem.

3. Remind yourself that even the worst child in your class deserves the best from you.

4. Plan to ignore the small stuff. Make a list of the behaviors that you can and should ignore.

5. Focus on the positive. Being negative will not make a situation any better; it will only make you feel miserable.

6. Be sincere. Adolescents have a special "teen radar" for phonies.

7. Do not engage in a confrontation with a student. Shouting is a sure way to ruin your day.

Step Four: Be Courteous and Alert

1. Stand at your door and greet your students. This gives you a chance to check the emotional weather as they enter.

2. Be aware of the messages your body language sends. Make eye contact and smile. Don't point at a student.

3. Be friendly and firm. If you have to say "no," do it pleasantly.

4. Never lose your cool. All kinds of bad things can and will happen when you indulge yourself in a petty tantrum.

5. Allow no disrespect. Treat your students with exquisite courtesy and expect the same from them.

6. Use those teacher-eyes that grew on the back of your head during student teaching. Pay attention to what is going on in your class at all times. Alert teachers can spot and nip trouble in the bud.

"Prevention is the daughter of intelligence."

—Sir Walter Raleigh

Section 6

DEALING WITH PROBLEMS
ONCE THEY OCCUR

In This Section . . .

This section gives you the opportunity to examine the various strategies you have available once a discipline problem has occurred in your classroom.

"Dealing with Problems Once They Occur" and "What Your Options Really Are"—and their accompanying reproducibles—will help you see the variety of choices you have available to you.

Reinforcement theory and how it can be successfully used in the secondary classroom is the topic of "Putting Reinforcement Theory into Practice" and "Rewards that Can Serve as Classroom Reinforcers."

Sometimes teachers are the direct cause of discipline problems. Learn how to avoid this in "How to Avoid the Most Common Discipline Mistakes," "When *We* Are the Cause of the Problem," and "Teacher Language: When What We Say Causes Problems."

Minimize many of your problems by using the information in "The Importance of Early Intervention" and the behavior recording reproducibles that go along with it.

Learn how to cope successfully with a large-scale problem in "Handling the Difficult Class," and use the accompanying behavior contract.

One of the most widespread problems we have to face is peer conflicts. Find out some useful ways to cope with it in "Helping Your Students Resolve Their Differences."

Four of the most troublesome problems are the next topics covered. Learn how to work successfully with students who are defiant, impulsive, tardy, and truant.

Possibly the most common problem we have to face is excessive talking. "Managing Excessive Talking Successfully" explores some of the ways to get students to overcome this bad habit.

The last three topics involve student-management techniques that have to take place outside of the normal classroom setting: detentions and referrals. Both can be managed successfully with a little preparation and forethought.

"Courage and perseverance have a magical talisman,
before which difficulties disappear and obstacles vanish into air."

—John Quincy Adams

DEALING WITH PROBLEMS ONCE THEY OCCUR

Without a doubt the most stressful part of our profession is not the long faculty meetings, the hours of grading papers, or yet another revision to the curriculum. Instead the most stressful part of the day for secondary teachers involves dealing with discipline problems once they occur in our classes. Since a discipline problem can run the gamut from a missing ink pen to a student with a weapon, discipline problems play a large part in our day.

Another reason that discipline problems cause us so much distress is that each one is unique—and difficult. We constantly have to balance the needs of the individual who has misbehaved against the needs of the rest of the students in the class.

Our determination to prevent the problem from being repeated is one of our unexpected strengths in dealing with problems. Another is the ability that successful secondary teachers have to repress our own human feelings of dismay, sorrow, or anger in order to deal calmly and professionally with a student who has misbehaved. We quickly develop our creativity, knowledge of human nature, and ability to make fast decisions under pressure.

Any discipline problem presents three big issues for teachers. First of all, we need to keep the disruption to a minimum. The fewer people who are disturbed by a student's misbehavior, the better.

The next issue we cope with is how to keep students from repeating their mistakes. Most of us spend a great deal of emotional energy trying to determine what we can do to help students solve their problems once and for all.

Finally, we have to help students learn that they have choices in their actions. Students who realize this are closer to becoming self-disciplined than those students who blame their friends, their enemies, mean teachers, unkind parents, and the dog that ate their homework last night. When students learn that the choices they make have a direct connection to their success or failure in our class, then we know that this part of our job is complete.

So what is it that successful teachers do when confronted with a tough discipline problem to create a positive outcome? Successful teachers cope with discipline problems by taking a problem-solving approach. Although a successful teacher may really want to indulge in anger or revenge or sarcasm, none of these will fix the situation.

When you take a problem-solving approach to a discipline dilemma, you have a better opportunity to settle it than those teachers who don't. When you can sit down with the misbehaving student and work through the problem in a calm and logical manner, you are on your way to a positive discipline climate in your classroom every day.

Here is a quick review of a common problem-solving approach that many teachers find helpful when dealing with discipline problems.

- *Step 1:* Define the problem. Determine the causes.
- *Step 2:* Generate as many solutions as you can.
- *Step 3:* Evaluate each solution.
- *Step 4:* Choose the best solution.
- *Step 5:* Decide how you plan to implement the solution.
- *Step 6:* After you have put the solution to work, evaluate its effectiveness.

WHAT YOUR OPTIONS REALLY ARE

When a student misbehaves there are many effective actions we can take that replace the harmful and outdated punishment practices of the past. We do not have to be abusive in order to make our students aware of their mistakes and the steps they need to take to correct them.

The creative secondary teacher practices many techniques during the school term in order to help students who have trouble behaving well. Sometimes what works for one student will not be effective for another. To complicate the issue further, sometimes what is effective for one student at one point may no longer work as well soon afterwards.

The complexity of the discipline process is one of the exciting challenges of teaching. Today's teachers have a wide range of options to take when misbehavior happens in a classroom. Some of the most commonly used strategies are listed here in order to guide you to make effective choices when you have to find successful ways to manage discipline problems.

Option 1: Ignore the Misbehavior

This is an effective option if you plan it, if the misbehavior is fleeting, and if other students are not seriously affected by it. Give thought to what kinds of behavior you find tolerable, what you find disruptive, and what you anticipate the result of ignoring will be before you decide to ignore misbehavior.

Option 2: Delay Taking Action

It is appropriate to delay taking action when the action you would take will cause further disruption. As an example, if it is the rule in your class that no one has permission to chew gum and you see a student with gum, you might choose to delay speaking to that student until you can do so quietly so that other students are not disturbed by your correction.

Option 3: Use Nonverbal Actions

Nonverbal actions such as physically moving closer, making eye contact, giving hand signals, or making positive facial expressions are nonintrusive ways to deal with student misbehavior. A more complete list of some nonverbal signals used by teachers can be found in Section 9.

Option 4: Praise the Entire Class for Its Good Behavior

When students who are misbehaving hear a teacher say to the room in general, "It is encouraging to see so many of you working hard to complete this assignment. I am sure you will all be finished by the end of the period," the off-task students will usually realize there are far more students doing what they are supposed to do than not. Praising the entire group for its positive behaviors will not only encourage those who are doing well to stay on track, it will remind those who are not behaving well of what they should be doing.

Option 5: Give a Gentle Reprimand

Giving a mild verbal reprimand when a student misbehaves will usually end the trouble. When you do this you need to move closer to the student if you can and be businesslike and firm. Try to be positive instead of negative. "Open your book and begin working" will be more effective than a more negative command such as "Stop playing around this instant." Don't allow the student to argue with you or to engage you further in an attempt to seek inappropriate attention. Be firm and friendly when reprimanding students.

Option 6: Confer Briefly with Students

There are many ways to hold a conference with a student. You could schedule time outside of class hours or you could meet briefly with the student while others are engaged in an independent activity. In a brief conference you can remind students of the rule they have broken, establish a signal to remind them to stay on task, redefine acceptable limits of behavior, encourage positive actions, and discuss the consequences of student misbehavior.

Option 7: Hold a Longer Conference with Students

Schedule a longer and more formal conference with students when there are several issues to be resolved or when misbehavior is serious. An appropriate time to do this is at an after-school detention. At this type of conference the emphasis should be on determining the causes of misbehavior and deciding what needs to be done in order to remediate them.

Option 8: Have Students Sign a Behavior Contract

There are several examples of behavior contracts in Section 5 that you could use or adapt for your students. A behavior contract will encourage students to learn to control their own behavior. It is an effective discipline option because it forces the student to acknowledge the problem and the steps that he or she must take to solve it.

Option 9: Move a Student's Seat

When students misbehave several times in a class period, often where they sit in the room is one of the causes. For example, if a student with attention deficit disorder sits in the back of the room, it will be harder for that student to stay focused. Immature students who sit with friends often distract each other with horseplay and talking. These problems and others can be improved by moving pupils. If you are going to move a student, try to do so as discreetly as possible; moving several students at the same time is one way to accomplish this. Warning students at the end of class one day that they will be moved the next day also gives them time to adjust.

Option 10: If Several Students in a Class Are Disruptive, Chart the Behavior of the Entire Class

One of the quickest ways to make a class aware of its positive and negative behaviors is to post a modeling chart and graph them so that everyone can see what they are doing right or wrong. There are many different ways to do this. If you want to be as discreet as possible, use a graph to note the negative behaviors you want to eliminate or the positive ones you want to encourage. Figure 6-1 gives an example of how a modeling chart can work for positive behaviors. The number shows how many students did the behavior each day. A *reproducible* "Behavior Modeling Chart" is provided on the next page.

FIGURE 6-1 **Modeling Chart**										
Positive Behavior	M	T	W	Th	F	M	T	W	Th	F
Working when the bell to start class rings	17	23	28	29	28	29	29	29	28	29
Bringing materials to class	20	20	25	27	28	29	29	29	29	29

Option 11: Arrange for a Time-out Room with Another Teacher

Sometimes a student who may be just having a terrible day does not hesitate to take it out on classmates. Students who normally are cooperative and willing to work hard on their assignments can become disruptive and unwilling to work if they are upset by something that may not even be related to class. In many instances the best course of action is to let these normally well-behaved students cool off somewhere else. If you have a cooperative colleague nearby, arrange for a student who is experiencing trouble to stay in that class until the end of the period or until he or she feels calm enough to participate in class.

Option 12: Contact a Parent or Guardian with a Phone Call or a Note Home

Helping students learn to behave well is a task that requires teamwork among all of the people involved: student, teacher, and parents or guardians. When the adults in a student's life work together to reinforce each other's expectations and beliefs, then everyone benefits. If you are having trouble helping a student learn to control behavior, involve parents or guardians with a note or a phone call. Too often teachers hesitate to do this or wait until the behavior has become serious. Early intervention with a request for help in solving the problem so that the child will benefit is always a good idea.

Option 13: Detain Students Who Are Having Problems

Keeping students after school is a time-honored practice with many merits. When students are experiencing difficulties in class, often sitting down with a teacher and working out those problems in a relatively private atmosphere will help. If you do decide to detain a student, be careful to follow the guidelines outlined later in this section.

BEHAVIOR MODELING CHART

NUMBER OF STUDENTS WHO DO THIS

Behavior	M	T	W	Th	F	M	T	W	Th	F

Additional Notes: _____

_____

_____

_____

_____

Option 14: Arrange for a Conference with Parents

Sometimes, in spite of our best efforts, a student continues to misbehave. After we have tried several times to remediate the situation, then spending more time with a parent than is possible over the phone or in a note is called for. Meeting with parents or guardians face to face is often a very useful technique for students who persist in misbehavior. There are many suggestions for arranging a successful parent conference in Section 4.

Option 15: Refer a Student to an Administrator

When you have exhausted all other possibilities or in the face of severe misbehavior, it is time to refer a student to an administrator. Students should know that you will do this, but that you will do it only if the situation is severe enough. Be careful not to abuse this discipline option by referring students for relatively minor offenses that you can handle with an organized discipline plan.

PUTTING REINFORCEMENT THEORY INTO PRACTICE

One of the most successful tools secondary teachers have in dealing with misbehavior in the classroom is the use of positive reinforcement. For those of us who may not be clear on an exact definition of reinforcement theory, it is sufficient to recall that teachers who want to encourage students to act in a certain way should reinforce that action.

It is also necessary to recall that positive reinforcement is a far stronger motivational tool than negative reinforcement. In other words, rewards and praise are more effective than punishment in helping students learn to control themselves—a fact well-known to secondary teachers.

What reinforcement theory gives the classroom teacher is a useful way to help students see that they have choices to make in every action they take. Every choice has a consequence that can be positive or negative. Students can be encouraged to see the benefits of choices that will result in a positive consequence. By immediately reinforcing behaviors that we want students to continue, we show them the connection between their behavior and a positive consequence.

Positive reinforcement is a powerful tool because it allows us to reach students who are so used to negativity that they are no longer strongly affected by it. Positive reinforcement, on the other hand, allows us to give valuable support to the student behavior, improvement, and effort that we want to see again.

When we set a supportive tone in our relationships with students through positive reinforcement, we tend to encourage their good behavior and discourage the bad. Finally, we also benefit when we establish a positive tone for our students because this type of reinforcement will move students away from a competitive atmosphere and towards the intrinsic motivation that is so necessary for self-discipline.

The importance of the two ways of expressing positive reinforcement—giving praise and giving rewards—is undeniable. In the lists on pages 211-213 you will find some of the fine points of both types of reinforcement so that you can charge your motivational techniques and discipline practices with positive energy.

HOW YOU CAN DETERMINE IF
A DISCIPLINE ACTION IS APPROPRIATE

Use this checklist to determine if an action you are considering taking to help students improve their behavior is one that is appropriate and will produce the results you want. You should be able to answer "yes" to all of these questions.

1.____ Is the action I want to take based on sound educational practices?

2.____ Is it consistent with school policy?

3.____ Is it part of the rules I have established in my classroom?

4.____ Can my students anticipate that this will be a consequence of their actions?

5.____ Is the discipline action I plan to take part of an hierarchy of consequences?

6.____ Is the action related to the offense? (*Example:* Incomplete homework—have to stay after school to do it)

7.____ Will my students regard this as a fair action?

8.____ Is this action geared to preventing or minimizing disruptions?

9.____ Are other adults involved if the situation warrants?

10.____ Does this action help students deal with the reasons for their misbehavior?

11.____ Will this action prevent further embarrassment or damage to self image for the students involved in the misbehavior?

12.____ Will this action help students begin the process of improvement?

13.____ Will students understand that this action will provide closure to their misbehavior?

14.____ Is this part of a long-term solution to the problem?

Praising Appropriate Behavior

1. When you praise a student, be careful not to overdo it. Being gushy or overdramatic will render your words of praise ineffective because students will regard them as insincere or as flattery. Overdoing praise can embarrass some sensitive students.

2. Be sincere and straightforward in what you say. Vary the words you use so that students will know you are paying attention to them as individuals.

3. Be sure that your approval is for the actions of your students, not for the worth of the students themselves if you want to encourage good behavior.

4. Heighten your awareness of whom you praise. Make a point of saying something positive to every student every day. Many of us unconsciously tend to favor one gender over another or some students over others. Be careful to reach everyone.

5. Make your approval specific. Students who have a clear idea of what they did right can continue that behavior. Don't say, "Nice job!" Instead give specific comments that will indicate what was "nice" so that students will have a clear sense of what they need to do to continue the good behavior.

6. Be aware of the connection between your body language and the praise you give. Pay attention to students when you praise them. Let your facial expression and tone express your approval and interest as well as your words do.

7. Be sensitive to whether students would prefer public recognition or private praise. Some students, shy or simply self-conscious, would prefer not to be in the limelight for any reason. Others thrive on public recognition. Be very careful to respect their preferences if you want your encouragement to continue.

8. Use praise to encourage students who are having problems with behavior and who need just a little boost to persevere and overcome problems. Focus on what they are doing well to encourage them to continue to strive. It is important to encourage effort.

9. Praise is most effective when it is specifically individual to the student. Don't compare students with their classmates. Let them see that you appreciate their behavior for its own worth.

10. Teach your students to show appreciation for each other. Counter the flood of negative messages they receive each day by teaching them to be kinder to each other. Positive reinforcement does not always have to come from you to be effective.

11. Be careful not to unconsciously belittle students by praising them for behavior that is more suited for younger students. High school seniors, for example, should not need to be reminded to bring materials and books to class every day, while this might be a valid point to praise in much younger students.

12. Greet your students at the door with pleasant comments as often as you can.

13. Make sure students are aware of the high expectations you have for them. Students whose teachers expect a great deal from them will soon be students who are confident that they will be able to accomplish a great deal. Overpraising students for minimally acceptable behavior sends the message that you don't really expect much.

14. Send a note or phone home whenever students have reached a major goal. Parents or guardians should be part of the reinforcement whenever possible.

15. Be clear with students that you do not want them to rest on their laurels after you have praised them. In order to remain successful, the effort they put into good behavior must continue.

Rewarding Appropriate Behavior

1. If rewards are to be valued by students, they must be given for the same criteria of success that you would praise them. Although it is important to recognize effort, rewards should not be given for inappropriate reasons if they are to continue to appeal to students.

2. One of the dangers of tangible rewards is that students may become so interested in the reward itself that they lose sight of the intrinsic motivation you want them to develop. Be careful not to overstress the rewards you might offer your students.

3. Be careful to pair a reward with praise. If you don't help students make this connection, they may not fully understand that they earn rewards through their own efforts and good behavior.

4. Another point to keep in mind when giving a reward is that it must be contingent upon good behavior, not just on the personality of a student.

5. Be sure to treat rewards in the same way you do praise in that you are very prompt in giving students this vital feedback.

REWARDS THAT CAN SERVE AS CLASSROOM REINFORCERS

Rewards that you can use to reinforce positive student behavior usually fall into two categories: items that students receive and activities that students enjoy. Use this list of both types of rewards to spice up your motivational techniques.

Items That Students Receive

■ An honor such as being voted "Most Improved Student"
■ Badges or buttons
■ Certificates
■ Bookmarks
■ Extra time to complete an assignment
■ Having their photographs in the school newspaper
■ Good grades
■ Peer recognition
■ Being included in the class honor roll

- Having their names displayed on a classroom Wall of Fame
- A treat
- A thank-you note from the teacher
- Having you send a positive note home
- Having you call home with a positive message
- Stickers
- Encouraging compliments on written work
- Smiles
- Permission to not do homework
- Verbal praise

Activities That Students Enjoy

- Earning extra credit
- Completing a checklist of tasks
- Tutoring other students
- Attending a breakfast banquet
- Creating a bulletin board
- Videotaping an activity
- Completing an alternative assignment
- Doing homework for another class
- Participating in a special project
- Watching a film
- Selecting the due date for an assignment
- Getting permission to miss a test
- Being team captain
- Displaying work for others to see
- Going on a field trip
- Spending a day observing at a local business
- Solving puzzles
- Writing notes to a classmate
- Being selected as discussion moderator
- Having a free reading period
- Attending a popcorn party
- Using the library during free time
- Being elected as class representative
- Being included in a class lottery for prizes
- Holding class outside
- Being allowed extra time on the computer
- Participating in games

HOW TO AVOID THE MOST COMMON
DISCIPLINE MISTAKES

1. Never confront a student in front of an entire class. You'll create a disruption that will upset everyone who watches. The misbehaving student will tend to act even worse in an effort to avoid greater embarrassment.

2. Do not lose your temper. When you lose your temper, you place yourself on the same level as your unruly student.

3. Speak Standard English when you speak with your students about misconduct. If you want your students to take a situation seriously, set the appropriate tone with the language you use.

4. Never order an angry student to comply with your demands. You'll get nowhere.

5. Avoid telling stories about your own misspent youth in an effort to bond with students who have misbehaved. They will either tune you out or retell the story with unkind embellishments.

6. Do not punish a group for the misbehaviors of some. This does not create the kind of positive peer pressure that will cause students to behave well. Instead it will generate anger.

7. Don't let poor behavior affect a student's grade. You should assess a student's progress in learning with a grade, not by his or her misbehavior.

8. Be careful not to assign double punishment. Keeping a student after school as well as missing a class outing is an example of a double punishment. This practice is not fair to the student who misbehaved.

9. Do not be confrontational. Help your student save face in front of peers. Backing a student into an emotional corner will only hurt the student.

10. Do not touch an angry student. Your actions may be misinterpreted by the student, who may strike out at you.

11. Don't allow yourself the miserable luxury of taking out your anger at a class or a disruptive student on others.

12. Do not let the intensity of a situation strip you of your objectivity. Remain calm and keep your thoughts collected no matter how frustrated you may be with a student.

13. Don't waste time trying to prove that you are right and your students are wrong. Instead of this time-consuming impossible task, spend your energy on finding a solution to the problem you and your students are having.

14. Be careful not to create win/lose situations with your students. Consequences should not cause your students to feel they have lost yet another confrontation with authority.

15. Never hide a serious problem—such as drug abuse—in a misguided effort to help a student. Involve other concerned adults and follow your school's policy when you have to deal with this type of problem.

16. Don't take student misbehavior personally. Your students do not regard you in the same way that you regard yourself or that you regard other adults. Distance yourself emotionally from their misdeeds and remain as objective as possible.

17. Do not force a student to apologize to you or to the class. Doing so will not only humiliate your student, but is not apt to be sincere.

18. Don't threaten a student. This is unproductive and unprofessional.

19. Never hit or even threaten to hit a student.

20. Don't punish in anger. Calm down and find a solution instead.

21. Don't argue with students. This only wastes time and energy that can be put to better use. Stay focused on correcting the problems you and your students are having.

22. Don't prolong a bad situation by acting incorrectly or by refusing to act. Be prompt in dealing with misbehavior. You don't need to discuss a situation for very long to get your point across.

23. Don't reward students for improper behavior. Often this is done unconsciously by ignoring it or through body language. Rolling your eyes while others laugh at a student's incorrect answer or allowing students to make fun of each other without stopping the insults are two examples of this type of mistake.

24. Don't assign work as punishment. Sentences to write, definitions to copy, and extra homework will promote a negative attitude towards school work and learning.

25. Don't make deals with your students to convince them to behave better. Enforce your rules instead.

26. Be as consistent as you can. The consistent enforcement of class rules and expectations will prevent many problems.

27. Don't ignore a small problem that can quickly turn into a much more serious one.

28. Don't be too quick to send a student to an administrator. You'll be more effective if you handle your own problems as often as you can.

29. Don't remain angry at a student. Once the situation has been settled, the student needs some reason to put forth the effort to behave. Knowing that you will remain angry will not encourage students to try.

30. Don't forget to tell students what they need to do to improve their behavior. It's not enough just to tell them to stop. You should also tell them what they need to do to get on the path to success.

31. Don't forget to remove temptation from your students. Don't leave valuables lying around, for instance. Prevent cheating by providing scratch paper for cover sheets or moving students' desks away from the bulletin board where they could be tempted into vandalism.

32. Don't try to scare students into behaving well. It doesn't work.

33. Don't go straight to severe negative consequences without a build-up of penalties for escalating misbehavior. Follow the plan you established when you posted your class rules.

34. Make sure your rules are clearly spelled out for your students.

35. Don't label your students in a negative way. Their *behavior* may be bad, but they are not bad *people*.

WHEN *YOU* ARE THE CAUSE OF THE PROBLEM

Sometimes teachers create their own discipline problems. We cause them because we inaccurately assess our students' needs, fail to plan adequately for emergencies and daily activities, misread our students' reactions, or unknowingly commit any number of mistakes.

The good news about the mistakes we make in our classrooms is that we have control over them. We can prevent them. Discipline problems that we do *not* cause ourselves are just not as easy to manage.

In the following list of 20 common teacher-made mistakes, you will find some of the reasons why you may have experienced discipline problems. With each mistake listed here you will also find a way to avoid making it into a discipline problem.

Mistake 1

You refuse to answer or give a poor answer when students question you about why they should learn the material you want them to master.

SOLUTION: We need to be careful to provide students at the start of a unit of study with the reasons why they need to learn the material in the unit. Start each class with a review of the purpose for learning the information in the day's lesson. Also make sure students are aware of the real-life applications for the learning you require of them.

Mistake 2

You present yourself in too tentative a fashion—too easily side-tracked, too tentative, too permissive.

SOLUTION: Approach your students with sincere courtesy and confidence. Set limits and take a positive approach to your students by preparing interesting lessons and attending to the classroom-management concerns that will make your students more successful in school.

Mistake 3

You are too vague in giving directions to your students.

SOLUTION: Be specific when telling students what they need to do. Instead of saying "Don't be annoying," a better choice is to say "Please stop tapping your pencil."

Mistake 4

You are unclear in the limits you set for your students, resulting in a constant testing of the boundaries and of your patience.

SOLUTION: Be as specific as possible in setting limits when you establish your class rules and procedures. Students need to know and understand just what they should do and what will happen if they choose not to follow the directions you have for them.

Mistake 5

You present yourself as less than professional by making mistakes on handouts or on the chalkboard.

> SOLUTION: Be careful to write as correctly as possible and to have someone proof-read your work if you are not as skilled at writing as you would like to be. When you make a mistake, graciously admit it when a student calls it to your attention and immediately correct it.

Mistake 6

You use inappropriate language with your students.

> SOLUTION: Present yourself as professionally in your speech as you do in your dress. You are a role model. Be careful to avoid using profanity. Don't overuse street language or slang in an effort to be friendly.

Mistake 7

You give too many negative directions. This sets an unpleasant tone for your students.

> SOLUTION: Make an effort to replace your negatives with positives. Instead of saying "Don't play around," you will be more positive if you say "Get started on your assignment now."

Mistake 8

You try to solve discipline problems without trying to determine the underlying causes.

> SOLUTION: Spend time trying to figure out what caused the problem to begin with. If you don't determine the root of the matter, you won't be successful in preventing it from reoccurring. You may also misread the situation and make a serious mistake in trying to solve it.

Mistake 9

You overreact to a discipline problem by becoming angry and upset.

> SOLUTION: Instead of spending your energy in anger, take time to examine the problem objectively before acting. Take a problem-solving approach to really deal with it.

Mistake 10

You refuse to listen to your students when they are trying to express their feelings about a problem.

> SOLUTION: Encourage students to express themselves in an appropriate manner and give them the opportunity to do this. Not allowing discussion or an airing of feelings is a serious mistake that will only cause the problem to become more serious as students grow increasingly frustrated.

Mistake 11

You neglect to command attention. Teachers who talk even though students aren't listening are not productive.

> SOLUTION: Refuse to give directions or instruction until you have your students' attention. There are many techniques you can follow for commanding attention: setting a timer, asking a leading question, holding up something unusual, and standing in the front of the room are just a few.

Mistake 12

You create problems by having lessons that are not interesting.

> SOLUTION: Take the time to plan stimulating lessons that have lots of varied activities. Well-planned lessons that engage students in meaningful activities from the time they enter your classroom until the time they are dismissed are an excellent defense against discipline problems.

Mistake 13

You have lessons that are poorly paced. Students either have too much work to do and give up or they don't have enough work. You also make this mistake when you have lectures that are so long that you can't keep your students' attention throughout.

> SOLUTION: Think of your class time in 15-minute blocks and schedule activities that can be completed in that time (or in a longer block with a brief break or change of pace) to keep students at their peak of learning.

Mistake 14

You make mistakes in assigning punishment by doing so without proof or by blaming the wrong student.

> SOLUTION: Determine who did what before you act. Punishing unfairly will create long-lasting bad feelings among your students. This will take longer than rushing to act, but taking your time to assign blame is always a good idea.

Mistake 15

You are inconsistent in enforcing consequences. This will lead students to a steady testing of the limits of good and bad behaviors.

> SOLUTION: Establish the consequences of rule-breaking at the start of the term and then be as consistent as possible in enforcing the rules. Make sure the consequences

are ones with which you will be comfortable in enforcing all term if you want to be consistent.

Mistake 16

You assign punishment that is not appropriate for the offense.

> SOLUTION: When you establish consequences for the rules of your class, make sure they match the seriousness of the offense if you want your students to learn from their mistakes.

Mistake 17

You neglect to create class rules or to have ones that are not workable.

> SOLUTION: Before the term begins plan the rules that you would like to govern your classroom. Make sure these rules are ones with which you are comfortable and that you know you can consistently enforce.

Mistake 18

You punish students for something while overlooking another, more serious, situation. For example, you reprimand a student for leaving a bookbag in the aisle during a test, but neglect to notice that others in the room are cheating on the test.

> SOLUTION: Take care to assess a situation as completely as you can before acting. Never punish unless you are absolutely sure of what the problem is and who is to blame. Be aware that it is easy to overlook misbehavior if you are distracted.

Mistake 19

You teach lessons where students are passive learners and therefore likely to become disruptive.

> SOLUTION: Plan activities where your students are up and doing. There should be lots of movement and noise and excitement in your class.

Mistake 20

You go to school each day without the belief you must have in order to help your students succeed: that students can learn and achieve the things you want for them.

> SOLUTION: There is no substitute for high expectations. If your students are to achieve success in your class, you must first demand it from them. Expect great things from your students and then help them achieve them.

TEACHER LANGUAGE:
WHEN WHAT YOU SAY CAUSES PROBLEMS

Although each region of the country may have its own dialect, there seems to be a common language that teachers from all regions have picked up as if by osmosis from our years in school, from our education classes, and from our teaching experiences. We know we can calm students and win them over to our side of a dispute by choosing our words carefully.

We also need to be aware of the power that our words can have to upset students. In the midst of a discipline problem, we need to be careful to use language that will help our students calm down and make a choice to behave better instead of worse.

In this list you will find some comments or questions that many teachers tend to use when exasperated with their students. These comments and questions will not make any discipline situation better. Instead, they have the power to frustrate students and result in an even worse disruption.

Examine this list in view of your own experience. If you know that these are unproductive, then you can choose words that will encourage rather than discourage your students.

- When I was your age . . .
- You don't want me to call your mom, do you?
- I'll send you to the principal . . .
- Now you've done it. Boy, am I mad!
- If you don't get to work this instant, you will fail!
- Who do you think you're talking to?
- Who do you think you are?
- How many times do I have to tell you . . .
- What am I going to do with you?
- If you think that I am going to take this, you are sadly mistaken.
- Why do you even bother coming to school with such a nasty attitude?
- I don't care what your father said . . .
- What's the matter with you? You know better than that!
- Why would you do such a stupid thing?
- Do I look like an idiot?

THE IMPORTANCE OF EARLY INTERVENTION

One of the most important responsibilities that teachers have is to help students who are in trouble get out of trouble as quickly as possible. We should strive to keep the time that our students are off-task to a minimum. Our goal is to do this without disrupting the other students in the class.

How do you begin? When you see a student misbehaving, you have three choices to make about how you want to deal with that problem.

Ignore the Problem

This is an appropriate course to take if the problem is minor and fleeting. Examples of misbehaviors that you can safely ignore most of the time include:

1. daydreaming briefly during independent worktime

2. rushing late to a seat when the bell rings, especially when the offense is infrequent and the student is contrite

3. having an unhappy nonverbal reaction to an assignment

4. tipping backwards in desk, but recalling the rule about this before you need to speak

5. talking loudly, but "shussed" by other students

Briefly Delay Acting on the Problem

This is an appropriate course to take when your intervention will cause more disruption than the misbehavior itself. Examples of misbehaviors where you can usually delay intervention include:

1. interrupting a lecture with minor off-task behavior

2. being tardy to class

3. having problems settling to work quickly

4. talking briefly during an independent assignment

5. packing up to leave a minute or two early (you can plan a better class closure for the following day)

Intervene to Stop the Problem

This should be a course of action you take if the problem is interfering with the learning of the student who is off-task or the learning of the other students in the room.

If you do choose to intervene, there are many reasons to do so promptly when you see that a student is misbehaving. Here is a list of some of the good reasons that should help you decide to intervene to stop disruptive behavior as quickly as you can.

YOU AVOID PROBLEMS THAT CAN BECOME MORE SERIOUS. An example of this type of problem is two students who begin with mild horseplay, then become angry, and finally engage in a fistfight.

YOU CONTAIN PROBLEMS TO ONE OR TWO STUDENTS. If students observe a classmate being reprimanded for a certain misbehavior, then they will be less likely to engage in that misbehavior. Misbehavior that is dealt with by early intervention rarely spreads to other students.

YOU SHOW YOUR STUDENTS THAT YOU ARE IN CONTROL. *You* are the classroom leader, not the unruly students in the room. This show of leadership and confidence will stop many problems from beginning.

YOU MAINTAIN A WELL-FUNCTIONING CLASSROOM. Your students will stay focused on learning rather than on disruptive behavior.

YOU EXPERIENCE LESS STRESS AND MORE ENJOYMENT. Your teaching responsibilities will be more pleasant as you cope successfully with each one.

10 Tips for Improving Interventions

There are many ways that you can intervene effectively to stop your students from misbehaving. Your intervention strategies will be more effective if you are positive with your students so that they know what they should be doing to succeed rather than having a teacher dwell on the negative aspects of their behavior.

If you are brief and positive in your intervention, you will accomplish more than if you engage the student in a lengthy discussion. If you follow your intervention with a brief reminder of the rule that your student should be following, then you are also putting that student in control of his or her own behavior.

The following strategies can improve the effectiveness of your interventions. Experiment with the ones you feel most comfortable with and continue to use the ones that you find valuable.

1. Use nonverbal language to get your point across. Move closer to a student. Make eye contact. Use these and other nonthreatening examples of body language to stop misbehavior.

2. Move to the student and quietly remind him or her of the rule that is being broken. Ask why the rule should be followed. How will following the rule benefit other students?

3. Make sure students know the next step in the sequence of their lesson so that they know what they should do next. This will give them a reason to work efficiently.

4. Change the seating arrangement if students are distracted from their work. It is best to do this at the start of class after giving the student who is being moved a warning the day before—if you want to avoid having a student angry at being moved.

5. Move to a student who is off-task and quietly ask if you can help. This will alert students to the fact that you are aware they are off-task.

6. Send students who may need a break on a errand or to get a drink of water.

7. Set a time limit for students who are distracted from finishing a task. Begin timing them.

8. Meet your students at the door and pay attention to their body language and other clues to their emotional states. If you can see at the start of class that a student is upset, then you should take action to prevent the problem from being more serious.

9. Call home to discuss a problem with the student's parents or guardians. Often the important adults in a student's life complain that teachers allow a problem to become serious before they call for help. Calling when you first notice that a student is beginning to have persistent problems is a sound management technique to follow.

10. Speak frankly with a student who is experiencing problems in your class. Offer help and encouragement. Stress that you will help, but that the student needs to take responsibility for behaving well.

ANECDOTAL BEHAVIOR RECORDS

Here you will find two forms that are designed to help you make better decisions about how you deal with behavior problems in your class.

Use the "Behavior Record Form" on the next page to keep a running account of the disruptive behaviors of each of your students. Photocopy it and slip a copy into the folder where you store the other important information about each student. When you need to make a referral for persistent misbehavior, you will have the needed information to make a fair evaluation of the student. You can also refer to it when you contact parents or guardians so that you can be specific about the problems their child is experiencing.

The second form, "Behavior Analysis Log" (page 225), will help you focus on the way you handle each behavior problem in class. Use it to record the important information about an incident and the steps taken to improve the situation.

50 WAYS TO HANDLE THE DIFFICULT CLASS

We all have one at some point in our careers—the class that is so difficult to manage that we daydream about a change in our profession on the way home from school. A difficult class turns our determination to help students succeed into a desire to just make it through one more class period. Fortunately for you and for your difficult students, there are many ways to turn a class like this into a successful one.

What causes a class to be difficult? There can be many reasons. Sometimes the class is too large for the room so that the seating arrangement can't be modified adequately. Sometimes there is an unpleasant chemistry among students and between students and teacher. There can be an unequal distribution in the ability levels of students so that the more capable ones are frustrated by the less motivated or less successful ones.

Many students in a difficult class lack goals for their lives or even for the successful completion of the course. Sometimes the time of day can have a negative effect on students. Many teachers will agree that classes that meet after lunch tend to be harder to settle than morning classes.

Peer conflicts can also disrupt a class. Students who are busy disagreeing with each other have little time for the successful completion of their class work. Sometimes, too, a class is given a negative label by teachers in earlier grades and that label becomes a harmful self-fulfilling prophecy.

Perhaps the most serious reason that classes are difficult lies in the way the students in the class regard themselves and their ability to succeed academically. Students who do not believe they will succeed have no reason to try. Successful teachers with difficult classes have found that they can turn the negative energy in the room into a positive force through patience and by persistently communicating their faith in their students' ability to succeed.

There are many ways to begin to overcome the problems posed by a difficult class. The specific strategies you choose will depend on your particular students and their needs. The ideas listed here are strategies that can start you on your way to turning a difficult class into a successful one.

BEHAVIOR RECORD FOR _____

Date	Time	Place	Disruption	Teacher Response

BEHAVIOR ANALYSIS LOG

Student's name: _____

Date of the incident: _____

Description of the incident:

_____

_____

_____

_____

What actions did I take?

_____

_____

_____

_____

What was happening just before the disruption?

_____

_____

_____

_____

What could I have done to prevent the incident?

_____

_____

_____

_____

What steps should I take in the future to make sure this does not happen again?

_____

_____

_____

_____

1. Attack the problem on as many fronts as possible as quickly as you can in order to gain control of the situation. Examine such factors as: the physical arrangement of the room, your relationship with troublemakers, the type of lessons you deliver, how your students handle transition times, and how consistently you enforce the rules and consequences you have established for your students.

2. Get help from a variety of sources. Even the smallest schools have many different resources that can help you cope with a difficult class. Some of these include: other teachers, coaches, counselors, administrators, non-faculty staff members, parents or guardians, siblings, other students, and community members.

3. Keep the expectations for all of your classes high. Lowering your expectations is the easiest and most painful mistake to make.

4. Establish from the first class meeting onwards that you are the person who controls the class. Demonstrate that you will regulate the behavior climate in your classroom for the benefit of everyone with the help of all students.

5. Work on the noise level every day until your students are willing to modulate their voices for the good of everyone. Teach students the volume that is acceptable and productive and the noise levels that are not. Establish signals for helping them stay quietly on track.

6. If your class is boisterous, regulate the kinds of activities that you give them. These students need lots of quiet, well-structured work, but this should be interspersed with activities that allow them to move about and interact with each other in positive ways.

7. Make sure your students know positive things about each other. It's easier to build trust and respect when students know their classmates.

8. Call parents or guardians as soon as you can when a problem arises. At best they will work with you in a teamwork approach to help their child. At worst you will have notified them of the problem. You have also protected yourself from an administrative reprimand if the problem escalates.

9. Teach ethical behavior. Don't preach, but encourage your students to make good choices in deciding how to live their lives.

10. Be prepared. Staying organized is an essential element in dealing with a class of students who can be unruly.

11. You must be able to call everyone by name if you want to gain control of the class early in the term.

12. Help your students get organized and stay that way. Make sure everyone has the materials they need to succeed in your class. Show them how to work quickly and efficiently.

13. If you are having trouble motivating your difficult class, consider giving them their work in the form of contracts where they are allowed a certain measure of freedom in how they accomplish their assignments. Students will regard a work contract as evidence of your trust in their maturity. A sample of an assignment contract is included on the next two pages for you to try.

ASSIGNMENT CONTRACT

I, _____, agree to complete all assignments necessary to earn a grade of _____ for this unit of study.

I realize all of the assignments must be completed to the degree of proficiency required, checked daily and that all assignments must be turned in by the date indicated for the grade that I choose.

My goal is to earn a grade of _____ on this unit of study.

Work required for an "A":

1. Any ten of these exercises by _____:

    1. _____
    2. _____
    3. _____
    4. _____
    5. _____
    6. _____
    7. _____
    8. _____
    9. _____
    10. _____
    11. _____
    12. _____

2. Any three of these by _____:

    1. _____
    2. _____
    3. _____
    4. _____
    5. _____

3. Successful notes on Chapter _____ by _____.

4. Quiz on _____ with a score of _____% or higher on _____ .

   Quiz on _____ with a score of _____% or higher on _____ .

5. Final test with a score of _____% or higher on _____ .

6. Two projects from this list:

   1. _____

   2. _____

   3. _____

   4. _____

   5. _____

   6. _____

   7. _____

   8. _____

   9. _____

   10. _____

Work required for a "B":

1. Any eight exercises

2. Any two choices

3. Successful notes on the chapter

4. Both quizzes passed with a score of _____% or higher

5. Final test with a score of _____% or higher

6. One project from the list

Student Signature _____

Witness _____

Date _____

14. Smile at your class. Share a good laugh together. If you were videotaped while teaching them, would your body language reveal your positive feelings or would it express your distrust and other negative emotions?

15. Be friendly, but firm. You are the adult in the room who is responsible for setting the successful tone that is appropriate to encourage your students.

16. Never lose your cool. Even in the face of serious student rudeness, never even consider raising your voice in anger. You won't make your point. Even if you succeed in cowering your students temporarily, your victory will be short-lived.

17. Don't allow any free time where your students just sit around waiting for class to end. Keep them productively engaged every moment of class.

18. Be unpredictable. Sometimes students misbehave in order to entertain themselves. Provide a safety net of routines and procedures, but spice up your lessons so that students will be interested in doing their work.

19. Play lots of games with your difficult students. Because they enjoy the variety and activity of games, these are successful learning tools. Be sure to establish and enforce rules of fair play in order to avoid trouble that might mar an otherwise productive experience.

20. Offer incentives other than grades. Some students who have never made a good grade are not really interested in them. Keep the rewards small, frequent, desirable, and tangible.

21. Plan activities around the short attention spans of many of your students. Be sure these activities include plenty of opportunities for practice and review.

22. Teach students how to be respectful to you, their classmates, and to themselves. Stress the importance of a pleasant tone of voice and a tolerance for others as ways to show respect.

23. Provide relevant work for your students. If adolescents can see a need for doing an assignment, they will engage themselves in it quickly.

24. Praise good behavior as often as you can. Difficult students need to know when they do well. If you praise an entire class for good behavior, that will help create a positive class image.

25. Make sure the work you assign is appropriate for the ability level of your students. No one wants to do work that is too hard or too easy.

26. Consider alternative methods of assessment for a difficult class. Portfolios and projects are among the many types of evaluation that will help build confidence. Also give frequent short quizzes and tests.

27. Celebrate your little triumphs. Focus on the positive changes in your students.

28. Make a list of the troublemakers in your class. Chances are, you won't have more than five. When you stop to consider the situation, you don't have a difficult class. You have a class with a few difficult students in it.

29. Use nonprint media to grab and sustain attention. Art, music, cartoons, and films are all things that will help you manage difficult students more easily.

30. Make sure your students can read well. School becomes more manageable for those students who are skillful readers. Teach, reteach, and reinforce reading skills no matter what your subject matter.

31. Create a persona for your class where they see themselves as helpful members of a team. Teach them what synergy (the whole is greater than its parts) is and show them the ways they can create this for themselves.

32. Arrange a time-out room with another teacher. Gently remove the offending student to that other teacher's classroom when the misbehavior becomes intolerable.

33. Stop frequently to review and to assess progress. Make sure everyone knows what to do.

34. Enable students to become competent. Work to this goal and you will see a change in their behavior if they have been unsuccessful in the past.

35. Stay on your feet and monitor everyone. Students who know that you are vigilant in watching over them will behave better than those students whose teacher is busy with paperwork.

36. Make sure you go over the rules and procedures of your class as often as you need to in order to have everyone understand them.

37. Model courtesy and the other qualities you want from your students.

38. Be straightforward with difficult students. This does not mean you have to be unkind, but tell them as specifically as possible what you want them to do and what they should not do.

39. Acknowledge the right of individuals in your class. Showing students that you are fair in enforcing rules is a good way to begin.

40. Have your students set goals for themselves at the start of the term and work towards those goals from then on. This will help them direct their learning and will give them the reason to keep trying when things become difficult for them.

41. Create a businesslike atmosphere in your class. Get off to a good start and make it evident to everyone that learning is the priority in your room.

42. Plan how to manage for the periods in your class when students are likely to be disruptive. Three of these are usually the beginning of class, transitions between activities, and the end of class.

43. Turn the ringleaders into your allies and the rest of the class will usually follow along. Create a sincere relationship with every student in the class so that they all feel valued. This is especially important for the class leaders who can influence other students in a positive way.

44. Don't threaten. Students should be aware that you mean what you say, but they should not be frightened into compliance.

45. Teach students to use a pleasant tone of voice when speaking with each other and with you. This will help reduce the number of angry outbursts you will have to mediate.

46. Get them involved in helping each other. Students who share their expertise with a classmate in a productive way will not disrupt while they are engaged in this activity.

47. Have your difficult students be the ones who run your errands and manage the daily business of the classroom. Giving troublemakers a sense of responsibility and of your trust will often encourage them to behave better.

48. Give difficult students who are seeking attention an opportunity to earn it for positive rather than negative reasons.

49. Be clear with your students that you expect them to do their work and that you will help them learn to do it well. Make this a priority in your classroom so that they understand there is no time to disrupt because they have bigger and better things to do.

50. Don't give up. Try to reach out in as many ways as you can. A difficult class calls for a creative and fearless teacher.

HELPING YOUR STUDENTS RESOLVE THEIR DIFFERENCES

As secondary-level educators we spend a significant portion of each school day involved in activities that seem to have little direct bearing on the subjects we are certified to teach. As irrelevant as they may seem, however, some of these activities can have a significant impact on our classes.

One of these important activities is how we work to help our students solve the inevitable conflicts that arise among them. Students who are in conflict with their peers will create an unpleasant discipline climate for everyone in the room. It is often up to the classroom teacher to mediate student conflicts so that the learning climate remains productive and positive for everyone.

There are many ways you can help students who are in conflict with each other. Some steps you can take are listed here. Use them to support the efforts that you and your students make in learning to work peacefully and successfully together.

Preventative Measures

1. Pay attention to the interactions of your students. When you see that relations are about to sour among a group of students, a quiet word or two from you will often put things right.

2. Teach your students that they have control over their moods. They can change an unpleasant attitude. They do not have to act out a negative feeling.

3. Make sure you fully understand your school's policy on student conflict and the teacher's role in mediation. You will be more comfortable in the role of conflict mediator if you understand what your supervisors expect you to do.

4. Make your stand of zero tolerance for threats, bullying, and intimidation well known.

5. It is better for you to teach your students how to settle their own differences rather than have you or other adults settle them.

6. Be careful about the activities in your classroom that set up a fierce competition that can go too far and turn into conflict.

Dealing with Peer Conflict

1. If you see that trouble is about to escalate, help students talk things over in a calm manner. Arrange for them to do this. Be the mediator if necessary.

2. If a conflict seems to be more involved than you feel comfortable handling, involve other adults in the mediation process. A good place to begin to seek help is the guidance department. Ask a counselor to help students who can't work out their differences.

3. When you work with students who are in conflict, it is essential for your own peace of mind and for the mediation process that you remain calm. Model the reasonable and open-minded attitude that you want your students to have.

4. Work to tone down the hurt feelings and anger in a conflict. Be careful not to take sides while you are doing this. Help students try to come together on issues.

5. When you work with students on ways to solve problems, lead them to understand that they should look for a fair solution. This does not mean they will always be right.

6. Use the active thinking skills that you teach your students to use in solving any problem to solve their own conflicts. Here is a 6-step approach students might use:

   ■ Define the problem from all points of view.

   ■ Generate as many solutions in a brainstorming session as possible.

   ■ After the brainstorming, study and evaluate the solutions generated.

   ■ Decide upon the best solution as a good course of action to follow.

   ■ After deciding what to do, decide how to implement the solution.

   ■ Finally, after trying the solution for a few days, meet again to assess the situation and evaluate how well the differences are being worked out.

WHAT TO DO WHEN STUDENTS ARE DEFIANT

The discipline problem secondary teachers dread most is students who lose control and become defiant—or even violent. These angry students can be loud, abusive, and confrontational or they may resort to muttering, showing disrespect, and refusing to work.

In some ways the more aggressive and confrontational student is easier to deal with because the intensity of the outburst demands immediate action. Because they often pose a danger to others with threats of violence, teachers don't ignore them. They significantly disrupt a class, but if handled quickly and well, the incident is over. Teachers of these students are also quick to involve parents or guardians, counselors, security personnel, and administrators—all adults who can help.

The less-violent confrontational student poses another type of problem for many secondary teachers. It's not easy to correct students who may only be mumbling under their breath. Attempts to correct this behavior can result in vehement denials and accusations that the teacher is picking on the student. Because of the nature of this problem, it is difficult to deal with and therefore is more common in secondary classrooms where many defiant students have had years of practice at being successfully disrespectful.

Defiant students of either type have a serious impact on the positive discipline climate we want to promote in our classrooms. Not only do they cause trouble for themselves, but they can perplex even the most caring teacher. The worst damage they do, however, is to the other students who watch the out-of-control behavior of their defiant classmates and wait to see what steps the teacher will take to deal with it.

To hone your classroom skills in dealing with defiant students, there are many things you can do to prepare yourself to successfully manage these students before they lose control and then to help them once an outburst has occurred. Use the following strategies to prevent defiant students from taking control of your class.

Strategy 1: Anticipate and Prevent as Many Problems as You Can

Many problems with confrontational students can be prevented or made less severe with early action. Monitor the emotional weather of your classroom as students enter the room and continue to do so throughout class. If you see that a student is frustrated or upset, offer help and support as quickly as you can. Too often we are so intent on the lesson we have to deliver that we ignore the unmistakable signs of stress in our students until it is too late. Some of these signs of trouble we need to attend to are:

1. refusing to work,
2. inattention,
3. muttering under the breath,
4. angry or exaggerated movements of the hands,
5. loud voice,
6. facial expressions that signal distress,
7. imminent tears,
8. work done poorly or not at all,
9. note passing, and
10. slamming books or materials.

Strategy 2: Plan What You Will Do if an Outburst Occurs

Even though it is unpleasant to contemplate, if you are a secondary teacher, you will have to deal with defiant students from time to time. Prepare yourself by planning what steps you will take to keep the disruption minimal. Some questions you should consider before a disruption occurs are:

1. How can I tell when I should act?
2. Where will I send an angry student to insure the safety of others?
3. What signs should I pay attention to that will let me know a problem is brewing?
4. Which of my students is already heading in this direction?
5. What can I do in class tomorrow that will ease some of the stress that my defiant students may be feeling?

Strategy 3: Stay Calm When a Student Is Defiant

Although you should take an angry outburst or other sign of defiance personally because the anger is directed at you, you should not lose control of your own emotions and of the classroom situation. Even though the outburst may have been provoked by something you did or that happened in class, it is up to you to assume control. Keep your voice low. Do not give into the temptation to threaten the student. Wait a moment or two to gather your thoughts. Often this will allow the student to calm down.

Strategy 4: Act Decisively

You must act calmly and quickly because the student has forced a showdown with you in front of the rest of the class. Those other students are now involved in that they are waiting to see what steps you will take to deal with the student and to protect them. Often defiant students will go to great lengths to engage in a power struggle. Be aware of this and keep it from happening. It will only make the situation worse. You should show you are serious, concerned, and in control.

Strategy 5: Remove the Defiant Student from the Room

As quietly and as undramatically as possible remove the defiant student from the room. This will not only keep the disruption under control, but will also save more embarrassment for the student who has misbehaved. You cannot begin to help a defiant student in front of an audience.

Strategy 6: Take a Problem-solving Approach, Not a Punitive One

When you begin to work with defiant students, acknowledge their feelings of anger and frustration as quickly as you can. While these are not an excuse for bad behavior, the student needs for you to pay attention to the reasons why the outburst happened. Students appreciate it, as we all do, when someone important to them takes them seriously, especially after they have been defiant. After this important first step, deal with the outburst and its causes.

Strategy 7: Work on Your Relationship with Defiant Students

It is up to you as the adult in the classroom to make sure you have a positive relationship with all of the students in your class, even those who are confrontational or defiant. The best discipline tool any secondary teacher can have is a positive relationship with students. All students need to be treated fairly. The same standards should apply to every student in your class—regardless of whether a student is frustrated or not.

10 WAYS TO DEAL WITH DEFIANT STUDENTS

While there are many techniques to dealing with the aftermath of an outburst in your classroom, the ones listed here are some that have been successful for many teachers in recent years. Experiment to see which ones will help you and your defiant students learn to work more productively together.

1. Send a defiant student to time-out. This can be an informal arrangement you have with another teacher nearby so that students can calm down and prevent further trouble.

2. Establish a signal with a defiant student to let you know that frustration is building. Once a student has said or shown the signal to you, take action to help that student.

3. Move a student's seat to another part of the room where it is easier for you to monitor and where the student's friends can't encourage trouble. Sometimes just the act of moving a student will end the frustration he or she may feel.

4. Make sure the work is appropriate to the ability level of students, who can be frustrated if it is too difficult or if it does not provide an interesting challenge. Having appropriate and meaningful work with a clear purpose will eliminate many problems.

5. If you have a student who persistently speaks to you and to others in a rude or inappropriate tone, tape-record that student so that he or she can hear how it sounds. A tape will also allow you to focus on what actions you do that may trigger the rudeness.

6. Hold a private conference with the student, preferably after school. At this conference work together to solve the problems that cause the defiant attitude and frustrations.

7. One of the outcomes of the private conference you hold with the students could be a behavior contract. This is an excellent technique to use with defiant students because behavior boundaries are clearly defined and their responsibilities are clear.

8. Another outcome of a student conference that could be a solution to the problem of defiance is to have the student write out a report of the incident from his or her point of view. This could even be in the form of a letter to parents or guardians. Having a student write a report is effective because it forces students to consider their actions and the effects of those actions on others and on their own futures.

9. If a problem is severe or persistent, you must involve the student's parents or guardians in the attempts to solve it. As with all conferences, the focus should not be to assign blame or punishment, but to resolve the conflicts that are causing the student to be confrontational.

10. If a confrontation is violent, severe, or if all other attempts to resolve a situation have not worked, then you should turn the matter over to an administrator for action. Be sure you can document all of the steps you took to resolve the situation before making a referral.

HELPING STUDENTS DEAL WITH IMPULSIVITY

Students with this learning problem are easy to recognize in any classroom. They are usually the ones soaking up all of the negative attention.

Impulsive students often act before thinking. They spend too much time in an unproductive attempt to get organized at the beginning of an assignment. The floor around their desks is littered with piles of balled-up paper that has been hastily scribbled on and discarded.

These students disturb others by calling out answers without regard to whether they are right or wrong. These are the students who seem to live frantic lives in a state of near crisis. Every request to leave the room is an emergency. Every bad grade is a sure sign they are going to fail the entire course. Undone homework—a nightly problem—is someone else's fault. They are fidgety and forgetful and their own worst enemies.

Impulsive students require the utmost in patient firmness from every teacher. With the help of teachers and other adults, these students can be transformed into well-behaved and successful students.

If you have one of these students, consider trying some of the strategies suggested here to help them get themselves under control and working productively.

1. Replace their negative behaviors with more appropriate ones. Teach them the correct behavior to follow in your class for the various times when impulsive students seem to have the most trouble staying focused in your room.

2. Be very specific about what is and what is not acceptable behavior. Begin consistent reinforcement as soon as you do this. If you are not consistent, you will only confuse them.

3. Simplify their lives by teaching them how to manage their materials. Teach these students how to get organized and then check their materials every day. Discourage them from the distractions that seem to go with these students—electronic toys and other gadgets, cosmetics, dried-up pens, headsets, tapes, or countless locker combinations on tiny scraps of paper. It will take weeks of checking before the older, disorganized habits are replaced by better ones, but be persistent.

4. Talk to parents or guardians about what they can do to help at home. Sometimes something as simple as showing adults a record of homework assignments each night or teaching their children to put their packed bookbags by the door will help reinforce the organizational skills that you want to promote.

5. Insist that they use a daily planner. Hold impulsive students accountable for keeping track of their work. Keep your standards high.

6. Reward and encourage improvement. Mark progress as it happens so that these students will have a reason to keep trying. These are the students in your class who become easily discouraged. Keep them upbeat and positive in their beliefs that they can overcome their bad habits.

7. Don't accept excuses that are clearly inappropriate. Impulsive students need to be sure of the boundaries of acceptable and unacceptable behavior. Be concrete and specific.

8. Make sure they see their assignments as small steps that lead to something bigger and that these small steps need to be accomplished one at a time.

9. Use plenty of positive reinforcement to build confidence and to reassure impulsive students that they are on the right track. They need lots of positive attention to replace the negative attention they have been used to receiving.

10. Impulsive students also usually respond well to a behavior contract because it is very specific about what they will be expected to do.

11. Teach impulsive students to self-evaluate themselves. They are usually so busily engaged in negative behavior that they haven't had a chance to learn this very natural act. Show them how. Use the Self-Evaluation Form that follows or design one that will better suit your impulsive students.

SELF-EVALUATION FORM

Name _____ Date _____

Rate your behavior today on a scale of 1 to 3:

A "1" means you were not as successful as you would like.

A "2" means you are getting better at the behavior.

A "3" means you were successful at that behavior.

1. _____ I followed written and oral directions.

2. _____ I did not make careless mistakes.

3. _____ I turned in all work on time.

4. _____ I worked independently.

5. _____ I paid attention to the lesson.

Circle the number that best reflects the percentage of class time you were productive today:

10%   20%   30%   40%   50%   60%   70%   75%   80%   85%   90%   95%   100%

What did you do in class today that helped your self-control?

_____

_____

_____

_____

_____

_____

_____

_____

_____

DEALING WITH THE TARDY STUDENT

For many teachers one of the most persistent discipline problems does not concern violent misbehavior or loud challenges of authority; instead, it involves students who are tardy to class. Although this problem is not as immediately urgent as an out-of-control student who is in the midst of a tantrum, a tardy student can disrupt a class almost as effectively. Alert teachers must be aware of the negative influence inherent in tardy students and work to minimize the troublesome potential in their disruptive behavior.

Strategies for coping with tardy students must include ways to prevent the problem from becoming a serious one in your class, some general guidelines for dealing with tardy students, and techniques for coping with the two types of tardy students. The following techniques can improve the effectiveness of how you treat this problem in your class.

Prevention Strategies

1. The first five class meetings are crucial in establishing the expectations you have concerning the prompt arrival of all students. Make tardiness control a strong priority on those five days and you will avoid many problems later in the term.

2. The most obvious way to promote promptness is to be on time yourself. Your students will follow your example.

3. You must make it important for your students to be on time to your class. Begin class the second the bell rings with an interesting and worthwhile assignment. When students rush to be on time, you know the tardiness problem is on its way to being solved.

4. Reward those students who are in their seats and already working when the bell rings to begin class. You don't have to do this every day. You could reward students early in the term until they are in the habit of being on time to class and less frequently later. Some quick little rewards you could offer are stickers, bonus points on a test or quiz, a treat, a grade on their warm-up assignments, reduced homework, or a chance to enter a class lottery for rewards.

5. Don't allow your students to lounge around the doorway between classes. They often slow down the arrival of other students and disrupt the smooth start of class with horseplay.

6. Post your procedures and go over them as often as necessary in order to educate your students about the importance of being on time to class and the consequences of being late to class.

General Guidelines

1. What do you mean by tardiness? Define it for your students. Most educators will agree that a student who is inside the room but not in a seat is not tardy; others are sticklers who insist that a student who is not sitting down is tardy. They have trouble justifying this interpretation to students and their parents. Be reasonable.

2. Encourage your students to help each other be on time to class. For example, if students are late because they have forgotten their books, other students could remind

them earlier in the day to bring their books to class. When you encourage your students to work together as a team, many of the problems you have with tardy students will disappear.

3. Praise your classes as often as you can for their promptness. This is a pleasant way to reinforce their good behavior.

4. Praise those individuals who overcome their tardiness problems. Express your appreciation for their maturing behavior.

5. Whenever you discuss the problems of tardiness with students, put the responsibility for their behavior where it belongs. Ask your tardy students what steps they intend to take to eliminate the problem. Offer support and encouragement, but don't accept the blame for their errors.

6. You must ask students why they are late. Do this privately later in the class period to minimize disruptions. When tardy students arrive in class, look at them and acknowledge their presence, but do not make all of the other students stop to watch as you interrogate the offending student.

7. Don't accept shabby excuses. Set your established procedures into motion if you hear excuses that are not legitimate.

8. Don't hesitate to ask parents or guardians for help with tardy students. These caring adults can often offer insights as well as some solutions to the problem.

9. Never embarrass your students with sarcastic remarks such as, "We're glad you could finally make it!" or "It's about time you got here!" These will not earn you respect nor will they solve the problem.

Specific Types of Tardiness

Tardy students usually fall into two categories: the occasionally late student and the student who is habitually tardy. Both can be remedied.

1. For the occasionally late student, allow one tardy to class per semester. Anyone could have a legitimate reason for being late to class one time. Forgiveness the first time shows a humanity and understanding that your students will appreciate and respect.

2. After students have used their allotment of one late arrival without penalty, you should then regard them as habitually tardy students. Enact a system of increasingly punitive steps aimed at eliminating the problem. You'll need to devise a step procedure with which you are comfortable. Here's a suggested one:

   First tardy: Warning

   Second tardy: 10-minute detention and phone call home

   Third tardy: 15-minute detention and phone call home

   Fourth tardy: 30-minute detention and phone call home

3. You and your habitually tardy students need to work together to understand the underlying reasons for their behavior. After you have done this, continue to hold them accountable for their actions.

REACHING THE TRUANT STUDENT

A child's attendance record is one of the most reliable indicators we have of the social and financial pressures that take a toll on stressed families. When a family is in turmoil, the children have difficulty attending school regularly.

Of course, family problems are not the only reason that a child is chronically absent from school. Illness is a frequent cause, especially during the times of the year when respiratory illnesses seem to affect every student in our classes.

There are many other reasons for a student to miss too much school. In some families an education is not valued and children are not expected to attend with regularity. In some others, older students are needed to help at home to take care of younger ones when a parent works. Students who are also parents find it very difficult to continue their own schooling with the additional responsibilities of a baby.

Some students miss several days in a row because of a legitimate reason and become so discouraged at the amount of work they have missed that they choose to sit out the rest of the term. We also all know of students whose educational needs are just not being met in the school setting where they are assigned and who unofficially drop out by refusing to attend.

Regardless of the causes, it is important that we encourage students to attend school regularly. Indeed, attendance is one of our most important responsibilities as educators and as adults who are concerned about the welfare of the young people in our care. Here are some suggestions that can help you cope with this serious discipline problem.

1. Talk to students to find out the reasons for their absence. Unless you do this you don't know whether to offer support or to involve other staff members in an effort to help the student.

2. Contact the students' parents or guardians to make sure you are working together on the truancy problem. Some parents will request a phone call whenever their child is absent. Although this is time consuming, it is worth it if the student realizes that he or she cannot cut class without getting caught.

3. Make sure all of your students feel successful and involved in class so that they will have a reason to attend regularly.

4. Create a policy for make-up work that will be useful in helping students stay caught up when they are out. This will prevent them from being too overwhelmed when they come back after an extended absence.

5. Make sure your records are accurate. It's not easy to keep accurate attendance records, but this must be done if you want to be as fair as possible to students.

6. Encourage students and their parents to keep a calendar of the days when they are out of school. Sometimes parents don't realize just how many days their children are out of school until they see such a reminder.

7. Follow your school district's policy for attendance procedures. If you are the only teacher in the building who is not doing this, you will open yourself to accusations of unfairness.

8. Send a letter home when students have missed the third day in your class. Keep a record of the letter as documentation that you contacted parents or guardians about a problem before it becomes serious.

9. Make sure students who are not doing well in school understand their options. Some students believe they can drop out and just pick up a GED certificate. They do not realize just how lengthy and rigorous the exam for this certificate is. Some students may be interested in attending classes at night to get ahead or to catch up if your district offers them. Have counselors speak to your students who are having trouble with attendance so that they understand the options that are available to them.

10. If you have students who are in trouble at home and who are missing school because of family or social problems, seek help for them. Start with the counselors at your school to help your students find the kinds of social support that will help them be able to attend school.

MANAGING EXCESSIVE TALKING SUCCESSFULLY

Every teacher is unique. We each have our own teaching methods, classroom management style, and learning philosophy. In spite of these individual differences, however, there is one problem that we all have in common. None of us—from the most skilled 20-year veteran to the recent graduate struggling with that difficult first semester—escapes this discipline problem. We all have to find ways to successfully manage the problem of excessive talking.

While the days of silent students have passed, the noise level in a class must still be appropriate for the activity that is underway. When students are off-task, they seldom amuse themselves quietly. The noise level in an unproductive class can be deafening. The students and the teacher suffer when this happens.

Although there are dozens of approaches to take when your students talk excessively, using just a few effective strategies will help you begin to solve this problem for yourself and for your students. Examine the following approaches in view of your own experience and use the ones you find useful.

1. Be emphatic with your students when you speak with them about this problem. You should make it very clear when it is okay for them to talk and when you want them to work silently. If you are clear in communicating your expectations to your students, they will not repeatedly test the limits of your tolerance for noise.

2. Avoid the sound-wave effect of a loud class time followed by a quiet one followed by a loud one again. Be consistent in the way you enforce the rules in your class about excessive talking. Teachers who aren't consistent spend their time getting a class quiet, allowing the noise level to build to an intolerable level, and then getting the class quiet again in an endless and ineffective cycle.

3. Make your students feel they can succeed in your class. Students who feel they are part of a worthwhile experience have a reason to stay on-task and to cooperate with you. They show respect for themselves and for their classmates when they have a reason to work. Students who do not care about their work, your expectations, and their classmates have no reason to respect the class rules about talking.

4. Sometimes *you* are the problem. When your students are working quietly and productively on an assignment, don't keep talking to the class in general. When you repeatedly interrupt their work by distracting them with your own conversation, you make it harder for your students to work quietly.

5. Begin every class with an activity that will focus your students' attention on the work they will be doing. This focusing activity will help them make a transition from the casual chatting they may have done in the hall on the way to your class to the purposeful work that you want them to begin.

6. Teach your students that they must be responsible for their talking if you do not want to spend all class period "shushing" them. Use a positive peer pressure to help them monitor each other's behavior so that your own monitoring efforts will be more effective.

7. Direct their conversation if you have a group that likes to talk. Get them talking productively about the lesson. If you are successful at doing this, their need to interact with each other and your need to have them master the material will both be satisfied.

8. Spend time observing your students to figure out why they are talking excessively so that you can turn this problem into an advantage. They may be talkative because they are excited, friendly, in need of more challenging work, unsure of the limits that you've set, or dozens of other reasons.

9. If your students tend to talk when they have finished an assignment and are waiting for others to finish, sequence your instruction so that there is always an overlapping activity for your students to begin right away. This could be another in a series of assignments, a homework exercise, or even an optional assignment for enrichment.

10. Sometimes when students are very excited, allow them to spend a minute or two talking about it to clear the air so that they can focus on their work. Be clear in setting time limits when you do this.

11. Stay on your feet when your class has a problem with talking. Eye contact, proximity, and other nonverbal cues will help. Persistent and careful monitoring will encourage students to stay focused on their work rather than on conversation.

12. During a movie or oral presentation when students may talk instead of listen, prevent this by giving them an activity to do. Students who are taking notes or filling out a worksheet will not have time for chatter.

13. If the noise level is too loud, give students quiet activities that require they write or read independently. These assignments should be designed to interest them, not just keep the class busy.

14. Shifting gears from one activity to another is difficult for many students. Make transition times as efficient as possible in your class to avoid this problem.

15. If the entire class persists in having a problem with excessive talking, chart their behavior for them to see tangible evidence of it. Create a bar graph each day where you rank their success at managing their problem with talking on a scale of 1 to 10. Sometimes students are not aware of the severity of a problem until they can see it in a format such as this.

16. Move students who talk too much away from each other. Placing one of them near where you spend most of your time will help your monitoring efforts.

17. Use good-natured, but firm signals to indicate that students should stop talking. Some signals that are appropriate for secondary-level students include writing a reminder on

the chalkboard, holding up a silly sign on a poster, saying a code word that your students recognize, counting backwards from ten, flicking the lights, ringing a bell, turning music on or off, putting your finger to your lips, holding your hands over your ears, writing a time-limit countdown on the board, holding your hand up and counting by folding your fingers, standing in the front of the room obviously waiting, having them put their pens down when you call for attention, or timing an activity and obviously watching the clock.

MAKING DETENTIONS BENEFICIAL FOR YOUR STUDENTS

Although it seems at times as if violent and disruptive behavior is too often the norm in schools across our nation, there are still many measures that we can take to control student behavior in our classes. Although the best discipline plan is one that prevents problems from beginning, some situations will inevitably arise that will need to be handled privately by teachers and students. One way to do this is by detaining students after school.

Plan to make detentions—the act of keeping students after school—productive times where the purpose is to resolve problems that the detained student is having in your class. Many teachers make the mistake of using detentions only to punish students. If it is your goal to help students improve their behavior, then you should plan detention activities that will help you reach that goal and that are not merely punishment for students.

Although there are dozens of approaches to take when detaining students, the following methods and suggestions should make the process easy to manage and effective in preventing more misbehavior.

How to Issue a Detention Notice

1. Find out what your district's policy on student detentions entails. If your district encourages you to use this method of disciplining students, educate yourself about the correct procedures to follow. Be meticulous in following them.

2. Decide what to do if a student does not serve the detention. What should happen next? What should you do? Determine what the policy is on this issue before you need to implement it.

3. Many students take detentions lightly, but most parents do not. Use this to your advantage. Getting parents or guardians to cooperate with you in having a child serve a detention is a sensible course of action. Call home to let them know a detention notice has been issued to their child. Ask for their cooperation in helping the student serve it.

4. If your district allows it and it's convenient for you, consider holding morning detentions.

5. Before you write out the detention notice, try to prevent the misbehavior. Privately warn the student of the rule he or she is breaking and that a detention is a consequence for breaking that rule. Students should not be surprised when you issue a detention for a misbehavior.

6. Be very clear with your students that a parent or guardian must sign the notice and that they must return it before they can serve the detention. You should never cause a parent worry because a child was late coming home from school and the parent had not been informed of the detention.

7. Avoid writing out the notice when you are upset, angry, or in a hurry. You will appear less than professional. Use a dark pen and write neatly. Correctly spell the names of the child and of the parents and guardians. Be specific so that parents will know what went wrong and what steps you have taken to correct the problem.

8. Issue the detention quietly and privately at the end of class. Do not embarrass the student.

9. Detentions do not have to be long in order to be effective. Thirty minutes set aside to solve a problem with a student should be sufficient.

What to Do During the Detention

1. Detention time should never be play time. Plan what you want to accomplish with your detained student and work to attain that goal.

2. You will accomplish more if you detain only one student at a time.

3. During a detention you should establish a very businesslike atmosphere. Do not tolerate less than acceptable behavior.

4. During the detention hold a conference with your student. Follow these steps:

   ■ Begin by asking the student to explain his or her point of view.

   ■ Discuss the situation to clarify any misunderstandings that either of you might have.

   ■ The student should generate a list of possible solutions to the problem.

   ■ Both of you should then discuss the possible solutions and agree on a course of action.

   ■ Have the student write out a brief explanation of the problem and the solution that you both have agreed upon.

   ■ After you have read the student's report, both of you should sign the agreement as a closure to the detention.

5. Make a phone call or send a letter home to notify parents or guardians of what you and the student have agreed upon as a resolution.

Mistakes Many Teachers Make

1. Do not give a student a ride home. If a parent has signed the detention notice, then transportation is not your responsibility.

2. Do not leave a student alone in an empty school. Wait with the student until his or her ride home arrives.

3. Keep a record of the conference on your personal calendar or on the back of the detention notice.

4. When you give students detention notices, have them write a brief sentence stating that they were given the notice and then sign it. Keep this in your records.

5. Never issue a detention to an entire class or to a large group of students. You will look ridiculous and the detention will be a waste of time for all concerned.

6. If a student loses control and crumples or tears the notice, continue to act in a very calm manner. If the student does not come back for the note and apologize before the end of the school day, contact his or her parents or guardians by phone at once. You should also lengthen the time of the detention since additional misbehavior now has to be resolved.

7. Be careful to protect yourself. Do not remain in your classroom with a student after school with your door closed. Keep the door open at all times to avoid being unfairly accused of misconduct.

Other Uses for Detention Time

Students do not have to misbehave to be detained after school. There are many reasons for you to work with students outside of class. Some academic reasons for detaining students are to make up work, to tutor or be tutored, and to get extra help on study habits.

ESSAY QUESTIONS THAT WILL HELP SOLVE DISCIPLINE PROBLEMS

Sometimes you will need to talk with your students about a particular problem they are having in class. One of the best ways to get students to think about what they have done and what they need to do to correct the situation is to have them write out their thoughts in a fairly organized manner before they try to talk with you about it. Such an essay is not busy work; rather, it is a useful tool to begin a dialogue with students.

Have students write these responses at an after-school detention or during a conference. They could even write them at home and bring them to the conference or detention if it seems appropriate to you and your students. Each of these should be used as a prelude to a conference, not just as punishments in themselves.

1. What steps can I take to make sure I get to class on time?

2. How can I improve the way I tackle the homework assignments I have each night so that I can benefit from them?

3. What other choices can I make rather than continue to hit or insult my classmates?

4. What steps should I take when I am having trouble with an assignment?

5. What are the reasons why I should turn in all work on time?

6. What are my goals for this class and how can I achieve them?

7. What methods can I use to help stay focused in class?

8. What are some of the ways I can show that I respect the rights of my classmates?

9. What are some of the ways I can show that I respect myself?

10. What are some of the appropriate behaviors I have used in this class in the past?

WHEN YOU HAVE TO REFER A STUDENT TO AN ADMINISTRATOR

At some point in your career, you will probably have to refer a student to an administrator for behavior that is either severely or persistently in violation of school or classroom rules. While no teacher likes to refer a student to an administrator, there are ways to make the process easier for everyone involved.

Some of these ways involve steps to take *before* the infraction occurs and some involve actions you can take *after* the student has misbehaved.

Before the Infraction Occurs

1. Make sure you are familiar with the school rules and procedures that apply to your students. Become aware of the ways the school board and your other supervisors expect you to handle student misconduct.

2. Prevent as many misbehaviors as you can through sound educational practices and consistent enforcement of rules.

3. Handle routine misbehaviors yourself. If a phone call to parents or guardians would be effective, there is no need in most cases to involve an administrator. Establish your rules, policies, and consequences early in the term and follow through when necessary. Document the methods you use to handle these routine misbehaviors. See the Behavior Analysis Log provided earlier in this section to make this process easier for you.

4. There are usually preliminary measures you should take before you refer a student to an administrator. Talking with the student, contacting parents or guardians, and putting the student on a behavior contract are three of the most important ones.

5. Make sure you have the necessary referral forms on hand so that you don't appear foolish or disorganized if a time comes when you have to refer a student to an administrator.

6. If you are not sure whether a misbehavior should be referred to an administrator, here are guidelines that can help you decide what to do about a specific misbehavior. Some behaviors that should be referred to an administrator are:

   ■ habitual tardiness
   ■ persistent disruptions
   ■ cheating
   ■ truancy
   ■ violent behavior
   ■ threats
   ■ substance abuse
   ■ weapons
   ■ deliberate profanity
   ■ vandalism

Some behaviors that you should handle yourself before involving an administrator are:

- excessive talking
- not working
- eating gum or candy
- poor work habits
- rude comments
- inattention
- scribbling on desks

After the Infraction Has Occurred

1. Once a student has misbehaved to the point that you will refer him or her to an administrator, make sure you prevent a bad situation from becoming worse by maintaining the student's dignity and privacy in front of classmates.

2. When you talk with a student about an infraction, don't threaten or bully the student even if you are angry. Calmly state your policy and the consequences for misbehavior.

3. Calm down before you write the referral. Your language should be as professional and objective as possible. Write the referral in language that is behavior-oriented and factual. Do not state your opinion of the student's behavior or sink to name calling.

4. Call the student's parents or guardians before the end of the day to inform them of the incident and of your action in referring their child to an administrator.

5. Make sure you also tell the student when you refer him or her to an administrator. The best way to do this is privately at the end of class.

6. Once you have referred a student to the office, let go of it emotionally. By completing and turning in a referral form, you have put the matter into someone else's hands. Some administrators may take a different approach to solving the problem from yours. Don't try to second-guess administrators when they need to make decisions about the best course of action to take.

7. Go back and examine the actions that led to the final referral. Was there anything you could have done early in your relationship with this student to have prevented this misbehavior from reaching the final point?

> *"Education makes a people easy to lead, but difficult to drive;*
> *easy to govern, but impossible to enslave."*
>
> —Lord Brougham

Section 7

STRATEGIES FOR SOLVING SPECIFIC PROBLEMS

In This Section . . .

You'll find suggestions for dealing with a variety of the most common problems affecting many secondary classrooms. Here are the topics covered in this section:

Bullying

School Assemblies

Fights

Intercom Announcements

Passing Notes in Class

After-School Jobs

A Visitor in the Classroom

Video Viewing

Cheating

New Students

Trips to the Library/Media Center

Good Citizenship

Fire Drills and Bomb Threats

Overcrowded Classrooms

Substance Abuse

Students with Special Needs

Hallway Misbehavior

Requests to See the School Nurse

Vandalism

Making Up Missed Work

Holidays and Vacations

Guest Speakers

Sleeping in Class

Chronic Illness

Personal Loss

Lack of Materials
Daydreaming
Cultural Diversity
Profanity
Stealing
When You Need a Substitute
Traveling with Your Students

> *"The spirited horse, which will of itself strive to beat in the race,*
> *will run more swiftly if encouraged."*
>
> —Ovid

BULLYING

It happens in the restrooms, in the hallways, at recess, on the playground, in the locker room, in the cafeteria . . . any place in a school where adult supervision is minimal. Generations of students have suffered verbal and physical abuse at the hands of other students. Unfortunately, too, bullying only gets worse as students enter the secondary grades.

How much worse? Each month thousands of secondary students report they have been attacked by a classmate at school. Many students report they have been afraid to attend school at least once because of the threat of violence by a classmate.

Bullying is a serious and growing problem for educators. As more and more violent scenes are played out in our daily lives—reported to us through our news programs, enacted in television shows and movies, and portrayed in popular songs—we have a generation of children who are rapidly becoming less sensitive to violence than preceding ones. Where schoolyard pranks of the past may have involved ugly name-calling or insults, today's can result in a much more violent consequence—murder or suicide.

The worst aspect of the problem of bullying, however, is that many teachers admit they are slow to react when they observe a student picking on a classmate. These teachers either react unsympathetically when a complaint about a bully is made or simply turn away when they hear or see this type of abuse. As a nation we have long been indoctrinated with the idea that some bullying, at least, is permissible because it forces students to be "tough" enough to handle the real world.

The weapons that make both of these effective in humiliating students are threats and fear. The misery that bullying brings to a hapless student who may just be different from the others in the class far outweighs the sense that this is a normal part of growing up.

This policy of neglect would not be so surprising if teachers also felt safe at school, but many of us do not. Many secondary teachers can report that they have been insulted, subjected to obscene gestures, or threatened by their students.

The first thing we need to do to stop this serious threat is to make sure we understand exactly what bullying is. Bullying can take two forms: physical abuse or verbal abuse. When physical abuse is involved, teachers are more likely to react to stop it. Verbal abuse is far more widespread and tolerated by teachers. Verbal abuse includes name-calling, teasing, racist remarks, rumors, and other insults or slurs.

There are 11 steps you can take in order to deal effectively with this problem. These strategies are designed to be followed in sequence when you have to deal with an incident involving bullying in your class.

Step 1

Make sure your school's policy is clear and up-to-date on this issue. Every staff member should have a copy and students should be aware of the school's policy and the consequences involved.

Step 2

A very positive step you can take with your students is to discuss the issue and to allow them to talk about their fears and beliefs on the topic of bullying. They can work together to establish peer group support and to help each other see how wrong verbal and physical abuse are.

Step 3

Be alert for the early signs of bullying. Often teachers only see the tip of the iceberg because bullies prefer to work in unsupervised areas. If, for example, you notice that several students have targeted one of their classmates for disrespect or that a child is having trouble making adjustments to your class at the beginning of the term, be alert that more may be going on that you see. Speak privately to the offending students to make sure they know that what they are doing is in violation of the school's policy on bullying.

Step 4

Make a special effort to patrol the areas in your school where bullying is likely to take place. Involve other teachers and administrators in this endeavor if a routine duty assignment schedule is not already in place.

Step 5

Continue to listen carefully and begin to document all incidents that you observe. Report your findings to an administrator or counselor.

Step 6

Put the school procedures into action when you speak to an administrator or counselor so that no time can be wasted in waiting for a response. Waiting for a response could allow the situation to escalate to more violence.

Step 7

Meet with the victim to discuss the incident and have that student write out a report of what happened. Just being able to talk about it with a concerned adult will help many victims.

Step 8

Lend your support to the victim. If an incident of physical abuse has occurred, act at once. Make sure victims are aware that you are working on their behalf.

Step 9

Meet with the bully and have that student also talk about what happened. Be firm, but don't lecture. Have that student also put the events of the incident in writing.

Step 10

Speak to the bully and his or her parents or guardians to let them know what you have witnessed or what has been reported. They should have a clear understanding that not only is the action not acceptable, but that there is a school policy against bullying and that the incident has been reported to an administrator.

Step 11

Involve both sets of parents or guardians. Either have them come to school for separate conferences or send them copies of the written statements made by both students. Parents or guardians can be valuable resources in stopping this problem.

SCHOOL ASSEMBLIES

School assemblies can cause trouble before, during, and after the actual assembly itself. Students are often so excited before an assembly that they are unable to focus on the lessons they have to do. During an assembly students who are not carefully prepared often misbehave, causing disruptions that their teachers have to handle. If the assembly has been a lively one, then students will return to class keyed up, excited, and difficult to settle down to work again.

Assemblies do not have to create discipline problems for you and your students. You can all enjoy them. Here are some guidelines for helping you and your students enjoy both types of assemblies that are common in many secondary schools.

Formal Assemblies: Awards Ceremonies, Performances, Etc.

1. Teach your students in advance of the assembly the behaviors you want to see from them. If they know what you expect them to do, your students will be more apt to act according to your expectations. Also discuss positive and negative consequences for their behavior in the assembly.

2. If you are not given a seating chart for your students, make up one for yourself. Determining where your students will sit in an assembly will help you control their behavior. Having an assigned seat will also make students more aware of the need for them to control their own behavior.

3. If you can, seat your students in a block where you can speak to each one. Stretching an entire class across the length of a row is not as effective as putting them in a smaller grouping where you can reach each one easily.

4. Make sure you remain with your students during the assembly. Model attentive behavior yourself. Grading papers during a presentation is not only rude, but it teaches your students poor behavior.

5. Be sure to discuss with your students the difference between the behaviors with which they are familiar when attending concerts or other teen-oriented events and the behaviors you expect to see from them in an assembly.

6. Encourage your students to leave in the classroom or in their lockers their bookbags, combs, mirrors, and other items that might distract them from the performance.

7. Make sure your students know why they should be polite to performers or to fellow audience members during an assembly:
   - everyone needs to hear,
   - the audience has a right to enjoy the performance without disruptions, and
   - you expect it from them.

8. Praise those students who behave well during an assembly.

Pep Rallies

1. Change your school-day mindset when you approach a pep rally. Expect noise, movement, and lots of student excitement. Pep rallies are designed to promote school spirit and spark student interest and pride. They are neither quiet nor dignified.

2. Student excitement before and after a pep rally can have an unpleasant effect in the classroom if you are not prepared. Help your students stay focused while they are in the classroom by planning an interesting lesson that requires more independent work than cooperation from excited students who are too keyed up to listen well to you or to their classmates.

3. Promote good sportsmanship by discouraging your students from booing, catcalls, throwing paper, or other unsportsmanlike behavior. Remind them how they are expected to behave during the pep rally if you have students who are not as mature as they should be.

4. Reinforce good behaviors by praising those students who behaved well during the pep rally.

FIGHTS

Every teacher's nightmare is that harm could come to our students while they are in our care. Our careers are based on the opposite idea. We want to help our students. Many of the rules and procedures we have established in our classes and in our schools are designed to help us protect our students from harm. A school fight is one of the most harmful events that our students can face.

Experienced teachers dread the first signs of a fight. If it is outside of our classroom, it usually begins with an increase in the noise level followed by students running and pushing each other to get to the fight scene. By the time teachers arrive, a large crowd is usually already gathered, blocking all attempts to stop the violence. At this point the noise and confusion become deafening as the crowd cheers on the students who are fighting.

When the fight is finally broken up, the energy level it generates affects the climate of the school and of our classes for the rest of the day. Our students do not want to settle down to work, preferring to discuss the fight blow-by-blow. An even worse effect is that often fights trigger a series of other conflicts as adrenaline and anger run high throughout the building.

In recent years the numbers of school fights have grown as more and more students bring their conflicts with others to school. As an educator, there are several things you can do to prevent fights from becoming an everyday occurrence and to lessen their adverse effect on the discipline climate of your classroom. An aware teacher can do a great deal to prevent a fight from beginning.

Fight Prevention

1. Watch for the signs of trouble building up among your students. Use your teacher's intuition to determine if violence is likely. Counsel students whom you suspect might be at-risk for fighting. Contact parents and administrators to get assistance.

2. Bullies often provoke violence. Refuse to allow any student to bully another in your presence. If you hear of an incident where one student teases or torments another, act at once to stop it. Sexual harassment is another form of bullying that can provoke a physical altercation. Make your students aware of the limits they should observe in how they treat members of the opposite sex.

3. Teach your students that angry words and "playing around" can lead to violence very quickly. Teach this at the same time you teach them the importance of tolerance and courtesy. Encourage good behavior as often as you can. Refer to "Arming Our Students: Teaching the Art of the Alternative Response to Rude Classmates" in Section Four to help you do this.

4. Make sure your students are aware of the schoolwide policies your school district has in place to deal with students who fight at school. Most schools have a zero tolerance for fighting and impose severe penalties in many instances. Make sure your students are well-informed so that they can make sensible judgments for themselves before they choose to fight.

5. Many schools also have programs in place that are designed to help students settle conflicts without violence. If your school does not have a conflict-resolution program, work with guidance counselors, other teachers, students, and administrators to establish one.

6. Teach your students how you want them to behave during a fight. Make sure they know they are not supposed to block the area so that adults can't get through to stop it. Less mature students who taunt and cheer on the participants in violence should be discouraged from inciting other students to fight.

7. A strong adult presence in the cafeteria, restrooms, hallways, bus ramps, and other less-supervised areas of a school will help deter fighting.

Once the Fight Has Begun

In addition to preventing school fights from beginning, you will probably be called on at some point in your career to break up a fight once angry students have lost control. This is one of the most stressful situations any teacher will have to face. The situation can be made even worse if there are injuries or weapons involved. Here are some suggestions to help you cope with this sad part of school life.

1. Make sure you are aware of the procedures your school district expects you to follow to protect the fighting students, the crowd, and yourself from harm.

2. If you are not physically able to stop the students who are fighting, immediately get help from nearby teachers or from the office. Do not leave the area to get help. Send a student if you can't get help any other way.

3. Once a fight begins, your first concern should be for the safety of all of the students involved either in the fight or who are in the area. Keep this safety issue in mind when you have to make crucial decisions quickly. You should also be careful how you attempt to restrain violent students so that no one, including you, is injured.

4. Be firm and clear with students who are watching the fight that you expect them to report back to class or to go to their seats if the fight takes place in your classroom.

5. You may be asked to appear in court as a result of witnessing a fight. As soon as you can after an incident, jot down notes that will help you recall important details you may need in court months later. Pay attention to what led to the fight. Get the names of any witnesses.

6. After a fight is over, model the calm, mature response that you want your students to have. Immediately resume teaching. Do not encourage a discussion of the fight in class: stick to your plans for the day's lesson if you possibly can.

7. If the fight took place while the participants were under your supervision, contact their parents or guardians to make sure they know how concerned you are about the situation, and so that you can work together to keep it from happening again.

A Fight with Injuries

1. Deal first with the injured student or students and then with the other students in the area. Send for the school nurse. Do not leave the scene. Send a calm student if necessary.

2. If more than one student is injured, help the more seriously wounded student first. Unless you are a trained emergency medical technician, be very careful that the aid you provide does not make the situation worse.

3. Protect yourself and others from contact with blood or other body fluids.

4. If you are injured, be sure to seek medical attention for yourself.

A Fight with Weapons

1. Work with other professionals to create a schoolwide policy on weapons at school. This policy should be one that all students are aware of, too.

2. Be aware that there are more weapons stored in students' cars than there are in lockers or bookbags. Contact a security guard or an administrator for help if you think an angry student is looking for a weapon.

3. Before there is any violence, talk with your students about the danger of weapons at school. Make sure they know why they need to report one at once and just how to go about doing so.

4. If you suspect a student is armed, contact a security guard or an administrator at once. This is definitely not a situation you should try to handle by yourself.

5. If a weapon is used during a fight, make sure other students don't take it afterwards. It will be used as evidence. If you are able, confiscate it until you can turn it over to an administrator.

INTERCOM ANNOUNCEMENTS

In some classrooms the beginning of the morning or afternoon announcements signals a free time for students to talk, pack their bookbags, and misbehave. In others the announcements are a time for students to stop what they are doing and listen attentively. The difference is not an accidental one—skillful teachers decide to use these few minutes as a productive learning experience instead of as a wasted time period where trouble is imminent.

Avoid discipline problems and wasted announcement time by teaching the behaviors you want to see from your students. The following techniques can improve the effectiveness of how you and your students use this opportunity each day.

1. Decide how you want your students to behave during the announcements. Are they supposed to be silent? Talking quietly? Which behaviors do you find acceptable and which ones are not acceptable?

2. If you want your students to listen attentively, then you must teach them that they are to stop talking at the start of the announcements and stay silent until the end.

3. Teach students why they should become more skilled at listening. They probably don't realize just how important good listening skills will be when they are employed. Good communication skills are necessary in the workplace as well as in school.

4. Reinforce your expectations by monitoring. Do not sit at your desk "shushing" your students. Stand up and walk around so that your students see that you are serious about how you want them to behave. Continue this until good behavior during announcements is ingrained in your students.

5. Turn this "wasted" time into a teaching tool and prevent discipline problems at the same time. Make a game of listening well and allow students to compete with each other to see who has the most accurate information from careful listening.

6. Have students practice their notetaking skills by taking notes during announcements. If you encourage them to practice their listening skills by quizzing them on the details of the announcements they just heard, then you will not only teach your students to listen carefully, but to take good notes while treating their classmates with courtesy. Reward those students who do well.

7. Another way to encourage self-discipline during this time is to use intercom announcements as an opportunity to discuss the importance of listening well in a variety of occupations. Have your students draw up a list of occupations where good listening skills are useful. After discussing this list, your students should understand that something as simple as listening to intercom announcements can help them become good future employees because they have learned to be active and skillful listeners.

PASSING NOTES IN CLASS

One of the cherished traditions of school-aged children is passing notes, often to the dismay of the hapless parents and teachers who come across these letters. If your students are writing and passing notes when they are supposed to be working, don't make the situation worse by overreacting.

In earlier days teachers would take the note from the student who happened to be holding it at the moment he or she was caught. The teacher then would either read the note to the class or post it for anyone to read. A more humiliating and demeaning punishment could not have been devised by even the most hard-hearted teacher.

In today's enlightened classrooms, such as abuse of power and such an invasion of privacy are not as common. Today we realize that it's not hard to convince students to stop passing notes. We also realize that it's really important to make sure that the way we handle the incident minimizes the disruption.

In fact there are many different ways you can capitalize on your students' enjoyment of writing notes. Use this enjoyment when you can to turn a potentially troublesome situation into a positive learning experience.

How to Handle It When It's a Disruption

1. You don't need to do anything else other than ask the students to put their notes away to make sure that everyone is back on track. Stand nearby to make sure notes have been put away.

2. Don't ever take notes from students; they were not written for you to read. Many students will bitterly resent the loss of dignity that occurs when a teacher violates their privacy. Don't read notes aloud. In fact, don't read them at all. If you find a note on the floor, simply drop it in the trash.

3. If you are still not convinced that you should not read student notes, ask yourself if you are prepared to deal with what you read. Students today are not shy about using very foul and graphic language. What will you do about the information you are not intended to know?

4. You should also ask yourself why your students have so much time to spend in writing and passing notes. If you provide them with engaging and challenging assignments to do instead, you will encourage your students to stay on-task.

Turning This into an Advantage

Passing notes does not have to be a discipline problem. Knowing that students enjoy writing and passing notes is something you can use to your advantage in your classroom in a variety of ways. Incorporate the desire students have to communicate with each other in this way into your lessons.

1. Have your students write you notes at the end of class to communicate personal information that they don't have a chance to tell you otherwise.

2. Have your students write informal notes to each other about a particular aspect of a lesson. Warn them that these notes will be monitored frequently and at random to insure that everyone stays on-task.

3. Consider having a "silent class." Plan to have your students communicate with each other and with you only by writing notes for an entire class period. This is particularly effective if you have a class of students who like to chat and who will enjoy the novelty of the experience.

4. Have your students write any questions they still might have at the end of a lesson and pass the note to a classmate who they think might answer it. When the people who answer the questions share their opinions with the rest of the class, everyone wins.

5. Set aside a particular spot on the board for students to record their concerns during group work. This is still note passing, but not in a one-on-one situation. Have your students tell you how this activity is like passing a note when you introduce it to your class.

6. Use students' enjoyment of passing notes to spark a discussion of various topics. Talk about privacy, respecting others, free speech, staying on-task, good classroom manners, and self-discipline, among other topics.

7. Some quick little assignments you could use to encourage your students to write notes to each other are:

   ■ Pay a compliment to someone in the class.

   ■ During a test allow each student to pass one note to a friend to ask for the answer to a question. They should turn in these notes with their test.

   ■ Students could write homework reminders to each other.

   ■ Students can ask one question that was not answered in the course of the day's lesson.

   ■ They can express an opinion about the homework or about the lesson to a classmate who will be more sympathetic than an adult might be.

   ■ They can give each other the answer to one of the homework problems.

   ■ They could complete sentences such as these:

     I wish . . .
     I regret . . .
     I think . . .
     I believe . . .
     I really should . . .
     I dread . . .

AFTER-SCHOOL JOBS

One of the most eagerly anticipated adolescent rites of passage is the after-school job. As soon as students are old enough to go to work, many of them do. Employers report that many teens are excellent workers—a fact that dumbfounds their teachers who can't even get them to turn in homework assignments!

Students who work after school often have to cope with additional stresses that can have an adverse effect on their school day. The problems with after-school jobs usually are caused by one of two things: long hours or problems on the job that students don't know how to handle. Signs of trouble can be exhaustion, inability to keep up with assignments, poor academic performance, sleepiness, and/or crankiness. As many teachers know, these trouble signs can have a serious negative impact on the discipline climate in any classroom.

In order to help students deal with these problems and to maintain the positive discipline climate that you want in your classroom, there are four steps you should take.

Talk to the Student

If you notice that a student is having problems trying to work and do well in school, talk to the student. Determine just what the problem is and whether it will be a temporary one. You should also determine just why the student needs to work at an after-school job.

If the student is working to help out with family expenses, then that student needs guidance and support. Involve other professionals, counselors, and social workers to ease the burden on that student. This student is burdened with more serious troubles than just wanting money for luxuries, so he or she needs caring adults who are willing and able to offer help.

On the other hand, if a student is working in order to earn more spending money, then the help you can offer is very different. In this case the student needs assistance in figuring out how to schedule time and how to prioritize tasks so that schoolwork remains an important part of the student's life.

Speak to Other Teachers

In addition to offering your support to the student, you can also speak to other teachers. Students who are involved in a work program through their vocational classes are warned about the stresses of long hours. Those teachers are excellent sources of information and guidance for you. You should also speak with other teachers who may be experiencing the same problems with the student that you are.

Contact Parents or Guardians

If speaking with the student and with other teachers does not seem to help the situation, then you should contact the teenager's parents or guardians. They may not be aware of just how adverse an effect working after school is having on their child's progress. They are also the people who can speak to the employer about job problems if the student is unable to do so. Parents or guardians can also work with you and other teachers to help the teenager overcome the problems that after-school jobs cause.

Continue to Maintain High Academic Standards

After you have done everything you can to help the student overcome work-related problems, you should still maintain high academic standards. You will do the students who work after school no favors if you allow them too many special courtesies just because they work after school. Keep your standards high, but reasonable. Continue to offer encouragement and support, but make it clear that school should be a priority in their lives during their teen years.

A VISITOR IN THE CLASSROOM

Classroom interruptions and visitors are a constant part of school life even in the most orderly and well-run schools. We must handle these frequent interruptions successfully so that the disruption they cause is minimal.

There are few things as humiliating for a secondary teacher as having students misbehave while there is a visitor in the classroom. Students who are normally well-behaved seem to think that when a visitor enters the room, it is acceptable to shout out greetings if they like the guest or insults if they don't.

The following six strategies will help you and your students turn this potential problem into an opportunity for your students to exhibit their maturity.

1. Be very clear with your students right from the start about what you expect them to do when there is a visitor in the room. Do this by teaching them the procedure you want all students to follow when someone enters the room, by practicing the procedure in two or three quick role-playing scenarios, and by imposing negative and positive consequences for their behavior.

2. Stress over and over the importance of polite behavior towards guests in your classroom. Teach your students that you want them to keep working when a visitor enters the room. Stress that they are not to call out the person's name or make other disruptive noises or gestures. Their behavior should remain the same as it was before the visitor entered the room.

3. Make things easier for your students by taking the time to introduce a visitor they may not know. Your students will appreciate this small courtesy.

4. Select one or two students to sit near the door and be in charge of opening it and referring visitors to you. Be clear with these students that you expect them to just open the door and refer the visitor to you. Be extra courteous and appreciative when they handle this task well.

5. No one should be allowed into your room to talk to a student without first clearing this with you. Teach the door greeters the importance of this. Go to the door to greet visitors whenever you can.

6. Praise your students when they do well with how they handle the interruptions in your class. It's as important for students to know when they have done well as it is for them to know when they have misbehaved if you want behaviors to continue to improve.

VIDEO VIEWING

"Wow! Are we having a movie today? Hey, everybody! We're having a movie today!" Teachers everywhere are used to this happy and hopeful reaction whenever students see us pushing audio-visual equipment into the classroom.

Students enjoy films and so do we. Watching videotapes and older films can reinforce what we want our students to learn and provide an enjoyable experience at the same time. In fact, this is one trend in recent years that almost all teachers can agree is a positive one. There are thousands of good audio-visual materials on almost any topic for all grade levels available to teachers.

Often, however, students want to focus only on the entertainment value of the viewing experience instead of learning what we want them to understand from movies. Some of the misbehaviors that can happen include: passing notes, sleeping, chatting, making inappropriate remarks about the film, doing homework for another class, and asking to leave the room because they are not interested in the movie. Instead of a pleasant and beneficial experience, we struggle to keep our students focused on the movie and on what they should learn from it.

There are many ways to make video viewing a much more enjoyable and beneficial experience for you and for your students. Pick the methods from the following short list that will help you create a positive learning experience for your students on "movie day."

1. Always preview the films you intend to show. More than one teacher has been unpleasantly surprised to find that the movie they are showing does not match the description of it in the film catalog or even on the box it came in.

2. Prepare students in advance of the viewing by reminding them of your expectations for their quiet and attentive behavior.

3. Don't have the room too dark. Students will beg to sit in total darkness to view films, but this is not a good idea, particularly if you want them to take notes or complete an assignment you have prepared for them. It will also be harder for you to monitor their behavior effectively in the dark.

4. Before the movie starts, students need to move their chairs where they can see the screen clearly. It will take a few minutes for them to settle down. Allow for it when you plan the lesson.

5. Students need to be taught that they are to behave differently while watching movies in school from how they might behave at home. They should not put their heads down. They should not talk during a film. Many teens are used to loud and rude behavior in movie theaters. Prepare them in advance so that they know how you expect them to behave during a film in your class.

6. Have an assignment prepared for your students to complete as they watch the movie. Use this assignment to guide their thinking and learning as they watch the movie. It will foster a positive learning environment because it encourages students to stay on-task. If you have the assignment photocopied for them in advance of the viewing, you'll find that they will be more engaged in the movie and in learning than if you wait to hand it to them afterwards.

7. When you preview the film, plan your stopping points for discussion. Stopping periodically to make sure everyone is on-task and learning what you want them to know from the movie is an effective way to encourage students to pay careful attention.

8. Hold your students accountable for their learning. Hold a closing activity after the movie and after any discussion that might have followed. Tell students this in advance so that they can be prepared and successful.

CHEATING

It's no secret to teachers, students, or parents that cheating is a widespread practice in classrooms. This plague affects all of us involved in education in one way or another. You do not have to stand by and let your students cheat. Honesty should be part of the culture of your classroom and, indeed, of all classrooms. You can prevent much of the cheating that could occur and lessen the negative impact of cheating once it does occur when you begin early to discuss this issue openly in your class.

You can take many positive actions to control this situation in the classroom. When you help your students feel confident about their mastery of the material and about their chances for success, you'll decrease the pressures on them to cheat. In addition to this, you can make sure your students know just how you stand and what you will do if they cheat.

There also are many unsuccessful ways to try to control cheating. The worst action you can take is to just ignore an incident of cheating. This makes you an accomplice. Another negative approach would be for you to just "talk things over" with the child and not put any sort of consequence into effect. This sends a clear message to the student that you are willing to allow cheating under certain circumstances.

When you deal successfully and consistently with cheating incidents as they arise, you make your students aware that cheating is just not going to be tolerated in your classroom. Dealing with cheating should be something you do consistently every day in your class, not just when you nab an offending student.

The most effective way to handle this issue is to use a two-step approach. The first step is to do everything you can to prevent cheating from happening at all. In the list that follows you should find some effective ways to do this. The second step involves the actions you can take once you discover a student has cheated. These tactics can improve the way you handle this serious discipline issue in your class.

Step One: Prevention

1. Know your school's policy on student cheating and follow it. If all teachers in a school consistently enforce a schoolwide policy on cheating, then the battle is almost won because students will know they are not supposed to cheat and what the consequences will be if they do.

2. Make sure your students know exactly how you stand on this issue. State your position early and often throughout the term.

3. Encourage students to talk about cheating during class discussions. They will surprise you with the insights and experiences they are willing to share with a concerned adult. There is a tremendous negative peer pressure at work in classrooms concerning cheating. Class discussions will give your students guidance on how to handle it.

4. One positive way to help your students become self-disciplined on this issue is to make a poster of their ideas on how to handle cheating. Ask your students to brainstorm some effective ways to prevent cheating.

5. Another tactic to help your students see that they have options on this topic is to arrange for them to role-play sensible ways to handle cheating in various situations.

6. Be a positive role model—Don't be guilty of cheating yourself. Model honest behavior by annotating photocopied material and by respecting copyright laws for films, software, books, and other material. Be sure to tell your students why you do this.

7. Discuss the need for honest behavior in all walks of life. Help your students see cheating as part of the big picture of life choices. Listen and advise. Don't lecture.

8. When students are engaged in any sort of research, they should credit their sources. Even very young children can be made aware of the breadth of plagiarism and the importance of avoiding it. Show students how simple it is to credit sources and reward them when they do so.

9. Tell your students whether it's okay to work together on an assignment or not. Don't assume that they know. State your expectations in advance of each assignment.

10. Keep desk tops and work areas clean so that you'll notice if answers are written on them or if a stray cheat note is visible. Make it a habit to do a quick survey several times a day. Keep paper towels and cleaner on hand to wipe away any notes or answers.

11. Before a test, ask students to neatly stow away their books, papers, and other materials as part of preparing for the test. Make it obvious that you are checking. If you do this, you can then monitor to make sure no tempting cheat notes are available.

12. Don't allow students to talk during a test or quiz.

13. Students should not turn sideways in their seats during a test. Talk to your students about taking a common-sense approach to avoiding the appearance of wrongdoing.

14. Don't leave tests or quizzes on your desk where anxious students might be tempted to peek.

15. If your students need a cover sheet for tests, provide it. Use recycled handouts or scrap paper.

16. Don't allow students to have extra paper on their desks as a writing pad. Allow them to fold the test paper or issue an extra sheet of recycled paper to create a softer writing surface instead. Extra paper is an obvious hiding place for disguising cheat notes.

17. Any questions your students may have during a test should be directed only to you. Walk to the student who has a question. Students should remain seated during tests in order to avoid inadvertently seeing another's paper.

18. Monitor your students very closely during a quiz or test. You can't do this by sitting at your desk. Move around the room frequently.

19. Give several different versions of a test—even during the same class period. Do this often at the start of a term and at unpredictable intervals later.

20. Don't use the same worksheets or tests year after year. Older students will frequently share these with younger ones.

21. For a test where you expect lots of detailed memorization, consider allowing your students to bring in a small legal cheat sheet. Determine the limits of size and information on it in advance. This will lessen their anxiety and reduce the temptation to cheat.

22. When students finish a test early, either have them keep their papers until you collect them all at once or have them turn them in and begin another assignment immediately. Bored students are far more likely to get into trouble than busy ones.

23. Ask your students to tell you about all of the ways they have seen or heard of people cheating. Even the most experienced teachers are surprised at some of the sophisticated lengths to which many students will go to cheat.

Step Two: Dealing with Cheating Once It Has Occurred

1. If you have caught a student cheating, the first thing you should do is arrange a private conference with the student to determine the reasons why he or she cheated. Sometimes students cheat because they have copied other students' work for so long

that they really don't understand that doing so is not just cooperating with a class-mate, but cheating. Others cheat because they have a very real fear of failure and are not prepared for class. Still others cheat because they do not see the relevance of the learning and of the tasks they are asked to perform. Whatever the reason, talk with the student in a calm manner to determine what went wrong and to help the student see other options that could prevent future cheating.

2. When you catch one of your students cheating, contact his or her parents or guardians at once. Cheating is, without question, an issue that involves parents, teacher, and child.

3. Put the school's policy on cheating incidents into action. Sometimes this means involving counselors and administrators. Make sure when you speak to parents or guardians that they understand what actions you will take.

4. Unless your school's policy prohibits it, you may want to allow the student to make up the missing assignment. This would be an effective action if the offense was a first one and if you determined that this would be beneficial to the student after talking with the student and with the parents or guardians.

5. If you suspect that a student is cheating on another teacher's assignment while under your supervision, don't accuse the child outright. Collect the work if you can and discuss it with the other teacher. If the child has cheated, you should work together to handle the problem.

6. If you do catch a child cheating, protect the child's privacy. Never publicly accuse a student of cheating. Don't chat about a cheating incident with other students. Cheating should be treated with confidentiality.

7. Don't ask a student to confide in you about another student's cheating. This is awkward and unfair to both students.

8. Never accuse a student unless you are absolutely sure that cheating has occurred. You must have proof before you act.

9. If a student confides in you that another is cheating, counsel that student in the best way to cope with this additional pressure. Make sure you take such confidences seriously and act with discretion to take the necessary steps to solve the problem.

10. Once you have settled an incident with a student, forgive and forget. Convey this attitude to all guilty students and you'll provide them with an incentive to start fresh and put their mistakes behind them.

NEW STUDENTS

Being the new kid in a school or in a class is especially difficult for adolescents. New students have trouble blending into the crowd as quickly as their emotional needs urge them to do. New schools mean unfamiliar standards of behavior and enormous stresses for students who are not accustomed to the overwhelming strangeness of the situation.

Often new students will have other problems related to the move. They may have family problems because of divorce or adjustments to make because of other family situations. New students not only face the loss of what is familiar to them at school, but also the support group of friends and teachers who helped them at the old school.

For teachers who meet new students for the first time, the situation can also be unsettling. We wonder what the teenager does and doesn't know about our subject. We wonder what the impact of this new student will be on the discipline climate we have established in our classrooms.

Having new students in class does not have to be an unpleasant experience for students or for teachers if we take a few simple steps to get them off to a good start so that they can quickly adjust to school and to our class.

If you want to help new students make a positive adjustment easily, here are some actions to help ease the transition for them.

1. Make sure your school has a packet to welcome new students at enrollment. This should be handled by the person who enrolls them in school. The packet could contain a variety of materials, but all of them should be aimed at helping the new student make adjustments as easily as possible. A school map, schedules, a school calendar, and other general information would be appropriate.

2. When a new student has been assigned to your class, take a few seconds to look at the situation from the viewpoint of that new student. That person doesn't know or care that your class is seriously overcrowded or difficult. All that student wants to do is fit in as easily and as quickly as possible. Treat the situation with the sensitivity that it demands.

3. Even if this is the one hundredth student to be enrolled in your first period class, do not indicate in any way that you are less than delighted to have that student in your class. Welcome that student into the room and quickly settle back into the class routine. If you have a problem with having another new student, take the issue to the source of the problem: the person who enrolled that student in the class. If you make a student feel uncomfortable on the first meeting with you, you will have a harder time trying to reach a pleasant understanding with that student during the rest of the term.

4. Introduce the student to the class matter-of-factly and quietly ask several of your more mature students to serve as escorts for the next day or so until the new student is comfortable with routines. Be especially sensitive to students who are non-English speaking or know very little English. If possible, try to enlist the aid of another student from that culture to help the new student.

5. At the end of the day's lesson, take the opportunity during the closing exercise to have your other students write quick little notes to the new student to welcome him or her to the class and to offer a bit of advice for doing well in your class and in school in general. Gather these notes into a large envelope for the student to read at home. Of course, depending on your class, you may want to review these notes to make sure there are no negative messages.

6. Make up a packet of information for new students to your class. Set aside several folders at the start of the term when you teach your rules and procedures to the class. File extra copies of these handouts for any future new students you might have. Also make sure new students fill out an information form like the one in Section Two and some interest inventories like the ones in Section Four. At the end of the first class for new students, you can slip the current syllabus in the folder and give them this information to take home.

7. One of the forms you might want to include in the packet for new students is the "New Student Information Form." (See following page.)

NEW STUDENT INFORMATION FORM

Name _____ **Date** _____

1. After reading all of the material you were given when you enrolled and when you entered this class, you may still have lots of questions. Please write any questions you might have on the back of this sheet and I will answer them for you.

2. Please check any of these areas that you are still uncertain about and would like for me to explain for you:

   _____ Notebook organization

   _____ Textbooks or other materials you may need

   _____ Class procedures

   _____ Homework assignments

   _____ Syllabus

   _____ Make-up work

   _____ Grading procedures

   _____ Seating arrangements

   _____ Other: _____

3. What topics did you cover in your previous class?

   _____

   _____

   _____

4. What are your strengths as a student in this subject?

   _____

   _____

   _____

5. With what part of this course will you need extra help?

   _____

   _____

   _____

6. What should I know about you so that I can be a good teacher for you?

   _____

   _____

   _____

TRIPS TO THE LIBRARY/MEDIA CENTER

More than ever our students need to know how to use the resources—both print and nonprint—that are available to help them with their schoolwork. Trips to the library/media center are necessary if students are to be part of the mainstream of education. Unfortunately, trips to the library/media center can also be disastrous for those teachers who do not anticipate the potential for negative behavior in such trips. Unprepared students can disturb other patrons, damage equipment, waste precious class time, distract other students who may want to be productive, and accomplish nothing productive themselves.

Here are some guidelines for making such trips productive and positive experiences for both you and your students.

Before the Visit

1. Teach your students that the library/media center is not only a shared resource but a public area and that both of these will affect their behavior. Teach them early the behaviors you want to see in your students.

2. Promote respect for the staff and for the rules and procedures of the library/media center. Teach your students the polite way to request information and advice and the other social and academic skills they will need to be successful patrons.

3. Plan an activity with your students in advance of the first trip to the library/media center so that they are aware they are there for a specific academic purpose and that they should work diligently on the lesson you have prepared for them.

4. Consult with the staff about the types of research you want your students to do if the project is a new one for you. They will be able to help you arrange your class groups so that the maximum use of shared resources—such as computers or microfiche readers—is possible.

5. If your school has a security system in place for preventing theft, teach your students about it in advance of your visit so that no one delays the entire class while bookbags are searched for offending material.

During the Visit

1. Remind your students that just as they are not permitted to roam about the classroom aimlessly chatting with their friends, they are not permitted to do this in the library/media center either.

2. Stay on your feet and monitor your students to make sure everyone is on-task and able to do the assignment.

3. Teach your students to work quickly and efficiently. For example, sitting down to take lengthy notes from one book instead of surveying the material first for other sources is not a good use of student time. When students understand the importance of using library time well, they will have a reason to stay on-task and you will have fewer discipline problems.

4. Your students should stay seated until the bell rings to dismiss them from class or until you give a signal.

5. Work closely with your school's librarians to make sure your students return shared books or other materials on time. School and public libraries are a tremendous resource for all of the people in a community. Students need to be taught early the importance of returning materials on time.

GOOD CITIZENSHIP

Almost every public school has a flag flying proudly in front of the building each school day. Many young students are taught the words to our national anthem and are expected to recite the "Pledge of Allegiance" as part of their school's opening exercises. Both the national anthem and a school song are played at school sporting events each week in thousands of schools across our nation.

If your school is one where students are expected to display good citizenship practices during the "Pledge of Allegiance" or during the singing of the national anthem or school song, then you need to make sure these parts of the school day are occasions where your students show a respectful attitude for the rights of others and for the citizenship responsibilities of all.

You can and should expect positive behavior from your students for these events. The following strategies can help you encourage your students to be good citizens.

The Flag

1. Check to make sure every student knows the "Pledge of Allegiance" and is able to recite it.

2. Teach your students that you want them to stand quietly and respectfully during this activity.

3. If you have students who refuse to participate, take their objections seriously. Contact their parents or guardians to make sure there is a valid reason for this refusal. Work with parents and students on this issue. Refusing to recite the "Pledge of Allegiance" is not a class disruption; however, disturbing others who want to participate in the recital *is* a disruption. Make this clear to both the students who refuse and to their parents or guardians.

4. If it is appropriate for your students' age group and for the subject you teach, have your students research the history of the "Pledge of Allegiance" and of the flag itself. You could also have students interview community members who have strong opinions on this topic.

The National Anthem and the School Song

1. Teach your students the history of and the words to these songs so that they can understand why so many people find them meaningful.

2. Help your students practice the polite behaviors we associate with these songs: standing still, removing headgear, and singing in harmony.

FIRE DRILLS AND BOMB THREATS

At least once during the first week of school and at unpredictable intervals thereafter, you and your students will be evacuated from your building. These evacuations inevitably come at the worst possible moment—during a major test or in the middle of a nervous student's first oral presentation.

Many experienced teachers can recall times when students and faculty members took fire drills and bomb threats seriously. Teachers hustled quiet students outdoors in orderly single file and stood well away from any possible danger while they took roll. This is not always what happens today in many secondary schools.

Students no longer exit the building in a safe manner. They rush out doors in a large noisy crowd, laughing and knocking into younger students and those with special needs. Fire drills and bomb threats have become an annual spring rite in many areas of the country where disruptive students want to cause just a little more trouble than usual.

Minimize the potential for trouble in these events by planning ahead and teaching your students some basic behaviors you would like to see during these times.

The following techniques will help you reduce the disruption caused by schoolwide evacuations for fire drills and bomb threats.

1. Teach your students just how you want them to behave during an evacuation. Many students just do not know how they are supposed to act safely.

2. Stress the importance of evacuating the building quickly and quietly. You might even hold a quick practice drill on your own with just your students. Praise the ones who take it seriously and who exit quickly and quietly. Convey the seriousness of the situation to your students so that they can see the importance of it, too. Your attitude should be consistently serious throughout the preparations for building evacuation.

3. During the first week of class, make sure you have the evacuation plan posted and your students know where they are supposed to go.

4. Select a responsible student to be the leader who knows where all of your students are to report for roll call. Make sure everyone follows that person out of the building to safety.

5. Teach your students how to help those students in your building who may be in wheelchairs or who may have trouble reaching safety. Discuss the issue with them so that they can see the need for helping everyone be safe.

6. Have your students meet you at a designated area where you can quickly tell if any of your students are missing. Teach them to remain there until you give them the signal to leave.

7. Take your roll book with you to call roll to make sure all of your students are safely out of the building. Teach them that you will call roll to provide for their safety and that you expect them to answer quickly. They should answer the roll by saying "Here" or some other agreed-upon signal so that you can do this with no fuss.

8. Don't forget to go over the procedures you want your students to follow while returning to your classroom. Don't allow them to dawdle just because of a drill. You could promote this idea by timing their return and by offering a reward to all of those students who are prompt in returning. You should also have a negative consequence for those students who are too slow to return to class.

9. If you are giving a test or quiz that is interrupted by an evacuation, you should assume that the integrity of the test or quiz has been compromised. You can consider either retesting the following day or disregarding the objective questions where cheating is most likely to occur.

OVERCROWDED CLASSROOMS

Rows of mobile classrooms beside a school are not an unusual sight today. Hundreds of new schools are under construction right now, much to the relief of the faculty members who have to teach in the overcrowded mobiles that will soon be replaced by new buildings. Because of a growing population and continuing budget cuts in education, most of us will have to deal with very large classes at some point in the course of our careers.

As inevitable as overcrowded classes may be, the discipline problems associated with them are not. Overcrowded classes can be managed successfully by those teachers who meet the unique challenges they present.

Even though we know that smaller classes are the preferred option for our students, a positive discipline climate and a pleasant learning environment are possible in overcrowded classes. The following strategies can start you on the way to successfully managing the problems of overcrowded classes.

1. The room arrangement is very important in overcrowded classes. Make sure you have enough desks. Move all equipment that you don't need to use right away to storage and do whatever else you can to further reduce the claustrophobic effects of clutter in the room.

2. You'll find it easier to maintain a positive environment if you do not allow students to put their desks against the walls where vandalism can occur. You should also pay careful attention to traffic patterns and student movement. Try to reduce this as much as possible. Teach your students to dispose of trash at the end of class and to sharpen pencils only at the start of class.

3. When you are dealing with the problems of room arrangement, remember that you will still need to be able to move around with ease. An overcrowded class requires more monitoring than a smaller one. Teach your students that they are to place their bookbags under their desks rather than in the aisle to make movement easier.

4. A seating chart is an absolute must in an overcrowded class if you want to reduce the amount of off-task behavior. A structured environment will reduce the number of problems you will face.

5. Prepare yourself for the noise level. A large class can be a noisy class if you don't establish some guidelines early in the year with your students to help them control the noise level.

6. Be extremely organized and a model of efficiency for your students who could be tempted to use overcrowding as an excuse not to do their best. Keep your personal space in good order and insist that your students leave their area tidy at the end of class. Encourage them to check to make sure their classmates don't leave personal belongings behind at the end of class.

7. It is important for you to avoid confusion and the discipline problems caused by failure to return papers promptly. Although it takes longer to grade papers for a large class, your students may feel lost in the crowd if you allow papers to pile up before you give them the feedback that all students need in order to stay focused on learning during class.

8. Routines are very important in a large class. Establish and teach them early in the term. Students should be able to predict what they are supposed to do in your class even though there are many students in the room.

9. Allow no horseplay. Even though you may be inclined to allow students some leeway in playing around, this is not a good idea when there are too many students in the room. Horseplay in a crowd is wasted time as well as dangerous. Stop it at the first sign it is about to begin.

10. Be especially careful in a crowded class to prevent the cheating that can happen because students have to sit close together. Provide a cover sheet and monitor carefully to prevent problems.

11. Enlist your students in a sense of togetherness and encourage a spirit of cooperation in solving the problems caused by an overcrowded class. A sense of humor and a positive attitude on your part will set a pleasant tone for your students to model.

12. It is important for you to speak with every student each day. Greeting them at the door is a good beginning to solving the problems of having to keep in touch with many students. Make a point to let your students know that you are aware of them as people, not just as faces in a crowd.

13. Creating permanent teams of study buddies is a good way to give students a sense of togetherness and connectedness in the midst of the larger group. When students have a few partners to turn to for help and support, they will feel like a part of the class instead of being just one of many.

14. Courtesy to each other and to you is especially important in a large class. Teach the importance of courtesy to the students in a large class and insist that they treat everyone with politeness. A large courteous class is much better and easier to deal with than a small rude one.

15. Your attitude is the most important factor in coping successfully with the demands of a large class. It's not the number of students occupying seats in the room, but the careful planning, interesting lessons, and sincere effort to connect with each student each day that will determine the success or failure of the discipline climate in a class.

SUBSTANCE ABUSE

Our social messages about drugs, alcohol, and tobacco are mixed. Teens are bombarded with messages that describe how grown up these are while being told in an equal barrage that they can be lethal. Being flooded with optimism, many adolescents simply can't believe that the negative messages about these seductive symbols of adulthood really apply to them. They may apply to some other teens, perhaps, but not to them.

By the time teenagers are in secondary-level classes, they have had plenty of time to become thoroughly confused about substances that are illegal for them to use. Many teachers do not know how to help teens with this issue. We are, however, familiar with the negative consequences of teen substance abuse in our classrooms: failing grades, apathy, degraded self-esteem, failure to complete assignments, defiance, and the rejection of social values, to name just a few.

Many of us don't know how to respond when students come to class reeking of smoke or bragging about the fun time they had had at a party over the weekend. Many of us are just not sure how far we should go in dealing with this issue. We don't want to overreact and make it impossible for students to come to us for help.

We want to think that educating students about drugs, alcohol, and tobacco are someone else's job: parents and family members. And it is, of course. But in many families the parents and other caregivers are just not aware of the problem or are not able to cope with it.

Educating students about substance abuse is one of our most important responsibilities. If teachers don't take a stand to help students understand all of their options about substance abuse and if family members can't, then who will?

If you want to help your students, but really aren't sure where to start, here is a list of ideas that could help you begin. After the list of suggestions for educating your students, you will find some procedures to follow if you suspect that one of your students is having trouble with illegal substances.

Preventing Substance Abuse

1. Make students aware of the problems of substance abuse so that they will be able to make choices that are based on facts and the opinions of experts rather than on just the opinions of their friends. A great deal of what many teens know about illegal substances involves information about the glamorous effects of drugs, tobacco, and alcohol and not the grim reality of addiction.

2. Hold discussions on the issues related to all three substances. Invite students to share their opinions as well as the information and misinformation they already have.

3. Having guest speakers who are older students is an excellent idea even if your own students are seniors. College students can be wonderful sources of information about this topic. Students will listen to older students who speak honestly to them while they will tune out teachers quickly.

4. Make sure your students are aware of the health risks and social consequences of substance abuse as well as the legal penalties. Many students are unsure of the laws governing illegal substances and of the penalties if they are caught. Local law enforcement officials are often willing to talk with students about their legal rights and responsibilities.

5. Your school district probably already has programs and policies in place to help students who struggle with this issue. The guidance office at your school is a good place to begin to find out about the community resources available to you and your students.

6. Make sure all of your students are aware of the school policies concerning all three substances. Students need to know what the consequences will be if they break the rules concerning alcohol, tobacco, and drugs.

7. The strongest defenses against teen substance abuse are education and a healthy self-esteem. Students who are confident in their ability to successfully manage their academic and social lives are well equipped to make sensible choices for themselves. Work with your students, their parents, and with the other professionals in your school to help students develop a strong positive self-image.

What to Do if You Suspect a Student Is Under the Influence

1. Don't be tempted to overlook the problem the first time you notice that a student is in trouble in class. Immediately and calmly put your school's policy into effect.

2. Remove the student from class at once as discreetly as you can. Speak to the student privately and in a nonaccusatory way in order to determine if a problem does exist.

3. Contact an administrator, security guard, or the school nurse—whoever is the person at your school designated to handle this problem and explain the situation as you see it. That person will conduct a search if one needs to be done and will then involve the parents and other appropriate school and community personnel.

4. You should not blame the student or project anything but a supportive attitude. Offer to help the student with this problem and to work together to solve it. Students who have problems with substance abuse need support and encouragement from their teachers, not blame or unpleasant labels.

5. Throughout your dealings with a student who is having problems because of substance abuse, keep in mind that this is a serious problem that needs to be handled with support from all of the adults in a student's life. You should not attempt to handle this situation without involving other adults.

STUDENTS WITH SPECIAL NEEDS

Although the "mainstreaming law"—PL 94-142—has certainly been controversial, no one who has been involved in helping students with special needs can deny that the law has changed the way public schools treat all students, not just those who have been mainstreamed or placed in inclusion classes.

We now have all sorts of students in our classes—from those with severe disabilities to those who only need a slight modification to help them learn. One of the best things to happen in public education in recent years is that we have come to regard *all* children as capable learners.

A wheelchair is not a symbol of stupidity. A student who has a physical problem or a learning disability is just as capable of succeeding in school as any child who has no outward sign of physical, emotional, mental, or social problems. Any teacher who has moved too slowly and risked getting a toe smashed by a student in a wheelchair hurrying to class can testify to the capabilities of all learners.

There are problems with how some teachers regard PL 94-142, however, that affect the discipline climate of our classrooms. Here are three unproductive and negative attitudes shown by some teachers who teach students with special needs. The problem with these attitudes is not that they are ones held by students, but that they are held by the people who are supposed to help these students. These attitudes harm everyone they touch.

Negative Attitude 1

STATEMENT. Some teachers believe the real problem with some students with disabilities, especially those problems that are not as visible as others, is that they just don't try hard enough. These teachers believe students who want to work hard will do well.

REBUTTAL. Trying hard does not guarantee success. Students who don't understand the work or who need help that they are not getting will not succeed no matter how much effort they put into it.

Negative Attitude 2

STATEMENT. Many teachers object to having the extra workload involved in modifying instruction. They resent having to spend so much time and effort on just one or two students when those students could be in a special education class.

REBUTTAL. If a student is placed in your class, that student deserves the best from you. Work with the special education teacher who is assigned to monitor those students to help share the workload and to figure out ways to streamline the additional duties while still meeting the needs of every student in the class.

Negative Attitude 3

STATEMENT. Many of us do not have enough training or experience to successfully deal with students with special needs.

REBUTTAL. We have been trained extensively in our content areas and, if we were fortunate, in educational methods. Few of us who are not special education majors have had even one course devoted to teaching students with special needs. But there are many resources available to us to help overcome this problem: attending workshops, asking colleagues to recommend materials and readings, observing a special educator teach a class, taking classes for more training, asking qualified professionals for advice, reading professional literature, working closely with inclusion teachers and monitors, speaking with the parents or guardians of the students, and taking responsibility for the solution to the problem.

General Guidelines

Here are several general guidelines that will help you successfully teach students with special needs.

1. You can make acceptance by the other students in the class much easier if you treat the student with a special need as openly and matter-of-factly as you do the other students. Create a relaxed but stimulating atmosphere in your classes so that all students, including those with special needs, are comfortable.

2. Be sensitive to the needs of the student and work to anticipate them whenever you can. For example, seat students with special needs in a part of the room where it is easy for them to see and hear you.

3. Talk with the student about any concerns he or she might have. Keeping the lines of communication between teacher and student open is important.

4. Talk with the other adults who deal with these students and keep talking until you are all working well together to the benefit of the students. Some of the other adults who can help you are the parents, the school nurse, the student's counselor, and other teachers who have worked with the student.

5. Study school records to help determine what has helped the student in the past. Use every resource available to you in your efforts to help all of your students, especially those with special needs.

6. Make sure your students with special needs are not socially isolated in the classroom. When you put your students into teams for various reasons, select a group of the most mature, tolerant, and cooperative students to be in the group with a student with a special need.

7. Speak with parents or guardians and with the student early in the term if you have planned an activity that may not be suitable for all students. Before you tell a student that he or she can't participate, work together to find solutions to the problems that would prevent all students from participating.

8. It is important for you to be proactive in dealing with students with special needs. Contact the special education teacher who is monitoring the students in your classes. Discuss the specific disabilities of your students and the methods you should use to help that student be successful.

9. Be alert to those students who experience significant distress or other learning problems, but who are not diagnosed as needing special help. Study records and talk to parents and other teachers to determine whether or not the student could benefit from a referral for special services. Often problems aren't found until the pressures of adolescence bring them to the attention of frustrated teachers.

Attention and Focusing Problems

Attention Deficit Disorder (ADD) and Attention Deficit/Hyperactivity Disorder (AD/HD) are both problems that can have a very negative impact on the positive learning climate you try to establish in your classroom. Although these disorders are under frequent debate as medical professionals try to find the best treatments, the following strategies will be effective in helping you teach ADD and AD/HD students.

1. Place ADD and AD/HD students near you. This will make frequent monitoring easier and less intrusive.

2. You will find that these students usually do better when they sit with their backs to other students who will be distracting. Other distractions will be windows, doors, pencil sharpeners, and other areas of high traffic flow.

3. Be careful to post rules and schedules for these students. They will benefit from hearing as well as seeing any written instructions.

4. Clearly define classroom procedures to help these students stay on-task. Make sure you plan and implement classroom procedures very carefully.

5. One of the most difficult times in the class for ADD and AD/HD students is the transition from one activity to another. Switching mental gears is not always easy for any student, but these students need extra attention at these times.

6. Photocopy the text and highlight the main points until your students with focusing problems can master this skill for themselves.

7. When you give directions to ADD and AD/HD students, be careful to give them one step at a time. Help them see that tasks are a series of small steps. If you write them on the board, say them aloud for your students.

8. Show ADD and AD/HD students how to use planners, schedules, and a syllabus to keep on track.

9. Set up peer tutoring situations in your class so that other students can share their methods of organizing materials and tackling assignments.

10. Provide an audiotape of the text for these students to listen to as they read. You don't have to create this tape for yourself. Contact either the publisher of the text or your state's textbook adoption committee for copies.

11. Be generous with extra time if students need to finish an assignment. Be sure, also, to break longer assignments into achievable steps.

12. ADD and AD/HD students usually do well when they develop computer skills. A computer not only makes it easier for them to stay focused, but it allows them to work competently and quickly once they have mastered the basics.

13. Review frequently and be sure to reinforce new knowledge with plenty of practice drills.

14. As always with students with special needs, focus on their strengths. In evaluating assignments use a variety of assessment measures to help you accurately determine the ADD and AD/HD student's grasp of the material.

15. Work with parents or guardians, who are the best source of advice in dealing with these students. They can offer help and advice to you as well as to the child.

16. Work with ADD and AD/HD students to help them understand how to succeed in school. They do not always have effective school-related skills such as keeping notes organized or figuring out how to complete assignments on time. A teacher who takes the time to show students how to succeed in school and who then takes time to help them accomplish their school tasks is providing students with the means to be successful in life as well as in school.

HALLWAY MISBEHAVIOR

Many secondary teachers who visit elementary or primary schools are amazed at how quiet it is when students are in the halls. We grin at all of the cute youngsters as they whisper "shush" at each other as they move through the halls on their way to lunch or to the library.

In the lower grades, it seems that the worst misbehavior in the halls is talking above a whisper or being in a crooked single-file line.

Our grins quickly fade, however, when we return to our schools and face the chaos of the halls. Our problems are much more serious. Common hallway misbehaviors in secondary schools include cursing, sexual harassment, bullying, fighting, shouting, running, knocking down other students, cutting classes, selling drugs, brandishing weapons, and vandalizing school property.

Many of us are reluctant to deal with these problems in the hallways because we don't know the students who are misbehaving. We are far more comfortable when we correct the behavior of our own students. We have a relationship with them and can anticipate a positive response from them.

What happens between the lower grades and secondary grades to cause this drastic breakdown in behavior? Part of the problem, of course, lies in the fact that our students are older and larger and coping with the many pangs of adolescence. But the real answer is in the fact that in the lower grades, students are not allowed in the public areas of the building without adult supervision. In secondary schools, for the most part, students are expected to behave well without adults marching them from place to place.

The Importance of Adult Supervision

While we should not be expected to put our students in orderly single files in the hallways, if misbehavior in the hallway is a problem, more adult supervision is necessary. There are several good reasons for increasing the number of adult supervisors in the public areas of a secondary school.

1. Areas with adult supervision are more orderly and quiet than those without an adult presence. Students know that in the presence of an adult they will be held accountable for their actions. They act more responsibly because of this.

2. Students know that an adult will help if another student is tormenting them. Supervised areas are safer for students than the unsupervised places in a school.

3. Behaviors that could grow into serious ones can be contained while they are still minor ones. Cross words between students are easier to deal with than the fistfight that could result from those cross words.

4. Students welcome the stress relief that comes from an orderly environment. Coping with the hallways and other public areas in a school can be very hard on students who are smaller or less aggressive than others. Adults in the hallways make life easier for everyone.

Importance of Students' Self-Discipline

In addition to increasing the number of adults who supervise the hallways in your school, there are also several actions you can take to help your own students learn to be self-disciplined about their behavior while in the public areas of the school.

1. Students may not be aware of what constitutes good behavior and what constitutes bad behavior while they are in the hallway. Make sure they are aware of any school policy they are expected to follow. You can do this early in the term in a positive and pleasant class discussion.

2. When you stand in the doorway to greet your students as they enter class, you are also supervising the hallway. Make sure your own students go to their desks to begin their opening assignments and do not lounge around in the doorway blocking traffic and causing hallway problems.

3. Make the behavior of all students in the hallways an open issue for your students. Brainstorm with them some of the good behaviors and bad behaviors that should and should not happen in the public areas of a school.

4. Since what happens in the hallway may have a negative effect on the behavior in your class during the first few minutes, make those first few minutes as meaningful and interesting to your students as you can. You want your students to feel they are missing out on something wonderful if they are late or not immediately on-task.

5. Make sure your students know they can count on your support if they experience trouble from other students in the hallway. Some students are the targets of repeated attacks by bullies and need your help in dealing with this problem.

6. Recognize that the hallways may be stressful for your students. Ask them how they cope successfully with the problem. You could do this as a quick closing exercise and as a positive way to interact with students to help them solve their problems.

REQUESTS TO SEE THE SCHOOL NURSE

The school nurse is a valuable ally for those teachers who want to create a positive climate in their classrooms. The school nurse can help in a variety of ways: by helping keep the lines of communication between school and home open, by keeping you informed about the health of your students, and working with you to learn what you can do to help every child be healthy enough to function well.

Many teachers do not see the role of the school nurse as important for the welfare of their students as they perceive their own role to be. These are the teachers who ignore health information from the nurse and who then treat every student alike regardless of the serious health issues that some students face.

Use the following five suggestions to help you deal with requests to see the school nurse in a sensible way.

1. Pay attention to the information you receive from the school nurse about your students. Keep it on file for quick reference when you need to deal with any problems that might arise.

2. Make yourself aware of the chronic diseases your students might have such as asthma, sickle cell anemia, or diabetes. While these diseases are not always visible, they profoundly affect the well-being of the students who have them. You should also contact the school nurse about the best way to help any pregnant students you might teach. You might think a student is misbehaving when that student is actually ill.

3. Ask the school nurse for a supply of adhesive bandages and safety pins to reduce the number of times students have to leave your room for minor problems.

4. If a student requests to see the nurse, respond at once. Let that student go with a properly filled-out pass. Be very sensitive to the embarrassment that a student might feel in asking your permission.

5. If you doubt that a student's request is legitimate, consult the school nurse after the visit to make sure. When students see that you and the other adults in the building are working well together, they are less apt to try to fool you. If the student is using a visit to the nurse as an excuse to leave the room, examine the cause of this behavior. Work to increase that student's self-esteem through improved work habits and an increased sense of cooperation with you and with other students in your class.

VANDALISM

Vandalism takes many forms. Spray paint on walls, broken windows, smashed lights, cigarette burns in the restrooms, damaged library books, damaged bulletin boards, broken equipment, and scribbles on desks tops are just a few examples of this problem.

Vandalism stems from a lack of respect for the school, from boredom, from insufficient adult supervision, and from a lack of accountability. Vandalism is an easy problem to stop—unlike so many of the other problems we face in education.

Use the following techniques to prevent vandalism from beginning and to cope with it once it happens.

Prevention

1. Monitor! At the end of class let students know that you will check their desk tops and other areas of the room for stray marks or other signs of destruction. Students who know that you are alert will not be as disposed to destroy school property as those students who know that they can get away with it. Holding students accountable for their actions is the best defense you have against future incidents of vandalism.

2. Discuss the problem of vandalism with your students and ask for their suggestions on how to prevent it. Those students who might not care will take notice when they hear their classmates express disgust at vandalism.

3. If your classroom is neat and clean, then students are going to respect this and keep it clean. Vandalism is not a crime to a student who writes with markers all over a bulletin board that has already been defaced by other students. A coat of fresh paint and a few small repairs will prevent a great deal of future vandalism.

4. Keep cleaning supplies on hand to clean stray marks right away.

5. Don't encourage your students to use illustrations in their reports and papers that they could have cut from books.

6. Pay attention to the length of time students are out of your class when they ask for a hall pass. Teach your students that they are expected to return promptly. Students who linger in the restrooms or halls will be more tempted to vandalize property than those who are aware that their teacher is waiting for them to return.

7. When you decide on the furniture arrangement in your classroom, don't allow your students to shove their desks too near the walls or bulletin boards where acts of vandalism are easy to commit.

8. Cover textbooks and encourage students to treat them well. Make informal checks as you walk around the room to see that students are taking care of them. You can teach

your students to take notes on self-sticking notes that they can keep on each page of the book. You can also show them how to make blank bookmarks from notebook paper as another way to take notes on the text without writing in their books.

9. Cover bulletin boards with background paper so that the damage students may do is just to the paper, not to the surface of the bulletin board itself.

What to Do When a Student Has Vandalized School Property

1. When you notice that a student has vandalized property, confront the student about it. Send a note home to let parents or guardians know that the incident has happened.

2. Use the technique of overcorrection to handle vandalism. If a student has marked on a desk, for example, that student should clean all of the desks in the room. If a student has defaced a bulletin board, then that student should not only recover that bulletin board, but the others in the room as well.

MAKING UP MISSED WORK

Very few students have perfect attendance. When students are absent for even one class period, the problem of making up missed work begins and doesn't seem to go away until the last bell of the term rings.

Make-up work can be a miserable experience that leads to serious discipline problems for teachers, parents, and students. When students do not make up their work promptly, their grades begin to drop and their desire to do well in class seems to vanish as they grow more and more overwhelmed.

The problem of make-up work does not have to be a tiresome task or a discipline problem for you and your students if you establish a fair policy, post it, teach it to your students, and then enforce it consistently. Here are some guidelines that will help you do all of these.

1. Make sure your policy is reasonable, workable, and in line with your school's policy.

2. If you provide your students with a syllabus, encourage them to follow it as closely as they can while they are absent to try to stay caught up.

3. Encourage your students to make up missed work as quickly as possible. Praise students who do so.

4. Discuss the issue of make-up work with your students. This will help you and your students in defining the limits of responsibility as well as in generating solutions to this problem.

5. Be sure to inform the parents of your students of your make-up work policy at the start of the school term.

6. Whenever you pass out handouts, put the leftover copies in a special folder for the convenience of those students who are absent. Encourage your students to check this folder when they return so that you won't have to search for extra copies for them.

7. Keep all returned papers for absent students in a folder. You'll have the papers right at hand when your students return.

8. A useful strategy is to divide your students into study teams. In each team, students share the responsibility for helping each other make up missing work by calling absent members, taking and sharing legible notes, reviewing difficult parts of an assignment, and just providing a bit of extra support.

9. Set aside a generous amount of time each week when you will be available to your students for make-up work. Post this information and make sure that it's also available for parents or guardians. Your students and their parents will appreciate this extra time and effort on your part.

10. Although the practice of allowing students to make up missed work during class time is certainly convenient for teachers and students, what you are really doing is causing that student to miss yet another day's work. Consider setting aside time before or after school for students to make up missing work instead.

11. Have your students rotate the task of recording the daily events from each class on a large calendar. This quick summary of what was done in class will help the absent class members quickly get back on track.

12. Set aside board space where you can keep a running record of missing work. In this space you could post your syllabus if you use one or a calendar with the daily assignments on it; a list of the students who owe missing work; and the final date on which you will accept missing work from them. A sample form, "Missing Work Reminder List," follows.

13. For long-term projects, you could post a modeling chart where you can mark off assignments as they are completed. Your students can check this to see what work they still need to complete. This is useful even for older students who have trouble staying organized and managing their time wisely.

14. Always make time to talk with your returning students about the work they owe. Make sure they understand what they need to do in order to complete the assignments satisfactorily and to get back on task quickly.

15. A time-consuming but very effective technique to keep students on track is to contact a parent if a due date for missing work is nearing and the student has made no effort to complete it. The word will get around quickly that you are serious about make-up work.

16. Don't allow students to make up work past your time limit simply to raise their grades. Enforce a reasonable policy and you'll teach responsibility.

17. If many of your students are absent due to an epidemic or some other catastrophe, then adjust your instruction and make-up work expectations.

18. Be prompt, detailed, and accurate when you are asked to send assignments home for a sick child. Writing a friendly note and offering assistance in making up missed work is courteous as well as professional.

19. When you assign a big project, give consideration to how you will grade one that students turn in late. Bear in mind that students who are not prepared will use absence as an excuse to create an extension for themselves unless you establish, teach, and enforce a policy for this situation. One solution is to deduct a certain number of percentage points for each day the project is late. Be sure that all of your students know about this in advance.

MISSING WORK REMINDER LIST

Student's Name	Missing Assignment	Due Date

20. Be consistent in teaching students to accept responsibility for missing work by asking them what steps they need to take in order to complete the assignment before the final due date.

21. There will always be situations where you have to use your best judgment. For example, if a student is absent because of a serious illness or because of the death of a family member, you should treat that student with compassion. You need to consider the overall benefit to the child and adjust the make-up work in some way.

22. Issue reminder slips to students upon their return so that they have a written record of what they owe. Figure 7-1 shows a sample reminder slip for you to adapt for your own class.

FIGURE 7-1
Make-Up Work Reminder

I, _____, understand that because of my absence from

class on _____, I owe the following assignments: _____

_____

_____

I agree to turn in this missing work on or before it is due: _____

HOLIDAYS AND VACATIONS

Some of the most stressful times of the school year occur just before a holiday or vacation break. Students are excited in anticipation of the upcoming event and find it difficult to focus on their schoolwork. Discipline problems multiply as students lose interest in school assignments.

When a holiday or vacation break is about to happen, you don't have to have a miserable experience with your students. Together you can make the days leading up to the break as pleasant and productive as the other days in your school year. Here are some guidelines to help you and your students enjoy the holidays or vacation break.

1. Attendance is often a problem right before a holiday or vacation break as parents or guardians who need to leave town will remove their children from school in order to get off to an early start. Be very careful that you are accurate in how you record attendance on the days before a holiday or vacation so that your records are in good shape. You will avoid many problems later in the year if you can be confident that you have accurate records of attendance for every day of class.

2. Making up missed work is a problem *after* a holiday or vacation break. Be careful to help all of your students make up missing work promptly to avoid the downward spi-

ral of failure and the resulting discipline problems that will occur. If the holiday has been a long one, some students will have forgotten that they have work due and will need help in scheduling their time so that they can accomplish all of their make-up work responsibilities with ease.

3. If you want to have a holiday party with your students and if your school permits such activities, be sure to make the occasion into a learning one. Structure some of the time into fun activities that are nevertheless related to your subject matter. Chalkboard games such as Hangman are terrific ways to review and have fun at the same time.

4. Remain focused on teaching the material in your curriculum. A wasted day right before a holiday or vacation break is not a good way to avoid discipline problems. Channel the excess energy into productive uses instead of just giving in to student excitement. Here are some ideas for activities that will engage students more easily than pen-and-paper exercises:

   ■ puzzles of all types
   ■ review drill games
   ■ chalkboard games
   ■ simulations
   ■ debates
   ■ logic problem solving
   ■ team games and activities

5. Don't relax your behavior standards on the days before a holiday or vacation break. While you should not be so strict that you would give a student a detention on the last day of school for a very minor offense, you should also not convey to your students that anything goes in terms of behavior.

6. Be sensitive to the fact that not all holidays are glorious ones for every student. Students who have experienced the loss of a family member, students moving away at the start of a school holiday, or students whose families will not be able to afford a lavish celebration are just three of the kinds of students for whom a holiday is stressful.

GUEST SPEAKERS

One of the most important trends in education in recent years is the inclusion of more real-life experiences in the material we teach. One of the best ways to do this is by inviting guest speakers to talk to our classes. Guest speakers can talk to students about a variety of topics, enhancing and enriching the information that you have taught.

Some guest speakers are more successful than others because of the material they present or because of their personal qualities. We can help all of the invited guest speakers so that the experience is a pleasant one for our students, the guest speaker, and for us. Those teachers who have not prepared wisely for a guest speaker have had to contend with students who were unprepared to ask intelligent questions or who were rude during the visit.

Here are some useful ways to make a guest speaker's visit a successful one by insuring that students act in a positive and productive manner.

1. Plan what you want students to gain from the guest speaker and gear instruction to that end. Design lesson plans that will successfully lead up to the visit and will provide a closure afterwards.

2. Prepare the guest speaker for your students if that person is not used to speaking in front of school-aged students.

3. Prepare your students for the guest speaker by teaching them the polite behavior you would like to see them show the speaker. They should pay even more attention than usual to their voice level, expression, and other courteous behaviors when there is a guest speaker present.

4. Address the importance of body language. Students who slump in their seats, turn aside to talk, or who otherwise convey their inattention are distracting to guest speakers. One useful way to emphasize this point is the role-play positive and negative behaviors you might see when there is a speaker present.

5. Have your students prepare questions in advance so that they will not only be knowledgeable about what the speaker is presenting, but they will also significantly extend their own learning during the visit.

6. Hold your students accountable for information they are expected to learn from the presentation. Expect them to take notes. Prepare them for this in advance.

7. Make it a point to evaluate your class's behavior with them after a guest speaker has come and gone. Discuss what they did that was good behavior and what they need to improve before the next speaker comes to the classroom. Praise the group and the individual students who helped make the visit worthwhile.

8. Teach your students the art of courteous behavior by requiring that they write individual thank-you notes to the guest speaker after a presentation. This not only teaches the necessity for polite behavior, but also reinforces the information that the speaker presented to the class. This is also an important workplace skill that students will need to know when they begin to interview for jobs.

SLEEPING IN CLASS

It is a damning indictment of a school when it is possible to walk through the hallways and see classroom after classroom where teachers allow some students to sleep through class day after day. The reason given by most teachers who allow students to sleep is simple: "At least they're not bothering anyone when they're asleep!"

What a tragic waste of student time and energy. There are two categories of students who sleep—one is acceptable and one is not. The acceptable one is illness. Sometimes a student comes to school and is too ill to participate in class, but who can't go home for whatever reason. At this point classroom teachers should use their best judgment about what is good for these students and may allow them to put their heads down.

On the other hand, chronic sleeping in class is a discipline problem that can be successfully managed with patience, persistence, and a step-by-step approach. Follow these steps if you want to have all of your students awake and participating every day.

Step One

Talk to the students who want to sleep in class to determine the cause. Many students will cite one of these as a reason for sleepiness: family problems, long hours at an after-school job, a late party, late television shows, or a late date. Counsel your students about better ways to manage time so that sleeping in class will not continue.

Step Two

Hold a goal-setting conference with the student who still has trouble staying awake in class. Show that student the importance of staying awake in order to meet the long-term goals that he or she may have. At this conference you should also help the student set short-term goals to help reach the longer one. Both types of goals should be put in writing and a behavior contract drawn up where the student can see in writing the steps he or she must take in order to solve this problem.

Step Three

Pay more positive attention to these students so that they will have a good reason to stay awake. Increase the number of positive interactions you have with them so that they know you care enough to take an active interest in their lives and well-being. When a student starts feeling successful and capable in a class, the problem of sleepiness will cure itself in most cases.

Step Four

If you have tried to work with a sleepy student and nothing has helped, then it is time to contact the parents or guardians. There may be an underlying cause you know nothing about and the student is not willing to share. Parents of students who are chronically sleepy can do much to modify the home environment so that the child will get the rest at home that he or she needs.

CHRONIC ILLNESS

Students with chronic illnesses have a harder time in school than students who are not ill. Not only are they not feeling well, but they are often isolated from their peers. The instruction that everyone else in the class receives—that will make the difference between whether instruction is easy or difficult—is denied the student who has to stay at home.

Ill students who are able to attend classes struggle not only with their ill health, but with the sense of being different from everyone else at a time when they long to be just a face in the crowd. These difficulties can manifest themselves in social, academic, and behavior problems that can have a very negative effect on the discipline climate in your classroom.

In order to help students with chronic illnesses and to help other students in your class accept them more readily, you must work to help all of your students—especially those with chronic illnesses—find academic success and acceptance from their peers. A compassionate teacher will find ways to make both of these a reality.

Students with chronic illnesses generally fall into two categories: those who must receive instruction at home and those who are able to attend school. The following ideas are designed to help you successfully meet the challenges of both types of students.

Homebound Students

1. If the homebound teacher or tutor requests work, send it immediately. Then, do all that you can to work with that teacher to help your student complete the work successfully. If you plan units at least three weeks ahead or if you use a syllabus, then you will find it much easier to cooperate with the homebound instructor.

2. Be flexible with timelines and other requirements for students who are homebound. You will prevent much frustration if you can adjust the picky requirements of an assignment to meet the needs of the student.

3. Maintain contact with the parents or guardians so that you can work together to help students who need extra help because of illness. Often they will be wonderful resources of information and guidance for you as you try to help their child.

4. Continue to have a positive relationship with homebound students by visiting them at home or in the hospital, by sending cards, and by having their classmates send cards. This courtesy will also help the ill child feel connected to the class and will make returning to class a much easier transition for everyone.

5. The ultimate goal is to have the child who has been out able to resume work immediately upon his or her return without having missed an assignment or an important part of the instruction. Unfortunately, this is not a reasonable expectation if the illness is a lengthy one. Be reasonable in your expectations and help the child make the adjustment back to the class a pleasant one instead of an overwhelming experience.

6. Be sensitive to the difficulty that a student who has been working one-on-one with a tutor at home will have in adjusting to the rules and procedures of a normal school day. Offer assistance and monitor the student's progress carefully for the first few days after he or she returns to class.

Ill Students Who Are Able to Attend Classes

1. Contact the school nurse and the parents or guardians of these students as soon as you can at the start of the term to make sure you are doing everything you should be in order to help them. Both the school nurse and the parents will help you learn more about the disease or condition that affects the health of the student.

2. If you need to make adjustments to lessons for students who are ill, be discreet about it to avoid problems with other students who may find this unfair and react negatively.

3. Make sure these students have plenty of peer support so that when they are absent, a classmate will take notes for them or be able to quickly tutor the ill student on the day's work. This will also help alleviate some of the negative behaviors that could arise from frustrated students who are overwhelmed by the work they are expected to complete.

4. Be careful to record attendance correctly and encourage chronically ill students to keep a calendar of the dates when they are absent from class. This will not only help them stay organized about any work they are missing, but will eliminate confusion about the number of days they have missed.

PERSONAL LOSS

There are many things we can do to let our students know we care about them. We can greet them at the classroom door, visit them at their after-school jobs, ask about their weekends, speak to them in the halls, write notes on their papers, call home, enforce fair rules, and call them by name.

We can also help our students cope with grief. We can help them deal with family problems such as divorce, separation, long-term illness, career changes, moving, or the loss of a home to fire or other disaster. We can and should also help our students cope with the death of a family member or a friend.

If times of loss are troubling ones for adults, then they are catastrophic for adolescents. Students who have a strong network of caring adults to help them through these difficult times will make the adjustment much more quickly than those students who do not. Some of the negative effects that personal loss can create for students and their teachers include: failure to complete work, peer conflicts, apathy, depression, mood swings, low grades, lack of focus or concentration, and poor attendance.

There are many ways to help students who are grieving. Select the ones from the following list that will best help you and your students.

1. Write a note or send a card to let your student know you are thinking of him or her and are willing to help, lend support, and listen.

2. Speak to the student in person to reiterate what you wrote in the card or note.

3. Speak with the student's guidance counselor and other teachers to let them know about the situation so that all of the caring adults in the child's life can work together to help.

4. Contact the student's parents or guardians to let them know you are concerned and care about the student. Offer to help however you can at school.

5. If it is not an invasion of the student's privacy, speak with the other class members. Perhaps they could send a card together. Ask them to share their ideas on how to help the grieving student cope with the situation. Often many teens have had serious losses in their own lives before they reached the secondary grades and have excellent insights about how they want to offer support.

6. Watch for signs of a delayed reaction. Often teachers are surprised to find this in a student who they had thought was coping well. If you are prepared for it, you will be better able to understand the student's reaction and to offer help.

LACK OF MATERIALS

When students *occasionally* forget their textbooks or other materials, this really isn't a problem that can't be solved by a quick trip to a locker, the loan of a book from the extras in the classroom, or sharing with a friend.

The problem with forgetting materials comes when students *repeatedly* "forget." This causes discipline problems in time off-task and in distractions. Students who regularly don't bring their materials to class have determined that there is no real reason to bring them.

There are several tactics you can use to deal with this problem. Look over the list below and pick the ones you think would be most helpful to you and your students.

1. Prevent problems with materials by reminding students what they will need to bring to class on the following day. You can do this by telling students what they will need at the beginning of class and then at the end asking them to tell you what they should bring. Post signs on the chalkboard and by the door on the way out. Make it part of their homework assignment and write it on the syllabus.

2. At the beginning of class when you are standing at the door, hold the book for the day in your hand to remind students who may have forgotten.

3. Reward those students who remembered their texts or other materials with a little treat at sporadic intervals to encourage them to remember. Praise those students who have remembered to bring their materials.

4. Try to have three extra textbooks in the classroom so that you will be able to lend one to almost any student who slips and forgets. Three are not too many to keep track of if you are busy, especially if you have the students who borrow books from you write their names on the board to remind you that they have one.

5. If forgotten materials continue to be a problem even after all that you do to prevent it, then you will need to call home to speak to parents or guardians about your concern. Perhaps you and the parents could work together on a behavior contract to help the student become responsible.

6. If missing ink pens or pencils are a problem in your classroom, set up a system where students can borrow from a shared bank of supplies. Ask every student to donate a new ink pen and put two or three students in charge of these. Wrap a strip of tape around the top and number each one. When students borrow these pens or pencils, the students who are in charge of distributing them should record the name of the borrower and the pen number on the board to remind them to return them at the end of class. This system promotes self-discipline because students run it themselves and are responsible for contributing to it.

7. If you have students who are unable to afford school supplies, lend them the materials that they need with collateral until they can purchase their own. You can do this discreetly if you see that a student is having trouble and would appreciate the help. You could also ask students who take materials from you to work in the classroom before or after school to defray the cost.

DAYDREAMING

Of all the discipline problems teachers have to face in the course of a school year, day-dreaming is the most gentle. This thought-crime does not involve other students or noise or weapons or even intentional discourtesy.

A daydreamer is simply a student who has more interesting things to think about than your class and the work you have assigned. Daydreamers only cause problems when their inattention is prolonged enough that they are off-task long enough to attract your attention.

There are six simple techniques to help daydreamers stay focused on learning while they are in your class. Use or adapt these to help your students be as productive in real life as they are in their dreams.

Step One

Close monitoring will keep many daydreamers focused on the task at hand. If the room is quiet, the lesson dull, and the teacher sitting at a desk, daydreamers will be encouraged to drift away. Stay on your feet and closely supervise everyone to keep all dreamers working. Call on daydreamers by name when the class is involved in a discussion.

Step Two

If monitoring and moving around does not work as well as you would like, focus all of your students on the work at hand, and then move close to the student who is daydreaming and stay there until he or she is on-task again. Offer assistance or ask a question to help day-dreamers stay focused on the assignment.

Step Three

Examine the lesson you have planned. Is it interesting? Are the activities varied, challenging, and engaging so that students will want to do the work? If the assignment requires that a student write or work in a team with other students, then daydreaming will be reduced. Reading silently and listening to lectures are prime times for daydreaming.

Step Four

If an upcoming event such as the prom, a championship game, or a holiday seems to cause more off-task behavior and daydreaming than usual, try to incorporate the event into the day's lesson in an attempt to redirect your students' thinking into productive work instead of daydreams.

Step Five

Examine your seating chart. Is the daydreamer facing away from you? At the back? Near a window? Move dreamers to a spot in the room where it will be difficult for them to lose focus of the lesson.

Step Six

If daydreaming is a chronic problem for a student, then you must schedule a conference with that student to discuss the problem and its solutions. You may be satisfied after talking with the student that the problem is solved. However, if you are not confident that the problem can be solved by just talking about it, then you and the daydreaming student should enter into a behavior contract designed to help the student stay focused on school work.

CULTURAL DIVERSITY

One of the enduring successes of our public school system lies in the variety of cultures that meet peacefully in thousands of classrooms each day: in small towns, suburbs, rural areas, big cities—wherever there are children in a school. We should be proud of how well so many cultural groups come together. In the classroom as well as in the rest of our country, cultural diversity is a fact of daily life.

While many people define culture solely in racial or ethnic terms, the truth is that culture is far more wide-reaching than this narrow definition would imply. We all belong to many cultural groups based on features such as: economics, geography, age, gender, religion, education level, past experiences, aspirations, or interests. Each one of these cultural groups affects how well we and our students interact with each other.

If we ignore the cultural differences we find in our students, we create the potential for a clash of values. Some of the discipline problems that arise from this result in students who are in conflict with each other, with their teachers, and with the expectations of a school environment.

If, instead of ignoring them, we choose to accept and celebrate those same cultural differences among our students, we will tap into rich resources that will help us create a classroom climate of shared trust, respect, and appreciation. There are three approaches you can take to dealing with cultural diversity. You could follow some general guidelines, explore cultural heritages, and create another culture for your students. These approaches are not exclusive of one another and can be used together successfully.

The first of these approaches, following general guidelines, can help you incorporate the many cultures in your classroom into a solidly successful working unit.

General Guidelines

1. Even if you have lived there all of your life, take time to find out about your community's various cultural groups. Understanding this and how those groups are represented in your school system will help you begin to understand your students better.

2. Accept the fact that you cannot stop racism or intolerance if that is what students are taught at home. However, you can and should stop it at school. Make your position clear through word and deed.

3. Allow no little "slips" from your students that indicate a less-than-respectful and appreciative attitude toward each other's culture.

4. Any successful school program requires the involvement of parents. If your students are having trouble relating to each other because of cultural differences, then get parents or guardians involved as quickly and as positively as possible.

5. Do all that you can to increase the self-esteem of your students. Students who are sure of themselves will be less likely to have to turn on others to feel better about themselves.

6. Don't ignore cultural differences. To do so is to make your students feel unappreciated and unworthy.

7. If your students are not behaving in ways that you like, examine the motives behind the actions. For example, if some of your students have trouble making eye contact with you, you need to determine if this is a way of showing deference for your role as a teacher before you assume this body language signals defiance or disrespect.

8. Stress the importance of open-mindedness and acceptance for people whose beliefs or lifestyles are not the same as those of your students. You can do this in your classroom every day by modeling those traits yourself.

9. Provide plenty of opportunities for discussion about the topic of cultures and the differences among people. These discussions do not have to involve hours of class time, but can be an important part of your closing or opening exercises.

10. Recognize that the concerns of a parent or guardian who is not part of your culture may not be the same concerns that you have. If you are sensitive to this when you speak with parents, you will find yourself asking questions to help determine what their goals for their children are before you impose the beliefs of another culture.

11. Don't challenge the cultural beliefs of your students in a mistaken attempt to make them choose between the values they hold and the ones you would like to impose. This heavy-handed strategy will only result in resentment or confusion, not enlightenment. It is better for you to expose your students to as wide a variety of beliefs and cultures as you can while guiding them to make wise choices for themselves.

Cultural Heritage Exploration

Another way many educators have found successful in dealing with cultural differences is to have their students explore their cultural heritages. While this is easier for teachers in disciplines such as social studies or language arts, it is still possible for teachers in other disciplines to incorporate this exploration into their lessons. Here are some strategies you could use to get started.

1. Emphasize the contributions that various cultural groups have made to the community and to your school. You can have students explore this in a variety of ways: skits, displays, interviews with community members, questionnaires about traditions and beliefs, writing assignments, and oral presentations.

2. Guest speakers are a valuable resource in a project such as this. You could invite representatives from several cultural groups to conduct a panel discussion where they compare their beliefs and lifestyles.

3. Whatever form you choose for exploring the cultural heritage of your students, the emphasis at the end of the project should be on the shared values and beliefs that all cultures have in common as well as on the contributions of the various members of a group.

Building a Classroom Culture

Time and time again people who have risen from the depths of poverty and adversity have credited their success to the importance that school played in their lives when they needed guidance. School provided them with the hope of a future away from the misery of their daily existence.

While the circumstances for your students may not be as extreme, there are students in your class who need support and guidance in their lives. One way to provide this for them is create a classroom culture that supersedes the various other cultures in the room.

In a classroom culture the teacher and students develop a sense of loyalty to the class and to the group that results in a positive and productive atmosphere. Students in this kind of classroom act as if they are in one large family of mutually supportive friends. The teamwork skills that your students will learn in a classroom culture are ones they will use later in their workplace experiences.

There are many ways to create a successful classroom culture. Pick those strategies from the following list that will best fit your teaching needs.

1. When a new student enters the class, have the other students write quick notes of welcome and advice on how to succeed in the class.

2. Have all students take part in determining the class rules by encouraging their active participation through class discussions.

3. Involve students in the daily tasks of the classroom. They can and should be responsible for a variety of tasks such as cleaning up, passing out papers, taking care of shared materials, running errands, and tutoring each other.

4. When there seems to be a conflict between what you want and what the group wants, allow students to speak up to present their side of the story through a spokesperson. This is an activity that would be appropriate only if the situation is one where you are willing to compromise, such as changing the due date of a term paper. It is also an activity that makes students feel you value their opinions when they are expressed clearly and logically.

5. Encourage students to help each other in understanding their lessons as often as possible. Students who take the time to tutor or assist each other with assignments not only learn the material better themselves, but they form a helpful bond with the students they are helping.

6. Your students could enter into a fund-raising event to help others who are less fortunate than themselves. Students who work together for the good of others will experience a real boost to their own self-esteem.

7. Instead of raising money, your students could also work together on a project outside of class. There are limitless opportunities for this. They could work at a soup kitchen, clean up a highway on Earth Day, send greeting cards to nursing home residents, or paint playground equipment in a local park.

8. Keep a chart of the good things you see your students doing and post this chart in a prominent place to remind them of their successes.

9. Put students in charge of shared materials. They will take better care of equipment and books if they are the ones responsible for them.

10. Encourage students to form study groups to get together to prepare for big tests and projects.

11. Use plural possessive pronouns often. Saying "our" room, "our" books, and "our" desks is much more friendly and inclusive than "mine, mine, mine."

12. Take their help when they offer it. If a student wants to help you carry something or run an errand, accept.

13. Have students contribute to the shared materials the school system does not provide for them. They can bring in tissues, pens, paper, and old magazines for everyone to use. They will value this more than if you provide these items for them.

14. Display their work. Few things increase a student's sense of pride than seeing his or her project displayed for all to see.

15. Take photographs of your students and display them. Make lists of your students in each class and display that with the photos to show your pride in each one. You can use computer calligraphy or other special effects to make the list and the photographs as attractive as possible.

16. Create a "wall of fame" to showcase the good things your students accomplish.

17. Have a class newsletter that the students themselves compose.

18. Engage them in as many real-life problems to solve as possible so that they can not only work together but your students can see that there is a place for this type of activity all through their lives.

19. Have a class goal for your students to work towards. They might all work to improve their behavior so that they could have a class outing or go on a field trip, for example. The emphasis here should be on the things they can do as a group to improve their behavior so that they can all share in the reward that they have worked to earn.

20. Teach your students the importance of saying kind things to each other. Picking on each other and saying insulting things is something that is too easy for many of our students to do. Steer them towards being as complimentary to each other as possible in an effort to get along with every member of the class.

21. Play ice-breaking games with your students so that they know each other well enough to learn to like each other. Make sure they know each other's names and a little bit about each other at the beginning of the term.

22. Ask their advice and opinions. Students often have useful insights to problems that perplex adults.

23. Use your sense of humor and encourage them to use theirs to have shared jokes and other friendly connections.

24. Celebrate birthdays and silly events as well as every success that you can.

25. Have students work together to help each other make up missed work. They should be the ones who remind each other of this so that you do not have to nag.

26. Stress the importance of courtesy as a mark of respect to each other, the class, you, and to themselves.

PROFANITY

Profanity is a fairly common problem in many secondary schools. Our society's standards about what is appropriate language to use at school have relaxed considerably in the last few years. Not too long ago, the expression, "School sucks!" was considered indecent language. Now most people regard it as rude, but not necessarily indecent.

Profanity may seem to be a perplexing problem at first, but it really isn't. While it is no longer considered educationally sound to wash a student's mouth out with soap, there are still many effective ways to deal with this problem.

Although there are dozens of ways to effectively deal with the problem of profanity in your classroom, most of the incidents of inappropriate language fall into one of the two most common categories described below. Use the guidelines for dealing with each type to get this problem under control in your classroom.

Category One: Unintentional Profanity

DESCRIPTION. In this category students simply make a slip of the tongue while they are chatting with one another. In this category students do not mean for you to overhear them. Sometimes this type happens in the hallways where students don't think they can be overheard by adults.

SOLUTIONS

1. Discuss the problem of swearing at the start of the term. Have students brainstorm reasons why this type of language is not acceptable everywhere. Explain that everyone has various levels of language and that students need to practice a more formal one at school so that they will be able to speak correctly in situations where it is expected. Have students discuss the ways they can break this habit.

2. Establish a hierarchy of consequences to help students remember not to swear. Here's a possible sequence:

   First Offense: Warning
   Second Offense: 10-minute detention
   Third Offense: 10-minute detention and phone call to parent
   Fourth Offense: Referral to administrator

3. Be careful when you overhear cursing not to turn to a student and say "What did you just say?" unless you want to hear the curse word again. You can usually tell by the shocked looks on the faces of the students near the guilty one that the word was inappropriate.

4. Be aware of those times in your class period when your students are more prone to forget and swear. Some potential trouble spots are at the start of class, at the end of class, between activities when students are switching mental gears and have time to chat, and when there is a loosely structured activity with lots of student movement and conversation.

5. Many times students who have cursed accidentally will try to convince you that they really said something else. Don't accept this.

6. Pay attention, however, if a student is genuinely remorseful and immediately apologizes. At that point the negative consequences should not have to be enacted because the student has enough self-discipline to realize that the mistake should not have happened and has tried to undo the error. If the student continues to forget, then you should enact the consequences.

7. Even though cursing is more common now than it used to be, you should not allow even mild words to just slip by without acting unless you want your students to believe that you think swearing in class is acceptable.

8. No matter how tempted or angry you may be, never swear in class yourself. Your students need for you to be a role model.

Category Two: Intentional Profanity

DESCRIPTION. Some words are bombs. As soon as students say them, they know they have gone over the line of what is and what isn't acceptable behavior. These are the hateful words that students throw at you or at other students when they are out of control with anger. This is a very different situation from the first category where a student does not mean to curse in front of you. In this type of incident, students deliberately use language to try to hurt the object of their anger. Most of the time these incidents also involve other problems: racial slurs or insults. Usually these incidents involve the "major" curse words . . . not just "hell" or "damn."

SOLUTION. You should not deal with this situation by yourself. This is a serious matter and should be taken seriously. You have two choices to make, depending on the severity of the offense.

1. If you are convinced the student is really out of control with anger, send for help and have the student removed from the classroom at once. You should then follow through with a written referral to an administrator and by contacting the student's parents.

2. If you think the student will not further disturb class, you may allow him or her to remain, but you should refer the student to the attention of an administrator before the school day is over. The situation should be dealt with before the student returns to your class. You should also phone the parents or guardians to let them know what happened and that you have referred the child to an administrator.

STEALING

In most secondary classrooms an act of theft will put to a halt even the most interesting lessons you have planned. The unpleasant consequences of stealing go beyond the thief and the victim as the rest of the class is involved in trying to figure out who is to blame and what the victim should do when the guilty person is discovered. All of your efforts to establish an atmosphere of trust vanish as your students stare suspiciously at each other.

The strategies for coping with the discipline problems caused by stealing can be divided into two categories: prevention and techniques for coping with theft once it has occurred.

Prevention

1. Be careful to remove temptation. Don't leave your personal belongs out in the open or on your desk. If you carry credit cards, be careful with them at school. Many street-smart teachers do not carry very much cash or take their credit cards to school.

2. If you have school money, be extra careful to deposit it if it is meant to be deposited or to keep it in a safe place until you can. If you have school equipment that would be attractive to thieves, be extra careful to lock it away safely and to establish an accounting system for when you check it out for student use.

3. Teach your students to be street smart also. Attractive school items that are often stolen are calculators, books, notebooks with notes, yearbooks, watches, jewelry, tapes, and electronic games.

4. Discourage your students from bringing large amounts of cash to school and then letting others know about it. Your school should already have a policy that bans headphones, games, and other electronic toys that are easy to steal. Be sure to enforce it if one is already in place.

5. Leave your classroom locked when you are not in it. Don't give your keys to students.

6. Don't allow students to take things from your desk, closet, file cabinet, or other personal space without your permission.

What to Do Once Stealing Has Happened

1. If your teacher's edition of the textbook or something else important to you is taken, offer a small reward for its return. State that you will ask no questions. Honor the "no question" rule even though you would like to know who took the item. What is important is that your belongings are returned to you.

2. When you catch a student stealing, keep this information as private as possible. If your school's policy is that you should report theft to an administrator, then you should do so. Certainly the student's parents or guardians should be involved. You should, however, try to help that student maintain a sense of dignity in front of his or her peers.

3. Try to find out why the student has stolen. Is there something you can do to help the student?

4. The best thing you can do after a student has been caught is to help the student learn from the mistake and then go forward. Improve your personal relationship with students who are caught stealing so that they can begin to improve their sense of self. Improved self-esteem will help many teens—who might be tempted to go along with the crowd—to resist temptation.

5. The most common mistake teachers who have an incident of stealing happen in their classrooms make is to keep all of the students in the room until either the item is found, someone tells on a classmate, or a student confesses. The lost class time involved in this procedure for an entire roomful of students is not usually worth the slim possibility of the item being returned.

WHEN YOU NEED A SUBSTITUTE

What do you want to think about while you are at home feverish with flu? Do you wonder if your students are working quietly or do you convince yourself that they are gleefully tormenting the hapless substitute? Have you created the kind of classroom environment where students are self-directed in your absence?

It's not easy to miss school if you are a responsible teacher. So much could go wrong that many of us just go to work even when we aren't well rather than have to deal with a substitute and the problems that missing a day of school can cause. However, you *can* maintain a climate of positive discipline when there is a substitute teacher in your place.

Instead of hoping that you'll never be absent, take an hour or so now to get organized and you will be able to trust your students to continue as if you were with them. While a large part of the discipline problems that occur when you are out can be attributed to the inability of the substitute teacher to maintain your standards and the high spirits of your students, the solution to these problems lies with you. There are many steps you can take to see that your class runs smoothly even though you are not in the room.

1. Make it a point to use your leave-time sparingly. You'll set a good example for your students; they need you in the classroom. You also need to have plenty of accumulated leave-time in case you are in an accident or some other serious misfortune befalls you.

2. As soon as you know that you are going to be absent, secure a substitute. The competent ones are usually booked weeks in advance.

3. Be kind to your sub. Don't leave lots of material to be photocopied or written on the board. If you don't have time to do it, chances are that your sub won't either. The most frequent substitute complaints are no lesson plans, plans that are impossible to follow, no seating chart, missing materials or equipment, and not enough for students to do.

4. Whenever possible, communicate directly with your students before or during your absence. They will appreciate this show of respect that you have for their maturity; and you will appreciate the lack of confusion and trouble that this simple act will save all of you.

5. Very early in the year set up a folder with the routine information any substitute would need to run your class smoothly. Include these items in it:
   - an up-to-date seating chart
   - a photocopy of your roll
   - a daily schedule
   - a copy of the *school* rules
   - a copy of *your* rules and procedures
   - fire drill and emergency information
   - the names of student helpers
   - the names of students with special needs (in case you have a sub who doesn't believe in sending ill children to the school nurse)
   - the names and room numbers of helpful colleagues

- hall passes
- a copy of your daily schedule
- where you would like for the sub to leave your plans
- a scratch pad so the sub can leave notes

6. You should also make a folder of emergency plans to be used in case you can't get your plans to school. These can be high-interest worksheets or activities that require very little instruction. If you are really cautious, you'll have enough for five days. Save time by using the same emergency plans every year. The time you spend early in the year on organizing materials for possible use by a substitute will save you stress when you are ill or rushed for time later.

7. Don't leave a film for a substitute to show while you are out. Students won't take it as seriously as when you are there and technical difficulties could cause problems. Don't assign a trip to the library, either. Students tend to be disruptive whenever there's a break in the routine. Use your common sense instead. Plan a quiet lesson of independent work that is easy for your sub and your students to follow.

8. Make the lesson you leave for your students meaningful. Drills and review exercises are good. Be sure your substitute knows to collect the papers for the day's work so that you can see who was on-task and who wasn't. You should also take a grade on the assignments your students do while you're out. Be sure you have the sub tell them that this will happen so that they will be encouraged to stay on-task.

9. Teach your students what to do when you are out. Hold them to the same standards of behavior and performance as when you are there with them. You might even want to role-play some scenarios of possible substitute problems with them. Select students to be substitute assistants early in the term. Discuss their duties so that they can help the substitute keep instruction running smoothly.

10. Be sure to specify in your plans whether or not you want students to work together during an activity. Many substitutes are just not comfortable with the noise level associated with group activities.

11. Put yourself in your sub's place. Would you be able to walk into an unfamiliar classroom filled with unfamiliar adolescents and immediately follow your plans?

12. If you need to be on an extended leave, stay in contact with your principal. Parents and other staff members will ask about you and your supervisor needs to be able to answer their questions. Work as closely as you can with your substitute to maintain the direction you want instruction to take. This is the only time you should leave your grade book with a substitute. Do everything you can to minimize the disruption in learning as well as to protect your professional reputation.

TRAVELING WITH YOUR STUDENTS

Field trips are an institution. Whether we went to the state fair in junior high or to the nation's capitol on our senior trip, some of our fondest memories of our own school days probably involve the fun we had on field trips.

Today there are more opportunities than ever for enrichment and fun through educational travel, whether the destination is a foreign country or a local point of interest. If field trips are handled well, everything goes smoothly and students and their chaperones can relax and enjoy the experience.

Unfortunately for many teachers, traveling with students is a huge headache that is just not worth the trouble. The kinds of misbehaviors that can ruin a field trip are daunting: being late for curfew, substance abuse, rowdy behavior in public places, shoplifting, missing a plane or bus, losing luggage or other personal belongings, serious safety issues . . . . The list of what can go wrong is endless. All of the planning, the enormous potential for misbehavior, the hassles with arranging transportation or lodging—coping with these and the other disasters that lie in wait for the poor teacher who did not plan the experience well may discourage many teachers who would like to travel with students.

If you would like to offer the exciting experience of educational travel to your students, you don't need to be intimidated by the thoughts of what could go wrong. Many, many teachers travel with their students and experience no problems at all.

Use the following techniques to move your students out of the classroom and into the world.

1. Make sure your field trips have an educational purpose and are not just for fun if you want to justify the experience for everyone involved. Students who have a serious purpose for a trip tend to behave better than those who are just on a fun-filled outing.

2. Work hard while planning the trip to keep the focus on learning, not just on playing as some of your students will try to convince you to do. A nice mixture of museums, guided tours, and rest times in a park, for example, will provide your students with the balance they need to make the trip an enjoyable learning experience.

3. Involve your students in planning and setting rules as much as is appropriate for their age. Students who have a say in what they're going to do are more likely to enjoy the trip and benefit from it. They will also be inclined to follow the rules and encourage their peers to do the same.

4. Make sure you have enough chaperones so that each student has quick access to an adult in case of need. You should have no fewer than one adult for every ten teens. The more chaperones you have, the better. Make sure the chaperones understand your behavior standards and will work with you and your students.

5. Make your plans well in advance of the travel date. Call the areas you intend to visit and make arrangements for guides, parking, and preliminary material to be sent to your students in order to prevent any problems.

6. After you have called ahead to the points of your destination, it would not hurt to call again a second time closer to the travel date to confirm your appointments and any arrangements you expect.

7. If you are traveling with students who have special needs, make sure they will be able to enjoy the trip, also. Be sure there are plenty of facilities available for them and you have enough help in managing wheelchairs or whatever other needs your students might have.

8. Be firm in setting the types of behaviors you *will* and *will not* tolerate on a trip. Small annoyances that can be tolerated in a classroom will quickly have you gritting your teeth on a long bus or plane ride.

9. Make sure to prepare your students for what they will learn on the trip. Students who are informed enough to have a basis of knowledge to relate what they see to what they have already learned will gain a great deal from the experience of traveling with you. They will pay better attention to speakers and announcements if they are well prepared.

10. Do not take students who you can't trust on a field trip. If they cannot control their behavior in the classroom, then they will be even less likely to behave admirably in a public place. Be careful to prevent problems even if it means not taking everyone on the trip or even not taking a trip at all.

11. One area you certainly need to discuss with your students in advance is food. Even veteran teachers are amazed at the amount of food very young children can consume. Plan out snacks and drinks with your students and accept the fact that they are not going to be thrilled with the same type of restaurants you would prefer. Before you leave school you also need to discuss table manners and civilized eating habits with any group you take out in public.

12. Set up rules in advance for the wearing of hats or clothing that might be offensive to people who are seeing you and your students as representatives of your school and community. Be as lenient as you can with their taste in music and other preferences when you can, but make it clear that you expect exemplary behavior from all participants.

13. Consider having your students sign a behavior agreement before the trip so that they and their parents or guardians know exactly what you expect their behavior to be. Stating your expectations in advance and in writing will eliminate many of the problems that could happen in a less-structured situation.

14. Rehearse with your students the behaviors you expect them to exhibit when they are in various situations. You can have lots of fun while getting your point across if you role-play situations where they have to listen to a dull docent, a boring lecture, or an excessively formal presentation while being extremely polite.

15. Teach your students the importance of promptness on trips. No one has the right to make an entire group waste precious time waiting for stragglers. Stress this over and over. Make sure everyone who needs one has a watch that has the same time as yours.

16. Establish a buddy system to keep up with your students. If you want to put them in groups or pairs, you'll do well if you let them pick their partners. Use the buddy system to make sure you don't leave anyone behind at any stop you make. Have frequent buddy checks to practice looking out for each other. Buddies can remind each other how to behave in museums and during the rest of the trip, too, if you encourage them to watch out for each other.

17. Don't allow your students to stop off at a mall or other shopping area just to spend money. The possibilities for trouble in these activities are endless, ranging from shoplifting to delaying the trip while you search for a missing student.

18. Stress the importance of courtesy. As representatives of your school, your students should be impressive in their courtesy to each other, to the chaperones, and to the adults and other people they meet. Small courtesies soothe all sorts of awkward situations. Promote this attitude all year and you'll be rewarded with a pleasant trip.

19. Be clear with your students about just how much money they will need to take with them on the trip. Planning ahead will prevent any awkwardness that might ruin a trip for an unprepared student. You will also avoid discipline problems that could arise from students who are upset.

20. Expect your students to pick up their own trash. Provide them with plenty of trash bags and encourage them to place even the tiniest scraps in them. Students who clean up after themselves are usually welcome to return to most places.

21. Set up a telephone chain for parents or guardians to notify each other if the bus is going to be late or if other problems arise. Once you have established a returning time, you certainly don't want to have parents sitting in a parking lot worrying about their children or even not coming to get them because you have not been clear about the time. A telephone chain will serve to relieve anxiety if you are late in returning.

22. If your students will be missing class time, be sure to stress the importance of making up any missed work promptly. Part of your job as an educator is to stress the importance of success in all classes, so see to it that your students know what they need to do to make up any assignment they have missed in other classes.

23. What happens if a problem arises? Contact your supervisor as soon as you can to get advice and to be the first one to explain. Do everything you can to prevent problems, but don't hesitate to contact your supervisor when you need help or when the situation warrants outside assistance.

> *"Instruction does not prevent waste of time or mistakes;*
> *and mistakes themselves are often the best teachers of all."*
>
> —Froude

Section 8

MOVING BEYOND CROWD CONTROL TO PROMOTE SELF-DISCIPLINE

In This Section . . .

This section gives you the opportunity to learn about the many ways you can promote self-discipline in your students. The reasons for doing this are given in "Moving Beyond Crowd Control to Promote Self-Discipline."

"The Importance of Giving Your Students a Future" is examined in the suggestions you'll find for using the five reproducibles that will help you get your students on the right track for success.

"Techniques for Increasing Intrinsic Motivation," "Putting Your High Expectations to Work," and "15 Ways Teachers Can Communicate Their Expectations" are explained so that you'll never have to worry about students who don't want to try their best on every assignment.

Learn how to be a consistent teacher who involves as many students as possible in authentic learning experiences in "The Consistent Teacher" and "Creating Self-Disciplined Students Through Problem-Solving Activities."

If you apply the techniques in "Holding Students Accountable for Their Own Success" and the reproducible that accompanies it, you'll find that students will rise to meet the challenge.

Also in this section are positive techniques for helping students improve their self-esteem in "Focusing on Your Students' Strengths," "Promoting Self-Discipline through Self-Image," and "Motivational Tools We Can All Use."

"No bird soars too high if he soars with his own wings."
—William Blake

MOVING BEYOND CROWD CONTROL TO PROMOTE SELF-DISCIPLINE

If the ultimate purpose of the enormous amount of energy, thought, and effort that we pour into our discipline policies and practices is to create students who are self-directed, at what point will we know we have been successful?

Unfortunately, as with most of our dealings with adolescent students, the process is not always an easy one. Often, just when we think that all of our discipline goals have been met, something will happen in class to remind us that our students still need us to help them from straying off-task.

In spite of the impossibility of ever knowing for certain just how successful our attempts to help students assume responsibility for their actions will be, we must work towards that goal. We should not only direct our students so that they understand what they should do, but we must encourage them to be willing to do the right thing at the right time.

Moving students towards the goal that we have for them—that they will become self-disciplined learners—requires a great deal from all of us. We have to use all of our skills and knowledge to take advantage of the opportunities that present themselves. This is easier for those teachers who prepare themselves.

Fortunately for teachers, we have countless chances to help students in their efforts to become self-disciplined. If you want to help your students mature into taking personal responsibility for themselves, you could pick two or three of these techniques to use now. When they have become an ingrained part of the culture of excellence you want to promote in your classroom, then you could try some of the others.

Model the Behavior You Want Your Students to Have

Our actions certainly speak louder than our words when it comes to teaching our students the behaviors we want to see from them. This is particularly true of self-directed behaviors.

If we want students to be articulate, then we must be articulate. If we want their work to be neatly done, then the handouts we give them must be models of neatly done work. If we expect our students to come to class on time, then we must encourage that promptness through our own punctuality.

Secondary students need strong positive role models who will show them the way to succeed. One of the greatest gifts we can give our students is to be the kind of role model they need day after day.

Maintain High Standards for All of Your Students

We are not going to be successful in moving our students towards self-directed behavior unless we have high academic and behavior standards for them. If students are going to stretch their limits and grow, then they need to be challenged to do this.

If you want to see just how capable your students can be, then set limits that are difficult but not impossible for them. You don't have to expect perfect academic or social behaviors all of the time, but too often our students are much more capable than we give them credit for being.

It is especially important to maintain these high standards when students seem to struggle or when less capable students are included in the class. It is a disservice to lower standards instead of helping students rise to meet them.

Motivate Your Students to Work Well

It is important for all of us to recall our own school years when large parts of the day were not as interesting for us as others. What made the difference for many of us was a determined and caring teacher who motivated us to want to learn.

These were the teachers whose homework we always did no matter what. We arranged our dentist appointments around their classes because we did not want to miss even one. What a contrast to those other classes where we perfected the fine art of sneaking peeks at the clock to see if another thirty seconds of tedium had passed yet.

The difference in those classes was not only in the subject matter under study. Those teachers who cared enough to motivate us to learn made the difference. We, too, can motivate our students to want to succeed. There are hundreds of techniques at hand for those teachers who use a bit of creativity to catch and sustain student interest. If you want your students to want to take responsibility for themselves, it is up to you to include as many motivating factors into each lesson as you can.

Be Encouraging and Positive with Your Students

Students whose teachers make it abundantly clear that they have confidence in their ability to succeed are students who are more apt to become self-disciplined than those whose teachers doubt their students' abilities.

If you want positive actions to come from your students, then you must show your own positive side. This does not mean you need to be falsely cheerful or to flatter your students; both of these will surely fail with a spectacular thud.

Secondary students are fragile creatures who need strong doses of support and encouragement (just like their teachers) in order to be at their best. If you want to help them move towards self-discipline, encouragement and a positive approach are critical for success.

Hold Your Students Accountable for Their Actions

In addition to high expectations and encouragement, students must be aware that there is also some level of negative consequence for their actions. It isn't enough to just have high standards for your students. You also must hold them accountable for their success or lack of it in meeting those standards.

Teachers can use many techniques to make sure students are learning to accept responsibility for themselves. These techniques should be part of the overall scheme by which you encourage students to perform at their best level academically and socially. If we never hold students accountable for their actions, then they will not develop into the resilient and self-disciplined pupils that we want them to be.

THE IMPORTANCE OF GIVING YOUR STUDENTS A FUTURE

According to the "American dream," anyone who wants to be a success can achieve that goal through a combination of persistence, hard work, and determination. This dream brought millions of immigrants to America in search of a better life. Sadly, the philosophy of violence and hopelessness permeating much of the popular culture avidly consumed by adolescents seems to have robbed many of them of the optimistic view of the future that guided so many earlier Americans to successful lives.

The widespread acceptance of this pessimistic attitude is not limited to inner-city street gangs. Teens who live in rural poverty, teens who are pregnant, teens who live in troubled homes, teens with substance abuse problems, teens in trouble with the law, teens who are unloved—almost every young person living in our country is at risk from this devastating hopelessness.

Adolescents need powerful and consistent messages from the caring adults in their lives to combat this national mood of weary despair. One of the most important tasks we can accomplish for our students is to help them grow and achieve their dreams.

If we are going to be successful at combating the negativity that seems to be so widespread among teens, we need to help them strengthen their feelings of self-worth by teaching them to set goals and then work to achieve them.

There are many benefits to teachers who do this. The most important one is the positive and purposeful class atmosphere that results from students who have a reason for attending school and have direction in their lives. This benefit has a profound effect on both teachers and students.

Here are some of the other benefits that can happen when teachers encourage students to become goal-oriented.

1. We can give support to students who are making serious efforts to learn to take control of their own lives and to achieve their dreams.

2. We can help students learn about career options so that they can make better choices about their lives after they leave school.

3. Our students will understand that what they do now will have an impact on their futures. They come to realize that there is a clear cause-and-effect correlation between their present and their future.

4. Students with clear goals have a reason to come to school and to learn. They are working for something, not just enduring another weary day at a desk. They achieve more than those students without goals.

5. Students will come to believe in their ability to make the productive choices that will help them fight peer pressure. The certainty of their decisions will help reduce many of the frustrations felt by teens today.

6. Students will develop marketable skills in secondary classes instead of waiting until they join the work force.

7. Secondary students of all ages need help in establishing realistic goals for themselves. We can help them with this at the same time we help them overcome the obstacles that stand in the way of their success.

8. Students who work towards achieving goals will learn to be successful. They will also learn that success comes from the act of taking responsibility for one's own actions and not from chance.

There are several ways you can begin the process of directing students to their futures. The most effective way is to begin with a structured lesson that will accomplish more than informal moments here and there. Here are ten steps for designing lessons that will help students establish goals and learn to work to accomplish them.

Step 1

Begin by having students discuss some of the famous people they know about. They can do this in a large-group or small-group discussion. Have them brainstorm about the qualities that cause some people to be successful. Eventually lead students to see that success does not happen by chance, but is created through planning and goal setting.

Step 2

Have students determine what personal qualities they already possess that could be classified as strengths and interests. You can do this informally or by using one of the student inventories in Section 4.

Step 3

Have students visualize their futures by imagining what they would like for their lives to be like five years and ten years from the present.

Step 4

Use the "Setting Long-Term Goals" form or design one of your own to have students write down the big goals they have for the future. Have them commit their dreams to paper along with the behaviors they will need to achieve their goals. Stress that long-term goals are those that are five or ten years away. (See next page.)

Step 5

Monitor carefully to make sure students' goals meet these criteria for success:
1. Goals should be specific.
2. Goals should be realistic.
3. Goals should be easy to explain.
4. Goals should be something the student really wants.
5. Goals should be attainable.

Step 6

Have students focus next on the mid-term goals they have to meet in order to achieve their long-term ones. Students can fill out the form provided or you can design one of your own. Stress that mid-term goals should be anywhere from six months to a year away. Use the sample form, "Setting Mid-Term Goals."

Step 7

Have students begin next on the short-term goals that will help them get started on the way to a successful future. Again, you can use the form included here or design one of your own. Short-term goals are ones students can accomplish today or within the week. Use the sample form, "Setting Short-Term Goals."

SETTING LONG-TERM GOALS

Name _____ Class _____

Goal 1: _____

Date when I achieve my goal: _____

Steps I will have to take to achieve my goal:

   1. _____

   2. _____

   3. _____

A problem I will have to manage to achieve my goal:

_____

_____

Goal 2: _____

Date when I will achieve my goal:

Steps I will have to take to achieve my goal:

   1. _____

   2. _____

   3. _____

A problem I will have to manage to achieve my goal:

_____

_____

Goal 3: _____

Date when I will achieve my goal:

Steps I will have to take to achieve my goal:

   1. _____

   2. _____

   3. _____

A problem I will have to manage to achieve my goal:

_____

_____

SETTING MID-TERM GOALS

Name _____ Class _____

Goal 1: _____

Date when I achieve my goal: _____

Steps I will have to take to achieve my goal:

   1. _____

   2. _____

   3. _____

A problem I will have to manage to achieve my goal:

_____

_____

Goal 2: _____

Date when I will achieve my goal:

Steps I will have to take to achieve my goal:

   1. _____

   2. _____

   3. _____

A problem I will have to manage to achieve my goal:

_____

_____

Goal 3: _____

Date when I will achieve my goal:

Steps I will have to take to achieve my goal:

   1. _____

   2. _____

   3. _____

A problem I will have to manage to achieve my goal:

_____

_____

SETTING SHORT-TERM GOALS

Name _____ Class _____

Target dates: _____ until _____

Goal 1: _____

How will I know when I have achieved my goal?

_____

_____

What specific steps must I take to achieve my goal?

1. _____
2. _____
3. _____
4. _____

What behavior might interfere with my goal?

_____

_____

Goal 2: _____

How will I know when I have achieved my goal?

_____

_____

What specific steps must I take to achieve my goal?

1. _____
2. _____
3. _____
4. _____

What behavior might interfere with my goal?

_____

_____

Are my goals:

_____ realistic?   _____ productive?   _____ attainable?

_____ specific?   _____ positive?   _____ timely?

Step 8

After students have committed themselves to their goals on paper, your next task is help them learn to become goal-directed. It's not enough to just write them down; people must learn to work to achieve their dreams. Do this by having students keep their goal commitments in their notebooks so that you can refer to them throughout the term.

Step 9

Use the flow chart included here or a similar activity to help your students understand that the only way to reach a long-term goal is by taking a series of smaller steps that lead from short-term goals to mid-term ones to the final ones. See "Goal-Setting Flow Chart" on the next page.

Step 10

Many teachers let the process drop at this point because they do not want to continue to spend class time on it. You don't have to spend more than a few minutes each week on helping your students stay focused on their weekly goals. This time will be regained several times over through the increased productivity of your students.

Other Activities You May Include

1. Help students who are having trouble staying focused identify the behaviors that are interfering with their goals. After they have done this, help them generate solutions to those problems.

2. Review their goals every now and then to see if students need to change direction. Are they taking the right steps? Are they still committed to these goals?

3. Ask students to determine the next steps in their personal growth. Do they need to seek more information about the goals they have for themselves? Do they need to find a mentor who will help them with guidance and support?

4. Use the "Goals and Strategies for School Success" form to help students focus on what they need to do to achieve in your class. They will find it easier to stay on task with this form because it takes a systematic approach to their class responsibilities. A sample form follows the flow chart.

5. Practice goal-setting techniques in the assignments you give your students. When they have a large project, ask them to break it down into smaller parts and then to set goals and timelines for each stage of the assignment.

GOAL-SETTING FLOW CHART

Name _____ Class _____

SHORT-TERM GOALS

1. _____
2. _____
3. _____
4. _____

MID-TERM GOALS

1. _____
2. _____
3. _____
4. _____

LONG-TERM GOALS

1. _____
2. _____
3. _____
4. _____

GOALS AND STRATEGIES FOR SCHOOL SUCCESS

Name _____ **Class** _____

I. Record the grade goal you have for this class.

_____

II. List the strategies you need to use to meet your goal.

1. _____
2. _____
3. _____
4. _____
5. _____

III. Keep a record of your progress here.

Date	*Assignment*	*Grade*

TECHNIQUES FOR INCREASING INTRINSIC MOTIVATION

Some of the greatest joys in a teacher's life are those happy moments when we realize all of our students want to do the work that we have assigned. We revel in the happy hum of their chatter as they settle down to tackle the problems posed in their assignments. The sense of satisfaction we feel when our students are excited about their work is one of the chief reasons that so many of us look forward to school each morning year after year.

Students who are busy doing their work just don't have time to misbehave. The challenge for all secondary teachers, of course, is how to create that desire to work in every student every day . . . day after day, week after week.

Much research has been done by many people to determine just what practices are useful in motivating students to be competent in school. It did not take long to discover that threats and intimidation don't work, while effective praise and tangible rewards do.

Even more effective than praise and tangible rewards, however, is intrinsic motivation. Intrinsic motivation is the incentive to work that is an essential part of the lesson plan or presentation. It is not a separate component, but rather, is built into the lesson itself.

Intrinsic motivation is the most effective stimulus to student achievement because its effect lasts much longer. Tangible rewards tend to be short-lived and not very useful once the student has or has not won a prize. For a long-term, fundamental change in students, intrinsic motivation has been proven to be successful over and over again.

There are many ways to include intrinsic motivation techniques in a lesson. Many effective teachers seem to do this instinctively by using a variety of strategies to sustain their students' interest in each assignment. All of us who want to motivate our students to achieve more or to perform at higher levels of success will follow their example and include more strategies for intrinsic motivation in our own lessons.

To boost your students' interest and desire to work productively, experiment with the following techniques that will help you build intrinsic motivation into your assignments. Try to include more than one in each lesson to reach as many students as possible.

50 Techniques for Increasing Intrinsic Motivation

1. Stimulate your students' curiosity by making your lessons suspenseful and novel. Most teens are interested in the new and different. Use this inclination to make a mystery out of old material. Have students solve puzzles or create solutions to problems. The anticipatory set component of your lesson plan is the ideal place to capture their curiosity with an intriguing question or brief puzzle.

2. Teach students to evaluate their own progress throughout a unit of study. Begin or end class by asking them to tell you what they have learned, what skill they have mastered, or what they have accomplished. You can even say to them, "You'll know you're on the right track when . . ." and have them finish the statement.

3. Don't work against the nature of your students. Instead, adapt their interests, hobbies, concerns, experiences, dreams, and cultural backgrounds into lessons as often as you can in order to make the material compelling for them.

4. Use your students' competitive instincts to your advantage. Instead of pitting one student against another, though, try putting students into teams to oppose other teams of students. The best sort of competition to foster, however, is the effort that a student can make to improve his or her own performance. Get students into the habit of asking themselves how they can improve each assignment so that it is better than the previous one.

5. When there is sufficient intrinsic motivation in an assignment, teachers do not have to answer the question we all dread, "Why do we have to learn this?" By making sure that our students have a real-life purpose for learning the material we teach, we will make them want to learn. As often as possible, our students should be engaged in real-world activities that will improve the skills they will need as adults.

6. Help students make a personal connection to the lesson. They should be able to identify with the people in the material under study. One simple way to do this is to use their names when creating worksheets or questions. Another is to use the writing-across-the-curriculum strategy of having students involve themselves in the material through a written response. An example of this strategy in a history class, for instance, would be to have students describe how they would find food, shelter, and clothing if they were to find themselves suddenly transported to ancient Greece. In written responses such as these students are forced to deal with compelling concerns rather than dry facts.

7. Surprise them! There are many things you can do that will make your students sit up and pay attention to the lesson. Try some of these just to get started:
   - say something startling
   - wear a costume
   - provide costumes for them
   - stage a reenactment
   - have them role play
   - hold up a message in a bottle
   - videotape them
   - give them something to eat

8. Make sure students know how they can apply the information they are learning. End class by asking them how to apply the information they've learned in your class to another class they are currently taking.

9. Issue a challenge. Ask them to beat their personal best on a test or other assignment. Or tell them that they must be finished by a certain time and then start watching the clock. Try telling them what a great student in the past has done well as a criteria for success on an assignment and challenge them to exceed that previous success.

10. Include assignments that require higher-level thinking skills. When students are asked to evaluate or judge material, they are doing much more interesting work than those students whose teachers only ask them to comprehend information. Open-ended questions are inherently interesting because they also do not risk a student's self-esteem. Students who are afraid of failure will be able to complete these questions successfully.

11. Expand on your students' previous learning. You could open class with an anticipatory set that will help students recall their previous knowledge about the new topic. Once you have done this, it shouldn't be too hard to help them move on to the new learning you want them to master.

12. Use a variety of media when you want to galvanize your students into paying close attention. Adapt these to the needs of your students: newspapers, advertisements, music, T-shirt slogans, cartoons, 3-D material, movies, art, computers, television, magazines, radio, and videos.

13. Play games with your students. There are many different kinds of games your students will enjoy playing in class. You could use sophisticated computer games or the dozens of low-tech ones that have been popular with students for years.

14. Put students who are in teams in charge of the successful learning of their teammates. A successful team project involves giving each student part of the information that they will all need to know. After each person has presented his or her part to the rest of the group, the entire group will benefit from the successful teaching by their teammates.

15. Make one assignment dependent on the successful completion of another. Tell students they won't be able to move on to the next project until they have acquired the learning they will need from the first assignment.

16. Be enthusiastic and project that enthusiasm to your students. Never admit that you find an assignment dull or that you fear they will find it less than intriguing or exciting themselves. Do all that you can to get students excited about what they have to learn. Hold a pep rally before a quiz if that is what it takes to generate enthusiasm.

17. Arrange for students to have a close, structured, and positive working relationship with their peers. Promote a team spirit in your class through such activities as creating a class motto or having students work together in study teams. Students who feel they are an important part of a learning community will feel encouraged to do their work well.

18. Show your students how to do their work. Often students do not know where to begin to manage their study time, organize their notes, or work efficiently. You can have students write detailed proposals for assignments or long-term projects. Some of the questions you should help students answer might include:

    ■ What steps do they need to take to get started?
    ■ What materials will they need?
    ■ How long will each step take?
    ■ What extra work can they do to make sure the project is a success?
    ■ How do they plan to get each part accomplished?

19. Include plenty of opportunities for discussion in your class. Students love to discuss issues and to debate topics of interest. One successful way to manage this is to have students work in teams to prepare for the discussion so that everyone's ideas will be included.

20. Remember the old saying, "Nothing succeeds like success." Design lessons that are easier at the beginning of the term so that your students can experience immediate success in your class. This will be much more effective than if they do poorly at first.

21. Hone your questioning techniques so that the oral drills and review sessions you conduct will engage every student. Some advice on this topic is included in Section 5 in "Perfecting the Art of Questioning."

22. Include opportunities for your students to use their imagination and to indulge in fantasy in your class. The enormous success of computer simulation games should show educators the power of our students' imaginations. Even in classes that don't appear to lend themselves to this type of work, a creative teacher will find a way. For example, in math class, teachers could ask students to imagine holding a conversation with Archimedes, Pascal, or Euclid and then write about it.

23. Have older students serve as mentors to younger ones. Either older students could mentor your students or yours could mentor younger students or, hopefully, both. What mentors do that is successful is show students what they need to know in order to succeed in school. In order to make good life choices for themselves, students need to see that others have done it and that they can, too.

24. Help students set goals for themselves and work towards the achievement of those goals. The smaller goals they set for themselves each week should be ones that enable them to work towards accomplishing the larger goals for their lives.

25. Invite community leaders to speak to your students as part of a unit of study. When other adults—coaches, other teachers, youth leaders, government officials, or counselors—talk about the importance of success in school, your students will be encouraged to stay focused on worthwhile goals.

26. Use plenty of models and examples when you show students how to do something. Your students need to know what you want for them to do and how you want them to do it.

27. Keep parents or guardians involved in class activities. Make sure you inform them of due dates for big projects and other information that will help them encourage their children to do well in your class.

28. Have students list on posters the reasons why school is important. Display these to remind students why they should strive to succeed in class.

29. Make sure the appreciation you show your students is focused on the positive qualities you observe about their work habits or their assignments. If they know exactly what they have been doing right, students will be encouraged to keep trying to do well.

30. Encourage open-mindedness and tolerance in your students so that they won't be afraid to take intellectual risks. Many students are so afraid of failure and rejection that they are not willing to share their ideas and expertise with others.

31. Pace your lesson delivery so that time doesn't drag for your students. Move quickly from one point to the next in a smooth flow of assignments so that students don't waste time.

32. Involve your students in projects of all types—simple and complicated, long-term and short-term.

33. Project an air of confidence in your students. They should feel you have unshakable faith in their ability to succeed at every assignment.

34. Too often students are kept in the dark about the "big picture." They don't understand how one assignment will lead to others. They don't see why they should learn certain skills or material. Combat this fragmented approach to their education by giving each one a course outline and by using a syllabus.

35. Be explicit about the criteria for success on each assignment so that students know what it is they have to do to be successful.

36. Break larger assignments into manageable amounts of work with clear deadlines. Provide checklists or other graphic organizers to help students stay focused. When students see each assignment as part of a progression of work, they will be more inclined to complete each assignment.

37. Include a variety of learning styles and modalities in each assignment. Students who are encouraged to learn in a variety of ways will be more successful than those who aren't.

38. Use a variety of assessment techniques so that if a student fails at one evaluation, he or she won't quit trying because of one low grade.

39. Give daily feedback to students. Return papers promptly. Monitor progress by staying on your feet and interacting with your students. Teach students to give each other feedback by proofreading or double-checking each other's work.

40. Reward effort. Not every pupil will master every lesson to your satisfaction, but you should recognize those who try their best.

41. Hold periodic conferences with your students. Make it a point to reach everyone through these conversations; where you can offer individual help and encouragement.

42. Have each student bring in a blank audio cassette tape. Use this tape to record comments to your students about their work. Students can also use the tape to respond to your comments and to ask questions.

43. Provide many opportunities for students to display their work and to be recognized for their accomplishments. This will keep them focused on the important things in class, not on misbehaving. This technique is especially effective for the troublemakers in your class who have grown accustomed to attention for the wrong reasons.

44. Hold your students accountable for their work. Use graphic organizers such as checklists, charts, and calendars. Have them assess their own progress and determine what they need to do to stay successful.

45. Assess progress frequently. If you only assess progress with a few large assignments, then students who are experiencing difficulty will be too discouraged to try their best. A daily quiz will keep students on their toes.

46. Get students involved in instruction. They can teach part of a lesson, design test questions, or offer helpful suggestions.

47. Inspiring messages, banners, posters, and "thoughts of the day" mean more to most students than we can ever imagine. You never know when the right words will help a struggling student.

48. Listen to your students and remain flexible. Students should have a strong voice in the classroom. Teachers who are able to successfully respond to student concerns will create the class climate where students are motivated to do their best.

49. Make sure the homework assignments you give are important to your students. Make them relevant, interesting, and based on higher-level thinking skills. An example would be not just to have students review for a test; instead, require that they prepare a review sheet of the 20 most relevant facts from the material that will be covered by the test.

50. Use technology. Computers are inherently interesting to most students who may quickly grow bored with applying pen to paper. Using technology can make even mundane tasks easier and more interesting.

PUTTING YOUR HIGH EXPECTATIONS TO WORK

When you walk through the halls of almost any secondary school, you will observe students engaged in a variety of activities as you peek into classrooms. In some, students are allowed to sleep or to chat with their friends because they have finished their classwork for the day, while in others you will find active students rushing to finish their assignments before the class ends.

What creates this difference in classroom activity? Why do some students become self-disciplined learners early in their school careers, while others never achieve more than just enough to get by? Why is one classroom a place where students have nothing better to do than rest (and be disruptive), while in others students have so much to do that they have to hurry to get it all done before the class is over?

The chief difference in these classes is not in the students nor is it in the subject matter. Instead, one of the biggest differences between teachers whose students perform well and those whose students perform poorly lies in the *expectations* that teachers have for their students. In many classrooms students do not reach their academic or behavioral potential because their teachers are satisfied with poor performance.

When teachers begin with the basic belief that their students are capable of doing meaningful work of high quality, they set the stage for a productive classroom environment. This is the first step in an important cycle of belief and behavior that permeates successful classrooms, promoting self-disciplined behavior in the students fortunate enough to be in those classes. Here's how this cycle works.

Teachers Believe Their Students Are Capable of the Successful Mastery of the Material They Plan to Teach Them

Common sense indicates that if teachers don't believe students are going to do well on an assignment, then they are just not going to deliver the kinds of well-structured lessons that students need to learn. These teachers are also not going to provide the supportive learning environment that will help motivate students to succeed.

Teachers Communicate Their Expectations to Students

We communicate our expectations for success to our students through a number of ways. The most important one is, of course, providing them with challenging work to do. When students have enough meaningful, accomplishable, and challenging work to do, then they are going to achieve at a higher performance level than those students whose teachers do not communicate their expectations for success to their students.

Our Expectations Indicate to Our Students That We Are Confident in Their Ability to Do Well

When we show our students that we have confidence in their ability to do the work we have planned for them to do, then we send a clear message to them that they are capable learners. More students than many teachers would believe are crippled by a lack of confidence in their ability to do well in school. Some give up early and turn into "at risk" students. Far too many others struggle on half-heartedly, never really learning or achieving very much. Still others, though, have teachers who convince them that they are good students who are capable of worthwhile efforts. These students are successful.

If Students Are Confident of Their Ability to Succeed, They Try Harder

Once students perceive that we regard them as capable and are willing to help them do their work, then they will soon assimilate this belief for themselves. Research and common sense both show that students who believe they can achieve at high performance levels will find it easier to keep on trying until they become successful.

When Students Start Achieving at Higher Levels, the Success Cycle Created by Expectations Begins Again Because Teachers Continue to Expect Students to Be Capable Learners Once More

Although it is easier to teach students who are ready for a challenge, the cycle of successful high expectations for both academic and behavioral success must begin with the teacher. When we give students the opportunities to succeed that will motivate them to try even harder, we are creating the kind of positive classroom climate that will help them all continue to move towards being self-directed learners.

15 WAYS TEACHERS CAN COMMUNICATE THEIR EXPECTATIONS

1. Make sure you have lots of friendly interactions with your students.

2. Spend much of your time monitoring your students for behavioral and academic success so that they can stay on-task.

3. Be careful to reward only responsible behavior and good work or efforts towards both behavioral and academic success.

4. Make sure students have enough work to do that is interesting, challenging, and achievable.

5. Show students how to succeed. Be specific in the criteria for success. Give them plenty of samples, models, and examples as well as sufficient practice.

6. Do not allow students to refuse to participate in class by sleeping or just not working. Call on every student every day.

7. Encourage your students to succeed by taking a "can do" approach. Communicate to them that the work you are asking them to do is worthy of their efforts and you expect them to do a good job on it.

8. Provide a time-management structure for students so that they know when they must hand in work to you. Use a syllabus, checklists, charts, reminders on the board, and student planners to help students stay on track.

9. Hold frequent conferences with students to talk over problems and to encourage them to do their best.

10. Give useful feedback as promptly as you can. Be specific about what students need to do to continue their success.

11. Keep misbehaviors minor.

12. Offer plenty of extra help to students who may be struggling with their work. You do not have to stay after school every day in order to do this, but you should make some time available to help students who need that extra little push.

13. Teach students to visualize their goals for assignments before they begin. Teach them to plan what they need to do to complete their work to a satisfactory standard.

14. Refuse to accept work that is messy or inaccurate. You do not have to be hateful about this, but students who try to turn in poorly done work should be stopped. One way to handle this is to have students redo their work and turn it in the next day.

15. Hold the same standards for all of your students. Don't let a student with a poor record for attendance or grades perform to a minimum standard if the other students in the class are expected to do their best. The negative message you send to students by allowing such poor work is a powerful one.

THE CONSISTENT TEACHER

Consistency is one of the most important variables in managing student behavior because it allows students a safe framework within which to operate while they struggle to become self-disciplined learners. Consistent classroom management allows a teacher to create a predictable environment where students know what to expect and thus can make choices based on established rules, boundaries, and consequences.

If we want our students to become self-disciplined, we must create a consistent environment for them. They have to know what to expect from their classmates and from their teachers if they are going to make intelligent decisions for themselves.

Even though consistency is so very important to the discipline climate in a classroom, it is also one of the most difficult struggles that many teachers face each day. It is not always easy to be as consistent as we should because teachers have to deal with the demands of many different personalities in each class.

Teachers have to make hundreds of decisions each day. Most of these, many of them critical to the future success of our discipline climates as well as to the success of our students, will be made in front of a room full of lively teenagers. We seldom have time for thoughtful reasoning because we have to think fast on our feet. No wonder it is so difficult to be as consistent as we should be every day.

In fact, here are some of the common mistakes in consistency that many of us find all to easy to make.

1. We overlook a broken rule "just this once."

2. When students have missed several days, we find it difficult to hold them to the same academic standards for make-up work that we would have had if they had been there for class.

3. We call one child's parents or guardians to report misbehavior that we have allowed from other students.

4. We allow a good student to slip into class tardy while we are on the alert for other students who try the same thing.

5. We expect less of the students whom we perceive to be less able than others.

If you want to become more consistent in the way you manage your class, there are some easy techniques that can help you get started. Here are ten quick ones for you to begin to use to create the consistent environment you want for your students.

1. Create routines and procedures for the day-to-day operation of your class and enforce them.

2. Post your class rules and teach them to your students.

3. Enforce your class rules for all students every day.

4. Don't threaten your students. When you tell them something, mean what you say.

5. Be a prepared and organized teacher so that you will find it easier to make those tough quick decisions each day.

6. Prevent discipline problems from starting or from getting out of hand.

7. Hold everyone accountable for the same high standards for behavior and academic performance.

8. Intervene early when students are having problems.

9. Use class time well. Keep all of your students engaged in meaningful work from the start of class until the end of class.

10. Listen carefully to your students, but don't be a pushover for too many excuses.

CREATING SELF-DISCIPLINED STUDENTS THROUGH PROBLEM-SOLVING ACTIVITIES

One of the best ways to help students make the transition from being part of an unruly mob to being trusted and valuable members of a community of self-directed learners is to involve them in making choices and decisions that solve problems. At this point in their lives, students are faced with countless important decisions to make.

Many times their futures depend on these choices. Many teens have to make important decisions about their careers, where they want to go to college, if they want to go to college, and other life-choice issues. Then they also have the tremendous additional pressures facing teens today: substance abuse, sexual activity, peer relationships, and self-confidence issues.

If what we want from our students is clear thinking on these issues and the ones that concern our subject matter and the behavior that we expect from them in class, then we need to give them plenty of practice in making viable decisions. There are three important things we can do to make this process part of our classroom.

1. We can teach students to recognize a good idea. Although there are many ways to determine this, we can at least show our students the necessity of looking ahead and predicting outcomes based on what they can anticipate as results.

2. We can teach students how to generate ideas by showing them how to brainstorm until they have exhausted all of the creative avenues available to them.

3. We can give students opportunities to have a strong voice in the decision-making process in our classrooms. Students who are on the way to becoming self-disciplined need the supervised practice in generating, evaluating, and implementing solutions to problems that we can offer.

If you are working towards having your students make wise choices for themselves as part of the classroom-management practices you use in your room, there are many opportunities to involve your students in problem-solving activities. Some problems you might have students solve include the following:

■ how they could improve the way they handle homework assignments

■ how they could improve student behavior in the public areas of the building: cafeteria, bus ramp, parking lot, hallways, restrooms

■ how to arrange a new due date for an assignment

■ how the rules of the class should be changed

■ how to plan class activities such as field trips or banquets

■ how to manage projects they have to complete as a group

■ how to manage class routines

■ how to improve student behavior in class

■ how to solve a community issue or problem

■ how to research information about a topic

■ how to obtain more materials needed for class: software, computers, calculators, books, tapes, magazines, pens, etc.

■ how to improve the traffic patterns in school

■ how to establish a peer-tutoring support system

■ how to resolve peer conflicts

■ how to monitor shared materials

HOLDING STUDENTS ACCOUNTABLE FOR THEIR OWN SUCCESS

In recent years one of the focal points in educational reform is the idea that in order to improve our students' chances for successful futures, we must set high standards for all of them, not just the ones who cause less trouble than others. Although this truth is surely self-evident, it is not the entire truth. It is not enough to have high expectations for our students if they do not know how to rise to meet those expectations.

We must hold our students accountable for meeting or exceeding the high standards that we have created for them. Setting high standards is simple. Holding students accountable for their success is not.

No matter how difficult it may be, however, helping students reach high standards is critical to the discipline climate in a secondary classroom. When students feel a sense of urgency about their work, they tend to be too busy to disrupt class. When a helpful and positive teacher is involved with hard-working students, the discipline climate reaches the potential we want for our students and for our own satisfaction.

An effective approach that can help all of your students reach the kinds of behavioral and academic success that you expect is to attack the problem on three fronts. The first area you must include in this approach involves the methods you use to build in and teach accountability to your students. The next is the behavioral expectations you have for them. The third approach is the academic performance standards you want your students to maintain.

Teaching Methods

1. Be clear with your students that you expect excellent behavior and work from them *at all times*. State this and then make it evident in the way you interact with every student in your class.

2. Involve parents or guardians as often as it takes for you to create an effective team of caring adults who want to help a child succeed.

3. Create a wide variety of fair assessments. A few objective tests or quizzes are not fair ways to hold students accountable for their learning. Employ as many creative and effective ways to evaluate student progress as you can in order to meet the needs and abilities of your students.

4. Be an organized teacher. You'll find yourself a much more credible role model if you can easily find important papers and materials.

5. Convey your faith in the ability of your students to achieve the standards of excellence you have established for them. If they think you doubt that they can succeed, then your students will give up.

6. Teach your students how to do their work. Students should be taught the study skills they need to reach the standards you have for them.

7. Call on every student every day. Allow no student to be invisible in your classroom.

8. Return papers promptly so that students know what they should do to improve.

9. Make sure your comments on assignments are geared to helping students correct their errors and improve their performance.

10. Be a good role model of the values you want to instill in your students. Hold yourself accountable for high standards and be the good example that your students should follow.

11. Foster responsibility through the daily routines and procedures you establish for your students. Involve them in routine classroom-management tasks.

12. When students have completed an assignment, give them another assignment to begin right away or allow them to choose among acceptable alternatives. No student should waste time by having nothing to do while others finish an assignment.

13. Review at the start and end of class so that students are aware of the material they should focus on learning.

14. Establish clear procedures to manage students who need to make up work, students who do not turn in completed work, students who do not complete homework assignments, and students who do unacceptable work.

15. Teach your students to pace themselves by paying attention to the time it takes for them to complete various types of assignments. Teach them how to estimate the amount of time it will take to complete assignments and how to time themselves.

16. Consistently enforce class rules, expectations, and procedures.

17. Keep your interactions with individual students brief enough so that your attention can stay focused on the rest of the class as well. Don't allow your time to be monopolized by one attention-seeking student at the expense of the others in the class.

Behavioral Expectations

1. Make sure your students know that you pay attention to what they do. Students who know their teacher is paying attention to their behavior are not going to misbehave as readily as those students who believe they can get away with bad behavior.

2. Teach your students to be organized and systematic in how they approach their work.

3. Encourage a team spirit in your class. If a student has reached success through hard work, then have that student share his or her newfound expertise with others who may be still struggling.

4. Refuse to repeat yourself needlessly. Set high standards for listening skills by thinking before you speak and by making sure your students are listening.

5. Hold your students to the same behavior standards for substitute teachers that you expect when you are in the room. Discuss this with them in advance of the time when you will be absent; you will find that your students behave much better than if you adopt a "kids will be kids" attitude.

6. Refuse to allow your students to sleep or to do homework for other classes in your class. They should be doing *your* work in *your* class.

Academic Performance Standards

1. Make it a point that you expect 100% accuracy in student work. Some students will aim to just get by with a minimum of work unless you encourage them to do otherwise.

2. Have students edit or double-check each other's work before turning it in. Peer editing works best if you provide students with a checklist of standards to follow while proofreading.

3. Be very specific about your criteria for success on an assignment so that students have a clear path for excellence before they begin to work.

4. Instead of having all of your students shout out answers in an oral activity, ask them to write their responses first and then answer when you call on them. This will force everyone to think before responding.

5. Plan the procedures you want your students to follow in case they don't have their materials or textbooks in class. Don't allow students to get away with not working because they don't have their materials.

6. When you are moving around the room to monitor activity, ask your students to underline the answers they think are correct and circle the ones that puzzle them so that you can work together to make sure they understand how to do all of their work well.

7. If you find that some of your students are reluctant to accomplish their work on schedule, contact their parents or guardians. If students know that their progress is being monitored at home as well as in class, they usually perform better.

8. If you see that students have trouble grasping an assignment, reteach the material. Don't allow students to rest on their ignorance.

9. When students miss the answer to a question, ask them to write the correct answer on their papers. Students should be held accountable for correcting their papers.

10. Make neatness an important component of the work in your classroom. You don't have to be a perfectionist, but you should expect your students to turn in neat work.

11. Create and use modeling charts so that students can see what they have done and what they need to do. These can be kept in their notebooks so that students can mark off work they have completed. An example of an "Assignment Checklist" that will help your students improve their performance is included here. (See next page.)

FOCUSING ON YOUR STUDENTS' STRENGTHS

It is no secret that the relationship we build with our students affects their success. A positive relationship with our students is one of our strongest defenses against disruptive behavior.

Often we try to stop misbehavior with a flurry of negative commands and injunctions against behaviors that students find more natural than the more formal or productive ones we try to teach. Students across the country can recite dozens of things they know they should not do. If those same students are asked to tell what their five greatest strengths are, however, many would be at a loss.

While it would be wrong to unfairly praise or encourage students for behaviors that are not acceptable to their future success, the negative attitudes that many of us carry to school with us are just as wrong. Although it is natural that we should spend so much time in our profession dealing with the errors our students make or with the things they should not do or with what's wrong, we do need to balance this negativity with focusing on our students' successes or strengths as well.

The long-term rewards that accrue when we focus on our students' strengths are partly the result of a self-fulfilling prophecy. When our students believe they can do some things correctly, they are going to be brave enough to take that extra risk that will generate even more success. Hateful or unkind comments, on the other hand, will destroy even the bravest student's confidence.

There are many ways to begin to include a more positive focus on your students' strengths in your lessons. Just a few to get you started can be found on page 330.

ASSIGNMENT CHECKLIST

Name _____ Month _____

Darken each block as you complete and turn in that assignment.

Week	1	2	3	4	5	6	7	8	9	10	11	12	13	14	15
1															
2															
3															
4															
5															

Remarks: _____

_____

_____

_____

_____

_____

_____

_____

1. Pay your students sincere compliments whenever you can. This is a pleasant and productive habit to encourage in them also.

2. Use positive body language to convey your respect and sincerity when you talk with students. Make eye contact. Pat a shoulder or a hand. Make sure your expression is pleasant.

3. Ask students to share a hidden talent or skill with you.

4. Be generous with praise. Students who are aware of what it is they are doing correctly will want to repeat it.

5. Open class by having students tell what they did well on their homework assignments.

6. End class by asking students to share the most important things they learned that day.

7. Ask students to tell others what they did right on a difficult assignment so that the good news can be shared to the benefit of everyone.

8. Do not compare one student with another, especially if you pit one student's weakness against another's strength.

9. Hand out brightly colored pieces of paper and ask students to write out a contribution they can make to the class. Post these contributions for all to see.

10. When students go over returned papers, have them correct their errors and list the things they did right, too.

11. An easy way to make sure all students have the extra help they need is to have the student experts in the room share their expertise with others.

12. Having students set and achieve goals is a good starting point for identifying the strong points of each. When students have a purpose for working, they tend to work well.

13. Be careful that the strengths you compliment your students on are ones that are appropriate for their age level, unless you inadvertently want to either insult them or send a message that your standards are very low.

14. Ask students for their advice or opinions. Students often have important insights and solutions to problems that surprise many adults, even those who know them well. Be obvious when you tap into this resource.

15. Some classes seem to take on a personality of their own. Use this to your advantage when you can. If classes are very talkative, turn this into a strong point by giving them lots of opportunity for debate and discussion. Some classes work very quickly, but not always accurately. Make sure you focus on their strengths while you help them eliminate their weaknesses.

PROMOTING SELF-DISCIPLINE THROUGH SELF-IMAGE

A healthy self-esteem is not handed out at birth—not even to those enviable individuals who were born with such advantages as intelligence, beauty, good health, and loving parents. A positive sense of self is something that caring adults help young people develop for themselves.

In secondary classes it is particularly apparent that students who are confident in their ability to master the daily challenges of school find it easier to succeed. When we boost this attitude in our students, our students learn more and behave better.

The reasons for this are not hard to determine. When students regard themselves as capable learners, they act in ways that perpetuate this belief. They resist the negative effects of peer pressure and learn to develop the social skills that will help them be positive members of class. Self-confident students are courteous, willing to offer help, tolerant of others, and willing to take risks.

Promoting self-esteem in our students is not something that should replace the curriculum; instead, it should be a natural part of the positive approach that we take with our students. When we let them see that we are concerned about them, we take an important first step.

It is also important to remember that in school self-esteem must be based on achievement—particularly for secondary-level students. It can't be founded just on personal qualities, but must be solidly based in the sense of satisfaction that comes from doing a job to the best of one's ability.

Although there are some simple activities that we can do to help our students focus on their successful achievements, the best ways to bolster a healthy self-image are the ones that will appeal most to your students. In the following lists, you will find general guidelines to help you work with your students. You will also find simple suggestions for specific activities so that the improved sense of self-esteem you want to foster will arise naturally from the positive relationship you develop with your students.

General Guidelines for Helping Students Develop a Healthy Self-Image

1. Improve your listening skills. Students are acutely sensitive to the nuances of body language. Treat your students as if they are important people in your lives. Attend to what they say, even in the frantic press of daily activities.

2. Pay attention to the way you talk to students. Use a pleasant, soft voice. Be friendly as well as firm with them. Encourage them through specific praise and encouragement, not just by saying, "Good Job!" no matter what a student does. It is also important to avoid needless negativity with students. For example, instead of saying "Don't interrupt me," try saying "I'll be with you in a minute" if you want to send a more positive message.

3. Offer help to those students who need special help and encouragement. Some students need that extra tutoring session or a bit of extra time with you in order to become competent in your class. You don't have to spend hours of personal after-school time to achieve this.

4. Hold your students accountable for participation in class. Do not let them sleep, refuse to work, neglect to make up work, forget homework, cut class, or ignore what you have assigned for all of your students. Students who opt out of participating in class may be relieved for the moment, but they are not going to feel good about themselves or about your class if you allow this behavior.

5. Involve your students in making decisions about the class. Students should have plenty of opportunities for supervised practice in making decisions about class issues, both large and small, that will affect their performance. Students who learn to speak up for

themselves and to participate in group decision making have a greater chance to develop self-confidence.

6. There is a great deal of personal reward to be found in activities that help others. Involve your students in class activities that are geared to helping other people. Students who tutor each other or younger students, collect money and goods for the needy, participate in Earth Day clean-up on school grounds, or involve other compassionate and helpful activities will reap tremendous benefits in the form of improved self-esteem.

7. Create a team spirit or classroom culture in your room. Students should feel they are part of a special group. When a class develops this strong sense of identity for themselves, everyone benefits from the confidence-enhancing effects.

8. Use praise and rewards to keep students focused on their accomplishments. Take a no-nonsense approach to how you provide correction for your students, but be gentle. Over and over again, research and common sense both prove that it is the positive actions we take with our students that promote a productive classroom climate. Students who have teachers who show sincere approval for their actions are more successful than those students whose teachers intimidate them into compliance.

9. Structure your lessons so that students have opportunities to succeed and then to enjoy the feelings of accomplishment that accompany success.

Simple Activities That Will Boost Self-Esteem

1. Create a class *Who's Who* entry about each student. Include the hobbies, interests, and skills of each in an effort to help students learn to relate to each other in a positive way.

2. Another way to increase the team spirit atmosphere in your room is to have students bring in words and photographs cut from newspapers or magazines. These should reflect their interests, talents, and skills. Use them to create a large wall collage to display the positive things your students have in common.

3. Create opportunities for students to reflect upon and recognize the contributions of their classmates after a shared assignment, project, or discussion. Teach the importance of recognizing each other's accomplishments.

4. Set aside space to create a "Wall of Fame" in your class where you can display excellent work.

5. At the end of class, ask students to tell you something important that they did well or learned.

6. Ask students to describe the most difficult part of a lesson and what they did to overcome that difficult part.

7. Take photographs of your students while they are working well and display them.

8. Ask students to share with you or with class members three things that will help them have positive feelings about themselves or their work.

9. After a particularly long or difficult unit of study, hold an awards ceremony to celebrate its successful completion.

10. At the end of the year, ask students to write a letter to a future teacher describing what they learned in your class.

11. Ask students to list the ways they can accept personal responsibility for becoming successful in school.

12. At the end of class, ask students to share with you what they think was the most successful part of the class.

60 MOTIVATIONAL TOOLS WE CAN ALL USE

As we write out our lesson plans each week, secondary teachers everywhere face the same dilemma. We know what we have to teach and how we want to deliver the instruction, but we usually have a harder job trying to figure out how to get our students to *want* to do the work. We all know that even the most well-planned lessons are wasted if our students are not interested in what we have to offer.

Successful teachers know they have to use motivational techniques in what they teach so that students will not only perform better academically, but behave better, too. Students who are interested in their work seldom disrupt class because they are just too busy. An added bonus for teachers and students is that motivation tends to have a long-lasting effect that will, over time, be effective in leading students to be self-disciplined learners.

Since it is important that we motivate students to do their work, it is indeed fortunate that there are so many techniques available for us to use. These motivational tools are ones that can benefit students of all types: from those who are reluctant to try to those who quickly lose interest in a lesson. Pick a few and experiment to see which ones appeal to your students. Since there are so many motivational tools available to us, feel free to add a few of your own.

1. Use a variety of media such as videos, art, music, or newspapers.
2. Return graded papers promptly.
3. Give sincere praise.
4. Give tangible rewards such as stickers, treats, or bookmarks.
5. Allow students to enjoy a classtime privilege such as a popcorn party.
6. Write more positive comments than negatives ones on papers.
7. Bring in interesting objects for students to puzzle over.
8. Reward the entire class for working together.
9. Help students who are struggling to meet your high expectations.
10. Make sure your expectations are high enough.
11. Consistently enforce class rules.
12. Encourage students to compliment their classmates.
13. Teach students to be courteous to everyone.
14. Videotape or photograph students at work or in class presentations.
15. Include lots of innovative and creative approaches to shake 'em up and wake 'em up.
16. Surprise students at the start and end of class.

17. Teach students how they will benefit from the lesson so that they will have a purpose for learning.

18. Display their work.

19. Create lots of opportunities for students to publish their work.

20. Include real-life problems or experiences.

21. Design activities for hands-on learning.

22. Be positive and upbeat with students.

23. Incorporate students' interests in lessons.

24. Help students be successful at the start of the term or of a unit of study so that they will want to continue this success.

25. Show students that you believe in their ability to succeed.

26. Inspire students with inspirational banners, posters, and quotations.

27. Pace your lessons so that activities don't drag.

28. Teach study skills so that the workload is more manageable.

29. Include a checklist or modeling chart so students can see what they have accomplished and what they have to do.

30. Send home a positive note.

31. Phone home as soon as trouble begins.

32. Use extra credit judiciously to encourage students to do that little extra that makes a big difference.

33. Show students how to organize their notebooks so that they can find their papers quickly.

34. Use students' names on practice worksheets.

35. Keep a shared store of materials so that students always have what they need to work.

36. Allow students to have a voice in class decisions.

37. Encourage peer tutoring.

38. Have students collaborate on their work.

39. Mentor students.

40. Use graphic organizers and other visual aids.

41. Help students improve their reading skills.

42. Use various modalities and learning styles.

43. Create a predictable routine.

44. Reward effort.

45. Ask students for their advice or opinions.

46. Show students how they can use their learning in other classes.

47. Give students problems to solve as well as facts to memorize.

48. Play games.

49. Use nonverbal language to convey your attention and interest.

50. Monitor students' behavior by moving away from the front of the room.

51. Have a sense of humor.

52. Ask, "How can I help you?"

53. Include higher-level thinking skills in every lesson.

54. Have students correct their errors on tests, quizzes, and other assignments instead of just looking over their papers to find out the grade.

55. Have students write a response to a question in a class discussion instead of just yelling out their first thought.

56. Help students develop goals for their lives and for school success so that they work with a purpose.

57. Refuse to speak until you have everyone's attention.

58. Gear activities so that students do more talking than you do.

59. Refuse to give up on misbehaving students.

60. Be so well-prepared each day that your inefficiency will not have a negative effect on your students.

"As he thinketh in his heart, so is he."

—Proverbs

Section 9

THE MOST IMPORTANT FACTOR IN DISCIPLINE: THE TEACHER

In This Section . . .

The most important factor in any discipline situation is the teacher, which is the focus of this section. The importance of your role can be found in "Successful Discipline Rests with You" and "Attitudes for Success." Use the reproducible checklist to help you examine your own attitude.

Body language is the topic of "Pay Attention to Body Language—Yours and Theirs." It is one of the most important tools successful teachers have.

The demands of our stressful daily lives and the way many teachers have found to be successful in overcoming stress are the topics of "Combating On-the-Job Distress" and "50 Quick Ways to Reduce School Stress."

Even the best plans go awry if students do not respect their teachers. This issue is the topic of "Earning Your Students' Respect" and its two accompanying self-checks.

You can also create a large learning environment for your students with the techniques included in "Enlarging the Learning Environment."

The final two topics in this section go hand in hand when teachers want to create a positive learning environment for their students. These teachers will act as professionally as possible and will work to create that extra quality that is so evident in outstanding classrooms: the culture of excellence.

"Not only is there an art in knowing a thing,
but also a certain art in teaching it."

—Cicero

SUCCESSFUL DISCIPLINE RESTS WITH YOU

Just as in those old Vaudeville jokes, there's bad news and there's good news about school discipline. The *bad news* is that the responsibility for a successful discipline climate rests with the teacher. We can't blame our students, society, their parents, or even the school board. The ultimate responsibility for creating a successful classroom is ours.

The *good news* is also that the responsibility for a successful discipline climate lies with the teacher. If we are the ones who are responsible for the discipline climate, then we are the ones who can make it successful. If we have the responsibility for the problem, then we also have the solutions to it. That's not just good news, it's wonderful news.

Luckily for those of us who are willing to accept the responsibility for what happens in our classrooms, the skills that make some teachers successful at creating a positive discipline climate can be learned. If we want to provide an atmosphere for achievement in our classes where we engage our students in actively acquiring knowledge through cooperation, curiosity, and hard work, then we have to realize that we are the keys to their success.

It is our "people skills" that will determine the success or failure of the classroom climate we want to establish. Students will respond to our personalities, our energy, our enthusiasm, our confidence, our warmth.

Accepting this responsibility does not mean that a career in education becomes any easier; we still face some unique problems. We have little or no chance for advancement and many of us are very poorly paid. We are seldom recognized publicly for our hard work. Parents and principals may be grateful, but they don't knock on our classroom doors every day to tell us what a good job we're doing.

So what keeps us going to school? It is an intangible—the satisfaction we get when our students finally master difficult material, or when we help an unruly student learn to like school, or when students' faces light up because they are interested in what they're learning. No paycheck can offer a comparable satisfaction.

ATTITUDES FOR SUCCESS

One of the most important factors in determining the success or failure of the discipline climate in a classroom is the collection of attitudes the teacher brings to work each day. Those upbeat and confident teachers who come to work convinced that their students can succeed are inspiring to us all. Their successful attitudes are invisible, but absolutely vital in the creation of a positive discipline climate in their classrooms.

We all know that in creating a productive classroom atmosphere, there are more actions we must take beyond teaching academic content. It is necessary that we take a positive approach to our students and to our teaching responsibilities if we want to make a difference in their lives. There are three significant steps you can take to communicate to your students your positive attitudes about their potential for success.

Have Confidence in Yourself

The first step is that you must have confidence in your own ability to reach your students and to make a difference in their lives. If you are to be successful in overcoming the barriers to positive discipline, you must communicate your belief that your students can grow and change for the better. Few students will try to succeed without a confident teacher who believes in them.

Show Your Students That You Care About Them

The second vital step in communicating your positive attitudes to your students is to show them you care about their success or failure in your class. To do this you must develop a personal relationship with each one. You do this when you show you are interested in their opinions and concerned about their welfare.

Plan Lessons That Are Attainable but Challenging

The third step you can take to let your students know you have confidence in their power to succeed is to design lessons where success is attainable. When you plan a unit of study, begin with information that students can relate to previous learning so that they immediately feel confident about what they already know. As the unit progresses, the work should gradually become more difficult so that those students who may have been reluctant to try at first are willing to take a chance and do the challenging work necessary for learning.

A Checklist to Examine Your Own Attitudes

Read "A Checklist of Positive Attitudes for Teachers" and be honest as you fill it out! (See next page.)

PAY ATTENTION TO BODY LANGUAGE— YOURS AND THEIRS

Even during the quietest class, we receive hundreds of signals from our students about their emotional states. There may be a boy in the back who sits with his hands folded on his chest while he looks out the window. A girl in the front row leans forward in her seat with her eyes on the teacher's face. The girl who always sits sideways in the middle row has her head propped on her hand while she idly traces her initials on her paper.

Just by glancing around the room, an alert teacher can tell which students are confused, bored, interested, angry, restless, tired, or excited. Our students also receive the same kinds of messages from us. They are just as aware of those times when they have our full attention as they are when something distracts us. Our actions definitely speak louder than our words when we deal with sensitive adolescents.

Knowing that nonverbal language is an important component of our classroom presentation makes it easy to us to see why we should focus on the ways we can improve how we use this hidden language to create a productive classroom. The teacher who takes time to observe the nonverbal cues in a classroom can then use that information to judge how involved students are in the lesson and to react accordingly.

Some of the nonverbal cues your students send are positive and others are negative. Here is a list of some common positive and negative nonverbal actions you can observe in your class.

Positive Nonverbal Actions of Students

Students who are interested in the lesson will signal this by:

1. waving or raising their hands *(continued on page 342)*

A CHECKLIST OF POSITIVE ATTITUDES
FOR TEACHERS

How positive are you? Use the 20 productive actions in this checklist to assess the positive image you already present to your students and to see where you can improve the way you communicate your confidence in your students.

Put a plus sign (+) in front of those statements that indicate strengths you already have. Place a minus sign (-) in front of those actions you need to improve if you want to be as positive as possible with your students.

_____ 1. Today I will encourage and motivate my students to be self-disciplined rather than demand compliance.

_____ 2. Today I will set a good example for my students by being in control of my emotions and my conduct.

_____ 3. Today I will provide my students with interesting, well-paced lessons that are designed to help as many of them learn as much as possible in the short time they are with me.

_____ 4. Today I will treat every student as a worthy individual whose contributions are important to the entire class.

_____ 5. Today I will be generous with praise and appreciation for the good things my students do.

_____ 6. Today I will be sure my students understand the immediate and future value of the material I teach.

_____ 7. Today I will be consistent in enforcing rules and in maintaining high standards.

_____ 8. Today I will convince my students that I believe they can all be successful in my class.

_____ 9. Today I will give prompt feedback so that my students know what they have done well and what they still need to do to improve.

_____10. Today I will ask questions before issuing a reprimand. I will make sure the reprimands I give are done privately.

_____11. Today I will assume responsibility for the discipline climate in my classroom.

_____12. Today I will plan ways to prevent discipline problems from disrupting the successful atmosphere I want in my classroom.

A CHECKLIST OF POSITIVE ATTITUDES
FOR TEACHERS *(cont'd)*

_____13. Today I will take a teamwork approach to the learning I want my students to have.

_____14. Today I will take actions that will keep misbehavior from escalating into larger problems.

_____15. Today I will provide lessons that will use my students' time wisely from the first minute of class until the last minute of class.

_____16. Today I will help my students set goals for themselves so that they have a larger reason for learning than just complying with my demands.

_____17. Today I will be organized and efficient because I know that a disorganized and inefficient teacher often creates academic and behavioral failure.

_____18. Today I will inform my students of what I expect of them so that they understand what they have to do in order to succeed academically and behaviorally.

_____19. Today I will help my students understand that they are part of a community that begins in our classroom and extends all over the globe.

_____20. Today I will take actions that will help my students learn to be self-disciplined.

2. moving around in their seats
3. turning their bodies to face you even when you move around the room
4. squint, smile, or make other exaggerated facial movements

Negative Nonverbal Actions of Students

Students who are not interested in the lesson will signal this by:

1. not making eye contact with the speaker
2. making faces or eye contact with classmates
3. slouching or turning away from the speaker
4. frowning or staring vacantly into space

If you observe the above negative behaviors in your class, you should pay attention to their implications for the success of your discipline climate. Be careful to interpret them as accurately as you can, however. Many teachers who teach students from cultures different from their own can mistake nonverbal cues that are neutral or positive in the student's culture, but are negative ones for the teacher.

Confusing or Negative Nonverbal Messages of Teachers

You should also pay attention to the nonverbal messages *you* send so that you show concern for and interest in your students. Make sure the nonverbal cues you send your students match your verbal ones. For example, if you frown while you tell students that they are doing well, you send a confusing mixed message. Here is a list of some other negative or confusing nonverbal messages you should avoid.

- no eye contact with certain students
- pointing at students
- laughing while delivering a serious message
- turning your back while a student is speaking to you
- slamming doors, books, anything
- rolling your eyes as if in disgust
- sharing "knowing looks" with other students when someone is having trouble with an answer
- staying behind a desk or at a lectern all class period
- hugging students who clearly don't want to be hugged
- snapping fingers at a student
- jabbing a finger at a student's chest to make a point
- ignoring students who fall asleep in class (sending a message that you don't care as long as they are quiet)
- staying seated all class period
- chewing gum or eating in front of students
- speaking too rapidly, too loudly, or in a monotone

- leaning away from students
- talking on and on and ignoring body language signals from students
- using a sarcastic tone
- ignoring a student who is obviously tearful or angry
- throwing anything at students, even in jest
- never smiling
- tapping fingers to show impatience with students
- putting your hands too close to a student's face—violating his or her personal space
- standing with your hands on your hips, obviously impatient or angry
- not responding to a student's answer to a question or when a student speaks to you

Nonverbal Signals to Stop Misbehavior

You can also use nonverbal language to send a clear message that you are in control of the class and aware of your students' activities. There are many signals you can use with misbehaving students that will convey your message without distracting other students. These nonverbal messages are effective because they get your point across and do not interfere with the learning process. Here is a list of the nonverbal signals you can send to deter your students from misbehaving without having to say a word.

- Pick up your book or grade book and move to the front of the room.
- Make eye contact with the student who is misbehaving.
- Stand up if you are sitting and face the students who are off-task.
- Turn music on or off.
- Move to the board and write a message.
- Hold up your hand with the palm facing the class.
- Frown at students who are misbehaving.
- Give a "thumbs up" or "thumbs down" signal.
- Shrug your shoulders and shake your head.
- Hand the misbehaving student something.
- Nod your head and raise your eyebrows.
- Smile.
- Put your hand on the object your student is touching.
- Lightly touch the student on the arm or hand.
- Move toward a student who is misbehaving.
- Lean forward to show you are interested in a student's activity.
- Stand or sit near students who are misbehaving.
- Pause in the middle of what you are saying until the offending student stops talking.
- Flick the lights or ring a bell as an arranged signal for attention.
- Go to a designated area of the room where students know they are supposed to stop talking when you are in this spot.

- Glance pointedly at the clock when students are either being timed or are dawdling.
- Point to the object you want them to focus on.
- Hold up an interesting object to catch attention and stop misbehavior.
- Put your hand on the desk of a student who is being disruptive.
- Raise your eyebrows and look surprised that one of your students would misbehave.

COMBATING ON-THE-JOB DISTRESS

Do you sometimes feel frustrated and impatient at school? Are you sometimes so exhausted by the end of the week that you feel you are just too tired to face Monday morning? You are not alone. Teaching is a very stressful profession. Many of us leave the profession for other careers because we become too burned-out to function well as teachers or as people. Worse yet, some teachers stay in the classroom and inflict us all with their high-stress gloom and doom.

Why is teaching so stressful? Research shows that teaching used to be easier. Less was demanded of teachers and students were easier to manage. Not too long ago, it was common for teachers to stay in the classroom past retirement age. Today's work pressures make this option less attractive to many veteran teachers. Indeed, many schools are full of teachers who count the years, months, weeks, and days until they can take early retirement.

Teachers are especially susceptible to occupational stress because we work in a rigidly structured career where pressures are exerted on us from students, administrators, parents, and the community. For most of us these outside pressures are minor when compared to the internal ones that drive us to try to reach every student entrusted to our care.

We spend our days caring for others with very little emotional support from a public that is unaware of just how demanding our jobs are. Here are just a few of the most common stress inducers unique to our profession: too many students, too little time to plan or even finish our work at school, little time for collegial support, changing curriculum demands, not enough money for salaries and materials/equipment, and our own confusion about the best course to follow in many discipline situations.

When you feel the negative emotions about your professional life begin to build, you should act quickly to avoid the misery of stress that has turned to distress. There are many strategies for coping with stress on the job as well as at home. Most of these suggestions can be divided into two categories: ways that will help you prevent stress from reaching dangerous levels and some simple techniques that you can use to change your attitude about your problems. If you can't change a situation at work, you can at least change your attitude to keep your stress levels manageable.

Techniques for Preventing Stress

1. Many school districts offer inservice classes or workshops. Take advantage of these courses to refresh your attitude. You could also take a correspondence course or a class at a local college. Being a student again will sharpen your professional skills.

2. Do your paperwork and other routine tasks as efficiently as possible. Learn to manage your clerical work so that you won't have to drag home hours of work each night.

3. Take pride in being a good teacher. Planning exciting lessons and carrying through with them won't leave you much time to brood on your problems.

4. Stay away from negative staff members—you can't change them. Even the most optimistic teachers have trouble remaining cheerful after a gripe session in the lounge.

5. Share your good ideas with colleagues. Start or contribute to a faculty newsletter in which you share good news and positive teaching ideas with other staff members. Or put up a bulletin board in a place where staff members congregate so that people can share teaching ideas that have been successful for them.

6. Set professional goals for yourself and then work to achieve them. Working towards the achievement of a goal will help you prevent or correct your teaching weaknesses rather than continue to suffer through them. This will keep you focused on something productive instead of your troubles.

7. Reward yourself when you have accomplished a particularly onerous task as school. Your reward doesn't have to be elaborate or expensive: rent a movie, order a pizza, visit a museum, go for a walk, pet a dog, go to a sporting event, browse through magazines at the public library, visit a public garden, call on old friends, go camping, plant a tree, or take a nap. Remember that teaching is not a profession where recognition is always dependable, so you should take care of your own need for recognition for a job done well.

8. Find the humor in the silly things your students do, especially when they are being most trying. Even a small chuckle is a good defense against stress.

9. Examine your daily tasks to see what you can eliminate, delegate, or make more pleasant. For instance, you do not have to grade every paper word for word in order to help your students learn. Learn to use a computer to average grades or make creating tests easier.

10. Plan relaxation time. Too much pressure from the "should haves" will destroy even the most determined soul. Many people plan their work days very carefully, but let their free time fly by. You need a balance in your life. Your personal life is just as important as your professional one.

11. Take time to enjoy your students. Too often we rush through our teaching chores without taking time to appreciate the unique qualities of each child. Make every adolescent in your class into a hero at least once. Celebrate their achievements with them.

12. Leave your problems at school, but take your successes home. If you don't learn to compartmentalize your professional and private lives, you will be, in effect, stressed out over your job 24 hours a day.

13. Take care of your health. Eat well. Get enough rest to function successfully at work. Practice deep breathing exercises to stay calm. Exercise will help you cope with the effects of stressful situations, too. Get outdoors and get moving. A sunshine-filled day will lighten a dark mood.

14. Learn a lesson from those who have suffered from great hardships and triumphed: Live one day at a time.

15. Set priorities for yourself and your workload and use these to get your daily jobs done well. Divide your daily work into manageable tasks that can be accomplished in a reasonable length of time. After all, since this is an important skill that you teach your students, shouldn't you benefit from it also?

16. Learn to work with the others in your department or your area of the building. Creating a community at work will make the day more congenial for you and your colleagues. Five ways to get started on this are to team teach, to share materials and good ideas, to celebrate each other's triumphs, to help each other out with various duty assignments, and to enjoy each other's fellowship at social gatherings, lunch, before school, and after school.

17. Solve your problems as quickly as you can. If you are stressed, because you have too many papers to grade, for example, divide them into reasonable stacks and get busy. Deal with misbehaviors before they can get to you. Return phone calls to parents or guardians within 24 hours. Settling down to solve a problem will prevent it from looming over you.

18. Give your students greater responsibility. There are many tasks even young students can do at school that will make any teacher's job easier. Some of these tasks include: running errands, handling shared materials, passing out papers, cleaning the chalkboard, putting information on the board, stapling papers, and posting notices or other items for display.

19. Politely say "no" when you are asked to do a task that will be too stressful. Teachers are, by nature, helpful people. Sometimes this tendency causes us distress because we take on too much. Do your part to be a concerned and dedicated faculty member, but be realistic about the time you have available. Teaching your students well should be your first priority.

20. Make using your planning time well a priority. Many of us enjoy chatting with our colleagues during this time. This is, of course, perfectly acceptable as long as we are not then stressed out because we haven't been able to finish our work. Use a "To Do" list to keep yourself on track.

21. Be aware of what causes you to be stressed and deal with the problem. Letting a stressful situation build will only increase your stress level. Here are some problems you should handle before they grow too large: not enough supplies, difficult students, difficult colleagues, poorly managed paperwork, and poorly planned lessons.

Techniques for Changing Your Perception

Sometimes the best way to handle a stressful situation is to accept it as something you cannot change. Once this happens, you will need to take a further step and change the way you perceive this problem.

Sometimes problems aren't really problems until we decide to react to them in a negative way. A student who we may regard as creative or funny may have another teacher who regards him as immature and irritating. The student hasn't changed, but the attitudes of the people who teach him have. One teacher enjoys this student; the other teacher is stressed.

There are many ways you can learn to see your job situation in a new light. All are deceptively simple. All can have a profound effect on the way you teach the students in your class and on the enjoyment you are able to find in your work day.

Experiment with some of these techniques to see which ones will help you in your current teaching situation. Discard the ones that don't seem to fit your needs and find creative ways to incorporate the ones that will help you take the stress out of your job.

1. Have a colleague with whom you can share problems. Talking with another teacher is helpful if that person is level-headed and not one of those grumpy people who will have a sour perspective on any problem. Having a colleague who will serve as an informal advisor/sounding board can help make sense of even the most complex problems.

2. Be sensible about your profession. Everyone has bad days, sometimes even bad weeks. The important thing to realize is that it is your attitude about those days and weeks that makes the difference.

3. Even the great teachers have had to realize they can't reach every child every day. Try your best, but be realistic about what you can and cannot accomplish.

4. On those really tough days, remind yourself that a year from now, today's problems will probably be forgotten.

5. Keep a box with a collection of those pleasant cards, notes, or little gifts your students have given you. When you are wondering why you chose this profession, pull out your memory box and remind yourself that you have had good times as a teacher in the past and probably will again.

6. Tell yourself that adversity causes character growth. Make a quick list of the benefits of a course of action when you are not sure of what to do. You will benefit from tough problems if you make the effort to learn valuable lessons from them.

7. Ask yourself: Is it the teaching profession that is making you miserable or is it the daily grind? Rising at dawn and heading off to a job with such heavy responsibilities is not always easy, but there are many other careers that are just as demanding and not nearly as rewarding. Before you allow your stress levels to build into burnout, consider carefully whether the grass is really greener on the other side of the career fence.

8. When you approach a time of the school term when you anticipate that your spirits will be low, plan to teach your favorite lesson. Involving yourself in a project that is exciting will help you and your students through a rough period.

9. Remember that *you* determine the dominant mood in your classroom and that no one, including a stressed-out teacher, has the right to ruin the learning opportunities for your students. A happy teacher can create happy students just as quickly as a grouch can offend every student in the room.

10. Refuse to take it personally when your students are disruptive or uninterested in a lesson. The cause of the problem probably has nothing to do with you.

11. If you find yourself reacting negatively at school, make an effort to change that attitude. Often when we practice acting in a positive way, even if we are not as sincere as we would like to be about it, our attitudes will gradually become positive. Paste a smile on your face and start looking for the silver lining in your school clouds.

12. Give up those heavy loads of teacher-guilt that we all carry around. We cannot make all of our students into happy and successful scholars in the course of a school term, no matter how diligently we try. Do your very best every day and do not allow yourself to feel guilty about all of the missed opportunities for improving your students' lives that you missed along the way.

13. Many of us suffer from being too optimistic. We sign up for every committee in the building and then agree to take on as many extra duties as we can. This naive attitude

will quickly lead to stress and teacher burnout. While you should be positive about your teaching situation, you should also be realistic about what you can accomplish each day.

14. When you have problems at school, maintain your perspective. Ask yourself what you did to cause the problem and what you can do in the future to avoid making the same mistake. Don't dwell on the things you have done wrong. Learn from them instead.

50 QUICK WAYS TO REDUCE SCHOOL STRESS

1. Clean out your desk. Do you really need to hang on to those dried-out markers?

2. Color-code your grade book so that it's easy to tell test grades from other averages. Use colored paper clips or folder labels to easily find the attendance records and grades for each class period you teach.

3. Join a professional organization. Read professional literature. You will learn many things that will make your school days easier.

4. Stay two weeks ahead in photocopying and planning.

5. Use a syllabus to help your students and yourself get organized. A syllabus will let your students and their parents or guardians see that you are a serious teacher who has a serious purpose in class.

6. Have enough supplies even if you have to purchase them yourself. It is annoying to have to hunt for the last paper clip or marking pen.

7. Leave your desk clean at the end of the day so that you can start the new one off fresh.

8. Make a real effort to grade all papers on the same day they are turned in to you.

9. Have an established routine at the start and ending of class so that your students can discipline themselves.

10. Have a set of emergency plans in a folder for a substitute to use in case you have to be absent and can't leave plans.

11. Keep a small kit of adhesive bandages, sewing supplies, cough drops or aspirin, and other personal items for your own use.

12. Take a copy of the teacher's edition of your texts home so that you won't have to carry one back and forth when you are planning lessons.

13. Be accurate in the way you keep attendance records.

14. Have a system for students to use to check out shared supplies.

15. Don't work through lunch. You need a break.

16. Have each student complete an information sheet so that you have all of the information you need to contact a parent or guardian without having to go to the office.

17. Be reasonable in the amount of homework you assign. Help students see that it is an important part of their learning process.

18. Use a seating chart from the first day of class until the last day of class.

19. Delegate as much work to your students as you can. This will not only improve their self-esteem, but it will free you from the tasks they are doing for you.

20. Share tasks with department members: clean out book storage areas together, hold term-paper grading parties, share monitoring duties, and exchange duty assignments when necessary. Many hands make light work of even the toughest tasks.

21. Have a "To Do" list that you follow each day. Planning how you need to accomplish the many chores we all face at school will make it easier to get them all done.

22. Keep accurate documentation of parent contacts.

23. Plan for the unexpected.

24. Don't procrastinate when it comes to paperwork or other dreaded tasks. You'll soon be overwhelmed.

25. If you can, use your most productive time of day to do your hardest tasks.

26. Eat a nutritious lunch. You need the energy. The universal teacher lunch of a soft drink and anything from a vending machine does not give you the energy needed to get through the afternoon.

27. Wisely use those small blocks of time you have between appointments. Don't arrive at meetings too early.

28. Listen and take notes at meetings. Take along your yearly planner and jot down upcoming events you need to remember.

29. Plan interesting lessons with lots of varied activities to hold your students' attention.

30. Have a place at school to safely store your keys and other personal belongings.

31. Take time to have well-written lesson plans that follow a logical format.

32. Plan for your students to do as much independent work as possible.

33. Arrive at school a little early and stay a little late.

34. File all papers when you are finished with them instead of letting them accumulate into disorganized stacks.

35. Jot quick notes on your lesson plans about what worked and what you need to improve before you teach the same unit of material again.

36. Dress professionally even on casual days. You don't want to attend an impromptu parent conference dressed in ragged jeans and old sneakers.

37. Carefully read the faculty handbook so that you know the rules and procedures you are expected to follow.

38. At the end of the day, keep your grade book in a safe place.

39. Set up a folder for each student so that you can store all of the paperwork that crosses your desk.

40. Learn each student's name quickly.

41. Photocopy your grade book so you will have a record of your students' names and progress to refer to after your original grade book has been placed in storage.

42. Share a laugh with your students and with your colleagues. Nothing chases stress away faster.

43. Plan your lessons by the year, the semester, the week, and the day.

44. Keep a book of inspirational sayings handy for you and your students to read on tough days.

45. Be flexible. Much of what you do at school just can't be done perfectly. Adjust your expectations for perfection if necessary.

46. Be friendly with everyone.

47. Add a green plant or flowers to your room to cheer up everyone's day.

48. Decorate your classroom with students' work.

49. When the task seems impossible, remind yourself that teachers made a difference in your life when you were younger. You can do the same for your students.

50. Make a list of the reasons why you chose education as your profession. Tuck it away in a safe place, but carry it in your heart.

EARNING YOUR STUDENTS' RESPECT

No matter how interesting our subject, how dynamic our instruction, or how well-planned our procedures, if we do not have the respect of our students, we are poor teachers. Respect is one of those vital intangibles that is difficult to define. It's the constant delicate balance among the many roles we assume in our workday: disciplinarian, motivator, humorist, listener, advisor, evaluator, entertainer, guide, comforter, lecturer, and role model.

When students respect us, they don't just see us as friendly adults who talk with them for several hours each week; instead we have met their ideal of what a teacher should be. Having your students' respect is the biggest asset you or any other teacher can bring to school each day. Without it, all of your other efforts will not be successful.

How do we lose the respect our students are willing to extend to us? There are lots of ways the unwary teacher can cause students to lose faith. Here are just a few of the more obvious mistakes that are all too easy to make:

- losing your temper
- refusing to admit it when you make a mistake
- treating students unfairly
- assigning an insufficient amount of work
- assigning work that is inappropriate or not challenging
- treating students harshly
- not knowing the material
- being insensitive to students' needs
- being emotionally unstable
- not being a good adult role model

If these are the mistakes that are easy for teachers to make, how then can we earn our students' respect? The best way to insure that we have earned our students' respect is to make sure we fulfill our roles as teachers.

There is no better substitute for improving the way we teach than to be self-critical. When teachers examine the way they fulfill their classroom roles—assessing their own strengths and weaknesses—then they can work systematically to improve the areas where they are not so strong as they would like to be.

You will find three assessments here to help you evaluate how well you earn your students' respect. The first one involves the issue of permissiveness, an area where many of us struggle to make good decisions for our students and ourselves. The second one is a way for you to examine your strengths and weaknesses in 20 important areas. The third assessment is one your students complete to help you determine how well you have earned their respect. (Sample assessments appear on following pages.)

ENLARGING THE LEARNING ENVIRONMENT

One of our most important tasks as educators is to help our students enlarge their lives. No matter where they live—in rural areas, suburbs, or cities—our students need our help to see that the world is a much larger place than the four walls of a classroom can ever contain. When we move our students into the larger world beyond their textbooks, we offer them benefits they can't learn by just sitting quietly at their desks.

First of all, when we help our students see that they are part of a large community, those students see that they can have more interesting lives than those of their classmates who either drop out or who do not succeed in school. Their lives can be enriched by possibilities rather than restricted by problems when they learn to see beyond their day-by-day concerns.

Students who are encouraged to explore a variety of interesting places and ideas have an opportunity to interact with many kinds of people. They then develop skills that will help them learn to get along well with others. Often students learn to appreciate their communities better just by learning about the many things other people do to make all of our lives easier.

The most welcome benefit, however, that comes to those students whose teachers take them beyond the classroom is an increased sense of self-confidence and an openness to new experiences. We know that our attempts to enlarge their worlds have been successful when we see that our students have become more self-confident and comfortable in the ways they relate to each other and to new situations.

There are many ways we can enlarge the learning environment for our students. Here is a list of some of the ways you can help your students begin to view themselves as citizens of a larger community. Many of these ideas are ones that caring teachers have used successfully for years. Pick a few that you think your students will enjoy and experiment to find the ones that will work best for you.

1. Have students write letters to pen pals. These pen pals can be from other states or even from other countries. You can also encourage students to go online to write to pen pals. *(continued on page 356.)*

SELF-CHECK FOR PERMISSIVENESS

One of the important areas we need to examine is how permissive we are. Do we let our students get away with misbehavior or are we too strict? Are we consistent in how we expect our students to behave? One of the most critical issues in earning student respect is the balance we must maintain between being too permissive and being too strict.

Use the items in this checklist to determine the areas where you are too permissive and where you may be too strict. Select the letter of the response that is closest to your own discipline style and put it in the blank. After you have finished all ten choices, check what your responses reveal about how permissive or strict you tend to be.

1. _____ Students jokingly insult each other while waiting for class to begin.

    a. Ignore the horseplay. Class hasn't started yet.

    b. Remind students of the procedure for starting class and the class rule about showing respect for others.

    c. Tell students to stop and to get to work.

2. _____ A student is lost in a daydream instead of finishing a reading assignment.

    a. Tell the student that if he or she doesn't get to work, there will be more to do for homework.

    b. Stay at your desk and wait to see how long it takes the dreamer to get back to work.

    c. Move to stand near the student.

3. _____ Students take too long to get their papers arranged for a test.

    a. Remind them to hurry.

    b. Start the test and let the slow ones catch up.

    c. Tell them they have one minute to get ready and then time them by watching the clock.

4. _____ Students ball up papers and toss them at the wastebasket while you are giving directions about an assignment.

    a. Shake your head, frown, and move near them.

    b. Stop what you are saying and reprimand them.

    c. Finish your directions. Go to the students and quietly ask them about the class rule they violated.

5. _____ Students chat while you are explaining the homework assignment.

    a. Ignore it.

    b. Stop and wait for them to pay attention.

    c. Tell them to stop talking and start paying attention.

6. _____ A student lacks a textbook, pen, or paper.

    a. Share materials from the class storehouse.

    b. Don't allow student to complete the work in class. He or she can do it at home. This will help all students remember to bring materials next time.

    c. Allow student to borrow from classmates.

7. _____ Students turn in sloppy or inaccurate work.

    a. Refuse to take it.

    b. Take it but give a lecture about work habits.

    c. Require that they redo the work.

8. _____ Students are tardy to class without a good reason.

    a. Enforce your rules regarding tardiness to class.

    b. Refuse to let them in.

    c. Meet them at the door and ask why they are tardy.

9. _____ Students talk back rudely when you have reprimanded them.

    a. Send them to the office.

    b. Reprimand them privately.

    c. Ignore it.

10. _____ Students ignore you when you call for the class to quiet down to work.

    a. Keep asking until they listen to you.

    b. Raise your voice until no one can ignore you.

    c. Give the signal that they recognize as a sign that they need to get quiet.

What Your Responses Reveal About Yourself

You might be *too permissive,* if you chose these answers:

1. a	6. c
2. b	7. b
3. a	8. c
4. a	9. c
5. a	10. a

You might be *too strict* if you chose these answers:

1. c	6. b
2. a	7. a
3. b	8. b
4. b	9. a
5. c	10. b

The best way to deal with the issue of permissiveness is to make yourself aware of the areas where you may be inclined to be permissive rather than sensible in your approach. If you are still not sure of the best course to take, ask yourself these questions:

1. Is this behavior appropriate?

2. What will happen if I choose to ignore this behavior?

3. What will happen if I choose to deal with this behavior?

4. What message about future behavior am I sending to my students in the way I handle this problem?

SELF-CHECK FOR STRENGTHS AND WEAKNESSES

Examine this list of positive teaching traits and rate yourself on each one. Use a number system to do this.

If you feel a statement describes one of your strengths, put a "3" in the blank in front of that statement.

If the statement describes how you are some of the time, but not as often as you would like to be, place a "2" in the blank.

If the statement is one that describes an area that is a weakness of yours, place a "1" in the blank.

1. _____ I know the material I am supposed to teach.

2. _____ I devise many ways to handle the discipline problems in my classroom.

3. _____ I have worked with my students to establish a pleasant class atmosphere.

4. _____ I almost always handle my own discipline problems.

5. _____ I am flexible.

6. _____ I spend time every day to let my students know that I care about their welfare.

7. _____ I focus my discipline energies on preventing problems rather than on having to deal with them.

8. _____ I provide my students with a sufficient number of challenging assignments so that they can successfully master the material they are studying.

9. _____ I am consistent and fair in the way I enforce the class rules.

10. _____ I motivate my students through a variety of methods.

11. _____ I show respect for the personalities of my students.

12. _____ I provide my students with the necessary training in social skills to reduce the conflicts they may experience.

13. _____ I have a clear purpose for the material I teach, and I communicate that purpose to my students.

14. _____ I work to promote a healthy self-esteem in my students.

15. _____ I strive to evaluate my students as fairly as possible with a wide assortment of assessment techniques.

16. _____ I work to become skilled at planning effective lessons.

17. _____ I provide prompt feedback so that my students understand what they need to do in order to succeed.

18. _____ I take a teamwork approach with my students, their parents or guardians, and other adults who will be able to help my students succeed.

19. _____ I use a variety of stimulating materials to keep my students interested and on-task.

20. _____ I work hard to engage every student in every assignment every day.

CLASSROOM CLIMATE STUDENT SURVEY

Please circle the appropriate number on the scale that best describes your teacher.

Gives enough meaningful work	1 2 3 4 5	Does not give meaningful work
Encourages personal responsibility	1 2 3 4 5	Encourages conformity
Is consistent in enforcing rules	1 2 3 4 5	Is inconsistent in enforcing rules
Motivates us to do our best	1 2 3 4 5	Does not make us want to try harder
Recognizes accomplishments	1 2 3 4 5	Disregards accomplishments
Is dynamic	1 2 3 4 5	Is not interesting
Prevents problems	1 2 3 4 5	Frequently has to deal with disruptions
Is organized	1 2 3 4 5	Is disorganized
Listens to us	1 2 3 4 5	Ignores helpful student suggestions
Sets high standards	1 2 3 4 5	Has low expectations
Treats everyone fairly	1 2 3 4 5	Plays favorites or is unkind to some students

2. Your students can tutor younger students in their community. Working with primary or elementary children will increase their own knowledge of what they are teaching as well as their sense of self-esteem.

3. Have your students speak out on community issues by writing letters to the editor of your local newspaper or attending local government meetings that are open to the public.

4. Bring newspapers and magazines into your classroom. Many students do not have access to these at home.

5. Help your students feel they belong to a school community by promoting school spirit. Show pride in your school and help your students see that it is important for them to become involved in school events also.

6. Take your students to both the school library and the public library. Libraries open the door to the world. Teach your students how to be responsible patrons so that they can benefit from these resources.

7. Use the Internet. Your students can enjoy exploring cyberspace and learning about the advantages of our information age.

8. Encourage students to join school clubs and organizations.

9. Students can also join community civic organizations. Many organizations will welcome the energy offered by secondary students.

10. Encourage your students to help others in the community who need assistance. Students can volunteer at soup kitchens, nursing homes, hospitals, blood drives, or at other community organizations and events.

11. Have older students mentor your students. Even college students with busy schedules will be willing to help out younger students who need the advice and guidance of more experienced friends.

12. Arrange an exchange program with another school. Even two schools in the same community can be very different from one another. Students who visit different schools have an opportunity to learn how others manage their daily responsibilities.

13. Arrange for guest speakers to share their expertise and experiences with your students.

14. Expose your students to art. Inexpensive prints of well-known paintings can add a great deal to your students' knowledge of the world of the arts.

15. Take your students on field trips to points of interest near and far. Certainly no students should graduate from high school without visiting their state capitol.

16. A tradition that has faded somewhat as students have become more difficult to manage is one that has enriched the lives of many: the class trip. Many students have enjoyed an excursion to Disneyland, to New York City, or to Washington, D.C.

17. Play music that students don't listen to on their radios. Classical music is something that even the most unsophisticated students grow to appreciate if they are exposed to it often enough.

18. Have your students find out about their communities by surveying community members about a variety of topics or issues.

19. Encourage students to visit a college campus even while they are still in middle school so that they can have an idea of what college is like for those students who work to earn a place there. For those who can't visit a campus, writing for information is a good idea. Students should not wait until their senior year to begin to explore their college options.

20. Encourage your students to serve as unofficial "big brothers" or "big sisters" to students who need someone to help them.

21. Help your students establish peer-tutoring sessions outside of class to help each other study.

22. Encourage your students to read for pleasure or to listen to books on tape to broaden their horizons.

23. Stress the importance of watching television sensibly. Educational television programs will help your students understand the worlds of nature, politics, the arts, history, and similar topics.

24. Publish your students' writing in as many different ways as possible. Encourage your students to enter contests.

25. Create a school newsletter to help students keep in touch with school events.

26. Work with your students to fund-raise for those people in your community who are less fortunate than your students. There are many service organizations—such as the United Way, the Red Cross, or the Salvation Army—that would benefit from your students' help.

27. Sponsor a group of students who will work together to clean up the school grounds or other areas in the community on Earth Day.

28. Help your students participate in their local City Hall Day where teens trade places with local officials for a day.

29. Connect your students with the rest of your region by shared projects—such as establishing a local weather station, acting troup, drill team—or other organizations and ideas that involve students sharing information and working together for a common cause.

30. Plan an imaginary field trip with your students to places they either know about or would like to learn about. Popular computer simulation games can give your students guidance about the kinds of things they should anticipate on their imaginary trip.

31. Help your students plan a banquet to celebrate academic success, raise money for an outing or other class event, or for some other special function. Local businesses are often generous with their time, expertise, and supplies when students are working for a good cause.

32. Hold a career fair so that students can see the types of careers that are available to them.

33. A growing trend in many areas is to have students participate in a Shadow Day. On this day students report to a local business instead of to school. They shadow an employee for the day, learning about the job skills they need to develop in order to become successful employees themselves.

34. Some ways of enlarging the classroom are much simpler than others. Put up a large map and have students talk about where they are from or places they have visited.

35. Have your students try foods that they don't normally eat. You don't have to force them to try exotic dishes that are so unusual that few people would enjoy them, but many students would enjoy trying out dishes from other countries.

36. Involve your students in a research project that they would enjoy. Learning about an event in the past or a group of people in an area of the world very different from their own will open their minds.

37. Have your students write letters to well-known people. Authors, entertainers, government officials, and sports figures are often generous in their willingness to write back to students to share the secrets of their success.

38. Have your students become involved in local, state, and national government issues. Even something as simple as encouraging them to join your school's PTA will be a good way to get students started on becoming involved in issues that can have a direct effect on them.

39. Your local chamber of commerce office has lots of information about your community that your students probably don't know about. Have students contact this organization to become aware of the many resources available to them in their communities.

40. Enlarge your classroom by team teaching with a colleague or by combining your classes for a project. Art students and English students can work together, for example, to produce a booklet or another project that combines the talents and skills of the two groups.

THE PROMISE OF PROFESSIONALISM

Older teachers often shake their heads at some of the things new teachers do in their classes that the wiser teachers wouldn't dream of doing now that they have years of classroom experience. While there may be some validity to this attitude, all of us—new teachers and veterans alike—need to be aware of the professional responsibilities we assumed when we chose our profession.

Exactly what is professional behavior? It means being the very best teacher and employee that you can every day. This is not always easy. Many things can distract us from our professional responsibilities. Poor planning, personal problems, lack of preparation, uncertainty about the right actions to take, stress, and fatigue are just a few. In order to be professional, we need to pay attention to these distractions and to the ill effects they can have on the discipline climate in our classrooms.

When we choose to conduct ourselves in a professional manner, we set an example for our students to follow that will also encourage them to behave in a productive way. Professionalism is an attitude that helps us earn the respect of our students because we send a message that we are in control of the classroom and of ourselves.

Consistently allow professionalism to be the underlying principle that governs your behavior towards your students. Use the following suggestions to improve the professional image you present to your students and to assume control of the discipline climate of your class.

1. Don't discount the importance of your appearance in creating a professional image. Dress neatly in a way that is comfortable for you but that is not distracting for your students. Because you are a role model of adult behavior for students in matters of grooming as well as conduct, you should take your workday appearance seriously.

2. Project an attitude of confidence even if you don't feel confident.

3. Treat all of your students fairly. Not the same. Fairly.

4. Separate your personal self from your professional self. This attitude change will help you accept criticism from your supervisors as helpful, not threatening.

5. Support student organizations and teams at your school. The members of the community will notice and appreciate your efforts. Your students will, too.

6. Acquaint yourself with the curriculum of the other grade levels in your discipline. If you are going to be an effective teacher, then you should know where your students are headed as well as what they are expected to have learned before they enrolled in your class.

7. Make a daily list of the paperwork that needs to be done and resolve to get it all turned in on time.

8. Be understanding and flexible, but not a pushover for too many ridiculous excuses.

9. Repeat as often as needed: "I am in charge of this classroom. Unruly children are not the leaders here; I am."

10. Teach your students the study skills they need to unlock the information in the textbook.

11. Let your students do the talking. Teachers who ask questions instead of lecturing will experience far fewer discipline problems than those teachers who drone on and on.

12. Be an example of a person who is always punctual. When you are late, you put an unfair burden on others who have to assume your responsibilities.

13. All teachers—young, old, cheerful, tired—affect classroom climate.

14. Students without enough to do will quickly annoy all nearby adults. Perhaps this is the most common mistake teachers make: not giving students enough meaningful work to do.

15. If you are angry enough to raise your voice in front of your students, stop and reassess the situation. Don't lose face in front of the class. Some of your students will be amused, some will be frightened, but all of them will lose faith in you.

16. Be excited about learning. Communicate that excitement to your students.

17. Ask questions if you are not sure about the best course of action to follow in a situation where you find yourself confused.

18. We don't teach a class; we teach individual students.

19. What you say in class today will be discussed at dinner tables all over town tonight.

20. Use humor to lighten a heavy lesson. Allow your students to enjoy life with you.

21. Treat all students with respect. Even the most difficult child has feelings that are easily hurt.

22. Accept responsibility for student learning. Teach your students to accept responsibility for themselves as fast as you can.

23. Don't join those legions of teachers who brag about how tough they are and how many students they have failed.

24. Accept into your heart and soul that all students can learn, even those who seem impossible to reach. Don't give up on them.

25. Be a force for positive change in your classroom. Don't allow yourself or your students to just drift through the term.

26. Make lessons relevant and goals attainable.

27. Learn from your mistakes. One of the hardest things about our profession is that it provides plenty of opportunities for this kind of learning.

28. Have a good answer ready when a student asks, "Why do we have to learn this stuff anyway?"

29. Have high expectations for your students. You must expect a great deal from them if you are to get a great deal from them.

30. Promote cooperation as often as you promote competition.

31. Don't allow students to curse in front of you. Don't tolerate even mild cursing.

32. It's often the small details that separate professional from unprofessional behavior. Be punctual, accurate, and precise in your work.

33. If a supervisor tells you that you have made a mistake, accept the correction with thanks. Work to correct the problem. Make sure your later success is evident.

34. Focus on your students' excuses. What can you learn about your students and how they see you?

35. Be consistent in your attempts to improve your students' behavior through patience and understanding. Don't give up on them.

36. Make your lessons as involved with real-life experiences as possible.

37. Help your students see the connection between their textbooks and their lives.

38. Speak out against teen substance abuse, *loudly, often.*

39. Open and end each class in a spectacular fashion.

40. Encourage your students to teach you.

41. Make all students see that they are important to the success of the entire class.

42. Take pride in your profession. Share this attitude with your students.

43. Be an active teacher with an active class.

44. Categorically refuse to accept certain behaviors such as name calling, insults, or other actions that will instantly disrupt your class.

45. Treat your students as worthy individuals. Let them know you care for them.

46. Make yourself aware of how your colleagues and students perceive you. Are you satisfied with the image you project?

47. Be careful not to insult your students with unconsciously negative body language.

48. Continually add to your base of knowledge about education. Read professional literature, attend workshops, and stay abreast of new developments in the field.

49. Make your students, colleagues, and supervisors look good. Support other staff members with praise in front of students.

50. When you make a mistake, admit it. Apologize and move on.

CREATING A CULTURE OF EXCELLENCE IN YOUR CLASSROOM

It is ironic that we have such different expectations for the various people we encounter in our daily lives. We expect that our daily newspapers will be delivered on time every day. We demand that other drivers stay on their side of the road. We require that doctors be accurate in diagnosing our ailments, and we certainly want the pharmacist to fill our prescriptions correctly.

We have the same expectations for the other adults we encounter: postal workers, repair personnel, telephone operators, technicians, bankers, lawyers, nurses, clerks, custodians, inspectors, manufacturers . . . in fact, we expect excellent service from everyone.

When it comes to our students, however, our expectations for academic and behavioral success drop drastically. Many of us are just glad to have made it through yet another long day at school.

Why are we willing to settle for so little from our students? Why can't we have the same performance expectations for these very important people in our lives that we have for the others we meet?

We can. In fact, it is up to us to show students how to achieve their best. An important part of a teacher's responsibility is to help students cultivate the habit of mind that will encourage them to always put forth their best efforts—even on the smallest tasks.

There are several techniques we can incorporate into the culture of our classrooms that will help us encourage this fundamental change in our students' thinking. Here are some techniques that will help you create the kind of classroom where students are encouraged to always put forth their best efforts.

Technique 1

Teach your students that it is not enough for them to just complete their assignments. Too often students seem to sleepwalk through assignments while not learning the information they are supposed to master. Teach students that they must review, recite, and actively study to learn the material in their lessons. Just doing the work is not enough.

Technique 2

Promote the desire to learn more about a subject in your students when you plan your lessons. Ask questions that are designed to arouse their curiosity. Comment on the appearance of their papers, the depth of thought evident in excellent work, and the importance of paying attention to details. If you incorporate these into every lesson, you and your students will soon be striving to achieve more than they thought they could.

Technique 3

Model this striving for excellence for your students and be sure to tell them that you do so. When you hand out papers that you took the time to type neatly, tell your students that you made an extra effort. Tell them how you try to use the small blocks of time in your day to improve a lesson or get your work done quickly and well.

Technique 4

Promote the concept of 100%+. When you teach your students to aim for 100%+ on every assignment, you are encouraging them to strive for excellence. Some of the ways you can indoctrinate your students into accepting this standard include:

1. Place posters and banners around the room to encourage students to do their work and then do a little extra.

2. Create a display area for papers that are extremely neat, accurately done, or go beyond the expectations for the assignment.

3. When you make an assignment, ask students to suggest some of the ways they can exceed the requirements.

4. Reward students' efforts at doing their best.

5. Help your students set goals for reaching their personal best on tests and other assignments.

6. Offer extra-credit questions on tests so that students can strive for more than the requirements.

7. Encourage students to be self-confident about what they achieve with just a bit more effort. Get them in the habit of asking themselves the question, "What is just one more thing I can do to make this assignment better?"

8. Teach your students the importance of focusing attention and concentrating their efforts, particularly at the end of an assignment when they may be tempted to rush to finish.

9. Share excellent papers with the class. Show them the reasons why some papers exceed the requirements for an assignment.

10. Discuss the standards your students will have to meet in the workplace. They should understand that taking a 100%+ attitude to their work now is something that will give them a competitive edge later.

"Say, 'I taught thee.'"

—William Shakespeare

NOTES

NOTES

NOTES

NOTES

NOTES

NOTES